Lecture Notes in Computer Science 4536

Commenced Publication in 1973
Founding and Former Series Editors:
Gerhard Goos, Juris Hartmanis, and Jan van Leeuwen

Editorial Board

David Hutchison
 Lancaster University, UK
Takeo Kanade
 Carnegie Mellon University, Pittsburgh, PA, USA
Josef Kittler
 University of Surrey, Guildford, UK
Jon M. Kleinberg
 Cornell University, Ithaca, NY, USA
Friedemann Mattern
 ETH Zurich, Switzerland
John C. Mitchell
 Stanford University, CA, USA
Moni Naor
 Weizmann Institute of Science, Rehovot, Israel
Oscar Nierstrasz
 University of Bern, Switzerland
C. Pandu Rangan
 Indian Institute of Technology, Madras, India
Bernhard Steffen
 University of Dortmund, Germany
Madhu Sudan
 Massachusetts Institute of Technology, MA, USA
Demetri Terzopoulos
 University of California, Los Angeles, CA, USA
Doug Tygar
 University of California, Berkeley, CA, USA
Moshe Y. Vardi
 Rice University, Houston, TX, USA
Gerhard Weikum
 Max-Planck Institute of Computer Science, Saarbruecken, Germany

Giulio Concas   Ernesto Damiani
Marco Scotto   Giancarlo Succi (Eds.)

Agile Processes in Software Engineering and Extreme Programming

8th International Conference, XP 2007
Como, Italy, June 18-22, 2007
Proceedings

Volume Editors

Giulio Concas
Università di Cagliari
Dipartimento di Ingegneria Elettrica ed Elettronica
Piazza d'Armi, 09123 Cagliari, Italy
E-mail: concas@diee.unica.it

Ernesto Damiani
Università degli Studi di Milano
Dipartimento di Tecnologie dell'Informazione
via Bramante 65, 26013 Crema, Italy
E-mail: damiani@dti.unimi.it

Marco Scotto
Giancarlo Succi
Free University of Bolzano-Bozen
Piazza Domenicani 3, 39100 Bolzano (BZ), Italy
E-mail: {Marco.Scotto, Giancarlo.Succi}@unibz.it

Library of Congress Control Number: 2007928867

CR Subject Classification (1998): D.2, D.1, D.3, K.6.3, K.6, K.4.3, F.3

LNCS Sublibrary: SL 2 – Programming and Software Engineering

ISSN   0302-9743
ISBN-10   3-540-73100-8 Springer Berlin Heidelberg New York
ISBN-13   978-3-540-73100-9 Springer Berlin Heidelberg New York

This work is subject to copyright. All rights are reserved, whether the whole or part of the material is concerned, specifically the rights of translation, reprinting, re-use of illustrations, recitation, broadcasting, reproduction on microfilms or in any other way, and storage in data banks. Duplication of this publication or parts thereof is permitted only under the provisions of the German Copyright Law of September 9, 1965, in its current version, and permission for use must always be obtained from Springer. Violations are liable to prosecution under the German Copyright Law.

Springer is a part of Springer Science+Business Media

springer.com

© Springer-Verlag Berlin Heidelberg 2007
Printed in Germany

Typesetting: Camera-ready by author, data conversion by Scientific Publishing Services, Chennai, India
Printed on acid-free paper   SPIN: 12078028   06/3180   5 4 3 2 1 0

Preface

"The Program Commitee of XP 2000 invites you to participate in this meeting of software development researchers, professionals, educators, managers, and students. The conference brings together people from industry and academia to share experiences and ideas and to provide an archival source for important papers on flexible process-related topics. The conference is also meant to provide information and education to practitioners, to identify directions for further research, and to be an ongoing platform for technology transfer."

This was the goal of the 1st XP 2000 Conference. The Organizing Committee expected around 60 people to attend, and they got 160. The subsequent conferences were held again in Sardinia and then all over Europe, maintaining the position of a leading world event on the topics of agility in software and system development. Now the International Conference on Agile Processes in Software Engineering and eXtreme Programming, XP 2007, is in its eighth edition.

During these years, the agile approach has become mainstream in the software industry. It is able to produce business value early in the project lifetime and to successfully deal with changing requirements. It focuses on the delivery of running, tested versions of the system at a constant pace, featuring a continuous interaction with customers, and paying extreme attention to the human component of software development. The rapidly growing scientific and practical evidence shows many quality gains, including increased productivity, fewer defects, and increased customer satisfaction.

The conference brings together both industrial practitioners and researchers. It is based not only on paper presentation, but also on workshops, tutorials, satellite symposia, such as the PhD Symposium, and activity sessions. These dynamic and interactive activities are the peculiarity of the Conferences on Agile Processes in Software Engineering and eXtreme Programming.

The topics of interest in the conference stress practical applications and implications of agile methodologies, with a particular focus on new openings, domains, and insights. They include theoretical, organizational, and practical aspects. Among the first, we may quote:

- Foundations and rationale for agile methods
- Digital ecosystems and agility
- Tailoring and building of agile processes
- Metrics, automated metrics, and analysis

Among the organizational aspects, both firm organization and team organization are covered. The former aspects include:

- Organizational change, management, and organizational issues
- Combining or streamlining the business processes and agile SW development
- Business agility

- Commitment, motivation, and culture in an agile SW development organization
- Contracting processes and issues, including subcontracting

Team organizational aspects include:

- Case studies, empirical experiments, and practitioners' experience reports
- Education and training
- Agile development on a large scale including scalability issues

Practical aspects covered by the conference are:

- Combining industry quality standards (e.g., CMMI) and agile approaches
- Experimenting with agile practices: pair programming, test-first design, continuous integration, refactoring, etc.
- Agile software development tools and environments
- Agile development of open source software
- Agile offshore and distributed development
- Embedded software (e.g., SW/HW co-design) and agile SW development

Forty-five papers were submitted to this year's conference. These papers went through a rigorous reviewing process, and only ten were accepted as full papers. We received 35 experience reports and research ideas, among which 20 were accepted for inclusion in this book as short reports. Many proposals were also submitted: 34 workshops, 35 tutorials, and 5 panels.

Overall, we believe that this book includes many rigorous, detailed and sound papers, able to give insights into the current state of the art of agile methodologies, and into its forecasted developments in the near future. Finally, on behalf of all members of the Organizing Committee, we would like to thank all authors of submitted papers, experience reports, research ideas, tutorials, workshops, panels, activities, papers to the PhD Symposium and all invited speakers for their contributions, our sponsors, all members of the Program Committee as well as other reviewers for their careful, critical, and thoughtful reviews, and all others involved in helping to make XP 2007 a success.

April 2007

Giulio Concas
Ernesto Damiani
Marco Scotto
Giancarlo Succi

Organization

XP 2007 was organized by research units of the MAPS (Agile Methodologies for Software Production) project: the Free University of Bolzano-Bozen, the University of Cagliari, CRS4 (Center for Advanced Studies, Research and Development in Sardinia), and the University of Milan.

Executive and Program Committee

General Chair	Michele Marchesi (University of Cagliari, Italy)
Program Chair	Giancarlo Succi (Free University of Bolzano-Bozen, Italy)
Program Co-chair	Marco Scotto (Free University of Bolzano-Bozen, Italy)
Organizing Chair	Ernesto Damiani (University of Milan, Italy)
Organizing Co-chair	Alberto Colombo (University of Milan, Italy)
Workshops Chair	Giulio Concas (University of Cagliari, Italy)
Tutorials Chair	Ernesto Damiani (University of Milan, Italy)
PhD Symposium Chair	Sandro Pinna (University of Cagliari, Italy)
Panels Chair	Jutta Eckstein (IT Communication, Germany)
	Frank Maurer (University of Calgary, Canada)
Web Chair	Alessandro Soro (CRS4, Italy)
Disruptive Activities Chairs	Steven Fraser (Qualcomm, USA)
Publicity and Industry Liaison Chair	Rachel Davies (Agile Experience Ltd.)
Publicity Team	Steven Fraser (Qualcomm, USA)

Review Committee

Marco Abis (Italy)
Pekka Abrahamsson (Finland)
Pär Ågerfalk (Ireland)
Scott Ambler (Canada)
Emily Bache (Sweden)
Geoff Bache (Sweden)
Hubert Baumeister (Denmark)
Stefan Biffl (Austria)
Lauren Bossavit (France)
Ko Dooms (The Netherlands)
Yael Dubinski (Israel)
Tore Dybå (Norway)

Jutta Eckstein (Germany)
John Favaro (Italy)
Steven Fraser (USA)
Steve Freeman (UK)
Paul Grünbacher (Austria)
Hakan Herdogmus (Canada)
David Hussman, (USA)
Jim Highsmith (USA)
Helena Holmström (Ireland)
Conboy Kieran (Ireland)
Filippo Lanubile (Italy)
Martin Lippert (Germany)

Frank Maurer (Canada)   Helen Sharp (UK)
Grigori Melnik (Canada) Alberto Sillitti (Italy)
Rick Mugridge (Canada)   Christoph Steindl (Austria)
Sandro Pinna (Italy)   Don Wells (USA)
Barbara Russo (Italy)   Laurie Williams (USA)

External Review Committee

Alberto Colombo (Italy)   Teresa Mallardo (Italy)
Irina Diana Coman (Italy)   Tadas Remencius (Italy)
Fulvio Frati (Italy)   Mario Scalas (Italy)

Sponsors

http://www.exoftware.com/

Google

http://www.google.com

http://www.microsoft.com/

agical

http://www.agical.se/

http://www.agilealliance.org/

Table of Contents

Managing Agile Processes

Comparing Decision Making in Agile and Non-agile Software
Organizations 1
  Carmen Zannier and Frank Maurer

Up-Front Interaction Design in Agile Development 9
  Jennifer Ferreira, James Noble, and Robert Biddle

British Telecom Experience Report: Agile Intervention – BT's Joining
the Dots Events for Organizational Change 17
  Sandra McDowell and Nicola Dourambeis

Agile Software Development Meets Corporate Deployment Procedures:
Stretching the Agile Envelope 24
  Olly Gotel and David Leip

Extending Agile Methodologies

Supporting Agile Reuse Through Extreme Harvesting 28
  Oliver Hummel and Colin Atkinson

Using Horizontal Displays for Distributed and Collocated Agile
Planning 38
  *Robert Morgan, Jagoda Walny, Henning Kolenda,
  Estaban Ginez, and Frank Maurer*

Applying Agile to Large Projects: New Agile Software Development
Practices for Large Projects 46
  Ahmed Elshamy and Amr Elssamadisy

Teaching and Introducing Agile Methodologies

Job Satisfaction and Motivation in a Large Agile Team 54
  Bjørnar Tessem and Frank Maurer

Motivation and Cohesion in Agile Teams 62
  Elizabeth Whitworth and Robert Biddle

How to Build Support for Distributed Pair Programming 70
  Jacek Dajda and Grzegorz Dobrowolski

Methods and Tools

A Metamodel for Modeling and Measuring Scrum Development
Process 74
  Ernesto Damiani, Alberto Colombo, Fulvio Frati, and Carlo Bellettini

Tracking the Evolution of Object-Oriented Quality Metrics on Agile
Projects 84
  Danilo Sato, Alfredo Goldman, and Fabio Kon

FitClipse: A Fit-Based Eclipse Plug-In for Executable Acceptance Test
Driven Development 93
  Chengyao Deng, Patrick Wilson, and Frank Maurer

EzUnit: A Framework for Associating Failed Unit Tests with Potential
Programming Errors 101
  Philipp Bouillon, Jens Krinke, Nils Meyer, and Friedrich Steimann

Empirical Studies

Does XP Deliver Quality and Maintainable Code? 105
  Raimund Moser, Marco Scotto, Alberto Sillitti, and Giancarlo Succi

Inspecting Automated Test Code: A Preliminary Study 115
  Filippo Lanubile and Teresa Mallardo

A Non-invasive Method for the Conformance Assessment of Pair
Programming Practices Based on Hierarchical Hidden Markov
Models 123
  Ernesto Damiani and Gabriele Gianini

Predicting Software Defect Density: A Case Study on Automated Static
Code Analysis 137
  Artem Marchenko and Pekka Abrahamsson

Empirical Evidence Principle and Joint Engagement Practice to
Introduce XP 141
  Lech Madeyski and Wojciech Biela

Methodology Issue

Power of Recognition: A Conceptual Framework for Agile Capstone
Project in Academic Environment 145
  Ville Isomöttönen, Vesa Korhonen, and Tommi Kärkkäinen

Agile Commitments: Enhancing Business Risk Management in Agile
Development Projects 149
  Mauricio Concha, Marcello Visconti, and Hernán Astudillo

Usability in Agile Software Development: Extending the Interaction
Design Process with Personas Approach 153
   Jukka Haikara

Defining an Integrated Agile Governance for Large Agile Software
Development Environments 157
   Asif Qumer

Ph.D. Symposium

Enhancing Creativity in Agile Software Teams 161
   Broderick Crawford and Claudio León de la Barra

Investigating Adoption of Agile Software Development Methodologies
in Organisations 163
   Antony Grinyer

Agile Software Assurance 165
   Noura Abbas, Andrew M. Gravell, and Gary B. Wills

Posters

User Stories and Acceptance Tests as Negotiation Tools in Offshore
Software Development 167
   Ivan Chubov and Dmitri Droujkov

A Case Study of the Implementation of Agile Methods in a
Bioinformatics Project 169
   Xueling Shu, Andrei Turinsky, Christoph Sensen, and Frank Maurer

Adapting Test-Driven Development for Innovative Software
Development Project 171
   Deepti Mishra and Alok Mishra

Learning Agile Methods in Practice: Advanced Educational Aspects of
the Varese XP-UG Experience 173
   Federico Gobbo, Piero Bozzolo, Jacopo Girardi, and
   Massimiliano Pepe

Experience Reports

Overcoming Brooks' Law 175
   Kealy Opelt

Project Bid on Iteration Basis 179
   Juanjuan Zang

Making the Whole Product Agile – A Product Owners Perspective 184
  Dharmesh Raithatha

Financial Organization Transformation Strategy 188
  Juanjuan Zang

An Agile Approach to Requirement Specification 193
  Tom J. Bang

The Application of User Stories for Strategic Planning 198
  Lawrence Ludlow

Introducing Agile Methods into a Project Organisation 203
  Tom J. Bang

Agile Development Meets Strategic Design in the Enterprise 208
  Eric Wilcox, Stefan Nusser, Jerald Schoudt, Julian Cerruti, and Hernan Badenes

An Agile Approach for Integration of an Open Source Health Information System 213
  Guido Porruvecchio, Giulio Concas, Daniele Palmas, and Roberta Quaresima

Agile Practices in a Large Organization: The Experience of Poste Italiane 219
  Mauro Sulfaro, Michele Marchesi, and Sandro Pinna

Multi-tasking Agile Projects: The Focal Point 222
  Ruud Wijnands and Ingmar van Dijk

Extreme Programming Security Practices 226
  Xiaocheng Ge, Richard F. Paige, Fiona Polack, and Phil Brooke

Multi-tasking Agile Projects: The Pressure Tank 231
  Ruud Wijnands and Ingmar van Dijk

The Creation of a Distributed Agile Team 235
  Paul Karsten and Fabrizio Cannizzo

Distributed Scrum in Research Project Management 240
  Michele Marchesi, Katiuscia Mannaro, Selene Uras, and Mario Locci

Multiple Perspectives on Executable Acceptance Test-Driven Development 245
  Grigori Melnik and Frank Maurer

Test Driving the Wrong Car 250
  Ingmar van Dijk and Ruud Wijnands

Epistemological Justification of Test Driven Development in Agile
Processes 253
  Francesco Gagliardi

Research Ideas

How Does Readiness for Agile Development Relate to Team Climate
and Individual Personality Attributes?............................. 257
  Tali Seger, Orit Hazzan, and Ronen Bar-Nahor

Communication Flow in Open Source Projects: An Analysis of
Developers' Mailing Lists 261
  Selene Uras, Giulio Concas, Manuela Lisci, Michele Marchesi, and
  Sandro Pinna

Panels

Community Reflections 266
  David Hussman

To Certify or Not to Certify 268
  Angela Martin, Rachel Davies, David Hussman, and
  Michael Feathers

Learning More About "Software Best Practices" 271
  Steven Fraser, Scott Ambler, Gilad Bornstein, Yael Dubinsky, and
  Giancarlo Succi

Author Index 275

Comparing Decision Making in Agile and Non-agile Software Organizations

Carmen Zannier and Frank Maurer

University of Calgary, Department of Computer Science, 2500 University Drive NW,
Calgary, AB, Canada, T2N 1N4
{zannierc,maurer}@cpsc.ucalgary.ca

Abstract. Our ability to improve decision making in software development hinges on understanding how decisions are made, and which approaches to decision making are better than others. However, as of yet there are few studies examining how software developers make decisions in software design, especially studies that place agile approaches in the context of decision making. In this paper, we present results of a multi-case study of design decision making in three software organizations of varying levels of agility. We show an agile organization produced a culture that supported communication and debate about alternatives to design decision more than 2 organizations of lesser agility.

Keywords: Consequential Choice, Serial Evaluation.

1 Introduction

We present an emergent multi-case study in which we compare the use of consequential choice [11, 12] and serial evaluation [9] in three small software organizations of varying levels of agility. Consequential choice is defined as the *concurrent* comparison and trade-off evaluation of more than one option in a decision [11, 12]. Serial evaluation is the *sequential* evaluation of options (n.b. no tradeoff evaluation and no concurrency) in a decision [9]. The results of our observations strongly suggest that small agile environments lead to more use of consequential choice (rather than serial evaluation) than small non-agile environments. This was a surprising result because consequential choice is rooted in "rational" approaches to decision making, typical of operations research, economic theory, and other seemingly "non-agile" fields of study. Our results show an agile environment was implicitly able to foster rational design decisions by emphasizing direct collaboration.

We conducted this study to continue learning how design decisions are made in software development. It is a relatively unexamined topic, despite recognition of its importance [1, 4, 8, 14, 18]. We also conducted this study to determine if agile methods were beneficial or detrimental to decision making, a question that has not been addressed empirically in the agile literature, to the best of our knowledge.

We present background work in Section 2 and describe our empirical study in Section 3. Results are presented in Section 4 and validity is described in Section 5. In Section 6, we conclude this work.

2 Background

We discuss four topics: decision making, problem structuring, qualitative studies of designers at work, and our past study on design decision making. First, we use rational and natural decision making as the conceptual frameworks to evaluate software design decision making processes. Rational decision making (RDM) is characterized by consequential choice of an alternative and an optimal selection among alternatives [11, 12]. Natural decision making (NDM) is characterized by serial evaluation of alternatives in dynamic and often turbulent situations [9]. *One alternative at a time* is evaluated and a satisficing goal is applied [9]. There are numerous perspectives from which to view design decision making (e.g. real options theory [3]) and we are in the process of comparing our data with different perspectives. For now we focus on the difference between consequential choice and serial evaluation provided by RDM and NDM.

Second, software design is a problem structuring activity accomplished throughout the software development lifecycle [5, 6, 7]. A well-structured problem (WSP) is a problem that has criteria that reveal relationships between the characteristics of a problem domain and the characteristics of a method by which to solve the problem [15]. An ill-structured problem (ISP) is a problem that is not well structured [15]. Most of problem solving is problem structuring, converting an ISP to a WSP [15].

Third, a survey of software design studies shows that five related factors impact software design: expertise, mental modeling, mental simulation, continual restructuring, and group interactions. Expertise is the knowledge and experience software designers bring to design [1]. Existing studies showed higher expertise resulted in an improved ability to create internal models and run mental simulations [1, 16]. Mental modeling is the creation of internal or external models by a designer. A mental model is capable of supporting mental simulation [1]. Mental simulation is the "ability to imagine people and objects consciously and to transform those people and objects through several transitions" [9]. Mental simulations occurred throughout the software design process at varying levels of quality dependent upon the skill of the designer and the quality of the model on which the mental simulation ran [1, 4, 5, 6]. Continual restructuring is the process of turning an ISP to a WSP. Group interactions are the dynamics of group work in software design. The terms "distributed" and "shared" cognition suggest that individual mental models coalesce via group work, resulting in strongly overlapping – mental model [5, 18].

Fourth, our previous study examined how agile developers make decisions [20]. We found that agile developers used NDM to a) recognize a design decision needed to be made, b) recall past experiences in design and c) apply external goals (e.g. marketing pressures) to the decision problem. We also found that agile developers used RDM to a) apply consequential choice in unstructured decisions and b) manage time pressure in decision problems. What was unclear from our study was when and how consequential choice was applied. We were only able to note that consequential choice was used in unstructured decisions [20]. However, exactly half of our interview subjects discussed the use of serial evaluation. Given the important role consequential choice and serial evaluation have in RDM and NDM respectively, and the frequency of each approach in our interviews, we pursued this specific topic via observations, to determine if our results were as mixed as in our first study.

3 The Empirical Study

The purpose of this empirical study is to address the question: Does consequential choice occur more, less or with equal frequency in small agile and small non-agile software development organizations? Our qualitative study used observations conducted from January to April 2006 and used convenience sampling [13]. At one organization we had a personal contact, at the other two organizations we advertised on a professional newsgroup. We spent 1-3 days with each developer depending on availability and environment. Developers in Company B pair programmed, thus we did not observe one developer at a time, as in Companies A and C.

Company A develops point of sale systems for the restaurant industry. There were 3 developers and development tasks were assigned to individual developers that specialized in certain components of the system: one developer focused on the back-end, another focused on the user interface. The third developer was also a manger and developed wherever was needed. Company A was not familiar with Agile methods, but due to the size of the organization they exhibited some traits of Agile methods such as direct verbal communication over heavy documentation [2].

Company B develops logistics software for the supply-chain industry. There were 6 developers and the breakdown of tasks was group-based. Company B followed Agile methods – specifically Extreme Programming – in a regimented fashion. Pair programming was performed, with 5 of the 6 developers sitting at two tables together.

Company C develops integration products for information technology operations management. There were between 11 and 14 developers (hiring occurred during our observations). Each developer was assigned their own mini-project and was matched with someone (called a "shadow") who had previous experience in the area or could take over the task should the primary developer not be available. Company C used a few agile practices such as standup meetings, story cards and iteration planning.

Table 1 provides a description of each company. At Company B we observed 6 developers plus 1 person who played the role of customer contact. This person was not a developer but interacted with the developers so often that it was impossible not to observe his role in the discussions. Table 2 describes the agile practices we observed at each company. We were unclear about the agility of Company C. They claimed to be agile and used some of the practices [2]. However, we did not observe traits we would expect of an agile culture. For example, we observed numerous developers who were *repeatedly* apologetic about interrupting work when asking questions of their colleagues; we observed developers who were so focused on their *own* tasks that they were unwilling to volunteer for new tasks or assist colleagues with new tasks; we observed a separation of development tasks among team members to the extent that an integral member of the team calmly referred to their development as a factory. The culture of Company C was so significantly different than the culture of Company B (whose agility was extremely apparent) that we report on the concepts presented in Table 3. Table 3 describes our observations of each company's ability to fulfill the principles of the Agile Manifesto [2]. We recognize the risk of using the word "culture" and the subjective nature of our classification of agile culture. Yet it is imperative that we express the difference between Company C's claim to agility and our observations. For Company C, where we found an agile culture was not supported, we have provided quotes from our field notes for support in Table 3.

Table 1. General Description of Each Company

Parameter	Company A	Company B	Company C
Breakdown of People Observed	2 Developers 1 Manager/Developer	5 Developers 1 Manager/Developer 1 Customer Contact	3 Developers 1 Lead Developer
Number of People Observed	3	7	4
Total Number of Developers at Organization	3	6	11-14
Days Spent with Each Participant	3	1-2	2
Days Spent at Organization	10	9	9
Division of Labour	Individual	Group-based	Individual

Table 2. Agile Practice Present in Company

Agile Practice	Company A	Company B	Company C
Iteration Planning	No	Yes	Yes
Pair Programming	No	Yes	No
Versioning System	No	Yes	Unsure
Stand Up meeting	No	Yes	Yes
Unit Test	No	Yes	Yes
Unit Test First	No	Yes	No
Collective Code Ownership	No	Yes	No
Move People Around	No	Yes	No
Integrate Often	No	Yes	No
Refactoring	No	Yes	No

We used content analysis to examine our field notes [10]. First we made case study summaries of 28 decision events we found in the field notes from our observations. Next, we used content analysis to classify a case study summary as using consequential choice or serial evaluation. Content analysis places phrases, sentences or paragraphs into codes (i.e. classifications) which can be predefined or interactively defined [10].

4 Results

The primary result of our study is that when observing design decision making, we observed more conversations in the small agile software team than in two small non-agile software teams. This led to more use of consequential choice in the small agile teams than in the small non-agile teams. We present quantitative and qualitative results to support this. Table 4 presents all our case studies showing the type of decision problem, the number of people involved and the approach to making a

Table 3. Agile Principle Present in Company

Agile Principle	Present in Company A	Present in Company B	Present in Company C
Individuals & Interactions over Processes & Tools	Clear	Very Clear	**Not Clear** O1: "[Developer] says they've just started the shadowing idea, but ...' it requires time and everyone is really busy. So it's the first thing to go.'" O2: "Assign big things to people and they go off to do individual planning. ... An Iteration Planning Meeting ends. ... No one shared what tasks they had or that they needed help with anything. E.g. [Developer] had her tasks on a piece of paper with yellow stick-its and they aren't on the [main] whiteboard. So those are tasks for her no one knows about."
Working Software over Comprehensive Documentation	Very Clear	Clear	**Not Clear** O3: Development team has a technical writer who writes all the documentation. O4: "During the meeting [Developer] reminds people of the documentation process. [Manager] adds that they should use [tracking system] and should also communicate [with technical writer]."
Customer Collaboration over Contract Negotiation	Did not Pursue Topic	Did not Pursue Topic	Did not Pursue Topic
Responding to Change over Following a Plan	Clear	Very Clear	**Not Clear** O5: "[Developer] ... said, 'Everybody is expected to meet their schedule. There is no room to fall behind.'" O6: "'One more day [of research phase].'"

decision. The case study ID is indicated with an A, B or C to identify the company, and a number of the order in which it is shown.

First, Company A (non-agile) used consequential choice in 4 of the 12 decision events we observed (33.3%). Company B (agile) used consequential choice in 9 of the 11 decision events we observed (81.8%). Company C (self-claimed agile, observed non-agile) used consequential choice in 2 of the 5 decision events we observed (40%).

We emphasize that our observations showed consequential choice when more than one developer contributed to the decision. In the 15 decision events where consequential choice was used, 14 of these involved more than 1 person contributing to the decision. In Company A more than one person was involved in decision making in 3 of the 12 decision events we observed. In Company B more than one person was involved in decision making in 9 of 11 decision events we observed. In Company C more than one person was involved in decision making in 1 of the 5 decision events we observed.

We acknowledge that there are numerous potential contributors to the approach to making a decision (e.g. the type of decision problem, the number of people involved,

Table 4. Quantitative Indicators of Consequential Choice in Agile Teams

Case ID	Motivator to Design Change	Number of Developers	Approach to Decision
A1	Bug Fix	1	Serial Evaluation
A2	Bug Fix, if done, halts release.	2	Consequential Choice
A3	Feature Request	1	Serial Evaluation
A4	Bug Fix	1	Serial Evaluation
A5	Feature Request	2	Consequential Choice
A6	Feature Request	1	Serial Evaluation
A7	Bug Fix	1	Serial Evaluation
A8	Bug Fix	1	Serial Evaluation
A9	Feature Request	1	Serial Evaluation
A10	Feature Request	1	Consequential Choice
A11	Feature Request	2	Consequential Choice
A12	Feature Request	1	Serial Evaluation
B1	Feature Request	1	Consequential Choice
B2	Bug Fix, if done, halts release.	4	Consequential Choice
B3	Feature Request	1*	Consequential Choice
B4	Bug Fix	1**	Serial Evaluation
B5	Feature Request	1	Consequential Choice
B6	Feature Request	2	Consequential Choice
B7	Feature Request	2	Serial Evaluation
B8	Feature Request	2	Consequential Choice
B9	Feature Request	3	Consequential Choice
B10	Bug Fix	2	Consequential Choice
B11	Feature Request	2	Consequential Choice
C1	Feature Request	1	Consequential Choice
C2	Feature Request	1	Serial Evaluation
C3	Bug Fix	1	Serial Evaluation
C4	Chose Programming Language	4	Consequential Choice
C5	Bug Fix	1	Serial Evaluation

* developer asked entire room open question.
** a 2nd developer helped part-way through task.

the culture of the organization). Our previous work has found the more structured the decision problem was (e.g. debugging), the less consequential choice was used [21].

Our results here are consistent with that. In 8 decision events that involved bug fixes (and as per [21], were well structured), only 1 decision event involved the use of consequential choice. These do not include decision events A2 and B2 listed in Table 4, which were bug fixes that had significant impact on the release of the software product. These decision events were not as well-structured as the other 8 bug fixes.

We provide excerpts from our field notes to show the different approaches to making a decision, in the different companies and to highlight that there was a cultural quality *not* present in Company A and Company C, but present in Company B. The cultural quality was an openness and willingness to challenge ideas. In Company A and Company C, more often than not, there was simply no one around to challenge an idea a developer had. Excerpts from our field notes are as follows:

"[Developer] has coded an idea like this before so he is going to copy and paste and modify what he needs. He says, 'It's faster, why waste my time?'" **Company A.**

"[Developer1] tells me they're looking at code from another project with another customer to see how they did something more complex but same sort of problem....'We can just take this [code from previous project]. Just change the table.' [Developer2] says. They look through what they need and talk out loud about what they need. They read a large section of code and talk about changes. ... [Developer1] says, 'How else are we going to do it?'... They're looking at how to sort days and months. ... Before they've just left it but 'it's a bit silly,' they say....[Developer3] comes over and says it's ok to put the number before it, like 01Jan. [Developer2] laughs like he's not impressed. ... [Developer3] agrees [to a suggestion from [Developer1]] but also says they've shown it to the customer in one way so if they can stay somewhat consistent with that it'd be good. ... [Developer1] says "Each row is going to be a customer, month, no, ... each row will be customer by day." He explains the "no" to [Developer2]. [Developer1] raises a question, if you ship an order over 2 days, it'll double count. [Develoepr2] asks "That happens?" [Developer1] says yes, [Developer1] says distinct count then. [Developer1] says need a month dimension. Create a fact table, it'll be a bit slower, [Developer1] says as an idea. ...[Developer2] proposes a solution ... and [Developer1] agrees." **Company B.**

*"[Developer] says he has never run into a situation where there was no SDK. If he can't find out that there **is** an SDK, the company is going to need a consultant."* **Company C.**

5 Validity

We address the validity and repeatability of our results. First, we selected observations for this study because it was the second step in a larger study on design decision making [21]. We recognize that our observations were only a glimpse into the life of an organization. While our observations occurred for 9-10 days, factors that affect our conclusions may have occurred before or after our arrival, without our knowledge. Future long-term studies are needed to validate our results. We addressed repeatability of our coding using a consensus estimate for our measure of inter-rater reliability [17]. We compared results of analysis performed by an external coder for 8 of the 28 case studies (29% of our data). We achieved a consensus estimate of 76%, comfortably above the recommended rate of 70% [17]. Lastly, we compared our results of this paper with the results presented in our previous work [20]. We found in our previous study, of the six agile developers who said they used serial evaluation in the decision event they described, only one described other people present during this decision. The other 5 agile developers described decisions they made by themselves. Thus, our theory that agile environments that lead to communication lead to the use of consequential choice, still applies. In comparison to our previous results [20, 21] this study shows multiple people involved in decision making leads to RDM in decision making, whereas fewer people involved in decision making leads to NDM.

6 Conclusion

We presented a multi-case study of software design decision making, examining the use of consequential choice and serial evaluation in small agile and non-agile software companies. We show a small agile company using consequential choice often while two small non-agile companies applied mostly serial evaluation. Our theory is that agile environments produce more open communication among developers, which results in developers challenging each other's ideas for solutions to design problems, thereby increasing consequential choice. This result is surprising given that the reduced amount of documentation produced by agile teams is often associated with a less rational approach to software design. However the approach to decision making we observed is arguably rational. We are also now motivated to ask: which approach results in better software design? We believe consequential choice provides an opportunity to find "better" alternatives to a design decision and serial evaluation limits this opportunity. Future work includes long term empirical studies examining the impact of design decisions.

References

1. Adelson, B., et al.: The Role of Domain Experience in Soft. Design. IEEE Trans. Soft. Eng., vol. 11 (November 11, 1985)
2. Manifesto, A.: (12/06/2005) www.agilemanifesto.org
3. Boehm, B., et al.: Software Economics, A Roadmap. Int. Conf. on S/W Eng. Proc. Conf. Future of S/W Eng., pp. 319–343, Limerick, Ireland (2000)
4. Curtis, B., et al.: A Field Study of the Soft. Des. Process for Large Systems. Comm. ACM, vol. 31 (November 11, 1988)
5. Gasson, S.: Framing Design: A Social Process View of Information System Development. In: Proc. Int. Conf. Information Systems, Helsinki, Finland, pp. 224–236 (1998)
6. Guindon, R.: Designing the Design Process. HCI 5, 305–344 (1990)
7. Herbsleb, J., et al.: Formulation and Preliminary Test of an Empirical Theory of Coord.in Soft. Eng., Eur. Soft. Eng. Conf./ACM SIGSOFT Symp. Found. Soft. Eng. (2003)
8. Highsmith, J., et al.: Agile Project Management. Add-Wesley, London, UK (2004)
9. Klein, G.: Sources of Power. MIT Press, Cambridge, MA (1998)
10. Krippendorff,: Content Analysis. V5, Sage Pub, London (1980)
11. Lipshitz, R.: Decision Making as Argument-Driven Action. In: Klein, et al. (eds.) Decision Making in Action, Ablex Publishing Corp., NJ (1993)
12. Luce, et al.: Games & Decisions. John Wiley & Sons, NY (1958)
13. Patton, M.Q.: Qualitative Research & Evaluation Methods, 3rd edn. Sage Pub., CA (2002)
14. Rugaber, S., et al.: Recognizing Design Decisions in Programs. IEEE Software (1990)
15. Simon, H.: The Structure of Ill Structured Problems. AI 4, 181–201 (1973)
16. Sonnetag, S.: Expertise in Professional Soft. Design. J. App. Psych. 83(5), 703–715 (1998)
17. Stemler, S.E.: A Comparison of Consensus, Consistency and Measurement Approaches to Estimating Interrater Reliability. Practical Assessment, Research & Evaluation, vol. 9(4). Retrieved (October 30, 2006) from http://PAREonline.net/getvn.asp?v=9&n=4
18. Walz, D.B., et al.: Inside a Software Design Team. Comm. ACM, vol. 36(10) (October 1993)
19. Yin, R.K.: Case Study Research: Design & Methods, 3rd edn. Sage Publications, CA (2003)
20. Zannier, et al.: Foundations of Agile Decision Making from Agile Developers & Mentors. 7th Int. Conf. Ext. Prog.& Agile Proc. in Soft. Eng, Finland. Springer, Heidelberg (2006)
21. Zannier, C., Chiasson, F., Maurer, F.: A Model of Design Decision Making based on Empirical Results of Interviews with Software Designers. Understanding the Social Side of Soft. Eng. A Special Issue of the J. of Info. and Soft. Tech. (To appear) (Spring 2007)

Up-Front Interaction Design in Agile Development

Jennifer Ferreira[1], James Noble[1], and Robert Biddle[2]

[1] Victoria University of Wellington, New Zealand
{jennifer,kjx}@mcs.vuw.ac.nz
[2] Human-Oriented Technology Laboratory
Carleton University, Ottawa, Canada
robert_biddle@carleton.ca

Abstract. In this paper we address how interaction design and agile development work together, with a focus on the issue of interaction design being done "up-front", before software development begins. Our study method used interviews with interaction designers and software developers on several agile teams. We used the qualitative approach of grounded theory to code and interpret the results. Our interpretation includes appreciation for benefits seen for a certain amount of up-front interaction design, and benefits from some levels of interaction design continuing with the iterations of software development.

1 Introduction

Interaction design and agile development have much in common, most importantly the fact that they will often both be involved in development of the same software. Despite this, there has been little investigation or discussion on how the two processes work together, and the issues that arise. We have been conducting studies of software teams that use both interaction design and agile development in order to better understand practice. In this paper, we focus on the issue of interaction design being done "up-front", before software development begins.

Interaction design and agile development have different perspectives on software. Whereas interaction design has a focus on how the end users will work with the software, agile development has a focus on how the software should be constructed. Both have major roles in making good software. The two processes also have in common an appreciation for the importance of evaluation of customer satisfaction, and how an iterative approach is the best way to accomplish this. However, how these two iterative processes are combined is unclear.

In the next section we outline other literature that addresses this issue. We then present our study method, team profiles, and our results, categorizing and quoting findings from our interviews. We then integrate these findings and produce an initial interpretation of the practice that emerges from our studies. We then present our conclusions and plans for future work.

2 Background

The way in which interaction designers[1] and agile developers should work together has been discussed surprisingly little. The debate between Kent Beck and Alan Cooper [1] did explicitly address the issue of when interaction design should occur relative to software development. They agree on many things, but Cooper argues that all the interaction design should be done before any programming, and Beck disagrees.

> Cooper: "So when I talk about organizational change, I'm not talking about having a more robust communication between two constituencies who are not addressing the appropriate problem. I'm talking about incorporating a new constituency that focuses exclusively on the behavioral issues. And the behavioral issues need to be addressed before construction begins."

> Beck: "The interaction designer becomes a bottleneck, because all the decision-making comes to this one central point. This creates a hierarchical communication structure, and my philosophy is more on the complex-system side — that software development shouldn't be composed of phases. ... The process, however, seems to be avoiding a problem that we've worked very hard to eliminate. The engineering practices of extreme programming are precisely there to eliminate that imbalance, to create an engineering team that can spin as fast as the interaction team."

Jeff Patton describes in several papers and tutorials how interaction design and agile development can work together by using a process where interaction design iterations fit in the iterative structure of agile development [2]. Lynn Miller describes similar experience in managing projects where the interaction design was of critical importance to the software [3]. Her approach is that both interaction design and programming use a common process, where the two kinds of work are done in parallel, but are one iteration out of phase. In this way, the interaction designers are doing detailed design for the iteration that the programmers will do next, and doing evaluation of the iteration that the programmers did last. Chamberlain, Sharp and Maiden [4] use a field study to ground their introduction of a broad framework for how interaction design and agile development can work together. In particular, their study shows, and their framework explains, how the general values and practices typical in interaction design and in agile development are quite similar and can assist teams in working together, but that efforts must be made to ensure balance, appropriate resource management, participation, and in general a coherence of purpose.

---

[1] Our interviewees used the terms interaction designer, user interface designer and UI designer variously; we use the term interaction designer to refer to the member of the development team, whose main responsibility it is to design the user experience and the user interface. The team members involved in mainly coding activities are referred to as the developers.

3 Method and Participants

Our research method was qualitative, using grounded theory based on interviews. We conducted our study using semi-structured in-depth one-on-one interviews with team members from software teams at several different companies, each in different countries. Our aim was to study actual practice, rather than any ideal or experimental situation. We selected teams that we felt confident would be regarded as using an agile process, and where the project did involve interaction designers. For each team, we interviewed both someone who concentrated on user interaction design and someone who concentrated on programming. The interviews were voice recorded and transcribed in detail. All persons interviewed were asked to validate the transcriptions. We began our analysis with the method known as open coding, and is used to identify the different categories present in the text. We then performed axial coding, where the relationships between the categories are established, and then began to build up the structure of what we found in the interviews.

The first team, T1, is based in the United States, and develops and markets web-based software for IT professionals. T1 is an XP team consisting of ten engineers and one product manager/user interface designer. At the time of the interviews, T1 was working on redesigning and enhancing one of its products. Their product manager/user interface designer described the previous version of the project as being "hacked together" and having user interaction that was "very cumbersome", and the next version was to address these concerns. We interviewed the engineering manager and product manager/user interface designer.

The second team, T2, is based in Ireland. They develop and sell software to support wealth management. T2 is also an XP team and includes four engineers, one domain expert/on-site customer and two interaction designers. One of the interaction designers explained that there were several smaller projects, but that their main effort was on a kind of application described as a "wealth planner", where both the size and the impending release to their first customer were their concerns at the time of the interviews. We interviewed their project manager and an interaction designer.

The third team, T3, is based in New Zealand and develop software that controls fruit sorting machines. Their team consists of five developers. Their main project was described as not only controlling machinery and reading sensor data, but "gathering this all together and presenting that information to our customer." We interviewed two developers, one of whom had a background in interaction design.

The final two participants, P1 and P2, are both employed by the same software consulting company based in Finland. At the time of the interviews, P1 was an interaction designer working on a system to manage teaching and course scheduling; the team consisted of a project manager, four developers and two interaction designers. P2 was a team lead/developer on a team consisting of five developers, who worked across several projects. P2's main project was developing a new web-based application.

4 Results

In this section we present some of the main concepts that emerged in our interviews that relate to the issue of up-front interaction design. In each of the subsections below, we identify a significant pattern, and provide some relevant passages from the interviews. We provide a more general interpretation in the next major section.

There are Advantages to Up-Front Interaction Design. The participants were clear about the advantages of doing interaction design before implementation begins. They saw up-front design as having a positive impact on the final product's user satisfaction and consistency, saying it helped mitigate risks and helped designers come up with the best possible design, while keeping to the customer's budget. Up-front design was also seen to contribute to cost and time savings by ensuring better project estimation and prioritization.

"And we have no help lines, or no support lines or anything like that to take calls on how to use the system ... So that's all because of the designers' up-front work, because of up-front design and also because of the agile process we use." — *interaction designer, T2*

"Just create some up-front consistency, like, what do buttons look like, where are they placed, what do tables look like, how do users interact with tables, what do forms look like, how do you get from a table to a form and then back to the table, like, basic interaction models. So, kinda like a style guide. And I did some of that before I even started." — *product manager/user interface designer, T1*

"The benefits are the fact that doing up-front design, you are not limited by any kind of technology. Of course we take into account the implementation technology. We're not going to do web interfaces that are not possible to do on the web, but we can go on the very, very bleeding edge, so that we can know that we're still in the limits but we're trying the best we can, so it creates, in this way, best designs." — *interaction designer, P1*

"There's also the fact that if you do up-front design, you can take your time for doing the design, meaning that if it would be tied into the iteration, the problem is if you design a part of the system and you don't know what the whole system is, then later on it might happen that you know new requirements of the system, they require a major refactoring of the user interface, something really huge, they might turn the whole concept upside down." — *interaction designer, P1*

Do Most, Though Not All, Interaction Design Up Front. Participants from most of the teams believed that having the user interface a certain percentage complete before development begins is essential, but also enough. A user interface that was not completely 100% specified up front left room for decisions to be made during implementation. All participants in the study brought up the fact that there were inevitable changes to the user interface during development, due to implementation issues or issues that were not known up-front.

"Before it gets into development, the user interface is more or less, ninety percent defined." — *interaction designer, T2*

"What we currently try to do here at [Organization], or what I try even sometimes to force through, is that interaction design should be completed at least ninety five percent of the whole system before starting the implementation at all because otherwise it's simply not going to work." — *interaction designer, P1*

"The UI designer actually can get away with not putting all the details and everything into it. Many things just work out during the iteration planning or during development ... he [the UI designer] doesn't have to make this absolute, final, ultimate thing that is then given to someone. You can get away with a seventy to eighty percent implementation." — *engineering manager, T1*

"[Change is] driven by the needs of the system or new things learned during the project and risks that didn't get identified in the beginning." — *team lead/developer, P2*

Much of the Interaction Design Involves Study of the Clients and Users. Participants emphasized the close collaboration that interaction designers had with business oriented people within their own organization, such as marketing, and with the clients and end-users before development begins.

"We'll hold a workshop with the project sponsors, we'd have them with end users of the product, we'd have them with IT people, with the actuaries in the company, with the compliance people, as many as we can who will have input into the product or are using it in some form, or who are developing it in some form. They come from our workshop. We gather the user stories via that." — *interaction designer, T2*

"So we're kind of using the user interface design as the requirement for the developers, because the idea of trying to come up with the user interface design while doing the same piece of software has proven that it is simply impossible. The current deal with the customers is that they ... we have now budget for this user interface design part and that is kind of labeled as requirements analysis." — *interaction designer, P1*

"... we use informal conversation with the customer, so someone tries to understand the domain that they're working in, what the problems are and why they're trying to achieve what they're doing." — *developer, T3*

Interaction Design is Informed by Software Implementation. Even with some up-front design, interaction designers did gain more insight as the software was actually implemented. In some cases, this allowed fine details to be polished, but in other cases it suggested changes in the higher level design. Also, implementation sometimes revealed that interaction designers would overspecify what the programmers were meant to tackle in an iteration.

"And with XP it's like, these are my cards, this is what I need to design for. I don't care about the next release. I'm not even thinking about that. And nine times out of ten for us, if we did try to think about the next release then when we designed it for that then we didn't end up implementing those features anyway. So I think the fundamental change in thinking is more just for this release ..."
— *product manager/user interface designer, T1*

"With the user interface you gather as much information as you need to do some kind of real thing and then you put it through an iteration ... you know enough about the kinds of interactions you need to perform a particular function so you do that, feed it back into real code and then you've got something that people can play with and look at and then you can go through another iteration or another cycle of 'Is that any good? What should we be thinking about there?' So you've got real working software that people can reflect on a lot better. And you can go through a number of cycles that are purely paper prototyping cycles as well." — *developer, T3*

"... it's not realistic and not a good way of working to try to specify things to the nitty gritty detail, meaning that there will always be some kind of feedback from the developers when they find out that, 'Hey, this is difficult to do,' or 'Have you thought of this kind of a situation, which came up now while trying to implement this?' They give a seed for a need for redesign or completing the design, which is not sensible to do beforehand, because there are so many of these exceptional situations that the user interface designer would never guess, because he would need to know the internals of the system." — *interaction designer, P1*

Cost and Time are the Issues. Participants saw no problem with up-front interaction design, as agile development only warns against up-front code design. They saw up-front interaction design as being very different to up-front code design, e.g. up-front code design produces a lot of costly waste, whereas it is essential to be able to refine the interaction design with the customer up-front to make sure it is correct, is essential. Most importantly, there is an understanding that the issues of cost and time are the *reasons* that determine whether the interaction design should have iterations with a prototype rather than programming. Using a light-weight prototype, in the form of pen and paper sketches or PowerPoint slides, was much quicker to develop than an actual application, and still allowed the interaction designer and development team to go through the design together for valuable feedback.

"With faster and quicker iterations in agile, maybe sometimes you need the slower ... With the user interface it takes longer to get feedback, so it doesn't always line up." — *developer, T3*

"The kind of issues that you get in up-front code design are not the issues you get in up-front interaction design at all. Code design comes out of just the amount of waste you get from people doing two, three jobs. Doing the same job two or three times in different forms ... There's an awful lot of waste involved in that, which is the main thing XP was trying to fix in the first place, but with regards to up-front interaction design, you know, putting together screens, in Photoshop or whatever and iteratively running it by customers and things, to make sure that the design itself is correct. So it's a whole different domain, basically." — *project manager, T2*

"We're not writing a specification that is not true, we're trying out the system in the cheapest possible way in a very agile fashion but we're doing it with pen and paper and it's to build a system. This pen and paper thing is not design up-front, it's defining what the system is in a faster and a cheaper way. If it would be as cheap to implement the system at the same time, well then go for it. But if I can draw in five minutes so much user interface that it takes two months to implement, I really do not think that that is the best way to tackle things." — *interaction designer, P1*

5 Interpretation

Working through our interviews, we found a structure emerged. The first step involves the interviewees' conviction about advantages of up-front interaction design. In particular, they held that there are problems mitigated with up-front design, such as poor design judgements that lead to costly redesign or no added value for the customer; budget issues; poor task prioritization; costly redesign problems uncovered late in development, due to new or changing requirements; usability problems; inaccurate work estimates. It was also regarded as understood how these problems are mitigated with up-front design: the team gain a high-level understanding through development of a style guide and navigation model; designs are kept technology free, but without the team completely disregarding the implementation technology. The whole system can be designed very fast, and the team can obtain early customer input about the system.

The second step involves agreement that although much interaction design should be done up front, this is not as simple an idea as it might appear. One important consideration is that what might be called "design" in fact involved close work with business analysts, markets, clients, and end users. This is necessary for several reasons: to determine the value of the business case for development, to appreciate the goals of the client, and to understand the work and mental models of the end users. This raises an important question about our shared terminology. Our participants agreed that this work was part of what they regarded as *design*. On the other hand, this kind of work might also be seen by developers as constituting *analysis* rather than design. Agile development advocates are wary of up-front design because it represents premature commitment, but if it is analysis and does not involve commitment, then it does not constitute the same kind of danger.

The third step involves understanding that there are benefits to interaction design that come from iterative development and delivery of working software. There is acknowledgment that even up-front interaction design must be done in the light of the software platform capability. And beyond this is an understanding that software development provides a different lens through which the interaction design can be examined, helping interaction designers identify strategies for improving and refactoring. Finally, there is also agreement that while prototypes do allow designers to return to clients and end users with something to evaluate, there are advantages to having actual software instead. Not only does it provide more functionality, but also more confidence that value has been delivered.

In summary, there is a conviction of advantages in up-front interaction design. But this turns out to include much that might be regarded as analysis. Moreover, there are also advantages to doing some interaction design together with software development iterations. The real insight is shown in the reasoning about why and when up-front design is advantageous and when it is not. This is shown to involve concern for risk management, not unlike that underlying agile development itself. In essence, up-front design is appropriate if it reduces risk, and inappropriate when it increases risk.

6 Conclusions

In this paper we have reported on our studies of up-front interaction design in agile projects. We employed a qualitative research strategy to better understand the practice in actual software development teams committed to both quality interaction design and an agile process for development. We presented some samples of our findings, and our initial interpretation. These reflect not our suggestions for practice, nor any ideal practice, but rather actual practice, together with understanding about how it came to be.

We find that up-front interaction design is commonplace in agile development, and indeed there is agreement that most interaction design be done up front. However, we also find that in interaction design, much business and end-user analysis is understood to be included. Moreover, there is recognition that there are benefits to some interaction design being done in the iterations together with the software development. Most important, there is evidence of understanding that the issue is not whether interaction design should be done up-front or not, but rather when up-front interaction design will reduce risk, and is therefore advisable, rather than increase risk by making premature design commitments.

References

1. Fawcett, E.: Extreme programming vs. interaction design. FTP Online (2002)
2. Patton, J.: Hitting the target: adding interaction design to agile software development. In: OOPSLA '02: OOPSLA 2002 Practitioners Reports, p. 1. ACM Press, New York, NY, USA (2002)
3. Miller, L.: Case study of customer input for a successful product. In: ADC '05: Proceedings of the Agile Development Conference, pp. 225–234. IEEE Computer Society, Washington, DC, USA (2005)
4. Chamberlain, S., Sharp, H., Maiden, N.A.M.: Towards a framework for integrating agile development and user-centred design. In: XP, vol. 143–153 (2006)

British Telecom Experience Report: Agile Intervention – BT's Joining the Dots Events for Organizational Change

Sandra McDowell[1] and Nicola Dourambeis[2]

[1] British Telecom
sandra.mcdowell@bt.com
[2] Exoftware
nicola@exoftware.com

Abstract. While British Telecom (BT) has been progressing the adoption of agile practices across teams for the last two years, the overall organizational transformation has been slow to emerge and a catalyst was needed. In November 2006, BT began running a series of one hundred person, one and a half day events called Joining the Dots 3, aimed at promoting the use of agile throughout the IT organization. The event's practical approach of embedding learning through the use of videos and activities on agile planning, user stories, customer collaboration and iterative delivery into a large scale end-to-end simulation has proven to be both fun and an excellent learning tool. Simulation retrospectives inside the event echo the learning points and feedback forms have confirmed that BT may have succeeded in generating large scale buy-in to using agile practices across thousands of people in their delivery organization.

Keywords: Agile transformation, Organizational Change, Agile Planning, Estimating, User stories, Retrospectives, Teamwork, Collaboration.

1 Introduction

There are enough books and articles about organizational transformation to acknowledge that it is neither easy to achieve nor straightforward. Such shifts usually encompass people, process and technology. Further still, to change an organization to one that is friendly to agile, one often must change the entire company culture. More than two years ago, British Telecom (BT) took on this challenge—and while there have been some exemplar projects showing agile successes, overarching company-wide acceptance and adoption results have been slow to appear.

This paper describes how the use of a highly engaging event with carefully selected embedded agile learning has been rolled out across thousands of the delivery organization in a short period of time. This event acts as an intervention catalyst for change.

2 Transformation History

BT is facing rapid marketplace changes that require it to radically increase its speed to market. BT now must compete with companies ranging from telecom providers to new technology companies like Google and Skype. From a strategic view, there is little alternative than to change the "old ways of working". But for a company with over 14,000 IT employees, embedded waterfall delivery techniques, large distributed projects and COTS applications, this a radical shift that requires a unique adoption to agile.

The first step in the transformation was the creation of an internal coaching community. The idea was sound; build up a specialist base of experts who could work with teams to determine which agile practices could be applied in each team, depending on their context. But agile coaching is a skill developed over time, and usually only through a combination of training, mentoring and experience. This community was not created quickly and needed the support of seasoned coaches.

New "apprentice" coaches were trained to augment the overall amount of agile support available. This succeeded in creating a small community of enthusiastic people, but as they were given only a brief level of training to start, many were soon faced with the daunting task of educating hundreds of others and pushing their programs to change. These apprentice coaches also faced a genuine fear that applying new techniques, even the most well intentioned ones, could disrupt already tight delivery deadlines. To help, the BT agile community took on a "baby steps" approach, encouraging teams to start using non-disruptive practices such as stand-ups and retrospectives. The difficulty with this approach has been that such non-disruptive changes cannot yield the speed-to-market improvements required.

There is one other major obstacle to BT's transformation—agile is not tool-based technique that can be easily rolled out across an organization. Agile is a values based approach that needs buy-in from teams in order for it to succeed. It can be a highly vulnerable way to work and team members have to want to do it. However, how can BT gain this buy-in in an accelerated fashion on a large-scale?

3 Joining the Dots as a Large-Scale Change Agent

It was in this context that Joining the Dots 3 was born.

Joining the Dots 1 was originally a series of one day, one hundred person communications events held for all of the IT staff to inform them of changes that had been made to the BT strategy in early 2006.

The agenda for Joining the Dots 3 is quite different from its predecessor. While the model of reaching one hundred people at a time is leveraged, the objective of the event has been to do more than communicate new ways of working—participants are invited to practice using agile techniques as a way of winning their buy-in and creating momentum for change. The target set for the first phase of Joining the Dots 3 is to reach 3000 people across 30 events, leaving an option to extend the reach based on the success of the events.

The event criteria included the following:

- Don't just talk about it—do it. Let the event excite people by having them give agile practices a try.
- Focus on agile values, principles and practices. Ensure that all participants understand the mindset shift required, rather than simply concentrate on

specific techniques that they can use. With that said, also give them practical techniques they could start doing immediately with their teams.
- Have leaders lead the event and ensure participants have a shared context so they can action-plan next steps. This strategy has the added benefit of gaining leader buy-in to using agile, a new framework for many of them too. They also get to witness the challenges and obstacles that their teams may face when they return to their regular roles.
- Make it fun. If participants enjoy themselves, they'll be more accepting to trying new things.

3.1 Learning Through Doing

Participants should be able to feel the benefits of using agile rather than having to trust that it works. Hence, the bulk of the event is created around a large-scale simulation where twelve teams must create contraptions that move a ball across an arena.

In it, they face the difficulty of meeting customer requirements as a single component while having to contribute to a multi-faceted end-to-end solution. This scenario mirrors the complexity of BT's large scale projects and is a great place to prove the benefit of using agile.

Participants start with an agile teach-in where in a half an hour, agile is raised out of buzz-word status and BT leaders describe their personal experiences with agile delivery, warts and all. The teach-in emphasizes the scale of the human transformation that agile delivery requires, but also reassures participants that some teams at BT are doing it with genuine results.

At this point, the talking is over and teams get to practice working in an agile environment. Unbeknownst to them, they will now participate in a non-software agile project—dispelling the myth that agile only applies to software. Teams are quickly run through tutorials on agile planning and given a set of user stories with which they must build a release plan for delivery of their components. This has been the first exposure to user stories, comparative estimation and commitment based planning for many of them. With the guidance of agile coaches who act as facilitators/customers, teams develop plans for two iterations of work.

Then comes execution and the learning really begins. Teams' working habits determine their success. Often teams quickly ignore plans in favor of using tactical approaches that mirror waterfall thinking. This contrasts nicely with those more attuned to applying agile.

Teams that deliver iteratively and get customer sign-off during the delivery cycle perform better than ones that ignore their customers and try to deliver everything and integrate at the end. Teams that continuously test have more stable structures than ones that defer testing. The results of everyone's efforts are clearly seen in the "show and tell" where all teams demonstrate their structure's contribution to the end-to-end solution.

Teams use retrospectives to record lessons learned that may corrected in their second iteration. To date, these retrospectives have consistently recorded even more learning points than what was expected to be gained—and they emerged naturally from team experiences. Invariably, teams that apply those lessons to their second iteration see far better results. It is worth noting that while many of the participants are not currently using agile delivery techniques, the merit of many common agile practices emerge as ways to improve.

Some common retrospective results are:

What's gone well?

- Continuous testing and lots of it
- Customer engagement for prioritization and sign-off
- Team collaboration
- Delivered business value early
- Shared best practice across teams

- Learning from retrospective
- Had fun

What did we learn?
- Involve the customer more
- Keep it simple
- Initially overestimated what they could deliver
- Establish realistic targets
- Getting agreement with customer at planning stage.
- Priority based on business value and complexity (Story points)
- Value of testing

What should we do differently?
- More inter-team co-ordination and collaboration.
- Customer engagement; involve the customer more and keep them up-to-date.
- More re-use of designs
- Stop delivering when it is done and working
- Apply learning points from previous iteration
- Test early and more frequently
- Prioritize user stories before the build

The event concludes with peer based action planning, where participants are asked to accept responsibility for applying new techniques moving forward. The use of peers is meant to provide reinforcement and support for ensuring the action plans are met in the days and months post event. The majority of the action plans involve either applying new practices such as planning, user stories, stand-ups and retrospectives into their routines immediately. Others choose to learn more and there has been an increased demand in agile training.

4 Event Challenges

There have been many challenges faced during the development and delivery of agile material for an event of this scale. Recognizing that agile is an already over-burdened word at BT, it has been critical to ensure that all events are delivered consistently. An important outcome is to create a common understanding of agile delivery for all participants. Moreover, despite the temptation to teach "everything", people can only absorb so much. To avoid overwhelming participants or diluting the key learning areas, it has been important to be selective in presenting specific content areas over others.

The key content pieces address highest impact opportunities for change. This involves agile planning and estimation (which infers iterative delivery and user stories), customer collaboration (a current gap with business partner involvement inside the delivery cycle) and inter/intra-team communication (how to ensure good communication with distributed teams). Short, nine minute videos have been created in each area to provide a uniform delivery of information. While these videos are run by agile coaches, the video format both ensures that every participant receives the same content as well as lessening the burden of having highly experienced presenters.

There has been a challenge in creating content that is both simple enough for someone unfamiliar and suitably engaging for the experienced, given the large number of participants who attend the event. The use of the large-scale simulation format has been very helpful in ensuring that everyone participates. Quite simply, it's fun. Where those new to agile learn new practices, experienced participants are encouraged to help mentor their teams.

Additionally, there are constraints surrounding the number of skilled coaches available to support the event, recalling their already heavy work schedules. This remains a challenge which continues to build, as groups run through the events and subsequently place heavier coaching demand on their program apprentice coaches. It has been partially overcome by leveraging the original team of agile coaches for support, but this is at the sacrifice of their other responsibilities. Given the complexity of orchestrating the event, it is difficult to train coaches if they can only support a small number of events.

5 Lessons Learned

Throughout this event, the project team has worked to apply the concept of continuous learning and improvement to itself. There are many lessons learned, which will continue to emerge as more events are run.

5.1 Make It Fun

The success of the event has largely been a credit to the engaging nature of the large-scale simulation. Had Joining the Dots 3 used a less engaging delivery mechanism, the amount of learning would have been significantly reduced.

Initial concerns that it may not appeal to such a wide range of people have proven unfounded. The format creates a dynamic where teams self organize to ensure everyone is involved. This dynamic cajoles even the most cynical into suspending disbelief in favor of participating and having fun. Since the agile practices are very tactically selected to ensure success of the task-at-hand, even those most resistant to using agile adopt the practices for the day.

5.2 Stay Focused on What Is Important

Especially with early positive feedback, there is a strong temptation to layer on many new lessons for participants. The simulation supports teaching almost all of the agile principles and practices in one way or another. This temptation has been strongly controlled. The key messages were originally selected to address the most compelling organizational needs. Teaching everything risks participants not learning the key messages. This event has never been intended to replace comprehensive training. It is meant to create momentum for teams to either begin or take the next step in their transformation.

5.3 Agile Transformation Requires Buy-in

BT has a "top-down" driver for teams to use agile. Executives believe that using agile will help the company become more competitive. However, in order for agile adoption to succeed, teams need to see the merit in the change and want to do it. Beyond simply showing participants new tools and techniques, the event is aimed at demonstrating the value of agile.

5.4 Create the Environment for Learning and Then Allow Discovery to Happen

If the event is well structured, it is possible to let lessons emerge rather than through direct instruction. The number of retrospective lessons recorded after the first iteration was initially surprising. There was an expectation that participants would see the importance of the video topics, however it is also apparent that cultural behaviors such as the importance of teamwork, customer engagement, cross team coordination and self organization are recognized.

5.5 Ensure Proper Follow-Up Is Available

Follow-up could be the weakest part of the execution of the event and cannot be forgotten. Without a dedicated team to support post-event follow-up, there is a reliance on using established feedback mechanisms to ensure follow-up and support. This is namely the apprentice coaches, BT leadership event sponsors/hosts, training courses and the peer/team based relationships formed during the events. In cases where partially in-tact teams have participated, there is greater confidence in ensuring behavioral change. For participants who have very little shared context, there is the risk of Joining the Dots 3 simply being a fun event with no resulting change. Measures are currently underway to determine impact of the event on early participants and a plan to be put in place to address results. To date, the only concrete data available is an increase in the demand for agile training.

6 Conclusion

BT has had success in creating an agile coaching competency but faces limitations with their capacity to work across the organization. Even though the roll-out of agile began more than two years ago, there is a wide variance in agile adoption company-wide. A means to reach a large number quickly, effectively and compellingly was needed to boost teams' use of agile. Joining the Dots 3 has been this method and will continue to be run for many months to come.

The event as an intervention, works. It opens people's minds, dispels misconceptions about agile and gets people excited and committed to using agile practices when they start work the following day. These results have been recorded through participant action-planning, anecdotes, simulation retrospective results and in feedback forms. Based on participant feedback to the event, increasing the number of events to a greater audience is likely.

However, the proof of an intervention's effectiveness is measured over time. Teams need to start using agile with positive results in order for the event to truly have an impact on the organization. These measures are slow to emerge and will require dedicated attention. High enthusiasm and increased demand for training are early indicators that momentum for change has been created and that BT teams are taking a bigger step forward in their transformation.

Agile Software Development Meets Corporate Deployment Procedures: Stretching the Agile Envelope

Olly Gotel[1] and David Leip[2]

[1] Department of Computer Science, Pace University, New York
ogotel@pace.edu
[2] ibm.com Chief Innovation Dude and Agile Methods Advocate, IBM Hawthorne
leip@us.ibm.com

Abstract. This paper describes a process initiative within IBM to make the Corporate Portal (*ibm.com*) development practices more responsive to changing customer needs and explains the bottlenecks that arose with application deployment when this agile approach was not initially extended throughout the wider solution delivery lifecycle. The paper details the simple process changes that were adopted to expand the agile philosophy beyond development.

Keywords: Agile Deployment, Agile Development, Extreme Programming.

1 Introduction

The IBM Corporate Portal (*ibm.com*) is an application-driven website that advertises and markets the products and services of IBM. Prior to 2004, the team responsible for its development followed a "waterfall-like" approach, attempting to capture and prioritize requirements for a new release before design and development. They found that, while straightforward to agree on the main requirements, reaching agreement on the complete set was problematic. Negotiations would introduce delays and slow down releases to customers. A more agile approach was viewed as a pragmatic way to tackle this issue; development would proceed from key requirements and additional requirements would be determined and prioritized as the product evolved.

In 2004, the IBM Corporate Webmaster's team adopted an agile approach to software development. The use of eXtreme Programming was trialed in the development of a major release of *ibm.com*, culminating in its successful roll-out in November 2004 [2]. The agile process has since been streamlined to develop and deliver software that addresses evolving customer needs within a reduced timescale. However, once a new release has been developed, it still has to be deployed to a production environment to deliver a fully operational solution. The deployment environment is maintained by a geographically distinct team. This team orchestrates the deployment of multiple applications from across IBM, so their work is subject to organizational-wide scheduling requirements and policies; the team has to ensure any new deploys do not impact other deployment schedules and live applications.

Limited improvements can be gained in end-to-end agility if there is a bottleneck between the development of a product and its eventual deployment. While there is advice on how to align agile with non-agile practices [3], there is less focus on deployment [1]. This paper reports on the issues surrounding the alignment of agile development practices with corporate deployment procedures and describes the agile-spirited end-to-end process adopted for *ibm.com*.

2   Agile Development for *ibm.com*

The Corporate Webmaster's team is responsible for developing and maintaining *ibm.com*. The requirements for *ibm.com* change frequently, driven by new business offerings, improvements in search engine technology, etc. Part of IBM Sales and Distribution, the team comprises some 20 personnel, skilled in Java and XML/XSL development, open and technical standards, and project management. The majority of the team is based in New York State, with other members based in Asia and Europe.

The deployment team is drawn from roughly 100 personnel within IBM Global Services. This team runs the technology for IBM-sponsored events, like Wimbledon, in addition to being responsible for the *ibm.com* infrastructure and operations. The Webmaster's team are hence one of a number of customers for the deployment team's services. The deployment team is responsible for estimating demand on servers, understanding network traffic requirements for new or changing applications, network settings and permissions, etc. They are also responsible for testing that new applications meet non-functional requirements, do not compromise the performance or availability of existing applications, and checking that applications are compliant with organizational security policies. The team is based in Raleigh, North Carolina.

The agile development process required the development team to work 7 week release cycles, each cycle comprising 3 iterations of 2 week duration followed by a week for deployment. Customer groups from across IBM submit high-level requirements to be reviewed and prioritized based on business value. Selected requirements are split into and/or reformulated as stories by customer representatives and written on index cards. The stories are sized by the development team according to the time they estimate they need to build the story and returned to the customer, together with their estimated velocity for the iteration. Since the development team is distributed, the velocity is for the extended team. The sizing is based on the expected development effort (Java and XML/XSL), not on the associated deployment effort. The customer selects stories to implement in the forthcoming iteration. This selection process takes place every first Monday in a meeting at the start of each 2 week cycle. Further interaction with the customer occurs as stories are clarified and developed, and any elaboration is written on the back of the card. The extended development team communicates via telephone and instant messaging during this time. Towards the end of the iteration, the team performs user/customer acceptance testing.

During this process, the deployment team should (ideally) be notified of any story that may have a deployment implication. One scheduled call takes place every Tuesday to give the deployment team an alert as to what may be coming through the process and some indication of timeline. The first formal notification the team has is when the development team submits a work request for a code review as a precursor to deploying into staging. This occurs around the beginning of the third iteration (i.e. week 5 in the cycle) but, as the development team began to take on more of the responsibility for code review, this removed the necessity to put in such a request. Once the application has been deployed, any issues are dealt with by the joint team.

3 Problem Description

A retrospective was undertaken at the end of 2004 and the benefits from the new process were seen to be the increased level of communication between the customer representatives and development team. Since the customers are able to determine and prioritize requirements on a regular basis, they had more control over the product's direction. This retrospective revealed tensions, however, at the bottlenecks in deployment. From the deployment team's perspective, the last minute hand-over of applications and expectation of a fast release into production indicated the developers were not cognizant of the other demands on their time and corporate constraints.

With the prior "waterfall-based" approach, the deployment team would receive a requirements document and use this to plan and estimate their work for scheduled deploys. Following the move to agile, this was replaced by paper-based story cards and the team would often only find out about deployment requirements with the request to deploy into staging. When this request came late, the seventh week in the overall cycle would get stretched, leading to delays; the deployment team could not abandon other work to accommodate this. With the move to agile there had been little focus on the processes required to manage the transition of products from the development environment to the corporate production environment. It relied on ad-hoc communications between individuals and tacit institutional knowledge.

4 End-to-End Agile

Both teams have demands on their time and conflicting priorities, and are in separate parts of the IBM organizational chart. It is therefore critical to gain an awareness of the wider culture, working practices, constituency and remit of each other to understand what is and is not feasible. A model of the prior end-to-end process was constructed to clarify the tasks, timelines and information needs of both teams. This included the role of artifacts that mediate communications and so help to synchronize efforts (e.g. meetings, phone calls, requirements documents, etc.) This was compared with a model of the agile process to get an idea of where there were significant changes in the cross-team communication and possible information gaps. It was found that the deployment team did not need intricate details about the application, just specific and quite regular information pertaining to deployment. It was anticipated the deployment team could provide an information checklist for development (acting like triggers to talk), thereby affording some lead time for planning and decision making.

The notion of who is a customer and who is a service provider changes throughout the end-to-end process. The development team effectively assumes a dual role as intermediary – supplier to the business customer and customer for the deployment team's services. The very nature of this shift in relationship means that the development team needs to rethink their interaction point: when they are customers, do they behave in an agile manner or does their agile thinking come to a stop? Examining how to reduce cycle times within this wider chain led to the introduction of timeboxes (with velocities) for the deployment team, which the development team could apportion in a "lock-and-load" manner. All the *ibm.com* deploys were thus scheduled to take place on a Monday/Thursday cycle (i.e. Monday to deploy to staging and Thursday to deploy to production). On a Friday, the development team would submit work requests for applications to be deployed in the following week's cycle. The deployment team would expect the code at 9am on Monday else release their time to other customers. Monday through Wednesday the development team would be in testing and on Wednesday the production request would go in for deployment on the Thursday. Extending the metaphor such that the development team received a set amount of scheduled effort, and making them responsible for deciding how to prioritize their demands and use this resource, extended the agile envelope.

5 Future Considerations

This paper has highlighted how deployment can easily be an afterthought in agile process initiatives. Since May 2006, the simple changes described above have resulted in a more agile end-to-end process for product development and solution delivery within *ibm.com*. A number of outstanding questions remain:

Scalability. Only one of the deployment team's customers works in an agile manner, while the other teams plan and pre-schedule releases up to a few months in advance. Would this model scale if all customers were to work in this way?

Whole team velocity. Is it more useful, in terms of end-to-end agility, to consider the teams separately or as one whole team with a single velocity?

Story structure. Does it make additional sense to augment customer stories with deployment aspects or to create separate deployment stories to chain with stories?

Accounting for the REAL end-to-end process. This initiative focuses on the latter stages of an evolving product's lifecycle. Are there initial upstream stakeholders and processes that can also be brought into better alignment for further agility?

Acknowledgments. We would like to thank the IBM staff who assisted in this work.

References

1. Ambler, S.: One Piece at a Time: Just because agile practitioners deliver working software weekly doesn't mean that they deploy it into production at the same rate. Dr. Dobbs Portal, November 9th (2004)
2. Grossman, F., Bergin, J., Leip, D., Merritt, S., Gotel, O.: One XP Experience: Introducing Agile (XP) Software Development into a Culture that is Willing but not Ready. In: Proceedings of CASCON, Markham, Ontario, Canada, pp. 242–254 (2004)
3. McMahon, P.E.: Bridging Agile and Traditional Development Methods: A Project Management Perspective. CrossTalk: The Journal of Defense Software Engineering (May 2004)

Supporting Agile Reuse Through Extreme Harvesting

Oliver Hummel and Colin Atkinson

University of Mannheim, Chair of Software Technology
68159 Mannheim, Germany
{hummel,atkinson}@informatik.uni-mannheim.de
http://swt.informatik.uni-mannheim.de

Abstract. Agile development and software reuse are both recognized as effective ways of improving time to market and quality in software engineering. However, they have traditionally been viewed as mutually exclusive technologies which are difficult if not impossible to use together. In this paper we show that, far from being incompatible, agile development and software reuse can be made to work together and, in fact, complement each other. The key is to tightly integrate reuse into the test-driven development cycles of agile methods and to use test cases - the agile measure of semantic acceptability - to influence the component search process. In this paper we discuss the issues involved in doing this in association with Extreme Programming, the most widely known agile development method, and Extreme Harvesting, a prototype technique for the test-driven harvesting of components from the Web. When combined in the appropriate way we believe they provide a good foundation for the fledgling concept of agile reuse.

1 Introduction

Agile development and software reuse are both strategies for building software systems more cost effectively. Agile methods do this by shunning activities which do not directly create executable code and by minimizing the risk of user dissatisfaction by means of tight validation cycles. Software reuse does this by simply reducing the amount of new code that has to be written to create a new application. Since they work towards the same goal it is natural to assume that they can easily be used together in everyday development projects. However, this is not the case. To date agile development and systematic software reuse have rarely been attempted in the same project. Moreover, there is very little if any mention of software reuse in the agile development literature, and at the time of writing there is only one published reuse concept whose stated aim is to reinforce agile development. This is the so called "agile reuse" approach of McCarey et. al. [12].

The reason for this lack of integration is the perceived incompatibility of agile approaches and software reuse. Whereas the former explicitly eschews the creation of software documentation, the latter is generally perceived as requiring it. And while agile methods usually regard class operations (i.e. methods) as defining the granularity of development increments, reuse methods typically regard classes as the smallest unit of reuse in object-oriented programming. As a third difference, reuse approaches tend to be more successful the "more" explicit architectural knowledge is reused (as in product line engineering), whereas agile development methods employ as little explicit architecture as possible. At first sight, therefore, there appears to be several fundamentally irreconcilable differences between the two approaches.

McCarey et. al suggest a way of promoting reuse in agile development through so-called "software recommendation" technology. Their "agile reuse" tool, RASCAL [10] is an Eclipse plug-in which uses collaborative and content-based filtering techniques [9] to proactively suggest method invocations to developers. It does this by attempting to cluster Java objects according to the methods they use, just as Amazon, for example, clusters its customers according to the books they buy. The tool monitors method invocations in the class currently under development to predict method calls that are likely to be soon needed and suggests them to the developer. To evaluate their system the authors experimentally predicted invocations of the Java Swing Library in common open source systems and claim precision rates of around 30%.

Although the concept of RASCAL fits well into the agile spirit of providing maximum support for "productive" activities, there is nothing in the technology which ties it specifically to agile development. The approach embodied in RASCAL can just as easily be used with any other development methodology that produces code, including traditional heavyweight processes. Moreover, the approach has the same fundamental weakness as other repository-based approaches – the quality of the recommendations is only as good as the quality of the code repository that is used to search for components. Unfortunately, to date there have been few if any successful attempts to set up and maintain viable component repositories [6]. The version of the tool described in [10] is clearly a prototype, but McCarey et el. do not present a strategy for solving this important problem. Moreover, although RASCAL showed impressive performance for the limited domain of Swing invocations, it is not clear whether this technique will work for other domains with many more classes that have much lower usage frequencies.

1.2 The Core Challenge

The core challenge of agile reuse lies in developing a reuse strategy that complements the principles of agile development and offers a way of promoting reuse in tandem with the key artifacts and practices of agile methods. Whilst proactive recommendation technology such as RASCAL is certainly valuable in complementing such a strategy it does not itself solve the issues mentioned above. In this paper we present an approach which we believe does address these challenges and thus represents a viable basis for the concept of agile reuse. The key idea is to use unit test cases, which in most agile methods should be defined before implementations, to influence the component searching process. Such test-driven development is one of the most fundamental principles of Extreme Programming, the most widely used agile method. Tests are used as the basic measure of a unit's semantic acceptability. Once a code unit passes the tests defining its required behaviour it is regarded as "satisfactory" for the job in hand.

Usually the code to satisfy the tests for a unit is implemented by hand. However, there is no specific requirement for this to be so. Since passing the corresponding tests is the measure of acceptability, any code module that passes the tests is functionally acceptable whether created from scratch or retrieved from a component repository. A search technology which can systematically deliver code that passes the tests defined for components will therefore make the implementation of new code unnecessary. In our opinion, the combination of test-driven development and test-driven retrieval, as proposed in a rudimentary form in [11], create a natural synergy between agile development and software reuse and provide a solid foundation for the notion of "agile reuse". Due to its roots in test-driven development we have called our solution "Extreme Harvesting".

The rest of this paper is structured as follows. In the next section we briefly review the key ideas of Extreme Programming and introduce a simple example from a well know book in the field. In the section after that we discuss the difficulties involved in promoting software reuse and introduce the notion of Extreme Harvesting, our test-driven technique for finding components on the Internet and other large scale component repositories. Section 4 then explains how Extreme Harvesting might be used to support software reuse in the context of agile development – so called "agile reuse". Section 5 presents some of the prototype tools that we have developed to explore this approach. Finally, we conclude our contribution in section 6.

2 Extreme Programming Revisited

In this paper we use Extreme Programming as the archetypical example of an agile development method. However, our approach is not limited to Extreme Programming (XP) but is in principle applicable to any other process where tests are written before the implementation as well (like Agile Modeling [2] for example). In this section we briefly highlight those aspects of XP that are of importance for the understanding of our approach. We assume that the reader is familiar with other fundamental principles of Extreme Programming such as the four values of communication, simplicity, feedback and courage and the many recommended practices. For further details we refer to [4], for instance.

The test-driven nature of XP requires in particular that unit tests be written before any code for that unit is developed. These tests are used as the primary measure for completion of the actual code. The maxim is that anything that can't be measured simply doesn't exist [14] and the only practical way to measure the acceptability of code is to test it. To illustrate how test-driven development works in practice let us consider a small example.

```
public class Movie {
    public Movie(String title, int priceCode) {}
    public String getTitle() {}
    public int getPriceCode() {}
    public void setPriceCode(int priceCode) {}
}
```

This class, Movie, offers a constructor with arguments for the title and price code of a movie and methods for accessing (i.e. getting) these values. It also provides a method for setting the price code to a new value. Together with classes Customer and Rental, it represents the initial version of the well-known video store example from Martin Fowler's refactoring book [3]. Beck [14] and others recommend that the methods be developed and tested sequentially. Thus, a typical XP development cycle applied to the class Movies might tackle the methods of the class in the following order -

- Constructor with title and price code
- Retrieve title
- Retrieve price code
- Change price code

The basic idea is to define tests to check that the constructor works correctly in tandem with the retrieval method. This can be done using one combined test or using a separate test for each retrieval method. In this example we choose the latter since it is the more realistic for larger components. Thus, a JUnit [5] test case for the retrieval of the movie's title of the following form is created (usually, the test case is created before the stub in XP, of course):

```
public void testTitleRetrieval() {
    Movie movie = new Movie("Star Wars", 0);
    assertTrue(movie.getTitle().equals("Star Wars"));
}
```

In practice, test cases would probably be more elaborate (for example, they might follow the principle of triangulation [14]) but due to a lack of space we stay with a simple example here. This should be enough to convey the core ideas. In the next step, a stubbed out version of the Movie class (similar to the signature above) with just the constructor and the getTitle method is generated and made to compile. After this, the test case and stub are compiled, and the test is run to verify that a red bar is obtained from JUnit. Once the failure of the test has been checked, the stub is filled with the simplest implementation that could possibly work, and the test is re-run until a green bar is received from JUnit. The to-do list is then updated accordingly:

- ~~Store title and price code~~
- ~~Retrieve title~~
- Retrieve price code
- Change price code

The same process is then applied to the next method(s) on the to-do list until the class as a whole has been completed. After each iteration, some design work may become necessary to refactor the implementation of the class.

3 Software Reuse and Extreme Harvesting

There is more or less general consensus on the two important prerequisites that need to be fulfilled to support the systematic reuse of small and medium-sized components of the kind typically handled in agile development environments. The first is the availability of a library or so-called repository that stores reuse candidates and the second is a query technique that allows components to be retrieved effectively [7]. At first sight, these may appear to be trivial, but in practice this is not the case. The effort involved in setting up and maintaining a suitable repository is typically so high that some researchers do not expect to see a working solution for a long time to come [6]. There are many examples of projects from the past in which researches and developers have tried to setup and maintain public component repositories of even just a few hundred components but have eventually failed due to the associated maintenance problems. The recent shutdown of the Universal Business Registry for web services is another high profile example of this. Lately a few commercial code search engines have emerged which focus on supporting searches for code on the Internet (e.g. google.com/codesearch, koders.com and merobase.com). These provide various techniques for retrieving components from software libraries but none of them have yet found the right combination of prescriptiveness, ease of use and performance to become widely used. The well-known survey of Mili et al. [1] describes the related problems in more detail.

To integrate a reusable software unit into a system one generally needs the unit's syntactical description (i.e. its interface) and a corresponding semantic description of its functional effects. In Extreme Programming, as with most other object-oriented development approaches, a unit's syntactic interface is represented by its method signatures. Where Extreme Programming differs from most other methods, and what makes it particularly suitable as a basis for systematic reuse, is its provision of a simplified semantic description of the behaviour of a unit's operations before they are actually implemented. Most other methods have no such semantic description of operations, since formal methods (for example based on pre- and post-conditions) have so far proven impractical in mainstream development. These semantic descriptions of operations (i.e. the test cases) in XP are the vital prerequisite for being able to establish whether discovered components are fit for the required purpose. At present, however, only merobase offers full support for intelligent interface-driven searches in which components are retrieved based on the abstractions that they represent rather than on the presence of certain strings in their code. Our Extreme Harvesting approach, however, revolves around the principle of using the test cases defined for a desired component to filter out discovered components which are not fit for the purpose in hand. Figure 1 below provides a schematic summary of the six basic steps involved:

a) define semantics of desired component in terms of JUnit test cases
b) derive interface (i.e. the class stub) of desired component from test cases
c) search candidate components in repository using search term derived from (b)
d) find source units which have signatures matching the one defined in (b)
e) filter out components which are not valid (i.e. compilable) source units
f) establish which components are semantically acceptable by applying the tests defined in (a)

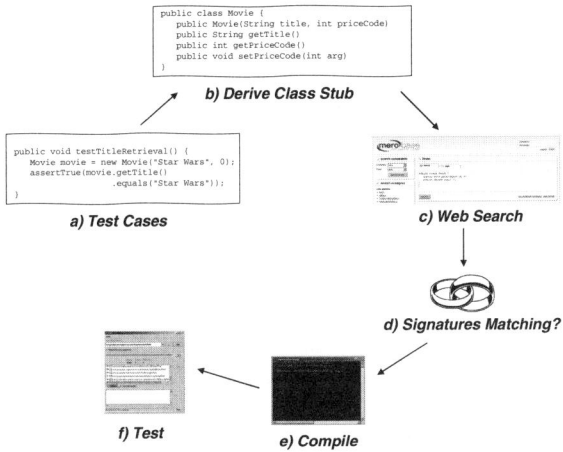

Fig. 1. Schematic process overview

4 Agile Reuse

As explained above, the basic idea behind our notion of agile (or extreme) reuse is to use test cases developed as part of the normal activity of Extreme Programming as the basis to search for suitable existing implementations. However, we believe there are two basic ways in which agile development could benefit from reuse, depending on the goals of the developer and the novelty of the application under development, namely definitive vs. speculative harvesting. In effect these approaches – which we will explain in the next two subsections – occupy opposite ends of a spectrum. At one end we have the situation in which the nature of the reused components is driven by a rigid design as it is typically used in traditional heavyweight approaches. We call it definitive harvesting. At the other end of the spectrum we have the situation in which the nature of the software design is influenced by the reused components what we call speculative harvesting. Practical software reuse activities will usually lie somewhere in between.

4.1 Definitive Harvesting

In projects in which the domain and requirements are well understood, or where the architecture is rigid, the interface and desired functionality of components might be fairly fixed and more importantly fairly common. When this is the case, it makes sense to develop all of the test cases and interface descriptions, for all of the items in the "to do" list, upfront, and then attempt to harvest as many suitable components as possible following the process shown in figure 1 above. If no suitable reuse candidates can be retrieved the required component has to be implemented in the regular way. However, if a reuse candidate can be found (e.g. a search for the interface of our Movie stub from section 2 on merobase delivers 25 candidates), a great deal of effort can be saved. Depending on the type of component and the size of the underlying repository the chances of finding something vary significantly, but since the overall amount of implementation effort (in the event that no suitable reusable component is found) is the same as in the unmodified case (i.e. in regular extreme programming) there would be no needless work involved.

4.2 Speculative Harvesting

Speculative harvesting, on the other hand, is best when the developer is unsure what the interface and complete functionality of the component should be, and is willing to adapt the rest of his/her system to the interface of any suitable component that may be found. This tends to occur more frequently in (agile) projects in an entirely new domain or with highly innovative characteristics. With this approach the developer creates test cases one after the other, working through the to-do list as recommended by Beck. However, before implementing the functionality to make the class pass the test (as in normal extreme development), a general search can be performed on the methods featured in the test case (e.g. a query for movie and getTitle on a search engine) to see if there are any existing classes from the Internet which might be able to pass it. If there are none, then obviously the developer has no choice but to go ahead and develop the component his/herself. If there are just a few, then the developer can quickly study and evaluate these to see if any of them provides the desired functionality for the whole class. If there are a large number of results, which is often the case when the query is very general, the developer can define the next test case according to the original to-do list and the implementations available. Then another test-driven search can be performed (using both exiting test cases), and the same decision process is applied again. This time, the set of results will be smaller, because by definition the set of components that pass both test cases will be a subset of the set which passed just one. However, if the result set is still very large, the developer can add another test case and continue in this fashion until either a suitable component is found or the set of results has been reduced to a number that can reasonably be analyzed. This process can be summarized as follows -

(1) Develop the next test on the "to do" list
(2) Perform a test driven search for the included functionality using all available tests
(3) See how many results there are

    a) None ➔ abandon all searching and implement whole class as normal
    b) A few ➔ analyze each class and

        (i) if there are any suitable– use one of them
        (ii) if not abandon searching and implement as normal

    c) A lot ➔ if the "to do" list is not empty, repeat the process from the start; if the "to do" list has been completed, abandon the process and implement whole class as normal

5 Prototypical Tool Support

Currently we are working in two directions to support this vision of Extreme Harvesting with appropriate tools. We have been developing an Eclipse plug-in which is able to harvest components from various code search engines from the Web with just a single mouse-click on the class stub once the developer has entered the desired method declarations and test cases as shown in figure 1. Proprietary repositories can also be used if they offer an API for programmatic access. For the videostore example, we were able to harvest multiple working implementations of the Movie class (Google: 16, Koders: 2, Merobase: 14) as shown in a screenshot below where our tool is used inside the well-known Eclipse IDE.

Fig. 2. Except of search results with a positively tested Movie class

The table at the bottom shows the URLs where reuse candidates have been found and the associated test result. A "0/3" with a green background denotes 3 test cases with 0 failures, a red "0/0" on black background is shown for classes that did not match syntactically and hence did not compile. These would not be shown to the user in a full version of the tool, but are currently kept for evaluation purposes. Like the "traditional" JUnit tool, the green "0/3" is the signal that a unit that has passed all tests and hence is appropriate for the required purpose. The editor above the table shows the code of an exemplary harvested class and the package explorer on the left contains all files that have been harvested.

As shown in the figure we obtained a version of Movie which depends on an additional class, Price, to work. Our tool automatically recognized this dependency and retrieved the Price class and its subclasses that were also needed. As mentioned in section 2, Fowler's videostore example in its initial version only involves two additional classes, Customer and Rental, which were also retrieved from the Web using the strategy outlined above. Missing dependencies to other classes can also be traced automatically to a limited extend, but we are currently working to further improve this capability. If the harvesting and the associated upfront "guessing" of the required functionality is successful, after stub and test case definition the only additional step is the invocation of our reuse tool for definitive harvesting. Our tool is also able to automatically create an object adapter [13] if this should become necessary. Further implementation work usually involved in building a component from scratch is thus avoided. Overall, the initial results from this approach are promising. During our initial experiments, we were able to retrieve multiple ADTs (like Stack etc.), implementations of a class for matrix calculations, a small ensemble of a deck and a card class for a card playing application, as well as various sorting algorithms, mathematical functions and other examples from the reuse literature. These results are described more fully in [8]. Results demonstrating the precision improvement of interface-driven searches and Extreme Harvesting compared with other approaches have recently been submitted elsewhere. Although our prototype currently focuses on Java it should be easily adaptable to other languages or even web services since they all offer a syntactic description of the interface to a piece of functionality and the possibility to test it.

The second prototype we are working on is intended to provide better support for the agile spirit of speculative harvesting. It is shown in figure 3 below. In the case when a developer starts with a very general search like a class movie with just a getTitle method (cf. figure 3) for example he will potentially receive a large number of results. They will all have at least some similarity to the component that the developer needs because they all pass at least one test. From these results it is possible to calculate a kind of "average search result" which collects together the features of the individual results and generates a representative summary. This tool is thus able to recommend canonical operations similar to the operation invocations delivered by RASCAL [10].

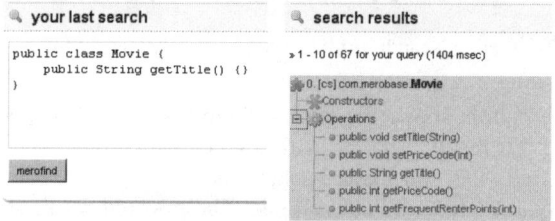

Fig. 3. Screenshot of a query and canonical operation recommendations derived from it

The developer can now choose from these canonical operations to constrain his next search in accordance with the to-do list. In the future this process might even support the creation of the to-do list itself by deriving common functionality for general concepts from a repository. We plan to elaborate on this on another occasion.

6 Conclusion

This paper has addressed the issue of promoting systematic reuse in agile development projects and explained how the use of a test-driven harvesting approach, known as Extreme Harvesting, can overcome the prima facea incompatibilities of the two paradigms. We presented an approach, based on the notion of Extreme Harvesting, which allows reuse and agile development to be combined in a complementary way. In short, the approach allows agile development to be enhanced through systematic reuse, and thus provides a solid basis for the notion of "agile reuse" coined by [12].

Due to this seamless integration in XP it is easy to use Extreme Harvesting in a reactive way (i.e. when the developer must explicitly invoke it) as well as in a proactive recommendation-oriented way in the spirit of RASCAL [10]. We believe that the presented approach therefore complements the work of McCarey et. al. We are currently working on improving our tool to proactively suggest code units that have been selected using automated clustering techniques of the form found in information retrieval research [9] and successfully applied in RASCAL. We hope that such an extension will also make it possible to anticipate possible refactorings in a given (or retrieved) code unit if only enough equivalent units could be retrieved from the repository. Furthermore, we are planning to conduct empirical studies with students to gain more experience about the value of our tool in practical settings.

References

1. Mili, A., Mili, R., Mittermeir, R.: A Survey of Software Reuse Libraries. Annals of Software Engineering, vol. 5 (1998)
2. Ambler, S., Jeffries, R.: Agile Modeling: Effective Practices for Extreme Programming and the Unified Process. John Wiley and Sons, Chichester (2001)
3. Fowler, M.: Refactoring: Improving the Design of Existing Code. Addison-Wesley, Reading (1999)
4. Beck, K.: Extreme Programming Explained: Embrace Change. Addison-Wesley, Reading (1999)
5. Beck, K., Gamma, E.: JUnit: A Cook's Tour. Java Report (August 1999)
6. Seacord, R.: Software Engineering Component Repositories. In: Proceedings of the International Workshop on Component-based Software Engineering, Los Angeles, USA (1999)
7. Frakes, W.B., Kang, K.: Software Reuse Research: Status and Future. IEEE Transactions on Software Eng., vol. 31(7) (2005)
8. Hummel, O., Atkinson, C.: Using the Web as a Reuse Repository. In: Proceedings of the International Conference on Software Reuse, Torino (2006)
9. Baeza-Yates, R., Ribeiro-Neto, B.: Modern Information Retrieval. Addison-Wesley, London, UK (1999)
10. McCarey, F., Ó Cinnéide, M., Kushmerick, N.: An Eclipse Plugin to Support Agile Reuse. In: Proc. of the 6th Int. Conf. on Extreme Progr. and Agile Processes, Sheffield (2005)
11. Podgurski, A., Pierce, L.: Retrieving Reusable Software by Sampling Behavior, ACM Transactions on Software Engineering and Methodology, vol. 2(3) (1993)
12. McCarey, F., Ó Cinnéide, M., Kushmerick, N.: RASCAL: A Recommender Agent for Agile Reuse. In: Artificial Intelligence Review, vol. 24(3-4), Kluwer, Dordrecht (2005)
13. Gamma, E., Helm, R., Johnson, R., Vlissides, J.: Design Patterns: Elements of Reusable Object-Oriented Software. Addison-Wesley, Reading (1995)
14. Beck, K.: Test Driven Development: By Example. Addison-Wesley, London, UK (2002)

Using Horizontal Displays for Distributed and Collocated Agile Planning

Robert Morgan, Jagoda Walny, Henning Kolenda, Estaban Ginez,
and Frank Maurer

Department of Computer Science, University of Calgary
2500 University Dr. NW, Calgary, AB
Canada T2N 1N4
{morganr,hkolenda,maurer}@cpsc.ucalgary.ca,
{jkwalny,eginez}@ucalgary.ca

Abstract. Computer-supported environments for agile project planning are often limited by the capability of the hardware to support collaborative work. We present DAP, a tool developed to aid distributed and collocated teams in agile planning meetings. Designed with a multi-client architecture, it works on standard desktop computers and digital tables. Using digital tables, DAP emulates index card based planning without requiring team members to be in the same room.

1 Introduction

Project planning in an agile team is a collaborative process relying on face-to-face communication and shared information to succeed. A common approach to planning involves teams sitting down at a large table and planning iterations using index cards to represent user stories or feature requests. One downside to this involves distributed teams. Using paper-based index cards requires all team members to be collocated during the meeting. Another issue is that the cards' location on the table and their proximity to other cards can contain important information for the iteration. When cards are moved from the table, their arrangement is often lost and with it so is the proximity and location information.

Our goal is to develop a digital environment for distributed agile planning while preserving the benefits of card-based planning. We began our endeavor by observing a team interacting with cards at a table during multiple planning meetings. The cards were organized into sub-projects and again organized so that related cards were grouped together. We rarely observed cards being lifted off of the table; rather, cards were rotated to allow for better viewing by people sitting across the table. These initial observations led us to consider using digital tables as part of a solution. [7] is based on the same idea but the tool does not support distributed settings and its usability is limited due to low screen resolution and issues surrounding the creation of new story cards. A refined approach was needed to overcome these issues.

We analyzed different designs of digital tables to overcome the screen resolution issue. One approach is to design a high-resolution table out of several LCD displays.

This implied that the table would have bezels between the displays. To investigate a bezeled design, we observed the same team conducting a planning meeting, this time using a table with physical bezels. Our observations showed that the containers created by the bezels benefited the teams with the organization of the cards. These observations and findings were part of the motivation behind the work presented here.

Distributed agile teams are a reality in today's world. Index cards cannot be used effectively in a planning meeting when team members are dispersed around the globe. While conducting planning meetings (using speaker phones and paper index cards) with team members at the other location, we noticed that information is often lost when not all team members see the same set of cards. In such a setting, awareness of card layout had to be verbalized for the benefit of distributed members. An approach was needed to support a more natural interaction so that no one is at a disadvantage.

DAP is a planning tool modeled after paper-based planning. It provides an intuitive way for teams working around digital tables to interact with digital story cards. The system supports both mouse- and keyboard-based computers in addition to pen and touch-based systems. This feature allows users to modify the cards as if they were modifying paper cards with a pen. DAP is designed to work with digital table displays as well as with standard vertical displays. Horizontal table displays add the requirement of supporting individuals sitting at different sides of the table. As a result, support for rotating planning artifacts is necessary. This paper reports on the design and implementation of DAP.

The remainder of this paper is structured as follows: Section 2 looks at existing solutions for distributed agile planning and provides an overview of digital table technology. Section 3 shows by example how the DAP environment can be used in a distributed planning meeting. Section 4 provides a description of the DAP digital table environment. In Section 5 we look at the next steps for this research. We summarize our work in Section 6.

2 Related Work

Over the last years, many commercial and open source tools have become available to support the agile planning process. Many of these are web-based[2][15][17]. In general, existing tools provide the ability to create, modify, and delete story cards, and to place them into iterations. However, these tools are usually designed to run on vertical displays that are controlled by a single user. Interaction with these tools is quite different compared to using index cards and handwriting on a table.

CardMeeting [1] attempts to bridge the gap between browser-based systems and physical card-based planning. It displays electronic index cards in a browser on a computer screen. However, it is primarily focused on the visual aspect of card-based planning: only one user per site can interact with the tool at the same time, and it does not provide the iterations and progress tracking that other agile planning tools have. In addition, it gives no support for handwriting-based input, making it unsuitable for digital table environments.

Morgan et al [9] proposed a card-based tool for distributed agile planning that supports a more natural interaction between the participants. This project attempts to exploit the benefits found in collocated and table-based environments. There is a large body of knowledge in the human computer interaction community on the topic of table-based interaction techniques that has been helpful to our investigation [13].

Several projects have studied how electronic boards support collaboration and group-based interactions. FlatLand [10] presents a way of supporting collaborative activities by using electronic boards, focusing primarily on improving same-site group interaction techniques. In [5], researchers investigated innovative ways of face-to-face collaboration through information sharing between multiple displays.

Recently, [11] investigated the tabletop capabilities in distributed meetings. It concluded that the use of digital tables enhances and encourages collaboration and interaction in a group setting, especially among distributed teams.

Wigdor's [16] investigation presents a solution that improves information sharing for domains in which real-time collaboration is essential. His investigation asserts that recent developments in digital tables can be valuable in supporting face-to-face real time collaborative environments. He reports a series of design requirements for building of an effective table-centered space, and by coupling all these with a real life scenario, he explains how table-based environments are to be utilized when creating collaborative applications.

3 Motivating Example

We present here an example of how DAP is used in a distributed planning meeting.

Suppose Alice, Bob, Charles, and Dan collaborate on a multi-iteration project between two companies. Alice and Bob work in Location X, while Charles and Dan work in Location Y. It is time for their next iteration planning meeting.

Alice and Bob gather around their digital table, connect to the server that contains their project data, and launch DAP. They place a phone call via speakerphone to Charles and Dan, who are already waiting around their digital table (Figure 1). Alice opens the previous iteration, and all team members see the story cards from the previous meeting, their arrangement unchanged. Alice now creates a new iteration.

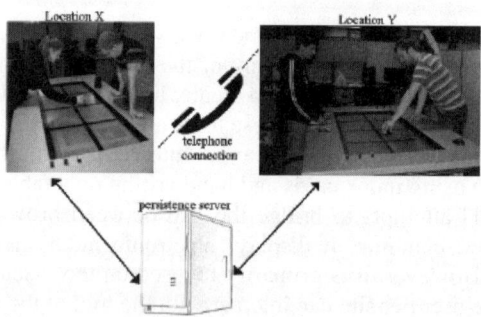

Fig. 1. Scenario for a distributed team meeting using DAP

While the team discusses the incomplete cards from the previous iteration, Alice points to a particular card that is assigned to Dan and asks a question. Dan immediately recognizes which card Alice is referring to because of the mouse pointer hovering over it. He indicates the card is incomplete and uses his finger to drag that card into the container for the new iteration. Charles asks Bob about a story card assigned to him. Bob drags the card to his side of the table and rotates it so that it faces him. The team decides that the card is not needed anymore, and Bob uses a simple hand gesture to delete the card.

After discussing the existing cards, it is time to create new ones. Charles uses his Tablet PC to create a new story, and quickly scribbles a few details about the task (Figure 2). Alice decides that she would like to work on the task as well, so she grabs the card that Charles just created with her Pocket PC. She then edits it to add her name, and places the Pocket PC back onto the iteration in order to save it. The changed card appears on the digital table in the same spot as her Pocket PC.

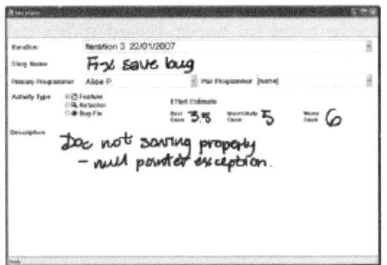

Fig. 2. Handwritten electronic story card

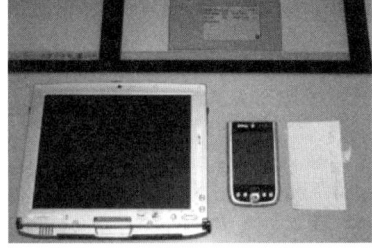

Fig. 3. Size comparison of Tablet PC, Pocket PC, paper, and digital story cards

4 DAP

DAP follows along the same line as work by Liu et. al.[6][7][8]. Their initial investigation looked at the impact of collocated planning on a digital tabletop environment. The investigation highlighted handwriting recognition and artifact organization as important functionality, and that areas which needed improvement included artifact creation, time estimation, and prioritization. The system presented here takes those recommendations into account but extends it in multiple aspects.

The current DAP provides various different methods of interaction to allow for a more flexible use and an increase in usability. We present DAP by highlighting the various methods of interaction to accomplish different tasks.

4.1 Environment Description

DAP is an amalgamation of software and hardware that, when combined, create a digital planning environment where story card based planning can be used by distributed and collocated teams alike. The planning environment makes use of visual representations for each type of planning artifact, with the iteration and backlog artifacts doubling as containers for story cards. To overcome the input resolution limitation of the digital table, DAP uses handwriting–enabled devices (Tablet PCs and Pocket PCs) to support creating and modifying story cards.

A central component to DAP is its use of digital tables. Our newly designed digital table provides a large, interactive, horizontal display surface. The output resolution of the table is approximately 10 MP. This large resolution allows displaying substantially more electronic index cards than conventional PC projectors. Interaction with digital tables is typically direct, using one's finger or other physical pointing device to control the on-screen mouse. The main advantage of a digital table is that it supports collaborative work environments: it allows many people to view and use a single display screen simultaneously in a face-to-face seating arrangement [13].

4.1.1 Story Card Creation and Modification

DAP supports a number of input mechanisms for creating and editing story cards. This is to allow team members to create and modify the cards in a way that is most comfortable and intuitive for them. Current digital tables do not provide an adequate input mechanism to support handwriting of the size used on paper-based index cards. A work around was found in using handwriting-enabled devices.

These small handwriting-enabled devices are employed to mimic card creation in a paper based planning meeting. Their primary purpose is to allow team members to quickly create and edit card content in a way that is similar to writing on an index card. The devices are well suited for these tasks as they can be easily held in one's hand or placed on the edge around our table. The DAP software for these hand-held devices focuses on creating and editing of card content; project and iteration information is limited to encourage interaction with the digital table DAP software.

DAP for the digital table is a full-featured planning tool. Its approach to creating card follows the idea of taking a card from a pile and placing it at the desired location on the table. This same approach is used for creating all other planning artifacts. The limitation with the digital table DAP is its ability to edit the card content.

4.1.2 Organization and Information Sharing

The digital table DAP focuses on allowing teams to organize planning artifacts. The visual representations of story cards, iterations, and backlog artifacts make it easy for anyone sitting around the table to place their finger on the artifact and drag it to a new location. Once again the interaction approach used tries to mimic the way teams move cards in a paper-based environment.

The moving of cards is not the only benefit that DAP brings to the table. A major component to DAP is its support of distributed teams. DAP's planning environment is shared with other DAP connected systems. Using existing tools, distributed planning presents some challenges when it comes to ensuring all team members see the same information at the same time. DAP shares the current state of the iteration plan in real time and pushes changes on one site out to all connected clients.

Live information updating is only part of DAP's consideration for distributed teams. Conversations taking place during planning meetings are often augmented by individuals gesturing with their hand to indicate context. This becomes very tricky when others can not see your hands. To overcome this limitation DAP uses telepointers, allowing for mouse gestures to be shared with other connected DAP tables. If a user moves a mouse on one site, the other sites see a mouse pointer moving too (i.e each display shows multiple mouse pointers).

We mentioned earlier that one advantage of digital tables is that some provide the ability for more then one individual to interact with the surface concurrently. This feature is important, as it is rarely the case that a single individual alone is interacting with the paper-based index cards on a (physical) table. DAP handles this situation by supporting multiple mice on the same site. This multiple mouse feature eliminates the need for any kind of turn taking mechanism and allows for collocated teams to work in a way that they are familiar with. The multiple mouse feature is combined with the telepointers to allow for everyone to see everyone else's interactions.

4.2 State of Implementation

DAP is heavily dependent on information exchange to provide its users access to the iteration plan in real time. To make everything work together seamlessly, DAP relies on a central persistence server to which all devices (PCs, digital tables, handheld devices) connect (see Figure 2). In order to synchronize clients in real time (as opposed to web-based systems that rely on repeated pull of information), DAP uses a push-based updating mechanism to provide near instantaneous feedback.

The use of digital tables is a central part of DAP and as such requires a digital table display. Our digital table is 8 x 4 feet with a 1-foot border for placing handheld devices and other meeting paraphernalia (e.g. coffee cups). Its display consists of 8 LCD screens. In total, we have an output resolution of approximate 10 megapixels. The placement of these 8 screens creates physical bezels useful for organizing story cards. Figure 2 shows the table in use.

In terms of handheld devices, we make use of Tablet PCs and Pocket PCs. It is important to note that handwriting recognition capability is limited by the state of the device's handwriting recognition technology.

DAP remains under development and features highlighted in our motivating example remain at various stages of completion. Features such as supporting distributed teams creating, editing, deleting and organizing cards are completed and are being used by us for distributed planning with our research partner. Multiple mouse support is in a prototype state and needs minor tweaking and stability enhancements. Card rotation is scheduled to be completed by summer 2007.

5 Discussion

DAP development has made significant strides towards reaching our goal of providing an environment that supports natural interaction for distributed agile planning meetings. DAP provides the benefits of a digital environment and preserves many advantages of paper based planning meetings by combining digital table technology and handheld devices with visual representations of planning artifacts.

Existing agile planning tools bring different aspects of card based planning to a digital environment. Web based tools provide project tracking and information storage to teams but they lose the spatial information provided by the location of planning artifacts. On the other hand, tools like [1] provide visual representations of cards that can be interacted with, but do not have a tracking aspect. DAP provides both project tracking and visual organization of cards at once, along with a natural way of inputting information and elements of non-verbal communication such as hand gestures (using telepointers). Telepointers, real-time synchronization, multi-use input on a single site, and handwritten index cards for distributed meetings are not available in any other agile planning tool.

Formal evaluation of DAP is scheduled for spring 2007 and we expect that the benefits of these features will result in improved team interactions for distributed agile planning meetings.

We note some limitations of the DAP environment. First, DAP does not provide an audio channel for communicating between teams in different locations. We do not plan to implement this functionality because this can easily be accomplished by a standard telephone conference call. Second, the handwriting recognition accuracy on the handheld devices is limited by the state of the art in that field.

It is important to note that DAP cannot solve all limitations of a distributed planning environment. There will surely be information lost by virtue of the fact that body language and facial expressions are a significant part of human communication, and much of what they convey is difficult to express over large distances. While this aspect may be important, dealing with it is outside the scope of our research.

6 Conclusion

We have presented DAP as a card–based planning tool to support distributed planning for teams sitting around a digital tabletop. Existing research highlights the importance of supporting natural interactions and encouraging face-to-face collaboration.

Existing planning tools provide limited support for interactions between distributed teams. Most tools do not provides support for keeping track of stories proximity to each other. DAP attempts to combine the benefits of digital tabletop environments and agile planning tools with the advantages of paper based story card planning.

DAP is still under development and so has a number of improvements planned. The two most notable are supporting gestures and changing seating arrangements. Gesture support would allow users to trigger actions such as deleting artifacts, cutting and pasting, and selecting groups of objects. Supporting changing seating locations would allow DAP to cater the orientations of cards based on the seating arrangement.

DAP is still work-in-progress and as such no formal evaluation has been completed. Through a formal evaluation, we would like to conclusively determine the benefits and drawbacks of using DAP. We believe that further examinations into the combination of digital tabletop environments and agile planning in both distributed and collocated settings is necessary. It is our sincere hope that tools like DAP will help agile teams in their distributed project planning endeavors.

References

[1] CardMeeting (2007) [Online] Viewed 2007, January 12. Available: http://www.cardmeeting.com
[2] Danube Technologies Inc. (2007) ScrumWorks – Product Overview. [Online]. Viewed 2007, January, 12. Available: http://danube.com/scrumworks
[3] Greenberg, S., Gutwin, C., Roseman, M.: Semantic Telepointers for Groupware. In: Proceedings of Australian Conference on Computer-Human Interaction, New Zealand, pp. 54–61 (1996)

[4] Greenberg, S., Tse, E.: SDGToolkit in Action. In: Video Proceedings of ACM CSCW'06 Conference on Computer Supported Cooperative Work, ACM Press, New York. Video and two-page summary (2006)
[5] Johanson, B., Fox, A., Winograd, T.: The Interactive Workspaces Project: Experiences with Ubiquitous Computing Rooms, IEEE Pervasive Computing Magazine, vol. 1(2) (April-June 2002)
[6] Liu, L.: An Environment for Collaborative Agile Planning, M.Sc. Thesis, University of Calgary, Department of Computer Science (2006)
[7] Liu, L., Erdogmous, H., Maurer, F.: An Environment for Collaborative Iteration Planning. In: Proceedings of Agile 2005, Denver, IEEE Press, New York (2005)
[8] Liu, L., Maurer, F.: Support Agile Project Planning. In: Proceedings of the Canadian Undergraduate Software Engineering Conference Ottawa 2005 (2005)
[9] Morgan, R., Maurer, F.: MasePlanner: A Card-Based Distributed Planning Tool for Agile Teams. In: Proceedings International Conference on Global Software Engineering (ICGSE 2006), IEEE Computer Society Press, Los Alamitos (2006)
[10] Mynatt, E., Igarashi, T., Edwards, W.K., LaMarca, A.: Flatland: New Dimensions in Office Whiteboards. In: Proc. of Human Factors in Computing Systems (CHI'97), pp. 346–353. ACM Press, New York (1997)
[11] Perron, R., Laborie, F.: Augmented tabletops, an incentive for distributed collaboration Horizontal Interactive Human-Computer Systems, TableTop 2006. First IEEE International Workshop on 5-7 January 2006, pages: 8 (2006)
[12] Rally Software Development Corp (2007) Software Development Life Cycle Management for Agile Development Teams. [Online]. Viewed 2007, January, 10. Available: www.rallydev.com/products.jsp
[13] Scott, S.D., Grant, K.D., Mandryk, R.L.: System Guidelines for Colocated, Collaborative Work on a Tabletop Display. In: Proceedings of European Conference Computer-Supported Cooperative Work (ECSCW), September 14-18, Helsinki, Finland, pp. 159–178 (2003)
[14] Tse, E., Greenberg, S., Shen, C., Forlines, C.: Multimodal Multiplayer Tabletop Gaming. In: Proceedings Third International Workshop on Pervasive Gaming Applications (PerGames'06), in conjunction with 4th Intl. Conference on Pervasive Computing, May 7th Dublin, Ireland, pp. 139–148 (2006)
[15] VersionOne LLC (2007) Agile Project Management Tool. [Online] Viewed 2007, January, 10. Available: www.versionone.net/products.asp
[16] Wigdor, D., Shen, C., Forlines, C., Balakrishnan, R.: Advanced interaction design: short papers: Table-centric interactive spaces for real-time collaboration. In: Proceedings of the working conference on Advanced visual interfaces (2006)
[17] XPlanner (2007) XPlanner Overview. [Online] Viewed 2007, January, 12. Available: http://xplanner.org

Applying Agile to Large Projects: New Agile Software Development Practices for Large Projects

Ahmed Elshamy[1] and Amr Elssamadisy[2]

[1] ThoughtWorks Inc.
Chicago, IL 60661 USA
Aselshamy@ThoughtWorks.com
[2] Valtech Technologies
Addison, TX 75001 USA
Amr@Elssamadisy.com

Abstract. Large software development projects are not agile by nature. Large projects are not easy to implement, they are even harder to implement using agile methodologies. Based on over seven years of experience building software systems using agile methodologies we found that large software projects require more practices than the usual used in small projects. In this paper, we will introduce a set of new and modified development practices, which will help developing a large agile project.

1 Introduction

Large software development projects have their own set of problems that need to be addressed [2,3,4,6,8,9,11]. For the purposes of this paper, let us consider a development project *large* if the development team is anywhere between 50 and 100 people (includes developers, testers, business analysts, and managers). Many of the standard development practices in agile methodologies do not provide their expected consequences [1,2,9].

In this paper we describe new and modified agile development practices, some of which we have used on different projects at multiple companies. Using this set of development practices along with the regular agile development practices will add to the success of a large project. At this point, many of these practices have only been used once or twice successfully – so use them at your own discretion.

2 Challenges in Applying Agile to Large Projects

One of the aspects common to many agile development methodologies is that the entire team (business analysts, developers, and testers) collaborate very heavily. With a large project, this type of collaboration is difficult at best. What we have found again and again is that we tend to break up into subteams for better communication. The downside to subteams is the possibility that the subteams build stove-piped subsystems if communication is insufficient among the teams. Problems of consistency and duplication may go undiscovered. Of course, there are other practices that help alleviate these problems such as rotating team members among the subteams, having an overall design document, etc. [4,6]. We are not invalidating these techniques, but in our experience they are not sufficient to alleviate the problems typical when separate subteams build separate parts of the system. Another way to state this problem is that the different subteams may result in a non-homogeneous and inconsistent architecture.

3 Divide After You Conquer

[11] Basically, instead of dividing the work first and then solving each sub-problem, start with a core team (usually about 20-30% of full team). The core team builds out a valid simple business case in a test-driven manner. This first phase lasts a nontrivial amount because we want to build out enough of the project that we touch all of the primary business areas (without dealing with alternative/exceptional scenarios) and build out most of the architecture. Because we have a small team, a full agile methodology works without modification. We end the first phase when we have a stable code base with a significant portion of the architecture built out and a broad swathe of business built. At this point we have *conquered* the problem and now it is time to *divide* by growing the development team and splitting up into smaller subteams to grow the project into a fully functional software system. Because the architecture has been built out in a test-driven manner we have the amount of complexity needed but no more. Teams now have a homogeneous architecture in the different subprojects. Unlike [2] we clearly define when we reach a more stable architecture as we have delivered business functionality at the end of the conquer phase. [2] recommends just declaring the architecture is stable to give the courage for developers to work on the existing code.

4 The Project Brain

After dividing the project into sub teams, a team of analysts, developers, QAs and managers are assigned to work on the big picture of the project *"The project brain team"*. After the division, each sub team starts to be in its own world. They act like different organs in a human body. Each has its own function but they all need a brain to interact together.

The overall project manager (or Scrum master) should have an over all vision of project. He is responsible for planning the whole project makes sure that sub-projects are going in parallel in a timely manner. Interdependent projects should have stories played according to the dependencies between these projects. The master project manager is responsible for making sure that these stories are played in a timely manner to resolve dependencies and to be able to test integration between sub projects as early as possible. Overall manager will have to manage the whole project plan according to sub teams' plans and their projected velocity. Mangers have to make sure the project will deliver on time. If a team needs extra resources due to missed requirements or underestimation of stories, resources may be acquired from other teams that are ahead of the plan.

Overall BAs (or customers) are responsible for creating integration and no-coding stories between sub projects. QAs have to test these stories and create test scenarios that will flow across project boundaries. Overall developers/architects are responsible for identifying integration points between projects and to work on or reassign defects to sub teams. Only overall project manager is required all the time once there are sub teams. Overall BAs, QAs, and developers can be assigned on as needed bases and rotate from different sub teams.

Developers on the brain team will maintain a master continuous integration build. They are also responsible for migrating DB and code changes to the master build. Issues with this build may be resolved with sub-teams.

5 Under the Hood Architect

There is no traditional architect role in most agile development methodologies. The design evolves through test driven development which involves a form of continuous design. Unfortunately subteams frequently cause a reinventing of the wheel. In traditional projects this was solved with upfront design. Upfront design is looked down upon (see a discussion below in 'Refactoring and Design Ahead'). With small teams, the architect role is frequently dropped. In large teams, however, it is often beneficial to reintroduce a modified version of this role. The two successful versions we have seen practiced are:

Keeper of the Theory of the Code: The architect is a member of the team with significant design and development talent and experience. A large part of the architect's role is to understand the 'whole' application code-base. The architect is hands-on and pairs with others on the team frequently and will be a participant in many agile modeling design sessions on the whiteboard. The architect understands the 'theory' of the code and can help guide others in new development to make sure that they are aware of how the part they are working on fits in the whole. This helps keep away redundancies and gives the code-base a homogenous reality.

Guiding hand: Here the architect is closer to a traditional role – all new major development efforts go through him. The architect is a participant in all major design and has veto power on how things are implemented. This architect is similar to the old command-and-control type with one major difference: design is still evolutionary.

6 No-Coding Stories

Stories are focusing on small parts of the system one at time. It is a good practice to focus on a small part of the system while developing it. Defining what needs to be done in small pieces would make the most complex system easy to develop. Developers, BA and QA will create their tests cases based on stories. Being that much story focused has an impact on test coverage and testing the interaction between different stories. Testing on the story level is not sufficient to test the system. The no-coding stories will depend on multiple individual stories and will be ready for testing only when all the dependant individual stories are done. Theoretically no-coding stories will not need any development efforts because it is an identification of a bigger test scenario that will combine multiple stories or an end-to-end test. Sometimes some development work might be done to get the full scenario to work or to prepare the test interface with the system. QA will create tests for the no-code story that will cover the overall scenario and the interaction of the individual stories. These stories will be played when all of individual stories are done. The main reason for the no-coding stories is to insure tests cases were created to cover more complex scenarios within one team and across multiple teams. No coding stories that run across multiple teams are created by the brain team.

7 Continuous Integration and the Build Process

Each sub-team will have their own build running. The brain team will have to create a master build that builds all sub-teams code and/or deploy their binary files. The master build will run frequently by pulling down the last successful builds for sub projects, compile and deploy the whole project and run the tests. In case of failure the brain team has to identify the problem and resolve it or take it to the responsible sub team to resolve it. Now when there is a failure the master build will rollback the sub-team(s) changes till the issue is resolved. It's highly recommended to use top of the line build machines for all of the subteams to save developers time. There are some requirements to get a smooth master build process. Functional tests for each sub team will run within a larger test suite by the brain team. There should not be any data conflict issues regarding this matter. Second functional tests should be solid tests.

There might be shared code between multiple projects, things like the main domain objects or libraries. Changes to these objects may affect other teams and would result in a rejected build from the master build. These changes have to be redone in accordance to having a rejected build. This is time consuming; it might take few cycles to get these changes right without breaking other team tests. Teams that use and change the shared code will have to run these tests to make changes on the shared code. Adding tests to verify usage of shared code by other sub teams that are just using it is also encouraged.

8 Two-Phase Commit Database Changes

Each sub team will have its own DB schema (that might extend to each developer will have his own). A master DB rebuild script will be used to rebuild the database with the build. This master file is shared by all sub-teams. Teams might have some shared db resource (table, stored procedures, trigger, etc…). Changes to these shared resources should be migrated across different teams. DB migration will be migrated in a two-phase-commit manner. Teams will make db changes by adding the changes into a predefined script file, the team build runs these changes automatically once it's there. The team will notify the brain team of these changes. The brain team will integrate these changes into the master script and run a full master build. If the master build is successful and every thing went fine they will integrate these changes into the master script and delete the changes file. If there are any issues, the brain team will notify any other team with the issues and wait on integration of the changes till the other team(s) resolved all the issues and try to rerun the changes again.

9 Communication Channels

Stand-ups are the most important communication channel. Sub teams will have their own stand-ups [13]. To ensure information exchange between teams everyday a member of each sub team should attend another team stand-up. A table should be created for the attendance so every team has a representative in the other team stand-up. The other team members should jump in anything related to their projects. Code reuse opportunity should be brought up in the meeting. Possible duplicate stories should also be identified. Team should discuss integration stories off-line.

Wikis, information radiators, group emails should also keep every body informed about other projects. Team outings, group lunch, similar activities should be scheduled every now and then. Such activities break the ice between teams, reduce *"us and them"* factor and improve teams' communication.

10 Refactoring and Design Ahead

In large projects Refactoring sometimes becomes very expensive process. Imagine a code base of a half million lines of code or more. A major refactoring to the code may take a month to be done. Some design ahead may be done to save expensive major refactoring later. Designing ahead has also its drawbacks as the design might not work for future requirements and then has to change or sometimes the design may be overkill to the requirements and will cause an overhead of maintaining extra complex code. There should be a compromise to make this decision of taking the chance of spending some time and effort of designing ahead for a design that might not work or may be more than what's really required for the project against spending time in refactoring existing code. Refactoring is still required to improve the design while implementing more functionality. For the conquer team when it's still early on the project, to avoid large complicated refactoring some extra time should be spent for designing for future known requirements. Having the overall picture of use cases will make it easier to predict future requirements and create a design that will handle them. This design ahead is allowed only during the conquer phase of the project and will only apply to core systems, frameworks and similar subsystems of the system which may be more expensive to be refactored. Designing ahead may require some future stories to be looked at and require analysis to be done for these future stories (out of order of the iteration planning).

11 Sharpening the Tools

Tools like functional tests, unit tests utilities, wiki pages, build scripts and DB scripts should be updated and made more efficient as much as possible. These tools are what being used to develop new functionality. If the cost to get a simple test to work is 30 minutes. If it's multiplied by 50 developers is 25 hours, if it happens over and over again, that's very expensive. Utilities and project library should be created to help writing tests and speed up implementing business stories. Using an object mother pattern for example is helpful in writing functional tests to set data up easily. Special attention should be given to build time. Keeping the build time low helps the project efficiency. Build time can be reduced by eliminating DB access in unit tests, use of in memory DB, using transactions in tests that rollback at test teardown and making the build script more efficient. Managers and team leaders should encourage tools sharpening activities. Tools will include hardware and software applications that help everyone on the project do his job more efficiently.

12 Unit Tests and Functional Tests

To reduce the coast of refactoring, the team may depend on functional tests more than unit tests. Functional tests test the functionality of the system and in general do not depend on the system design. Applying refactoring should not change the functional tests, but it will affect most of the unit tests related to the area being refactored.

Unit tests are still important and are very helpful for test driven development. Unit tests should still be created for test driven development and for critical pieces of the system that may cause the system to break. Tests that are created after the development and tests created for reported bugs should be functional tests. As functional tests will allow refactoring more often and still keep the system in a good working state. Having less unit tests will lead to more time spent in debugging issues and functional tests cannot pin point problems but having a better design through constant refactoring will reduce the development time much more than the extra time being spent in debugging issues. Functional test should be documented in each test to describe the test scenario, expected results and differences between test scenarios. Documentation helps fixing issues with functional tests and these tests will become good live behavior documentation for the system.

13 External Interfaces

Dependencies on external systems are normally points of failure for large projects. In many cases delivery dates were delayed because external interfaces were not completed or they did not work the way it's supposed to be. The system should be developed in a way to tackle external interfaces as early as possible. There should be enough time to test the external interfaces before the project delivery. The system should be developed horizontally to interact with the external interfaces as early as possible. Stubs may be created to allow the system to be tested while external groups are still working on implementing their part. The stubs should be removed and replaced with an actual access to the external system. Integration functional tests should be created on both sides to ensure the correctness of the system after the external groups finished implementing their part of the external interface. Teams may exchange functional tests as a contract for interacting with an external interface.

14 Night Watching

For a small project, it's easy for a team leader to QA code quality and coding standards. For a large project it may be much harder to achieve the same results without using coding style checking tools. Running code metrics is also extremely helpful. Checking the number of unit tests (make sure it's increasing), application layers are respected, lines of code, lines of test code and cyclomatic complexity [12] of the code. Running these code metrics tool on a nightly build and presenting the data in a graph over time would show hints for areas of improvements within the project. Noticing the number of unit tests declining of certain part of the system may need some explanation of team members working on this area. Performance tests may run with the nightly build to indicate any change in performance.

15 Keeping It Real

Testing with real data and real life scenarios is always encouraged. Brain team should schedule runs against massive real data in a nightly run style. Log should be investigated to find errors and issues. The purpose of these runs is to find issues when using real data. You will be surprised of how many data issues you may find. Testing should run on production like environment using the same database, operating system and application server. Real life test scenarios should be used in the no-coding stories and end to end testing.

16 Challenges in Applying These Practices

As we mentioned earlier the recommended practices in this paper will help mediate some of the problems in applying agile to large projects. There are also some difficulties in applying these practices that we should be aware of and try to avoid.

Having a master build is not as easy at it seams. The setup may take a couple of weeks, but the hard part is sustaining a successful master build. Sharing code between running sub projects is difficult and requires extra efforts in writing extra tests by sub teams to test usage of the shared code to avoid issues resulting from another team making changes to the shared code.

Still there should be more practices to improve communication between teams. With member rotation, standup attendance, wikis, emails and teams outing it's still not enough. Code duplication and missing possible refactoring might still occur. Teams have to be proactive about communication with other teams.

Designing ahead may get into the extreme of building useless frameworks. We suggested a compromise between just in time design and designing ahead. It's on case by case bases mainly for the conquer team. But there is no fine line to make the decision much easier.

Testing external systems might not be as easy. Accessibility to external systems might not be possible. There might be a charge each time there is an access to external system. Issues like that with external systems should be identified and associated with risks. Try to resolve these issues and still plan to test with external systems as early as possible.

References

1. Cockburn, A.: Agile Software Development, Pearson Education, Indianapolis, IN (2002)
2. Eckstein, J.: Agile Software Development in the Large: Diving into the Deep. Dorset House Publishing, New York, NY (2004)
3. Elssamadisy, A.: XP on a Large Project- A Developer's View. In: Marchesi, et al., (eds.) Extreme Programming Perspectives. Pearson Education, Indianapolis, IN (2003)
4. Elssamadisy, A., Schalliol, G.: Recognizing and Responding to "Bad Smells" in Extreme Programming, presented in International Conference on Software Engineering (2002)
5. Evans, E.: Domain-Driven Design: Tackling Complexity in the Heart of Software, Pearson Education, Indianapolis, IN (2004)
6. Jacobi, C., Rumpe, B.: Hierarchical XP: Improving XP for Large-Scale Reorganization Processes. In: Succi, et al., (eds.) Extreme Programming Examined, Pearson Education, Indianapolis, IN (2001)
7. Larman, C.: Applying UML and Patterns. Prentice Hall, Upper Saddle River, NJ (2001)
8. Rogers, O.: Scaling Continuous Integration, presented in XP 2004 (2004)
9. Schalliol, G.: Challenges for Analysts on a Large XP Project. In: Marchesi, et al., (eds.) Extreme Programming Perspectives, Pearson Education, Indianapolis, IN (2003)
10. Scott, K.: The Unified Process Explained, Pearson Education, Indianapolis, IN (2001)
11. Elshamy, A., Elssamadisy, E.: Divide after You Conquer, presented in XP 2006 (2006)
12. McCabe, T., Butler, C.: Design Complexity Measurement and Testing, Communications of the ACM 32, 12 (1989)
13. Schwaber, K.: Agile Project Management with Scrum. Microsoft Press, Redmond Washington (2004)

Job Satisfaction and Motivation in a Large Agile Team

Bjørnar Tessem[1] and Frank Maurer[2]

[1] Department of Information Science and Media Studies,
University of Bergen, NO-5020 Bergen, Norway
bjornar.tessem@uib.no
[2] Department of Computer Science,
University of Calgary,
2500 University Drive NW
Calgary, Alberta,T2N 1N4 Canada
maurer@cpsc.ucalgary.ca

Abstract. Agile software development processes emphasize team work in small groups as one of the features that contribute to high software quality and knowledge dispersion among developers. Research supports claims that agile methods also lead to higher motivation and job satisfaction among developers. Research in workplace psychology indicates that factors like autonomy, variety, significance, feedback, and ability to complete a whole task are significant factors to ensure satisfaction and motivation among workers. In this case study, we show, through the analysis of semi structured interviews with software developers and business representatives, that large teams continuously adapting the SCRUM methodology are able to ensure these empowering factors, and thus ensure a staff of motivated and satisfied software developers. The study presented is based on data from an agile project involving 70 people (including 30 developers) building a software product for the oil & gas industry.

Keywords: agile software development, large teams, SCRUM, job satisfaction, motivation, qualitative case study.

1 Introduction

Agile methods have become increasingly popular in the industry, but have also been struggling with the perception that they are not applicable for larger projects. Some have tried to show how agility can be ensured also in larger projects [4], but research on what factors are essential to help with agility in larger teams are scarce.

In this paper, we use knowledge from workplace psychology combined with data from a detailed case study to understand whether essential factors for agility can be present in large development projects and how these factors can be ensured in such a project. Our chosen approach is to look for the five critical factors of Hackman and Oldham's Job Characteristics Model (JCM) [5] in our interview data and explain why and how these factors are maintained in our case study.

We continue by presenting the SCRUM methodology and attempts to scale agile methods in the next section, and proceed with a more thorough description of JCM in

Section 3. In Section 4 we describe the case, which is a team that develops software for the oil & gas industry. We describe our analysis and arguments in Section 5, and discuss the results in Section 6, before concluding.

2 Agile Methods and SCRUM

Quite a few agile methods are used in industry. XP [2] is perhaps the most well-known and most widely used approach, but others also have their adherents. In particular, the SCRUM framework for managing projects [8] is commonly used. In a sense, SCRUM is more of a management methodology that encapsulates the daily practices of software engineers into a project structure. Many or all of the practices found in XP can thus be included in a SCRUM process, or the team may find other ways of doing the daily engineering work.

A SCRUM project is divided into iterations called sprints, lasting about four weeks. A backlog of things do be done is basis for planning. These "things-to-be-done" are usually called user stories, which are to be considered requirements for the software system, but may also be other tasks like bug fixes. The team estimates the work needed to do the jobs in the backlog, and a subset of them are prioritized and scheduled for the next sprint. The developers choose jobs to work on from the prioritized set of jobs, and report to the team on progress and impediments in short daily meetings. At the end of the sprint, the team goes through a retrospective meeting, where they demonstrate the software, assess the progress of the team and its work practices, and suggest and decide on improvements to be tried.

One issue in agile software development is how well methodologies scale to large projects with more than about 10-15 developers. Some authors, like Cockburn [3], indicate that scaling of agile methods is problematic, and difficult to realize due to the coordination issues met. Still, a concept like "SCRUM of SCRUMS" is found to be useful for making larger teams agile. Such teams are split into smaller sub-teams who run local a SCRUM process, and the team leads from each sub-team participate in the higher level coordinating SCRUM process - called "The SCRUM of SCRUMS" [8].

3 Group Work Research and Agile Methods

Within psychology, studies of the organization of work in groups and teamwork are many [1]. Using such perspectives, our concern is on how well-organized groups will display properties that result in employees who are more motivated and satisfied with their jobs. The assumption is that this in the next step will lead to productivity gains or other gains for the business. Within this research tradition, the factors

- Autonomy: the ability to define and solve your own work tasks
- Variety: the ability over time to work on different tasks.
- Significance: The ability to influence the result of the work process.
- Feedback: The ability to get meaningful responses to your efforts.
- Ability to complete a whole task: The ability to work on a task until it is complete without being removed or reassigned to other work.

are shown empirically to result in both higher motivation and job satisfaction for the employees (Job Characteristics Model (JCM), [5]), which again has been shown to lower turnover in the workplace [7]. Lower turnover has a significant cost effect on companies.

Job satisfaction and motivation are claimed to be one of the main effects of using agile software development methods, and this is confirmed by Melnik and Maurer [6] in a comparison of agile and non-agile software developers. In an ethnographic study of an XP team by Sharp and Robinson [9], we see how and why agile methods in fact contribute to create a work environment where the developers are highly motivated and satisfied with their work situation.

We can assume that the five factors of Hackman and Oldham's JCM model are present in smaller agile teams. But as small agile teams use the physical proximity and direct communication as means to ensure these factors, we are interested in how they are ensured in larger agile projects, where the number of participants requires more structured coordination and communication across sub-teams. This is the goal of the rest of this paper, where we see in a case study how motivation and job satisfaction is assured in a large scale SCRUM project.

4 The Case

The development project we are referring to in this study, was run within a large ICT company. The project's goal was to develop a production accounting system for the petroleum industry to distribute produced value among shareholders in oil and gas wells, using the terms gas allocation/oil allocation. While old legacy software for this area exists, several oil companies formed a consortium to develop common oil and gas allocation software using Java™ technology. The project started in 2005 and was supposed to deliver the complete software in early 2007 with a total effort of about 150 person years. The project started with only a few developers, and grew until it was the work place of a total of 70 persons including 30 developers plus business representatives, quality assurance people, managers, and technical support.

The development team followed a SCRUM methodology using XP practices like user stories, pair programming, and test-first design. In the beginning, the project was run as one single team with traditional SCRUM practices. At one time in the process, the team became too big because of an increasing amount of requested features from the business side. A need for specialization was recognized, and the development team was divided into three sub-teams. In addition, the project managers appointed an architecture and refactoring team consisting of earlier team leads, a user interface team, and several persons with specialized assignments. The project thus was run as a SCRUM of SCRUMS project. Working with the development teams were eight spocs (SPOC = Single Point Of Contact), as they were called in the project. The spocs were representatives from the industry and customer representatives in the team. They had the responsibility to come up with requirements or user stories. Also working with the developers were quality assurance persons (QAs), who also had substantial business experience and knowledge. Their responsibility was to test the software to see if it fit the intentions of the requirements and report bugs to the developers. Each development team had a couple of spocs and a couple of QAs assigned to them.

The physical setting of the team was a large open space where teams of developers were placed with computers around a large table, together with the associated spocs and QAs. Around this open space there were meeting rooms, management offices, and rooms for equipment, as well as other facilities.

5 Observations and Findings

The data we use for our analysis is mainly five semi-structured interviews gathered in this company. The interviews are part of a larger study where we focus on studying team work, decision making, and empowerment in software engineering. The interviewees either volunteered, or were appointed by agreement in the team after we asked for a QA and a woman developer. We interviewed three developers, of which one has a special role as a database migration specialist, one QA person, and one spoc. The interviews were done in fall 2006, a few months before the end of the project. Each interview took 30-60 minutes. In addition, we use general knowledge about the company gathered from observations at the locations, and various conversations with people involved in the project. The interviews are rich in context and opinions about the project as seen from interviewees' perspective.

The interviews were transcribed into about 40 pages of text, and analyzed through several rereads. In the presentation of our analysis, we particularly indicate support of the factors of the JCM model, as well as argue for how these factors are realized in the project. In addition we will indicate how we have used the data for looking for evidence of motivation and job satisfaction among project participants.

5.1 Autonomy

The developers' daily work was mainly pairing up with a colleague, picking a story, do some initial work to get an understanding of the story, divide into tasks, and then program tests and production code. This way of working gives the developer significant autonomy in the daily work. In between stories, developers fixed bugs. Ideally, they selected bugs from a bug registration system. However, it seems as if the QAs had a lot of influence on who was going to fix which bugs, and when. The developers respected this, but they also seemed to feel a small dislike for this.

As in other jobs, there are of course some limitations to autonomy for these developers. There are, for instance, architectural guidelines for the implementations, or the pair programming practice which is strongly encouraged by management. On the other hand, we see that confidence in people's abilities made leaders trust them with advanced tasks. One example was the database migration developer who together with another developer was responsible for developing the database migration process mainly on their own, choosing tools and automating solutions.

The spocs and QAs seemed to have a higher level of autonomy than developers, as they very much were able to work with their primary tasks their own way. In early stages, spocs did work in a single team separate from developers, but split up and specialized into different parts of the system like the developers. The QAs also seemed to be working individually, the one we interviewed had specialized in having the large picture of the development organization, and the tasks people were working on. That way she was, for instance, able to influence the assignment of bug fixes to the right people across teams, and also ensure that related bugs were handled together. Thus, she did through her own initiatives take an informal, but important role in the organization which gave her much influence on the project's progress.

5.2 Variety

Developers in this team worked with a variety of tasks, mainly implementing user stories and bug fixes, but their job was not only pure coding: they also had to create tests, get a precise understanding of user stories in collaboration with spocs and QAs, estimate user stories, and assess & improve work processes in the project. This brought them in contact with other issues than the purely technical, and thus contributed to a varied job. In the early stages of the project, all developers would also work on all parts of the system, as they all were part of a single team. However, for efficiency reasons, the project managers – during the project - split the developers into the several specialized teams. This has of course led to less variation in the kind of business domain issues or technical problems that developers meet.

Of course the spocs and QAs also participated in a variety of tasks, but in fact it seems as if they specialized somewhat more than the developers, as they really had a narrower focus in their daily work.

5.3 Significance

All the interviewees showed a clear understanding of the significance of their own and the other project members' role, although they also were aware of their own personal replaceability due to the spreading of knowledge in the team. Everybody's knowledge was considered important at meetings, which were highly informal.

Developers were occasionally able to influence the content of user stories, because by combining their domain and technological knowledge they were able to see simplifications or improvements to the requirements. There is an asymmetry here, because spocs and QAs were not able to influence the developers' way of solving problems. The spoc reported some frustration about this, because he felt that with his knowledge of the domain he could see software designs that obviously would have to be refactored later when new stories came up.

The team members were also able to significantly affect the work of the other teams through the project wiki. Another example is the QA interviewed, who had an understanding of special knowledge within the different teams, and were then able to distribute work to the right person not only in her own team, but in the whole project.

The interviews indicate that many of the changes in the organization seemed to originate in dissatisfaction among the project members, and when the pressure built up, the issue would be attacked by someone. This happened around the demo sessions that were held at the end of sprint. The number of participants and the amount that should be demoed made this event grow to a size so that many felt it was a waste of time. The demo meetings were removed from the process and today the developers only have ad hoc demos with the appropriate spoc(s) when user stories are completed.

5.4 Feedback

The most important form of feedback found in the project was the daily feedback given in the direct communications between developers, QAs, and spocs in order to get a common understanding about what the content of the user stories was. The QAs and spocs also had direct contact with their colleagues in the other teams to get feedback on their work. The role of feedback in the sub-teams seemed to be invaluable. Developers tried to get feedback on their work results often and early.

From our data, there seemed to be little feedback about solutions and technological issues between developers in different teams. Such feedback would presumably take the way around the team leads. The project members, however, did get regular feedback on their own progress from the project management.

All the interviewees mentioned the very friendly tone among team members, indicating that the project was almost conflict free. Although there were misunderstandings and disagreements, these were solved in an open way, with respect for each others views and with good solutions as common goals.

5.5 Ability to Complete Whole Tasks

The allocation of work in many agile teams and also in this team makes it easy for developers to identify with tasks that have been fulfilled. The user story represents a task that produces a visible part of the software. This is somehow opposed to some other practices for work assignment within software engineering where developers are given a specification for parts of the solutions, and do not have full responsibility in completing the whole requirement. In this project, the completion of user stories was involving some ceremony as the developers would give a demo to the spocs. Thus, the surrounding organization acknowledged their contribution. Spocs and QAs did not have this type of task completion, but worked more continuously on providing user stories and testing the software. Still, in particular for the spocs, the completion of a sprint marked a completion of work, as they worked both alone and collectively to finalize new user stories for development in the next sprint.

An interesting story suggesting the importance of identifying with a task, and developer's ability to complete it, is when the project due to time pressure, started a practice that was called double pair programming. Two developers would work on a user story each, whereas a third developer would alternate in supporting the two programmers. Soon, people were all doing single programming. Most likely this was due to the fact that the third programmer did not feel responsible for any of the stories the two others worked on. The practice was abandoned because of this, they returned to pair programming, and the interviewee telling about this reported a significant improvement in both productivity and quality as a consequence.

5.6 Motivation and Job Satisfaction

Statements from the interviewees about a willingness to work hard to complete their tasks within the defined sprints indicated high motivation among the team members. The interviewees used positive phrases like challenging, 'I like the software', friendly, and gently about the project and the development environment. A very positive statement from one of the developers verifies high job motivation and satisfaction:

"I think the work, the environment that we have here is quite interesting. I think I'm very happy to be here. I'm honored to be on this project. I think it is a big challenge to me. I don't think there are a lot of companies out there doing something like this." (Developer, woman)

While discussions with some team members indicate that there was low turnover in the project, we do not have any hard data whether this perception was actually real.

6 The Project as a Growing Organism

Through the analysis, we have seen that this particular project has been able to maintain the critical factors of JCM, as well as job satisfaction and motivation, and thus the JCM theory has been shown to be applicable. A perhaps more challenging problem is to explain what has happened in this project to keep the agile values, at the same time as coordination and efficiency issues had to be considered for the growing team. Our suggestion is to use of an analogy to growing organisms. They are initially small. As they grow, they adapt their shape to the surroundings or go through a restructuring. But as the organism approaches its end of life, it stabilizes into a fixed form which is not changed much in the last phases of life.

To see how this fits, let us go through the project history. The team first started with only a few programmers, with everyone working in the same group. However, as the need for more developers led to a larger team, it was evident for the management that a division into specialized sub-teams was needed. This way, daily work in small teams was maintained. When that split occurred, spocs worked in a separate team to create user stories. This lead to a distance between developers and spocs, and important feedback disappeared. The solution was that spocs specialized too and were placed together with the separate teams. Thus, direct communication between developers and business representatives was strengthened again. A significant change for all parties seems to have been the removal of the large demo sessions. This was a change that was initiated from within the teams, but was accepted as management saw that the demos did have little value. A late change was the introduction of the database migration task, which involved one and a half person. A more efficient method for repopulating the test databases was needed, and the management asked for volunteers for this task. Towards the end of the project, we also see that people were expected to stay within their special fields. The mature process did not change much anymore and team members just didn't see any value in the retrospectives. A more rigid organization developed as everybody worked hard towards delivery.

Case studies are often problematic to transfer to other circumstances, and whether this growing organism model may transfer to other projects remains to be seen, as the same practical solutions may not be possible in other projects. However, in our analysis, we see that essential values of agile teams like small team size, open communication, participation in decisions, and voluntarily choosing tasks has been maintained, and ensured the motivation and job satisfaction we would like to see.

7 Conclusion

In this qualitative case study, we have shown how a large SCRUM team can show properties usually found in smaller agile teams, namely high degrees of motivation and job satisfaction. We have looked for the essential factors supporting these and verified their presence in the case project. We demonstrated that autonomy, variety, significance, feedback, and the ability to complete a whole task were factors prevalent in the project. The study suggests that one way of maintaining agility in software development as the software and the developer team grows, is to let it grow slowly like an organism, where management continuously takes into consideration both business value and motivation and job satisfaction issues when deciding upon changes.

References

1. Batt, R., Doellgast, V.: Groups, Teams, and the Division of Labour: Interdisciplinary Perspectives on the Organization of Work. In: Ackroyd, S., Batt, R., Thompson, P., Tolbert, P. (eds.) The Oxford Handbook of Work Organization, Oxford University Press, Oxford (2004)
2. Beck, K., Andres, C.: Extreme Programming Explained: Embrace Change, 2nd edn. Addison-Wesley Professional, London (2004)
3. Cockburn, A.: Agile Software Development. Addison-Wesley Longman Publishing Co. Inc., Redwood City (2002)
4. Eckstein, J.: Agile Software Development in the Large: Diving Into the Deep. Dorset House Publishing Co., New York (2004)
5. Hackman, J.R., Oldham, G.R.: Work Redesign. Addison-Wesley, Reading, MA (1980)
6. Melnik, G., Maurer, F.: Comparative Analysis of Job Satisfaction in Agile and Non-agile Software Development Teams. In: Abrahamsson, P., Marchesi, M., Succi, G. (eds.) XP 2006. LNCS, vol. 4044, pp. 32–42. Springer-Verlag, Heidelberg (2006)
7. Mobley, W.H.: Employee Turnover: Causes, Consequences and Control. Addison-Wesley, Reading (1982)
8. Schwaber, K.: Agile Project Management with Scrum. Microsoft Press (2004)
9. Sharp, H., Robinson, H.: An Ethnographic Study of XP Practice. Empirical Softw. Eng. 9(4), 353–375 (2004)

Motivation and Cohesion in Agile Teams

Elizabeth Whitworth and Robert Biddle

Human-Oriented Technology Laboratory
Carleton University, Ottawa, Canada
elizabethwhitworth@gmail.com, robert_biddle@carleton.ca

Abstract. This research explored aspects of agile teamwork initiatives associated with positive socio-psychological phenomena, with a focus on phenomena outside the scope of traditional management, organizational, and software engineering research. Agile teams were viewed as complex adaptive socio-technical systems. Qualitative grounded theory was used to explore the socio-psychological characteristics of agile teams under the umbrella research question: What is the experience of being in an agile software development team? Results included a deeper understanding of the link between agile practices and positive team outcomes such as motivation and cohesion.

1 Introduction

A growing body of evidence suggests that participants in agile team environments find the experience particularly rewarding; more so than most other software development environments. A survey by Cockburn and Highsmith [1], for example, found that agile methodologies were rated higher than other methodologies in terms of morale. Although the 'hype' surrounding agile methods is likely a strong contributor to such enthusiasm, there seems to be a solid basis for the association of agile practices with the idea of 'project chemistry' or positive 'team climate' that can contribute to high performance.

Pockets of literature surrounding software development methodologies contain strong references to socio-psychological issues, such as ego, well-being, control, and team conflict [2]. Even so, there is a lack of basic research into the socio-psychological experience of individuals in agile software development teams — or any other type of software development team, for that matter. Agile and software engineering literature was found to be overwhelmingly based on management and engineering perspectives, concerning the practicalities of software construction, software development processes management, and the hurdles of making it all work within a business context.

The motivation for this research, therefore, was to better explore the animation and excitement observed in practitioners of agile software development. We hoped that examination of positive experiences in agile teams would yield a deeper understanding of the aspects of agile methods that support cohesive team activity. It should be noted that the view of agile in this study is based on, but not limited to, Extreme Programming (XP) practices [3].

2 Theoretical Framework

The framework for this study defines agile software development teams as complex adaptive socio-technical systems. Systems theory [4], on which the framework is based, is a determining influence in small group interaction theory [5,6], and already used in some instantiations of agile software development. Exploration of system properties, such as feedback and feedforward loops, was valuable in that it supported an understanding of invariant relationships that remained constant despite complex and evolving systems, and would be difficult to obtain through use of simple cause and effect paradigms. Advances in systems theory related to human agency further outlined the importance of considering the team itself as a holistic entity that has an impact on individuals. We found the socio-technical perspective valuable in that it highlights the importance of considering agile teams as systems comprised of both social and technological components. The use of physical artifacts in agile, for example, such as interactive wall charts and automated testing tools, is integral to team coordination and motivation. Practices such as daily stand-ups and pair programming were also viewed as technology, in that they too structure and mediate team interaction. Socio-technical thinking addresses that fact that management and engineering perspectives tend to focus on either the social or the technical aspects of team activity respectively, and thus fail to account for the fact that human and technical subsystems interact and mutually adjust, often with dramatic effect.

3 Method — Grounded Theory

Grounded theory [7,8,9] is a research methodology that provides a set of procedures for the systematic collection and analysis of qualitative data. Grounded theory is characterized by use of the constant comparative method of analysis. Data and abstract concepts are constantly compared to each other, ensuring the development of an integrative theory that is firmly and empirically grounded in raw data. Twenty-two participants were recruited through networking with members of the agile software development community. Participants included a variety of roles, including developers, interaction designers, project managers, coaches, and quality assurance specialists. All but two of the participants had previously worked in non-agile teams. There were sixteen male participants, and six female participants. Participant interviews investigated the subjective experiences of individuals in agile software development teams. Semi-structured interviews were chosen in order to maintain focus on the theoretical framework, while still leaving room for phenomena significant to participants to emerge. Each interview was audio recorded and transcribed. The transcriptions were broken down into discrete parts and incidents were identified, conceptualized, and named in the process of open coding. Open coding was conducted line by line to ensure thorough grounding and critical thinking about the data. Axial coding was then used to examine the relationships between data. Open and axial coding were performed in parallel as data were gathered, analyzed, and reanalyzed in light of the emerging theory or concepts.

4 Results

Participants in this study, when asked about software development teams characterized by strong feelings of excitement, discussed well functioning teams that 'clicked,' 'gelled,' or 'really worked together' to successfully develop software. Such 'cohesive' teams can be held in comparison to non-cohesive teams, which were not associated with feelings of excitement. The distinction between cohesive and non-cohesive teams in this study was separate from the distinction between agile and non-agile teams. Examination of results therefore involved the question: what characteristics of agile teams are related to team cohesion? The following sections outline key aspects of the answer. Interview segments are referred to by three radixes, for example (L.4.35), identifying the interview batch, the number of the quoted participant within each batch, and the interview paragraph.

Ease of Interaction. One of the main factors associated with enjoyment and excitement in agile software development teams was the ease and speed by which team members could get things done; questions were answered, problems were resolved, and collaborative opportunities were quickly grasped.

(T.3.33/44) And so once we started adopting some of the agile techniques in the previous product I was working on, they were very welcomed. It was instantly recognizable as a pleasant way to work for the people, for the developers, for the managers, for everybody involved; because there is less crisis, it's easier to manage, you have a better idea of what it really takes to deliver what people are asking for. It's so much more manageable... I mean it takes out uncertainty, it reduces the risk, crisis management, it's easy to schedule and plan — everyone's happier.

A Clear Objective. What was found to be one of the most valuable aspects of agile software development methodologies in supporting cohesive teamwork was that they provide a clear team goal — to deliver the most business value to the customer in a certain amount of time. Cohesive agile teams were also seen to maintain a strong focus on developing quality software code. The value of such goals from a team perspective is that they are objectives that most everyone in the team will agree to and happily work towards, without the reservations or divisiveness commonly associated with specifications-driven objectives.

(L.1.82) "Have you been on a really dysfunctional team?" In some ways that spec driven team was a bit dysfunctional, but that might have just been my perceptions. Um — it's bits like there's more push to meet the spec than to meet the customer needs. I mean, in my view that's dysfunctional, but in terms of most software engineering teams, it's not.

The Planning Game. In addition, the team goal is instantiated in a clearly visible and rigorous process as outlined by the agile practices such as the "planning game". Participants often noted the agile prioritization and planning procedure as a point of pride in their team process, and expressed feelings of excitement in that it allowed them to negotiate to create a plausible plan to develop software:

(T.1.11) There is a lot of tension is just when you develop a feature; there is only so much you can do ... the product specialist will often come in with a list of a 1000 items on it, [and] there is this dance that takes place and the developer estimates, they say 'well I can do 50 of those' ... And so we will have discussions about that a lot earlier and that also causes a little bit of tension because you know, now the product specialists realize the implications of all they are asking for. And then likewise the developers realize that they actually do need to put some thought into how they are going to do something so that they can provide reasonable feedback and reasonable estimates.

Agile planning was noted as especially valuable as a means of generating group agreement, and was seen to greatly reduce the tension and conflict traditionally surrounding requirements specification and planning. Collective participation and negotiation, in particular, rather than top-down mandates, was seen to strongly support individual involvement, engagement, and buy-in to project planning and activity.

The ability of the agile plan to adjust and allow for specific project and team needs was particularly related to cohesive team activity. The agile practices of allowing developers to estimate their own stories, for example, and the fact that the project plan would then be constructed around these estimates, seemed associated with the feel of 'rhythm' or 'flow' often discussed with regard to agile teams. Planning in this manner was seen to allow individual pace and team pace to be highly synchronized, where tasks to be completed were neither too difficult nor too easy for individuals in the time allotted. Such team momentum and responsiveness was highly related to excitement and motivation in the agile team environment.

(T.5.5) What I have done in the past has been different, like at other companies where it was more waterfall where you created an obnoxious UI stack from now until next year; and then stuff changed, and I am not a big fan of that. You know there is a lot of investment in terms of writing stuff out and then once you have done all that, the commitment is really high to keep all of that in, even though it may not be the best solution.

Long term planning was also associated with pressure for individuals to ensure that their specific needs were met in a plan that they would have to live by for the course of development. In comparison, iteration-based plans spanning a week, two weeks, or a month, seemed to increase the perception of the current situation as temporary or non-fatal. Flexible and short term planning was therefore seen to allow for more relaxed team relations in planning and implementation, seemingly because there is less at stake. Customization of the agile plan was seen as reducing preoccupation with personal tasks and goals, and allowing a focus on generating agreement and succeeding in team-based software development around a small number of tasks. Interestingly, while the agile plan was seen to highly regulate individual behavior over the course of an iteration, the relatively constrained nature of the agile environment was related to feelings of liberation:

(O.2.15) It's invigorating, because for the first time in your career you know exactly what is expected of you.

Regular Iterative Delivery. Iterative delivery was seen to increase the sense of immediacy in the team environment; particularly through the prioritization process, which meant that the majority of the team would always be working on the most important thing. The fact that team members had to deliver a working product at the end of the week or month was further seen to increase the sense of urgency in team interactions, and the capacity for team members to resolve or put aside personal differences in order to work together to deliver. The ability to deliver regularly was several times noted as the main motivator related to agile software development:

(O.2.8) You are working on something and at the end of the week it goes out to the customer and you get feedback right away. And that's great, because your work matters; every day matters. You notice when we have a new product and you are working on it for 6 months and then it is really tough going; because you are not delivering.

Agile practitioners, in delivering working software on a regular basis, were increasingly able to see the purpose and value of their efforts outside the context of development tasks, as well as outside of the context of project activity. Holistic understanding in the larger context of development was seen to provide meaning to low-level tasks, and to support the ability and willingness of team members to create software that would be of value to customers and users:

(T.2.48) You know I am trying to think back in the old way when I was on [another larger project]. I think those user issues were very much filtered. So by the time it got to me [there was] not a lot of background as to what the original task was and what the original situation was, [which] makes it harder to question ... Whereas I think definitely on this product there is a lot more interaction that way and we can go back and forth and say 'You know I know a customer said he wanted this but I think really it would work better if we gave him this,' which to me makes a better product definitely. I really got the sense of that being a problem in [on the old team]; where you work, you work and work and work on a feature, in the end it isn't exactly what they want but at that point it's too late; and I think in agile you at least modify it on the way and get, end up with a better solution. Does that motivate me better? Yeah I think so.

Thus splitting the planning and development activity into small chunks was related to increased motivation and enjoyment surrounding project activity as a whole:

(T.3.18) On other projects or teams that I was on, it was very much you define a bunch of features and then you worked on them for months and then you bug fix for twice as long and that was the release. So you really didn't know what the big picture was, ever. You just knew that one of these or a couple of these features were what you were supposed to work on for however long and then you are just fixing bugs for ten months or — well that's an exaggeration, but that's pretty much what it felt like.

Splitting the development process into iterations was seen to increase energy in the team environment and allow the team to work together more cohesively. Finally, consistent iterative delivery was seen as a source of pride, and highly related to the motivation to maintain team standards. It was additionally associated with high levels of trust and security, in that agile team members were well practiced and assured in their ability to work together as a team to produce results:

(X.4.11) I don't think that we would have been so consistent in our releases if we had done it otherwise ... The main point is that I feel more secure about what I'm doing. Very strongly. It's also what they tell you the basic reasons behind unit testing, continuous integration. And it's basically that. And I really feel it like that. You really prove after two weeks that this thing is really working, in a more or less stable way.

(O.2.13) We will do it. We always do it.

5 Interpretation

The main value of agile methods in supporting team cohesion, as well as motivation and excitement, was found to be their ability to support collective team culture. Collective team functioning, where each individual is aware of and invested in the activity of the team as a whole was seen to support feelings of personal security and control; feelings that seem to be absent in many instances of software development in teams.

The stability provided by agile planning and iterative development as a team was seen to offset increasingly unpredictable development environments. Team-based software development is an unstructured, complex, creative, and social, problem-solving and design activity (see Warr & O'Neill [10]). Software development outcomes are further dependent on the resolution of interdependences between team members, the synergy resulting from team-wide discussion and collaboration, and the ability of all team members to share a common vision for the software to be developed. Such activity and coordination must be differentiated from 'knowledge work'. Cohesive software development teams in this study were set apart, not by their ability to 'leverage specialist knowledge' or 'utilize human resources,' but by their ability to get all members of the development team to work closely together towards a common goal. Agile methodologies were seen to allow, support, and even *require* the development of a collective culture over time.

The instantiation of such a culture seems highly dependent on feedback and feedforward mechanisms in the agile socio-technical system, where agile practices support heightened team member awareness of collective tasks, goals, and progress. A study by Eby and Dobbins [11], for example, found that personal preference towards collective group activity is related to positive past experience working in teams and self-efficacy for teamwork, as well as the need for social approval. Positive experience can be seen to result from agile planning and iterative delivery. Positive experience results from agile planning and iterative delivery, which allows teams to develop a history of success, and thus increase the likelihood of team member involvement in collective activity.

Self-efficacy for teamwork was also seen to be particularly well maintained by agile methodologies. Eby and Dobbins discuss team self-efficacy with regards to efficacy expectations and locus of control [12]. Efficacy expectations involve perceived self-efficacy regarding effort or skill expended in effecting change in a specific context. The related but distinct concept of locus of causality or control, on the other hand, involves the amount of controllability or modifiability of one's environment. Agile practices such as daily team meetings and continuous integration and testing, which focus daily activity on the collective goal of working software, and which provide constant feedback on the validity of individual actions in relation to team goals, were seen to greatly increase perceptions of self-efficacy and control in the team environment.

The negotiation of a flexible plan well suited to team capabilities was further seen to increase individual perceptions of team-wide self-efficacy and control. Other factors such as positive feedback in the agile social and development environment (see Bandura [13]), and detailed and holistic awareness and involvement in project activity, particularly by way of information radiators and the evolutionary development of a working software product, also supported such feelings of self-efficacy. In contrast, software development environments where those conducting development tasks were relatively uninvolved in the development of a detailed project plan, or where team members were not clued-in to the day-to-day activities of others, were related to high levels of discomfort, dissatisfaction, and the absence of perceived team self-efficacy and control, seemingly regardless of the actual state of the project.

This study was not focused on measures of performance, but it should be noted that the presence of self-efficacy in the agile team environment indicates a socio-psychological environment of high-performance. It is generally accepted, for example, that performance in both physical and academic tasks is enhanced by feelings of self-efficacy [14], with effects ranging from the physiological [15] to the socio-psychological. The Collective Effort Model of Karau and Williams [16] adds to such findings. According to this model, individuals will work hard on a given task only to the extent that a) they believe that their hard work will lead to better performance, b) they believe that this performance will be recognized and rewarded, and c) the rewards are ones that they value and desire: "individuals working alone will exert effort only to the extent that they perceive direct links between hard work and the outcomes they want" [14].

Aspects of agile teams, such as transparency, highly focused iterative delivery, and noticeable measures of progress can therefore be seen to increase perceived linkages between day-to-day effort and valued collective goals, such as delivery. Agile environments thus provide motivation for individuals to work harder towards team goals when compared to environments where team members are less aware of the activity of others, or where it is less clear how the team is working together to produce results.

6 Conclusions

This paper has described our study of positive socio-psychological phenomena in agile teamwork. Our theoretical framework was complex adaptive socio-technical systems, and we used the qualitative approach of grounded theory based on interviews with members of agile teams. Our results lead to a deeper understanding of the link between agile practices and positive team outcomes such as motivation and cohesion. In particular, it appears that these positive outcomes are strongly linked to operation and effect of agile practices.

References

1. Cockburn, A., Highsmith, J.: Agile software development: The people factor. IEEE Computer, vol. 34 (2001)
2. DeMarco, T., Lister, T.: Peopleware: Productive projects and teams. Dorset House Publishing Co., Inc., New York (1999)
3. Beck, K., Andres, C.: Extreme programming explained: Embrace change, 2nd edn. Addison-Wesley Professional, Reading, MA, USA (2004)
4. von Bertalanffy, L.: An outline of general system theory. Britisch Journal of Philosophie of Science (1950)
5. Arrow, H., McGrath, J.E., Berdahl, J.L.: Small groups as complex systems: Formation, coordination, development and adaptation. Sage, Thousand Oaks (2000)
6. Ilgen, D.R., Hollenbeck, J.R., Johnson, M., Jundt, D.: Teams in organizations: From input-process-output models to IMOI models. Annual Review of Psychology 56, 517–543 (2005)
7. Charmaz, K.: Grounded theory. In: Smith, J.A., Harré, R., Van Langenhove, L. (eds.) Rethinking methods in psychology, Sage Publications, Thousand Oaks (1995)
8. Glaser, B.G., Strauss, A.: The Discovery of Grounded Theory. Aldine, Chicago, IL, USA (1967)
9. Strauss, A., Corbin, J.: Basics of Qualitative Research. Sage, Thousand Oaks (1990)
10. Warr, A., O'Neill, E.: Understanding design as a social creative process. In: Proceedings of the 5th Conference on Creativity and Cognition(C&C '05), London, UK (2005)
11. Eby, L., Dobbins, G.: Collectivistic orientation in teams: An individual and group-level analysis. Journal of Organizational Behaviour, vol. 18 (1997)
12. Bandura, A.: Self-regulation of motivation and action through anticipatory and self-reactive mechanisms. In: Dienstbier, R. (ed.) Nebraska Symposium on Motivation 1990, vol. 38, University of Nebraska Press, Lincoln, NB, USA (1991)
13. Bandura, A.: The explanatory and predictive scope of self-efficacy theory. Journal of Social and Clinical Psychology, vol. 4 (1986)
14. Baron, R.A., Byrne, D.: Social Psychology, 9th edn. Allyn and Bacon, Needham Heights, MA, USA (2000)
15. Bandura, A., Cioffi, D., Taylor, C.B., Brouillard, M.E.: Perceived self-efficacy in coping with cognitive stressors and opioid activation. Journal of Personality and Social Psychology, vol. 55 (1988)
16. Karau, S.J., Williams, K.: Social loafing: A meta-analytic review and theoretical integration. Journal of Personality and Social Psychology, vol. 65 (1993)

How to Build Support for Distributed Pair Programming

Jacek Dajda and Grzegorz Dobrowolski

Department of Computer Science
University of Science and Technology
Cracow, Poland
dajda@agh.edu.pl, grzela@agh.edu.pl

Abstract. Agile methodologies with their close collaboration principle remain in conflict with the present trends of developing software in geographically distributed teams. To resolve it, a suitable tool support for certain lightweight practices must be provided. Although systems of this kind are reported to exist, they do not meet the expectations. Presented paper proposes an iterative approach to developing discussed support. As a verification of the presented assumptions, a dedicated Distributed Pair Programmers Editor was developed and experimentally verified.

Keywords: distributed pair programming, methodology and tools.

1 Introduction

Agile programming reflects a new direction in the philosophy and techniques of modern software development. The close physical proximity, considered a crucial factor in the success of agile project, is also often pointed out as a significant limitation of agile methodologies. The globalization of computer science industry and growing costs of software development cause companies to locate software development centers in geographically distributed sites. Therefore, a problem arises to maintain close collaboration practices and run agile project in a distributed setting. As a solution to this problem, a suitable tool support is usually employed, however, it seems insufficient at the moment.

The aim of this paper is to propose an iterative approach to building efficient supporting systems of this kind. The paper presents a set of general requirements that become a basis for further investigation into distributed collaboration needs and challenges. As a verification of initial assumptions, a new system was designed and part of it, that is responsible for supporting distributed pair programmers, implemented and experimentally evaluated.

The paper first introduces available solutions, then proceeds to propose a set of general requirements of discussed support and present Distributed Pair Programmers Editor that was developed. Finally, experimental evaluation results and further work plan are included.

2 Existing Solutions for Distributed Pair Programmers

The support for distributed pair programmers can be realized by tools of general purpose and dedicated solutions. The first group includes conferencing applications (e.g. Microsoft NetMeeting), virtual whiteboards and desktop sharing solutions. The example of second group tool is TUKAN environment with a pair programming oriented tool consisting of voice-video connection and other communication means. In [1] authors present another solution: Sangam plug-in to Eclipse IDE with a dedicated editor and basic synchronization. A novel concept of transparent video interface is introduced by Facetop project [2]. It integrates and lines up side-by-side the video streams of distant programmers, overlying them over the transparent desktop at the same time. Not only can they see each other pointing to some spot at the shared screen but also manually control the mouse pointer. In order to join the advantages of Sangam and Facetop projects, [3] proposes a prototype combination of these tools.

Although presented solutions provide support for distant collaboration, their efficiency does not meet expectations. Strict firewall restrictions, long latencies and poor quality can hamper a pair programming session with a use of video conferencing approach. Sangam plugin for Eclipse claims to provide a solution for these limitations. It does not require high network bandwidth as it sends only significant session changes, not the whole screen image. However, it does not meet authors' expectations due to lack of significant features such as write blockade in navigator's editor. What is more, Sangam project is no longer maintained. Intern, Facetop project, while still under development, is not available for PC and download.

3 The General Requirements for the Discussed Support

As the available tool support is not satisfactory, the need for its further development arises. In spite of high variety of existing solutions, there is no common subject on how pair programming should be maintained in distributed setting. This paper proposes the following general requirements for discussed support, a computer system in turn:

1. The system must support (preserve, stimulate, not suppress) the phenomenon of synergy which is not only the most valuable but also crucial factor, especially under the circumstances of a team and distribution of its pairs.
2. The system ought to cover all functions that are recognized as necessary or useful in the *geographically collocated* mode, which stay in accordance with the primary requirement, including also functions which are decisive only for the *friendliness* of it.
3. The system must fulfill all requirements for a modern computer system of its type as long as a conflict with the primary or secondary requirements (necessary ones) does not arise.

A very interesting observation arises, that as long as requirements 2 and 3 can be fulfilled based on usual practice, the primary requirement needs a special approach. It is proposed here to take advantage of a real-life experiment. A thoroughly monitored team trying to realize a real task using the system under consideration. It is expected that, without significant intervention in the process of software development, it is possible to formulate the detailed functions of the system, tune its parameters and, finally, to tailor it to the needs. This approach, iteratively driven, is expected to provide informative feedback, necessary for system enhancement.

In [4] authors identified 7 synergetic behaviors of pair programming. One of them is Negotiation behavior. It refers to common observation that pair programmers inspect greater number of alternatives and consider different approaches to the same problem, elaborating better solutions in result. To maintain it, the supporting tool must provide efficient communication channels. The question of their types and implementation arises.

In order to sustain the phenomenon of the synergy in distributed setting, all of the synergetic behaviors should be supported. However, due to space limitations of this paper, the attention is put to Negotiation only.

4 System Design and Implementation

The general requirements became a base for developing Distributed Pair Programmers Editor. Based on previous experiences [5], the following communication channels were pointed out: video and voice connection, text chat and code based pointers. This proposal was done with an intention of experimental verification and assessment.

The editor was developed as a part of a larger system called Agile Studio, meant for supporting selected agile practices. It has been observed that every collaboration is likely to take advantage of certain shared objects. Therefore, the editor is based on server-client architecture, where server side is responsible for sharing synchronized instances of the session objects. In case of the editor, these are source files.

As a result of previous experiments and proposed enhancements, authors decided to implement the editor in the form of plugin to Eclipse IDE. It consists of three views and an editor wrapper. The editor wrapper can be attached to any Eclipse editor and handle its synchronization with the remote instance. This includes: code changes, marking, scrolling and folding. To improve programmers' Negotiation their cursors are visible in the remote partner's editor. This serves as another communication channel. Figure 1 presents all these functions in action.

Among others, Figure 1 emphasizes the feature of colored editor background, which indicates the current role of the programmer. Green editor background indicates the programmer is a Driver and can modify the shared code. Blue color informs about Navigator role and read-only access. This feature was added based on the feedback received during previous experiment and can be treated as an additional communication channel enhancing the Negotiation process.

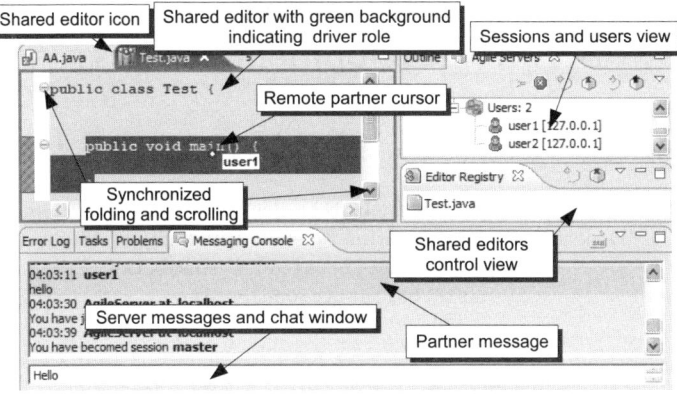

Fig. 1. Distributed Pair Programmers Editor

5 Experimental Verification and Further Work

The plan for evaluation experiment assumed a simulation of production environment, with 6 students working for 30 hours in a standard *collocated* mode and with the use of developed editor. According to observations and feedback questionnaire, the editor proved capable of supporting distant pair programming. Among others, internet co-navigation and more IDE synchronization (e.g. opening pop-ups) were suggested as possible enhancements. In addition, participants confirmed the usability of the remote cursor functionality and keyboard ownership background notification, which is useful during frequent changes of session master (e.g. hot discussions and negotiations on specific code fragments).

Future work includes further development of the editor based on the obtained feedback and further experiments. In addition, thorough tests regarding various settings and operating systems are planned, as well as introducing the project into the Open Source community.

References

1. Ho, C.W., Raha, S., Gehringer, E., Williams, L.: Sangam: a distributed pair programming plug-in for eclipse. In: Eclipse '04: Proceedings of the 2004 OOPSLA workshop on eclipse technology eXchange, pp. 73–77. ACM Press, New York (2004)
2. Stotts, P.D., Smith, J.M., Gyllstrom, K.: Support for distributed pair programming in the transparent video facetop. In: XP/Agile Universe, pp. 92–104 (2004)
3. Navoraphan, K., Gehringer, E.F., Culp, J., Gyllstrom, K., Stotts, D.: Next-generation dpp with sangam and facetop. In: Eclipse '06: Proceedings of the 2006 OOPSLA workshop on eclipse technology eXchange, pp. 6–10. ACM Press, New York, NY, USA (2006)
4. Williams, L., Kessler, R.: Pair Programming Illuminated. Addison-Wesley Longman Publishing Co. Inc., Boston, MA, USA (2002)
5. Dajda, J., Ciszewski, S.: Supporting extreme programming in distributed setting. AGH Computer Science, pp. 49–62 (2005)

A Metamodel for Modeling and Measuring Scrum Development Process

Ernesto Damiani[1], Alberto Colombo[1], Fulvio Frati[1], and Carlo Bellettini[2]

[1]Department of Information Technology, University of Milan
[2]Department of Information Science, University of Milan
{colombo,damiani,frati}@dti.unimi.it
carlo.bellettini@unimi.it

Abstract. Many organizations using agile processes would like to adopt a process measurement framework, e.g. for assessing their process maturity. In this paper we propose a *meta-model* supporting derivation of specific data models for agile development processes. Then, we show how our meta-model can be used to derive a model of the Scrum process.

Keywords: Software development process, Scrum, MOF, meta-model.

1 Introduction

Software Process Management (SPM) is aimed at controlling and managing all the resources involved in software production. Four core SPM responsibilities can be defined [6]:

- *Process Definition*, including the creation of the environment required for controlling the process;
- *Process Measurement*, including all measurement activities needed to detect deviations from the process expected performance or behavior;
- *Process Control*, including all actions taken to control the process behavior;
- *Process Improvement*, including all changes to the process that can improve its capabilities and performance.

In this paper, we focus on the first two responsibilities, describing *i)* a generic environment for modeling agile development processes, and *ii)* a generic measurement framework, that can be applied to any process instantiated in the environment.

As an application, we describe a roadmap to achieve the formalization of the agile development process Scrum using the OMG *Meta-Object Facility* (MOF). The paper is organized as follows. Section 2 discusses some related works about development process measuring and modeling. Then, Section 3 describes our meta-model and the related measurement framework, while Section 4 uses the proposed schema to model the agile process Scrum, showing how a measurement framework can be applied to Scrum. Finally, Section 5 presents our conclusions.

2 Related Work

The idea of a meta-model for the development process is well established in literature. Seminal work by *Mi and Scacchi* [7] defined meta-modeling as "a constructing and refining a process concept vocabulary and logic for representing families of processes and process instances in terms of object classes, attributes, relations, constraints, control flow, rules, and computational methods". Mi and Scacchi's meta-model was developed for representing generic knowledge about the software process. Other approaches, like the *SD packages*, were specifically aimed at representing statistical or numerical information. The latter approaches have given rise to sophisticated, performance-related process analysis tools (see http://www.intelsystech.com/), while generic process meta-models have targeted extensibility, relying on process vocabularies represented as ontologies [10].

More recently, a need for standardizing process descriptions in order to support interchange and fusion of process data emerged. *Piattini et al.* [9] described the advantages of using Object Management Group's standard Meta Object Facility (MOF) to represent software processes. MOF (Meta-Object Facility) is a standard supported by OMG [8]: it defines a generic pattern for the construction of systems based on metadata.

Conceptually, MOF can be described as a layered structure composed of four levels: at the top there is *i)* the definition of all the concepts and attributes of the MOF language itself, which is used to build *ii)* meta-models, which define the structure and semantic of the metadata describing a generic environment; then, meta-models are used to create *iii)* models, that depict specific objects and describes the structure (e.g., the relational schema) for *iv)* representing and storing the user data.

Recent work by *Ventura Martins et al.* [13] presents the *ProjectIT* initiative, including a complete software development workbench and an example of development process meta-model.

All these approaches are based on the MOF-based SPEM (*Software Process Engineering Meta-model*) specification [12] proposed by OMG to describe a concrete software development process or a family of related software development processes. While in this paper we focus on applying the meta-model notion to agile processes, a general, detailed description of our own SPEM-based proposal for a measurement framework and of a set of metrics for the assessment of a generic software process is reported in [5].

3 Process Development and Measurement Meta-Model

In this Section we show how MOF is used to define two meta-models: one used to generate models for describing the development process and the other used to generate models for describing a measurement framework. Again at the meta-model level, we also define a simple *trigger* layer that connect the two meta-models.

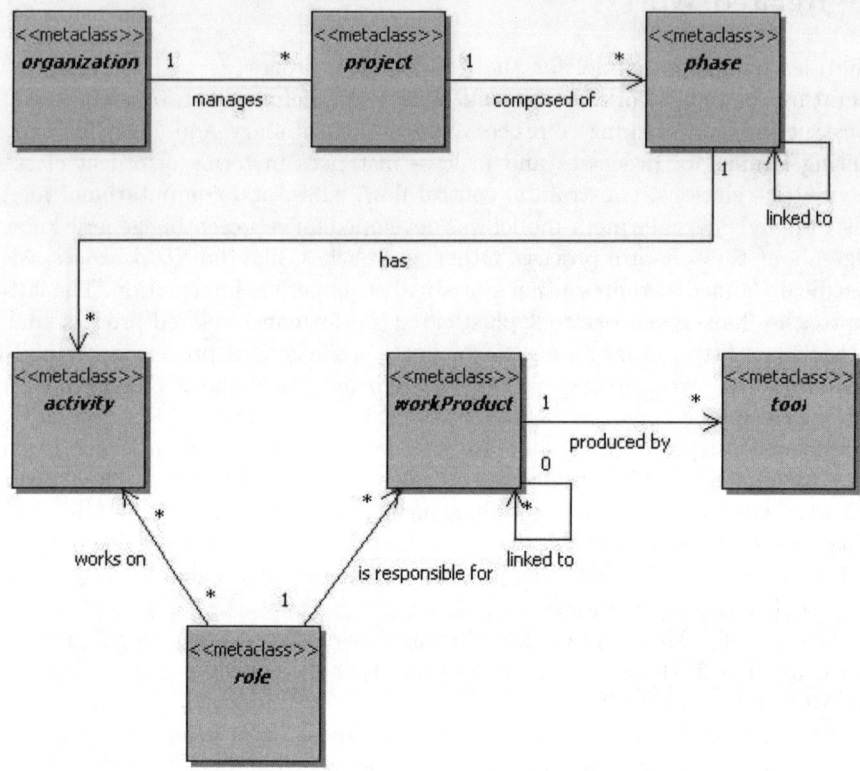

Fig. 1. Development Process Meta-model

3.1 Development Process Meta-Model

The meta-model that describes the development process has been designed to be as generic as possible. We took SPEM [12] as a basis of our work and simplified it by considering only meta-classes that can be interesting for measurement purposes.

To facilitate meta-model description, Fig. 1 contains a graphical representation of our process meta-model, where the boxes depict meta-classes, and arches indicate relations. The top element of the meta-model is the class[1] *Organization*, that gathers all the *Project* nodes and supports enterprise-wide analyses across projects. The class *Project* represents a single project of an organization; each project is associated to a specific development process, that is defined as a set of phases.

A development process is presented as a non-empty set of *Phase* classes. Each phase can be linked to another phase, to allow iterations in the development process, and is composed by a series of *Activity* classes; depending on the level

---

[1] Note that, for the sake of simplicity, in the remainder of the paper, the terms *class*, *entity*, and *node* are used in place of *meta-class* to denote meta-model elements.

of granularity chosen, each activity could be itself decomposed in *Task* or *Subactivity*. Here, for the sake of conciseness, we limit our description to activity classes.

Further, each activity is in relation (many-to-many) with the following classes:

- *Workproduct*, that represents the set of workproducts the activities are expected to produce
- *Role*, that defines the roles that cooperate to carry out a specified activity and produce a set of workproducts;
- *Tool*, that indicates the tools required to use and produce workproducts within activities.

3.2 Measurement Framework Meta-Model

The measurement meta-model, depicted in Fig. 2, is based on the Goal/Question/Metric paradigm (GQM) [1] that establishes a mechanism for defining and interpreting software measurements. In particular, the GQM approach requires

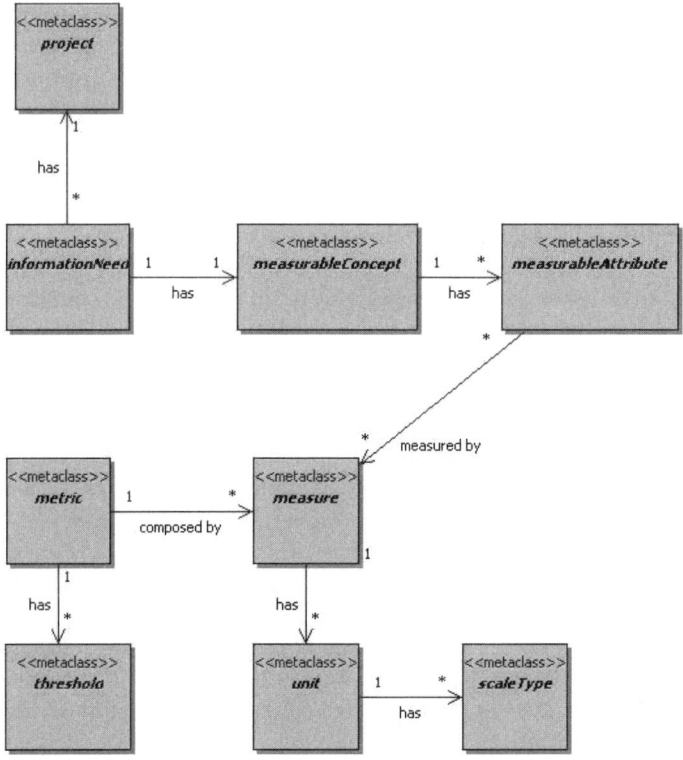

Fig. 2. Measurement Framework Meta-model

organizations to specify the goals for their projects, and traces these goals to the data that are intended to define these goals operationally, providing a framework to interpret the data and understand the goals.

Specifically, our measurement meta-model is defined as a skeletal generic framework exploitable to get measures from any development process.

The *InformationNeed* node is the container node that identifies the information need over which all the measuring actions are based, as for instance an internal process assessment. This node is used as a conceptual link between the two meta-models.

Following the GQM paradigm, the *measurableConcept* class defines the areas over which the analysis is based; examples of measurableConcept data instances could be "Software Reuse" or "Software Quality", indicating as goals an assessment of software reuse and software quality level within the organization.

The *measurableAttributes* node defines which attributes have to be measured in order to accomplish the analysis goals. Furthermore, this element specifies the way how attribute values could be collected: indeed, there a strict relation between *workProduct* and *measurableAttribute* classes.

The *measure* class defines the structure of measurement values observed during a measurement campaign. *Measure* is strictly related to *unit* and *scaleType* classes, that define, respectively, the unit of measurement used and the type of scale adopted (nominal, ordinal, and so forth). In particular, *measure* is in relation with the *metric* class, that defines conditioning and pre-processing of measurements in order to provide meaningful indicators. Finally, the *metric* class is in relation with the *threshold* node that specifies the threshold values for each metric when needed for qualitative evaluation.

3.3 Trigger Meta-Model

The trigger meta-model defines a skeletal middle layer that connects development process and measurement framework meta-models, factoring out entities that model application of measures to attributes. Fig. 3 shows the trigger meta-model and its relation with the other two meta-models.

The trigger meta-model is composed of two entities: *trigger* and *triggerData*.

Trigger is the class that represents a specific question, component, or probe that evaluates a specific attribute in a given moment of the development process. Indeed, *trigger* is related to the *measurableAttribute* class in order to specify which attributes are to be measured, and with *organization, project, phase*, and *activity* classes to indicate the organizational coordinates where attributes have to be measured.

Finally, the *triggerData* class identifies a single result of a measurement action performed by a trigger instance. There is a slight but important difference between data represented by *triggerData* and raw measures: measure instances supply triggerData values to metrics applying, whenever necessary, suitable aggregations to reduce the cardinality of triggerData result set.

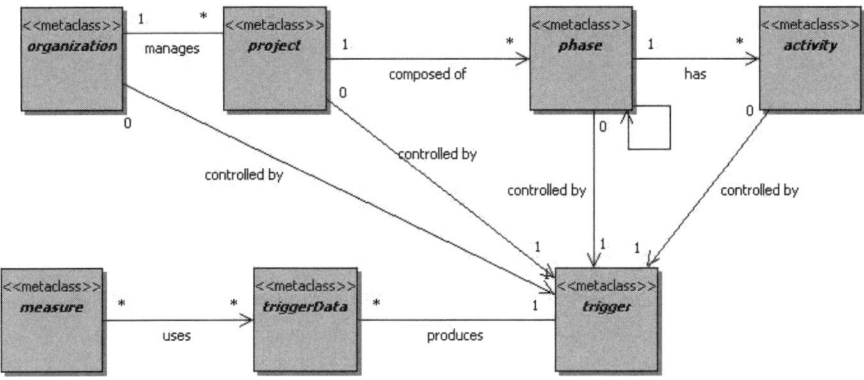

Fig. 3. Trigger Meta-model

4 Scrum Model

In this section we use our software process meta-model to model an agile process and couple it with measurement framework. As a proof-of-concept, we shall focus on the Scrum development process [2,4]. A major difference between traditional development processes and empirical ones like Scrum is that analysis, design, and development activities during a Scrum process are intrinsically unpredictable; however, a distributed control mechanism is used to manage unpredictability and to guarantee flexibility, responsiveness, and reliability of the results. At first sight, it may seem that Scrum's unpredictability could make it difficult to use a measurement framework to assess a Scrum process. However, we shall see that our meta-model seamlessly superimposes a measurement framework to Scrum activities.

4.1 The Scrum Development Process

In the following sections we propose an instance of our development process meta-model based on Scrum, defining phases, activities, and workproducts of it. Our description of Scrum is based on the work of *Schwaber* [11] that clearly defines Scrum phases and workproducts and gives guidelines for defining its activities.

Phases and Activities. The Scrum process is composed by the following five phases (see Fig. 4):

1. *Planning*, whose main tasks are the preparation of a comprehensive Backlog list (see Section 4.1), the definition of delivering dates, the assessment of the risk, the definition of project teams, and the estimation of the costs. For this phase, none activity has been formalized; to maintain coherence with the proposed meta-model, we define a generic *planningActivity*.

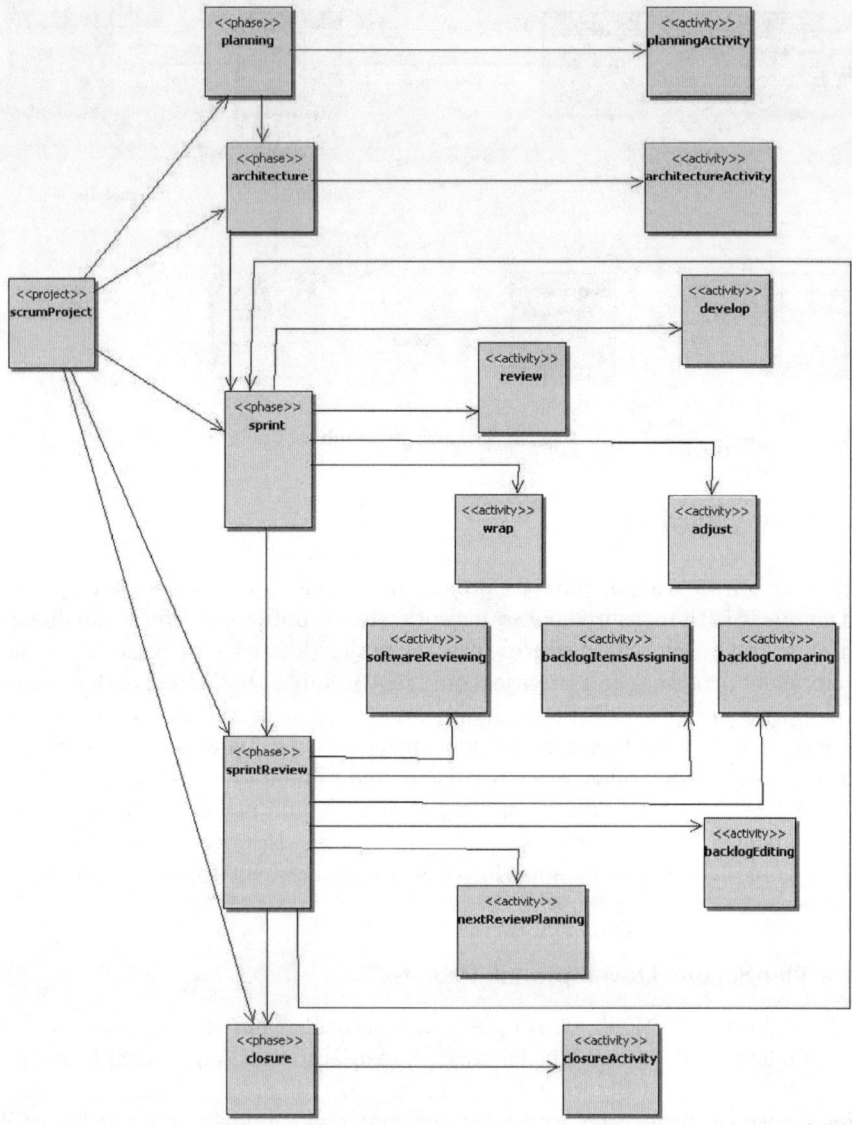

Fig. 4. Scrum model

2. *Architecture*, that includes the designing of the structure of Backlog items and the definition and design of the system structure; also for this phase we have instanced a generic *architectureActivity*.
3. *Sprint*, that is a set of development activities conducted over a predefined period, in the course of the risk is assessed continuously and adequate risk controls and responses put in place. Each Sprint phase consists of one or more teams performing the following activities:

- *Develop:* that defines all the development actions needed to implement Backlog requirements into packets, performing changes, adding new features or fixings old bugs, and documenting the changes;
- *Wrap:* that consists in closing the modified packets and creating an executable version of them showing the implementation of requirements;
- *Review:* that includes a review of the release by team members, which raise and resolve issues and problems, and add new Backlog items to the Backlog list;
- *Adjust:* that permits to consolidate in modified packets all the information gathered during Sprint meetings.
4. *Sprint Review*, that follows each Sprint phase, whereby it is defined an iteration within the Scrum process. Recent literature [11] identified a series of activities also for the Sprint Review phase:
    - *Software Reviewing:* the whole team, product management and, possibly, customers jointly review the executable provided by the developers team and occurred changes;
    - *Backlog Comparing:* the implementation of Backlog requirements in the product is verified;
    - *Backlog Editing:* the review activities described above yield to the formalization of new Backlog items that are inserted into the Backlog list;
    - *Backlog Items Assigning:* new Backlog items are assigned to developers teams, changing the content and direction of deliverables;
    - *Next Review Planning:* the time of the next review is defined based on the progress and the complexity of the work.
5. *Closure*, that occurs when the expected requirements have been implemented or the project manager "feels" that the product can be released. For this phase, a generic *closureActivity* has been provided.

Workproducts. A typical Scrum work product is the *Backlog*, a prioritized list of *Backlog Items* [3] that defines the requirements that drive further work to be performed on a product. The Backlog is a dynamic entity, constantly changed by management, and evolves as the product and its environment change. The Backlog is accessed during all activities of process and modified only in during Review and Backlog Editing.

Backlog Items define the structure and the changes to apply to the software. We identified as instances of our workproduct class the entities *Release* composed by a set of *Packet* that includes all the software components implemented. Fig. 5 shows an excerpt of the Scrum model showing relation with our activity and workproduct instances. It is important to note that each workproduct instance is characterized by a list of measured attributes that are themselfes instances of the *measurableAttribute* class of our measurement meta-model. During the configuration of the data representation and storage environment, it is necessary to point out which attributes to measure and which workproducts consider in measuring these attributes.

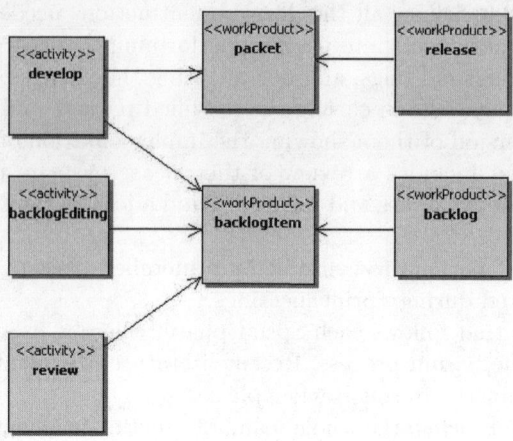

Fig. 5. Relations with workproducts and activities

```
BACKLOGITEM(id, name, description, priority, category, version, state,
            estimatedEffort)

BG-DEV(backlogItemID, developID)

DEVELOP(id, startDate, finishDate, sprintID)

SPRINT(id, startDate, finishDate)

PROJECT(id, name, description, startDate, finishDate)
```

Fig. 6. A database schema for Scrum data complying with our data model. The table *BG-DEV* implements the many-to-many relation between the *BACKLOGITEM* and *DEVELOP* tables.

5 Conclusion

In this paper we have laid the basis for a framework to model a generic software process meta-model and related measures, and we propose an instance of the meta-model modeling the agile process Scrum, showing how the assessment of such a process is possible without deranging the approach at the basis of this methodology. It is important to remark that the data model we generated for Scrum supports creating and maintaining Scrum process data, e.g. using a relational database. A sample set of tables complying to the model are shown in Fig. 6.

Having been generated from our standard meta-model, the Scrum model can be easily connected to similar models generated for different agile processes like XP, supporting enterprise-wide measurement campaigns in organizations that adopt multiple agile methodologies. We shall explore this issue in a future paper.

Acknowledgments

This work was partly founded by the Italian Ministry of Research under FIRB contracts n. RBNE05FKZ2_004 TEKNE and n. RBNE01JRK8_003 MAPS.

References

1. Basili, V.R.: Software Modeling and Measurement: The Goal Question Metric Paradigm. Computer Science Technical Report Series, CS-TR-2956 (UMIACS-TR-92-96), University of Maryland, College Park, MD (1992)
2. Beedle, M., Schwaber, K.: Agile Software Development with SCRUM. Prentice Hall, Englewood Cliffs (2001)
3. Beedle, M., Devos, M., Sharon, Y., Schwaber, K., Sutherland, J.: SCRUM: An Extension Pattern Language for Hyperproductive Software Development. In: Harrison, N., Foote, B., Rohnert, H. (eds.) Pattern Languages of Program Design 4, pp. 637–651. Addison-Wesley, Reading, MA (2000)
4. Cockburn, A.: Agile Software Development. Addison-Wesley, London, UK (2001)
5. Colombo, A., Damiani, E., and Frati, F.: Processo di Sviluppo Software e Metriche Correlate: Metamodello dei Dati e Architettura di Analisi. Nota del Polo - Ricerca n. 101, Italy (available in italian only) (February 2007)
6. Florac, W.A., Carleton, A.D.: Measuring the Software Process: statistical process control for software process improvement. Addison-Wesley Professional, Boston, USA (1999)
7. Mi, P., Scacchi, W.: A Meta-Model for Formulating Knowledge-Based Models of Software Development. Special issue: Decision Support Systems 17(4), 313–330 (1996)
8. OMG Meta Object Facility (MOF) Home Page (2006) www.omg.org/mof/
9. Ruíz, F., Vizcaíno, A., García, F., Piattini, M.: Using XMI and MOF for Representation and Interchange of Software Processes. In: Proc. of 14th International Workshop on Database and Expert Systems Applications (DEXA'03), Prague, Czech Republic (2003)
10. Scacchi, W., Noll, J.: Process-Driven Intranets: Life-Cycle Support for Process Reengineering. IEEE Internet Computing 1(5), 42–49 (1997)
11. Schwaber, K.: SCRUM Development Process. In: Proc. of OOPSLA'95 Workshop on Business Object Design and Implementation, Austin, TX (1995)
12. SPEM Software Process Engineering Metamodel (2006) www.omg.org/technology/documents/formal/spem.htm
13. P. Ventura Martins, A.R. da Silva.: PIT-P2M: ProjectIT Process and Project Metamodel. In: Proc. of OTM Workshops, Cyprus, pp. 516–525 (October 31-November 4, 2005)

Tracking the Evolution of Object-Oriented Quality Metrics on Agile Projects

Danilo Sato, Alfredo Goldman, and Fabio Kon

Department of Computer Science
University of São Paulo, Brazil
{dtsato,gold,kon}@ime.usp.br

Abstract. The automated collection of source code metrics can help agile teams to understand the software they are producing, allowing them to adapt their daily practices towards an environment of continuous improvement. This paper describes the evolution of some object-oriented metrics in several agile projects we conducted recently in both academic and governmental environments. We analyze seven different projects, some where agile methods were used since the beginning and others where some agile practices were introduced later. We analyze and compare the evolution of such metrics in these projects and evaluate how the different project context factors have impacted the source code.

Keywords: Agile Methods, Extreme Programming, Object-Oriented Metrics, Tracking.

1 Introduction

In recent years, the adoption of agile methods, such as Extreme Programming (XP) [4], in the industry has increased. The approach proposed by agile methods is based on a set of principles and practices that value the interactions among people collaborating to deliver high-quality software that creates business value on a frequent basis [5]. Many metrics have been proposed to evaluate the quality of object-oriented (OO) systems, claiming that they can aid developers in understanding design complexity, in detecting design flaws, and in predicting certain quality outcomes such as software defects, testing, and maintenance effort [8,11,14]. Many empirical studies evaluated those metrics in projects from different contexts [3,6,7,10,13,17,18] but there are a few in agile projects [1,2]. This paper describes the evolution of OO metrics in seven agile projects. Our goal is to analyze and compare the evolution of such metrics in those projects and evaluate how the different project context factors have impacted the source code.

The remainder of this paper is organized as follows. Section 2 describes the projects and their adoption of agile practices. Section 3 presents the techniques we used to collect data and the OO metrics chosen to be analyzed. Section 4 analyzes and discusses the evolution of such metrics. Finally, we conclude in Sect. 5 providing guidelines for future work.

2 Projects

This paper analyzes five academic projects conducted in a full-semester course on XP and two governmental projects conducted at the São Paulo State Legislative Body (ALESP). Factors such as schedule, personnel experience, culture, domain knowledge, and technical skills may differ between academic and real-life projects. These and other factors were discussed more deeply in a recent study [16] that classified the projects in terms of the Extreme Programming Evaluation Framework [20]. This section will briefly describe each project, highlighting the relevant differences to this study as well as the different approaches of adopting agile methods.

2.1 Academic Projects

We have been offering an XP course at the University of São Paulo since 2001 [9]. The schedule of the course demanded 6 to 8 hours of weekly work per student, on average. All academic projects, except for projects 3 and 5, have started during the XP class, in the first semester of 2006. The semester represents a release and the projects were developed in 2 to 4 iterations. We recommended 1 month iterations but the exact duration varied due to the team experience with the technologies, holidays, and the amount of learning required by projects with a legacy code base.

- **Project 1** (*Archimedes*): An open source computer-aided design (CAD) software focused on the needs of professional architects. We analyze the initial 4 iterations.
- **Project 2** (*Grid Video Converter*): A Web-based application that leverages the processing power of a computational grid to convert video files among several video encodings, qualities, and formats. We analyze the initial 3 iterations.
- **Project 3** (*Colméia*): A library management system that has been developed during the last four offerings of the XP class. Here, we analyze 2 iterations of the project. Other system modules were already deployed. Hence, the team had to spend some time studying the existing system before starting to develop the new module.
- **Project 4** (*Ginástica Laboral*): A stand-alone application to assist in the recovery and prevention of Repetitive Strain Injury (RSI), by frequently alerting the user to take breaks and perform some pre-configured routines of exercises. We analyze the initial 3 iterations.
- **Project 5** (*Borboleta*): A mobile client-server system for hand-held devices to assist in medical appointments provided at the patients' home. The project started in 2005 with three undergraduate students and new features were implemented during the first semester of 2006. We analyze 3 iterations during the second development phase in the XP class.

2.2 Governmental Projects

The governmental schedule demanded 30 hours of weekly work per employee. In addition, some members of our team were working in the projects with partial-time availability.

- **Project 6** (*Chinchilla*): A human resources system to manage information of all ALESP employees. This project started with initial support from our team, by providing training and being responsible for the coach and tracker roles. After some iterations, we started to hand over these roles to the ALESP team and provided support through partial-time interns from our team. We analyze the initial 8 iterations, developed from October/2005 to May/2006.
- **Project 7** (*SPL*): A work-flow system to manage documents (bills, acts, laws, amendments, etc.) through the legislative process. The initial development of this system was outsourced and deployed after 2 years, when the ALESP employees were trained and took over its maintenance. Due to the lack of experience on the system's technologies and to the large number of production defects, they were struggling to provide support for end-users, to fix defects, and to implement new features. When we were called to assist them, we introduced some of the primary XP practices, such as Continuous Integration, Testing (automated unit and acceptance tests), and Informative Workspace [4]. We analyze 3 iterations after the introduction of these practices, from March/2006 to June/2006.

2.3 XP Radar Chart

To evaluate the level of adoption of the various agile practices, we conducted an adapted version of Kreb's survey [12]. We included questions about the adoption of tracking, the team education, and level of experience[1]. The detailed results of the survey were presented and analyzed in a recent study [16]. However, it is important to describe the different aspects of agile adoption in each project. To evaluate that, we chose Wake's XP Radar Chart [19] as a good visual indicator. Table 1 shows the XP radar chart for all projects. The value of each axis represents the average of the corresponding practices, retrieved from the survey and rounded to the nearest integer to improve readability. Some practices overlap multiple chart axis.

3 Metrics and Method

Chidamber and Kemerer proposed a suite of OO metrics, known as the CK suite [8], that has been widely validated in the literature [3,6]. Our metrics were collected by the Eclipse Metrics plug-in[2]. We chose to analyze a subset of the available metrics collected by the plug-in, comprising four of six metrics from

---

[1] Survey available at http://www.agilcoop.org.br/portal/Artigos/Survey.pdf
[2] http://metrics.sourceforge.net

Table 1. XP Radar Chart (some practices overlap multiple axis)

Radar Axis	XP Practices
Programming	Testing, Refactoring, and Simple Design
Planning	Small Releases, Planning Game, Sustainable Pace, Lessons Learned, and Tracking
Customer	Testing, Planning Game, and On-site Customer
Pair	Pair Programming, Continuous Integration, and Collective Code Ownership
Team	Continuous Integration, Testing, Coding Standards, Metaphor, and Lessons Learned

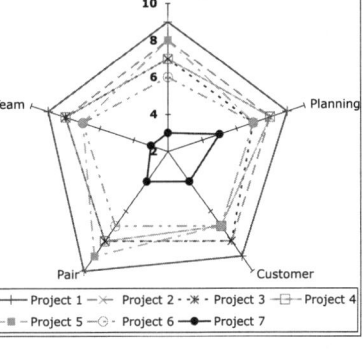

the CK suite (WMC, LCOM, DIT, and NOC) and two from Martin's suite [14] (AC and EC). We were also interested in controlling for size, so we analyzed LOC and $v(G)$.

The files were checked out from the code repository, retrieving the revisions at the end of each iteration. The plug-in exported an XML file with raw data about each metric that was post-processed by a Ruby script to filter production data (ignoring test code) and generate the final statistics for each metric.

- **Lines of Code** (LOC): the total number of non-blank, non-comment lines of source code in a class of the system. Scope: class.
- **McCabe's Cyclomatic Complexity** ($v(G)$): measures the amount of decision logic in a single software module. It is defined for a module (class method) as $e - n + 2$, where e and n are the number of edges and nodes in the module's control flow graph [15]. Scope: method.
- **Weighted Methods per Class** (WMC): measures the complexity of classes. It is defined as the weighted sum of all class' methods [8]. We are using $v(G)$ as the weighting factor, so WMC can be calculated as $\sum c_i$, where c_i is the Cyclomatic Complexity of the class' i^{th} method. Scope: class.
- **Lack of Cohesion of Methods** ($LCOM$): measures the cohesiveness of a class and is calculated using the Henderson-Sellers method [11]. If $m(F)$ is the number of methods accessing a field F, LCOM is calculated as the average of $m(F)$ for all fields, subtracting the number of methods m and dividing the result by $(1 - m)$. A low value indicates a cohesive class and a value close to 1 indicates a lack of cohesion. Scope: class.
- **Depth of Inheritance Tree** (DIT): the length of the longest path from a given class to the root class (ignoring the base `Object` class in Java) in the hierarchy. Scope: class.
- **Number of Children** (NOC): the total number of immediate child classes inherited by a given class. Scope: class.

- **Afferent Coupling** (*AC*): the total number of classes outside a package that depend on classes inside the package. When calculated at the class level, this metric is also known as the *Fan-in* of a class. Scope: package.
- **Efferent Coupling** (*EC*): the total number of classes inside a package that depend on classes outside the package. When calculated at the class level, this metric is also known as the *Fan-out* of a class, or as the CBO (Coupling Between Objects) metric in the CK suite. Scope: package.

4 Results and Discussion

4.1 Size and Complexity Metrics: LOC, $v(G)$, and WMC

The mean value of LOC, $v(G)$, and WMC for each iteration were plotted in Fig. 1(a), Fig. 1(b), and Fig. 1(c) respectively. The shapes of these 3 graphs display a similar evolution. In fact, the value of Spearman's rank correlation between these metrics (Table 2) shows that these metrics are highly dependent. Several studies found that classes with higher LOC and WMC are more prone to faults [3,10,17,18].

Project 7 had a significantly higher average LOC, $v(G)$, and WMC than the other projects. This was the project where just some agile practices were adopted.

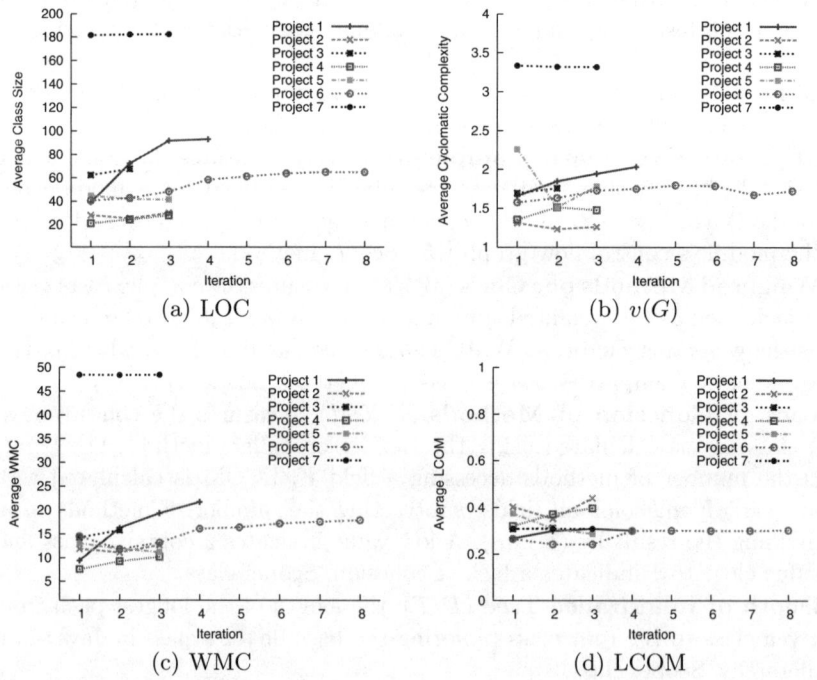

Fig. 1. Evolution of mean values for LOC, $v(G)$, WMC, and LCOM

Table 2. Spearman's Rank Correlation test results

Metrics	Correlation (ρ)	p-value
LOC vs. $v(G)$	0.861	< 0.000001
LOC vs. WMC	0.936	< 0.000001
$v(G)$ vs. WMC	0.774	< 0.00001

In fact, it had the most defective XP implementation, depicted in Tab. 1. This suggests that Project 7 will be more prone to errors and will require more testing and maintenance effort. By comparing Project 7 with data from the literature, we found that projects with similar mean LOC (183.27 [10] and 135.95 [17]) have a significantly lower WMC (17.36 [10] and 12.15 [17]). Other studies show similar WMC values, but without controlling for size: 13.40 [3], 11.85, 6.81, and 10.37 [18]. These values of WMC are more consistent with the other six agile projects, although our projects have smaller classes (lower LOC).

We can also notice a growing trend through the iterations. This tendency is more accentuated in the initial iterations of green field projects (such as Project 1), supporting the results from Alshayeb and Li [1]. After some iterations the growing rate seems to stabilize. The only exception was Project 5, showing a decrease in size and complexity. This can be explained by the lack of focus on testing and refactoring during the first development phase. The team was not skillful on writing automated tests in J2ME before the XP class. This suggests that testing and refactoring are good practices for controlling size and complexity and these metrics are good indicators to be tracked by the team.

4.2 Cohesion Metric: LCOM

The mean value of LCOM for each iteration was plotted in Fig. 1(d), however we could not draw any interesting result from this metric, due to the similar values between all projects. In fact, the relationship between this metric and the source code quality is controversial: while Basili et al. has shown that LCOM was insignificant [3], Gyimóthy et al. found it to be significant [10].

4.3 Inheritance Metrics: DIT and NOC

The mean value of DIT and NOC for each iteration were plotted in Fig. 2(a) and Fig. 2(b) respectively. The use of these metrics as predictors for fault-proness of classes is also controversial in the literature [7,10]. Table 3 shows the average DIT and NOC from several studies for comparison.

None of our projects show high values for DIT or NOC, showing that the use of inheritance was not abused. Mean values of DIT around 1.0 can be explained by the use of frameworks such as Struts and Swing, that provide functionality through extension of their base classes. In particular, a large part of the code base from Project 5 was a mobile application, and some of its base classes inherited directly from the J2ME UI classes, resulting in a higher value of DIT. NOC was usually lower for green field projects, and a growing trend can be observed in

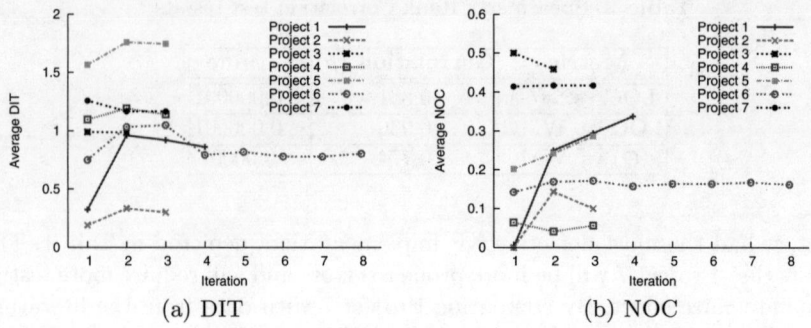

Fig. 2. Evolution of mean values for DIT and NOC

Table 3. DIT and NOC mean values on the literature

Metric	[3]	[10]	[18] A	[18] B	[18] C	[17]	[7]
DIT	1.32	3.13	1.25	1.54	0.89	1.02	0.44
NOC	0.23	0.92	0.20	0.70	0.24	N/A	0.31

most of the projects. This can be explained by the fact that a large part of the evolution of a system involves extending and adapting existing behavior.

4.4 Coupling Metrics: AC and EC

The mean value of AC and EC for each iteration were plotted in Fig. 3(a) and Fig. 3(b) respectively. The shapes of these 2 graphs display a similar evolution. In fact, there is a high dependency between these metrics. Spearman's rank correlation of 0.971 was determined with statistical significance at a 95% confidence level (p-value $< 10^{-14}$). Unfortunately, we can not compare our results with other studies because we used different coupling metrics at a different scope

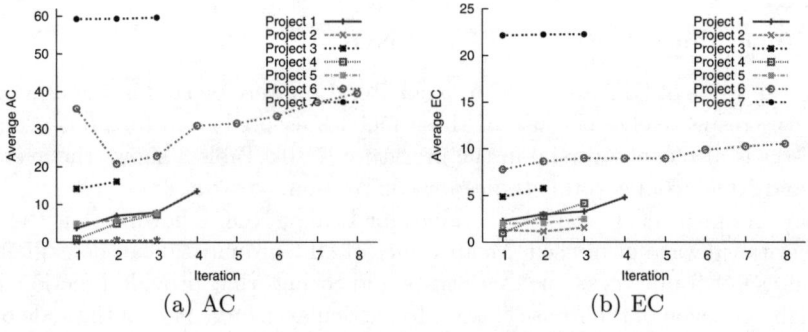

Fig. 3. Evolution of mean values for AC and EC

level (package). The most usual metric in the literature is CBO, which is similar to EC but calculated at the class level.

Project 7 have again a higher average AC and EC than the other projects. Binkley and Schach found that coupling measures are good predictors for maintenance effort [6]. In this case, due to the outsourced development, the team was already struggling with maintenance. There were also no automated tests to act as a safety net for changing the source code. We had some improvements in the adoption of Continuous Integration [16] by automating the build and deploy process, but the adoption of automated testing was not very successful. Writing unit tests for a large legacy code project is much harder and requires technical skills. However, we had some success on the adoption of automated acceptance tests with Selenium[3] and Selenium IDE[3].

5 Conclusions

In this paper, we analyzed the evolution of eight OO metrics in seven projects with different adoption approaches of agile methods. By comparing our results with others in the literature, we found that the project with less agile practices in place (Project 7) presented higher size, complexity, and coupling measures (LOC, $v(G)$, WMC, AC, and EC), suggesting that it would be more prone to defects and would require more testing and maintenance efforts. We also found that there is a high correlation between size and complexity metrics (LOC, $v(G)$ and WMC) and coupling metrics (AC and EC). We think that the automated collection of these metrics can support the tracker of an agile team, acting as good indicators of source code quality attributes, such as size (LOC), complexity (WMC), and coupling (AC and EC). In our study we found that these curves are smooth, and changes to the curves can indicate the progress, or lack of progress, on practices such as testing and refactoring.

In future work, we plan to gather more data from different agile projects. We are interested in measuring defects and bugs after deployment to analyze their relationship with the collected metrics. We are also interested in studying similar projects, adopting agile and non-agile methods, to understand the impact of the development process on the evolution of the OO metrics.

References

1. Alshayeb, M., Li, W.: An empirical validation of object-oriented metrics in two different iterative software processes. IEEE Transactions on Software Engineering 29(11), 1043–1049 (2003)
2. Ambu, W., Concas, G., Marchesi, M., Pinna, S.: Studying the evolution of quality metrics in an agile/distributed project. In: 7th International Conference on Extreme Programming and Agile Processes in Software Engineering (XP '06), pp. 85–93 (2006)

---

[3] http://www.openqa.org/selenium and http://www.openqa.org/selenium-ide

3. Victor, R., Basili, L.C., Briand, W.L.: A validation of object-oriented design metrics as quality indicators. IEEE Transactions on Software Engineering 22(10), 751–761 (1996)
4. Beck, K., Andres, C.: Extreme Programming Explained: Embrace Change, 2nd edn. Addison-Wesley, Boston (2004)
5. Beck, K., et al.: Manifesto for agile software development (February 2001) (Last Access: Janaury 2007) http://agilemanifesto.org
6. Binkley, A.B., Schach, S.R.: Validation of the coupling dependency metric as a predictor of run-time failures and maintenance measures. In: 20th International Conference on Software Engineering, pp. 452–455 (1998)
7. Cartwright, M., Shepperd, M.: An empirical investigation of an object-oriented software system. IEEE Transactions on Software Engineering 26(7), 786–796 (2000)
8. Chidamber, S.R., Kemerer, C.F.: A metrics suite for object oriented design. IEEE Transactions on Software Engineering 20(6), 476–493 (1994)
9. Goldman, A., Kon, F., Silva, P.J.S., Yoder, J.: Being extreme in the classroom: Experiences teaching XP. Journal of the Brazilian Computer Society 10(2), 1–17 (2004)
10. Gyimóthy, T., Ferenc, R., Siket, I.: Empirical validation of object-oriented metrics on open source software for fault prediction. IEEE Transactions on Software Engineering 31(10), 897–910 (2005)
11. Henderson-Sellers, B.: Object-Oriented Metrics: Measures of Complexity. Prentice Hall PTR, Upper Saddle River, NJ, USA (1996)
12. Krebs, W.: Turning the knobs: A coaching pattern for XP through agile metrics. In: Extreme Programming and Agile Methods - XP/Agile Universe 2002, pp. 60–69 (2002)
13. Li, W., Henry, S.: Object oriented metrics that predict maintainability. J. Systems and Software 23, 111–122 (1993)
14. Martin, R.C.: Agile Software Development: Principles, Patterns, and Practices. Prentice Hall PTR, Upper Saddle River, NJ, USA (2002)
15. McCabe, T.J., Watson, A.H.: Software complexity. Crosstalk: Journal of Defense Software Engineering 7, 5–9 (1994)
16. Sato, D., Bassi, D., Bravo, M., Goldman, A., Kon, F.: Experiences tracking agile projects: an empirical study. To be published in: Journal of the Brazilian Computer Society (2007) http://www.dtsato.com/resources/default/jbcs-ese-2007.pdf
17. Subramanyam, R., Krishnan, M.S.: Empirical analysis of CK metrics for object-oriented design complexity: Implications for software defects. IEEE Transactions on Software Engineering 29(4), 297–310 (2003)
18. Tang, M.-H., Kao, M.-H., Chen, M.-H.: An empirical study on object-oriented metrics. In: 6th International Software Metrics Symposium, pp. 242–249 (1999)
19. Wake, W.: XP radar chart (January 2001) (Last Access: January 2007) http://www.xp123.com/xplor/xp0012b/index.shtml
20. Williams, L., Layman, L., Krebs, W.: Extreme Programming evaluation framework for object-oriented languages – version 1.4. Technical report, North Carolina State University Department of Computer Science (2004)

FitClipse: A Fit-Based Eclipse Plug-In for Executable Acceptance Test Driven Development

Chengyao Deng, Patrick Wilson, and Frank Maurer

University of Calgary
Department of Computer Science
2500 University Dr. NW
Calgary, Alberta T2N 1N4 Canada
{cdeng,piwilson,maurer}@cpsc.ucalgary.ca

Abstract. We conducted a survey on Executable Acceptance Test Driven Development (or: Story Test Driven Development). The results show that there is often a substantial delay between defining an acceptance test and its first successful pass. Therefore, it becomes important for teams to easily be able to distinguish between tasks that were never tackled before and tasks that were already completed but whose tests are now failing again. We then describe our FitClipse tool that extends Fit by maintaining a history of acceptance test results. Based on the history, FitClipse is able to generate reports that show when an acceptance test is suddenly failing again.

Keywords: Executable Acceptance Test-Driven Development (EATDD), executable acceptance test, Fit.

1 Introduction

In Extreme Programming, two sets of test techniques are used for double checking the performance of a system, unit testing and acceptance testing. [7] With unit testing, detailed tests from the developer's perspective are conducted to make sure all system components are working well. Acceptance testing is the process of customers testing the functionality of a system in order to determine whether the system meets the requirements. Acceptance tests are defined by or with the customers and are the concrete examples of system features. Recent literature on agile methods suggests that executable acceptance tests should be created for all stories and that a story should not be considered to be completed until all the acceptance tests are passing successfully. [3][10] Acceptance tests should be expressed in the customer language (i.e. customers should be able to understand what they mean) and should be executable (i.e. automated) and be included in the continuous integration process.

Executable Acceptance Test Driven-Development (EATDD), which is also known as Story Test-Driven Development (STDD) or Customer Test-Driven Development, is an extension of Test-Driven Development (TDD). While TDD focuses on unit tests to ensure the system is performing correctly from a developer's perspective, EATDD starts from business-facing tests to help developers better understand the requirements, to ensure that the system meets those requirements and to express development progress in a language that is understandable to the customers. [11]

From the customer's perspective, EATDD provides the customer with an "executable and readable contract that the programmers have to obey" if they want to declare that the system meets the given requirements. [12] Observing acceptance tests also gives the customers more confidence in the functionality of the system. From the perspective of programmers, EATDD helps the programmers to make sure they are delivering what the customers want. In addition, the results help the team to understand if they are on track with the expected development progress. Further, as EATDD propagates automated acceptance test, these tests can play the role of regression tests in later development.

This paper is organized as follows: section 2 discusses a survey and the motivations for building such a tool; section 3 presents the related work and Eclipse plug-ins based on Fit; section 4 describes the overall design of FitClipse; section 5 talks about how FitClipse works for EATDD; section 6 demonstrates our initial evaluation of FitClipse.

2 Survey Results and Motivation

We conducted a survey to find out how EATDD is being used in industry by sending questionnaires to mailing lists and discussion groups of Agile communities. The comprehensive findings of this study will be published in the future. One specific part of that study is relevant for this paper: We asked about the time frame between defining an acceptance test and its fist successful passing. The findings of this questionnaire are a core motivation underlying the development of FitClipse.

2.1 Timeframe of EATDD

A major difference between TDD using unit tests and EATDD is the timeframe between the definition of a test and its first successful pass. Usually, in TDD the expectation is that all unit tests pass all the time and that it only takes a few minutes between defining a new test and making it pass [8]. As a result, any failed test is seen as a problem that needs to be resolved immediately. Unit tests cover very fine grained details which makes this expectation reasonable in a TDD context.

Acceptance tests, on the other hand, cover larger pieces of functionality. Therefore, we expected that it may often take developers several hours or days, sometimes even more than one iteration, to make them pass.

For validating our hypothesis, we conducted a survey by sending a questionnaire to email groups of Agile Communities (such as the Yahoo agile-usability group and the Yahoo agile-testing group etc.). One goal of the survey was to find out the timeframe between the definition of an acceptance test and making it pass successfully. We were expecting the following results:

- The *average* timeframe between defining one acceptance test and making it pass successfully, following EATDD, is more than 4 hours (half a day).
- The *maximum* timeframe between defining one acceptance test and making it pass successfully, following EATDD, may be the majority of an iteration or even more than one iteration.

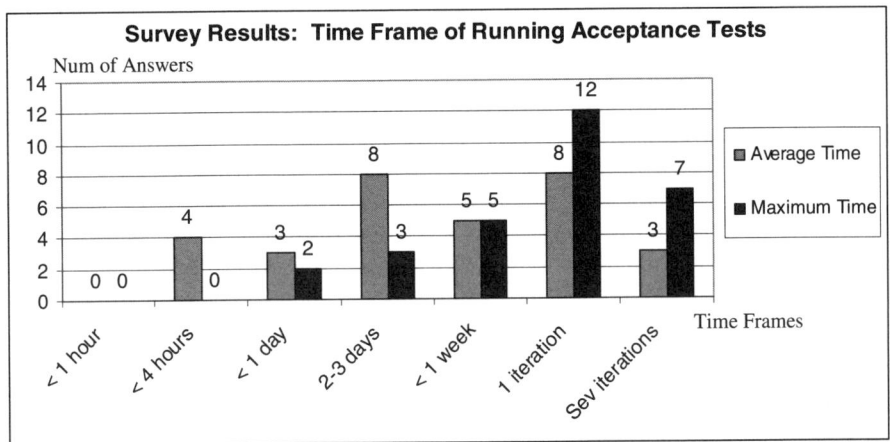

Fig. 1. This Chart shows the survey results of the time frame between the definition of an acceptance and making it pass successfully

Overall, we received 33 responses, among which 31 were valid. Fig. 1 shows the detailed findings of the survey according to the above expectations.

The result of the survey strongly supports our first expectation. About 87.1% (27/31) of the participants reported the average timeframe to be more than 4 hours for defining an acceptance test and making it pass and the number increased to 100% when they reported the maximum time.

Our second expectation is also supported by the survey result. 41.4% (12/29, two participants did not answer) of the participants spent most of an iteration to finish one acceptance test, and about 24.1% (7/29) of the participants reported the time frame to be several iterations. One of the participants even spent several months working on making a single acceptance test pass.

Therefore, both of our expectations were substantiated by the evidence gathered in this survey. We can also draw the conclusion that the time frame between the definition of an acceptance test and its first successful pass is much longer than that of unit test.

2.2 Motivation of FitClipse

Due to the substantial delay between the definition and the first successful pass of an acceptance test, a development team can NOT expect that all acceptance tests pass all the time. A failing acceptance test can actually mean one of two things:

- The development team has not yet finished working on the story with the failing acceptance test (including the developer has not even started working on it).
- The test has passed in the past and is suddenly failing – i.e. a change to the system has triggered unwanted side effects and the team has lost some of the existing functionalities.

The first case is simply a part of the normal test-driven development process: It is expected that a test that has never passed before should fail if no change has been made to the system code. The later case should be raising flags and should be highlighted in progress reports to the team. Otherwise the users have to rely on their recollection of past test results to determine the meaning of a failing test. For anything but very small projects, this recollection will not be reliable.

FitClipse raises a flag for the condition that a test that is failing but was passing in the past. It identifies this condition by storing the results of previous test executions and is, thus, able to distinguish these two cases and splits up the "failed" state of Fit into two states: "still failing" and "now failing after passing earlier".

3 Related Work

There are several open source frameworks and tools that support EATDD, with Fit [4], FitLibrary and FitNesse [5] being three of the most relevant to our work.

Fit is a framework for integrated testing. "It is well suited to testing from a business perspective, using tables to represent tests and automatically reporting the results of those tests."[9] Fixtures, made by the programmers to execute the business logic tables, map the table contents to calls into the software system. Test results are displayed using three different colors for different states of the test: green for passing tests; yellow for tests that can not be executed and red for failing tests. FitLibrary is a collection of extensions for the fixtures in Fit. Other than test styles that Fit provides, it also supports testing grids and images. FitNesse is a Wiki front-end testing tool which supports team collaboration for creating and editing acceptance tests. FitNesse uses the Fit framework to enable running acceptance tests via a web browser. It also integrates FitLibrary fixtures for writing and running acceptance tests.

Our FitClipse tool is an Eclipse plug-in that uses the Fit framework for writing and running the acceptance tests. There are several other Eclipse plug-ins which also use Fit or FitNesse, including FitRunner [6], conFIT [2] and AutAT [1]. FitRunner contributes to Eclipse a Fit launch configuration that enables people to run automated acceptance tests. ConFIT uses a FitNesse server, which can run either locally or remotely, to perform acceptance tests. AutAT enables non-technical users to write and execute automated acceptance tests for web applications using a user-friendly graphical editor. [1]

Compared to the above tools and in addition to running acceptance tests with the Fit frame work, FitClipse extends the Fit tests result schema with historical result information for the users. In FitClipse, instead of one single test failure state, two kinds of acceptance test failure states are distinguished automatically: unimplemented failure and regression failure.

4 FitClipse

FitClipse [13] is an Eclipse plug-in supporting the creation, modification and execution of acceptance tests using the FIT/FitNesse frame work.

FitClipse works as a client side application and communicates with a Wiki repository, which works as the server. The repository has been implemented with FitNesse. The FitClipse tool consists of (multiple) FitClipse clients for editing and running acceptance tests, the Wiki repository for storing acceptance test definitions and the Database for storing the test execution history (See Fig. 2). Using FitClipse, acceptance tests are written, on the client side, in the form of executable tables with Wiki syntax and then saved on the server side as Wiki pages. FitClipse uses the Fit engine to run the acceptance tests.

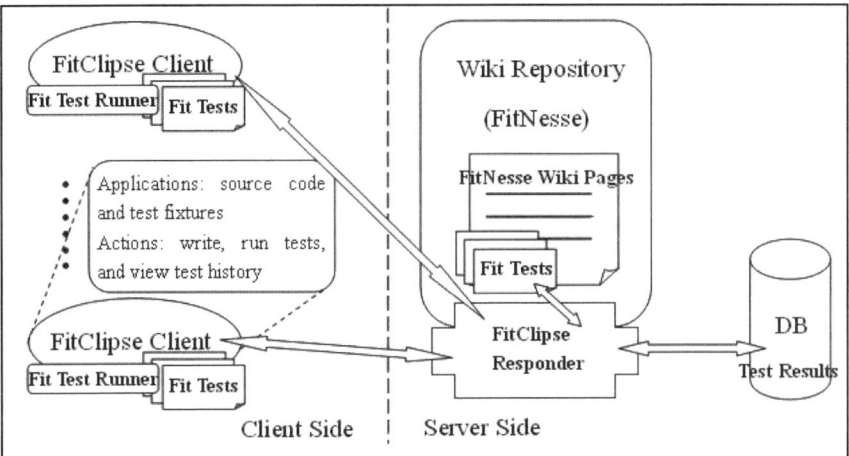

Fig. 2. Overview of FitClipse framework with FitNesse as the backend. We extend FitNesse server by adding a FitClipse Responder to handle the requests from FitClipse clients and to talk with the database for saving and retrieving the test results.

In order to distinguish two test failure states, FitClipse, coupled with a Wiki repository server, stores the results of each test run and can retrieve the result histories for each test and each test suite. The algorithm for distinguishing two test result failures is as follows:

```
for (each test t){
    t.run();
    PersistTestResult (t.result);
    if (t.isFailing){
       getResultHistory(t);
       If (hasPassedBefore(t)){
          displayRegressionFeature();
       }else
          displayUnimplementedFailure(t);
}}}
```

FitClipse splits up the test failure state in Fit or FitNesse into two: Unimplemented failure and Regression failure. Table 1 shows the four test result states in FitClipse comparing them to the three states of Fit or FitNesse.

Table 1. Comparison of test result states of FitClipse and Fit or FitNesse

Test Result States	Fit or FitNesse	FitClipse
Failure (the tests fail)	Color Red	Regression Failure – failure as a result of a recent change losing previously working functionality (color red)
		Unimplemented Feature – not really a failure as it might simply mean that the development team hasn't started to work on this feature (color orange)
Passing (the tests pass)	Color Green	test page with green bar – no difference to Fit/FitNesse (color green)
Exception (the tests can not be executed)	Color Yellow	test page with yellow bar – no difference to Fit/FitNesse (color yellow)

5 FitClipse and EATDD

FitClipse provides the following core functionalities for EATDD:

1) *Create and modify Acceptance Tests*: In the FitClipse environment (as shown in Fig. 3), customer representatives, testers and developers collaborate on creating acceptance tests for each story. Users can create, delete and restructure acceptance tests in FitClipse.
2) *Creating Fixtures*: The programmers create fixtures that translate Fit tables into calls to the system under development. Based on a given acceptance test, FitClipse can generate the fixture code stubs automatically. Fig. 3 shows sample Fit tests and corresponding fixture code in FitClipse.

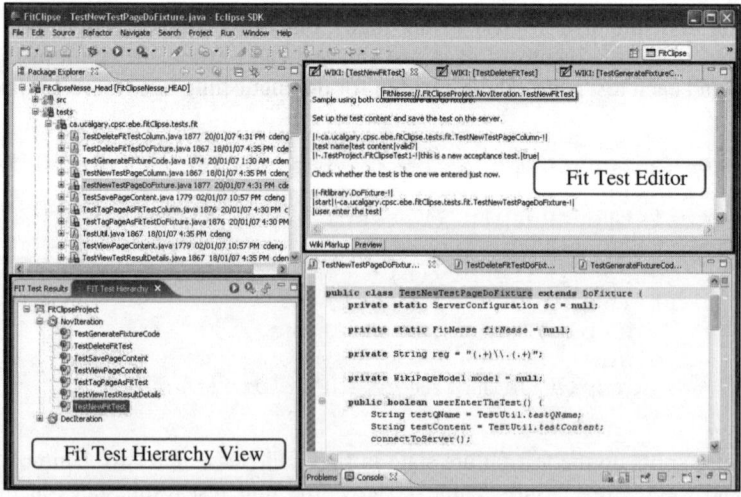

Fig. 3. Fit tests and fixture code in FitClipse environment

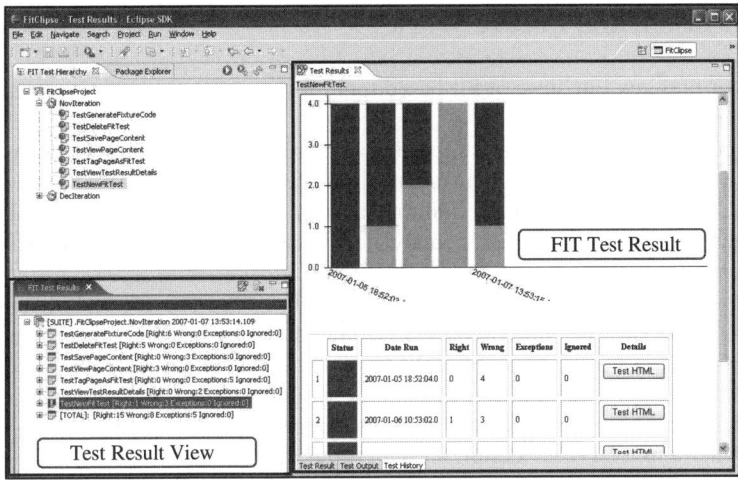

Fig. 4. Test result states and test result history for an acceptance test

3) *Implementation*: In this step, unit test-driven development is utilized in conjunction with EATDD. Programmers follow TDD to implement features of the system. After several unit tests are passing, one acceptance test will pass, too. All through the implementation of acceptance tests, FitClipse provides two kinds of test failure states and maintains the test result history. Fig. 4 shows all test states and a sample test result history in FitClipse.

6 Initial Evaluation

We ran an initial self-evaluation on FitClipse by using it for two iterations. The evaluation lasted for 6 weeks and had several findings.

We followed EATDD process in our development process. In all, we spent about 150 programming hours and created 14 acceptance tests with 40 assertions.

Our first observation confirms our expectations. The distinction between two test failure states was helpful when the number of acceptance tests increased. When we broke the system by adding new code, the second failure state warned us at once by showing the special flag. We did not have to trace in a test history record or rely on our memory to recognize which test was passing before and broken by ourselves.

Second, the test result history provided helpful information for us to understand the development progress. In FitClipse, we can generate a test result history chart for a suite which includes all the acceptance tests in the iteration. From the number of passing and failing acceptance test we could see how our development was progressing.

Even though we only have limited time to evaluate FitClipse, we find that it was worth the effort as the distinction between two test failure states is useful. We believe that if we had spent a longer time for the evaluation with more acceptance tests, we would find the tool even more helpful.

To address the self-confirmation bias of the initial self evaluation, we will conduct a controlled experiment using outsiders in February and March 2007.

7 Conclusion and Future Work

This paper presents FitClipse, a Fit-based tool for automated acceptance testing and a self-evaluation of the tool.

Existing tools are limited in supporting Acceptance Test Driven Development as they do not provide enough information to distinguish two different kinds of test failures. FitClipse distinguishes these failure states by maintaining a test result history on the server, which is valuable for analyzing the existing progress and making improvements.

From the self-evaluation, we can see that FitClipse can provide useful support for EATDD. However, this self-evaluation is limited in time and the number of acceptance tests. Therefore, the next research step is to conduct a more formal evaluation of the approach to assess if FitClipse as a whole is useful for development teams to practice Executable Acceptance Test Driven Development. In the future, FitClipse will also provide a WYGIWYS editor for supporting the users to edit the Fit test documents.

References

1. Schwarz, C., Skytteren, S.K., Øvstetun, T.M.: AutAT – An Eclipse Plugin for Automatic Acceptance Testing of Web applications. OOPSLA'05. October 16–20, 2005, San Diego, California, USA (2005) ACM 1-59593-193-7/05/0010 (See also: http://boss.bekk.no/autat/)
2. conFIT: A FitNesse for Eclipse Plugin (http://www.bandxi.com/fitnesse/)
3. Extreme Programmin: Acceptance Tests, (http://www.extremeprogramming.org/rules/functionaltests.html)
4. Fit: Framework for Integrated Test (http://fit.c2.com/)
5. FitNesse Web site (http://fitnesse.org/)
6. FitRunner: an Eclipse plug-in for Fit (http://fitrunner.sourceforge.net)
7. Beck, K.: Extreme Programming Explained: Embrace Change. Addison Wesley, Boston (2000)
8. Beck, K.: Test-Driven Development: By example, p. 11. Addison –Wesley, London (2003)
9. Mugridge, R., Cunningham, W.: Fit for Developing Software: Framework for Integrated Tests, p. 1. Prentice Hall, Englewood Cliffs (2005)
10. Miller, R.W., Collins, C.T.: Acceptance Testing, 2001 XP Universe Conference, Raleigh, NC, USA (July 23–25, 2001)
11. Story Test Driven Development (http://sangam.sourceforge.net/StoryTestDrivenDevelopment)
12. Tracy Reppert, Do't Just Break Software, Make Software, Better Software Magazine (July/August 2004) available on line: http://industriallogic.com/papers/storytest.pdf
13. University of Calgary, EBE website: FitClipse, (http://ebe.cpsc.ucalgary.ca/ebe/Wiki.jsp?page=.FitClipse)

EzUnit: A Framework for Associating Failed Unit Tests with Potential Programming Errors

Philipp Bouillon, Jens Krinke, Nils Meyer, and Friedrich Steimann

Schwerpunkt Software Engineering
Fakultät für Mathematik und Informatik
Fernuniversität in Hagen
D-58084 Hagen
Philipp.Bouillon@gmail.com, krinke@acm.org,
nils.meyer@jcom1.com, steimann@acm.org

Abstract. Unit testing is essential in the agile context. A unit test case written long ago may uncover an error introduced only recently, at a time at which awareness of the test and the requirement it expresses may have long vanished. Popular unit testing frameworks such as JUnit may then detect the error at little more cost than the run of a static program checker (compiler). However, unlike such checkers current unit testing frameworks can only detect the presence of errors, they cannot locate them. With EzUnit, we present an extension to the JUnit Eclipse plug-in that serves to narrow down error locations, and that marks these locations in the source code in very much the same way syntactic and typing errors are displayed. Because EzUnit is itself designed as a framework, it can be extended by algorithms further narrowing down error locations.

1 Introduction

All contemporary integrated development environments (IDEs) mark syntax errors in the source code, in close proximity of where they occur. In addition, static type-checking lets the compiler find certain logical errors (sometimes called semantic errors) and assign them to locations in the source in much the same way as syntax errors. Today, remaining errors in a program are mostly found by code reviews and by testing, in the context of XP and other agile approaches especially by pair programming and by executing unit tests.

JUnit is a popular unit testing framework. It is based on the automatic execution of methods designated as test cases. A test case usually sets up a known object structure, called test fixture, executes one or more methods to be tested on the fixture, and compares the obtained result with the expected one (including the possible throwing of exceptions). Because the expected result must be determined by some other way than executing the method(s) under test (the test oracle), test cases are usually rather simple. However, there is no theoretic limitation on the complexity of test cases, other than that they must run without user interaction and that the result must be repeatable.

JUnit as currently designed reports errors in the form of failed tests. Contemporary IDE integration of JUnit lets the developer navigate from the test report to the failed test case, that is, to the test method that discovered an unexpected result. However, the test method only detects the presence of a programming error — it does not contain it. The developer must infer the location of the error from the failed test case, which is not necessarily trivial. But even if it is, navigating from the error report to the source of the error currently requires a detour via the test case. Transferred to syntax and type checking, this would correspond to navigating from an error report to the error source via the syntax or typing rule violated, which would clearly be considered impractical.

Our ultimate goal is to lift unit testing to the level of syntactic and semantic checking: a logical error detected by a unit test should be flagged in the source code as close as possible to the location where it occurred. As a first step in this direction, we present here for the first time an extension of the JUNIT integration in ECLIPSE, named EZUNIT, that provides basic reporting and navigation facilities, and that accommodates for algorithms and procedures serving to narrow an error location.

2 The Framework

In JUNIT 4, test cases are tagged with the @Test annotation. When adding a test case through ECLIPSE's New > JUnit Test Case... menu and selecting a method to be tested, the test method is automatically annotated with a Javadoc tag saying that this method is a test method for the method for which it was created. We raise this comment to the level of an annotation, named @MUT (for method under test), and allow more than one method under test to be listed. This accommodates for the fact that the tested method may call other methods, which may also be tested by the test case, and that the initially called method may be known to be correct, while other methods it calls are not. To help the programmer with generating the annotations, a static call graph analysis of the test method is provided, listing all methods the test method potentially calls. From this the developer can select the methods intended to be tested by this test case. The generated list can be automatically filtered by an exclusion/inclusion of packages expression (e.g., excluding all calls to the JUNIT framework).

The @MUT annotations are exploited in various ways. Firstly, they aid with the navigation between test methods and methods under test: via a new context menu in the Outline view of an editor, the developer can switch from a method under test to the methods testing it and vice versa, without knowing or looking at the implementation of a method. Secondly, and more importantly, whenever a test case fails during a test run, corresponding markers are set in the gutter of the editor, in the Package Explorer, and in the Problems view. Fig. 1 shows a test method (from the well-known Money example distributed with JUNIT) with a corresponding @MUT annotation, and the hints provided by a test run after an error has been seeded in the add() method of Money.

Surely, in the given example associating the failed testSimpleAdd() with add() in Money is not a big deal, but then spotting the error in add() without knowledge of the test method isn't either, so that the developer saves one step in pinning down and navigating to the error. In more complex cases, especially where there is more than one method to which blame could be assigned, checking all methods that may have contributed to the failure requires more intimate knowledge of the test case.

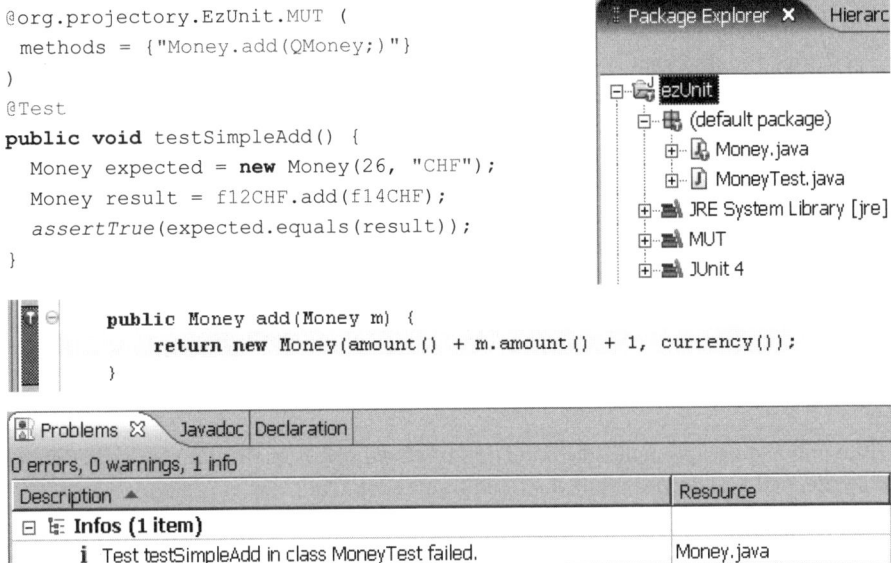

Fig. 1. An @MUT annotated test case and the markers it creates if the method under test is faulty

With EZUNIT, the essence of this knowledge, namely which methods are being tested by the test case, is contained in the Problems view and the various error adornments. By going through these methods one by one, the developer can look for a potential error, fix it, and rerun the test cases until the problem disappears. During this process, the developer can always consult the test case to get additional hints, simply by using the quick navigation facilities offered by the EZUNIT framework.

The basic functionality offered by EZUNIT is rather simple, one may even say simplistic. However, because EZUNIT is designed as a framework, this basic functionality can be extended by adding methods capable of narrowing the possible source of the error, thereby providing assistance to the developer that is as yet unavailable. We are currently exploring various such extensions. The framework is downloadable as an ECLIPSE bundle from the EZUNIT update site found at http://www.fernuni-hagen.de/ps/prjs/EzUnit/update.

3 Discussion and Related Work

Our approach is simple. Its appeal comes from the fact that we can exploit the special character of unit tests, namely that they are 100% repeatable (in that every run creates exactly the same object structure and calls exactly the same methods on it): several approaches to error locating practically intractable for the general case (such as program slicing [1, 2]) can therefore likely be used in our setting, simply because there is no dependency on input or other uncontrollable variation. With the provision of our framework, we hope to attract other researchers to contribute their ideas.

Our approach is somewhat related to David Saff's work on continuous testing [1, 4]. Continuous testing pursues the idea that test execution, like compilation, can be performed incrementally and in the background. Whenever a developer changes something and triggers a (successful) compilation, all tests whose outcome is possibly affected by that change are automatically rerun. Thus, like our own work Saff's raises unit testing to the level of syntactic and semantic (type) checking, yet it does so in an *orthogonal dimension*: continuous testing is about *when tests are executed*, our work is about *how the results are interpreted and presented*. It should be interesting to see whether and how the two approaches can be combined into one, particularly since the mutual dependency of testing and program units under test is common to both of them.

4 Conclusion

While unit testing automates the detection of errors, their localization is currently still an intellectual act. By providing a simple framework that

- allows the developer to select — based on the result of a static call graph analysis — which methods are being tested by each test case, that
- enables rapid switching between test methods and methods under test, and that
- marks failed tests as adornments in the editor and other representations of the source code,

we have laid the technical groundwork for a symptom-to-diagnosis mapping for programming errors. Extensions helping to narrow down error locations are easily conceived and added. In fact, we believe that the best results can be expected from applying several algorithms in parallel, and from combining the evidence collected from each. We have provided the framework for this.

References

1. Agrawal, H., Horgan, J.R.: Dynamic program slicing. In: Proceedings of the ACM SIGPLAN '90 Conference on Programming Language Design and Implementation, pp. 246–256 (1990)
2. Korel, B., Laski, J.: Dynamic program slicing. Information Processing Letters 29(3), 155–163 (1998)
3. Saff, D., Ernst, M.D.: Reducing wasted development time via continuous testing. In: ISSRE 2003, 14th International Symposium on Software Reliability Engineering, pp. 281–292 (2003)
4. Saff, D., Ernst, M.D.: An experimental evaluation of continuous testing during development. In: ISSTA 2004, International Symposium on Software Testing and Analysis, pp. 76–85 (2004)

Does XP Deliver Quality and Maintainable Code?

Raimund Moser, Marco Scotto, Alberto Sillitti, and Giancarlo Succi

Center for Applied Software Engineering, Free University of Bolzano-Bozen,
Piazza Domenicani 3, Italy
{rmoser,mscotto,asillitti,gsucci}@unibz.it

Abstract. Extreme Programming aims at delivering working software for less money and still of high quality. It is well known that software maintainability is one of the most important concerns and cost factors of the software industry. The question of this research is whether Extreme Programming intrinsically delivers easily maintainable code or not. We propose a model on how to evaluate the evolution of source code quality and in particular maintainability in an Extreme Programming environment and evaluate it with a small case study. The results obtained from the case study seem to sustain the hypothesis that Extreme Programming enhances quality and in particular maintainability of a software product. Given such promising results, additional experimentation is required to validate and generalize the results of this work.

Keywords: quality, maintainability, metrics.

1 Introduction

In Extreme Programming (XP) much emphasis is given on an agile, iterative and customer oriented way of how to develop software. Among the top priorities of XP are to satisfy the customer through continuous delivery of valuable software and to welcome changing requirements (http://agilemanifesto.org). XP practices are tailored to achieve such goals: iterative and informal planning, simple design, continuous refactoring of the code, pair programming, test first and continuous integration – just to mention a few [2]. Most of these practices are intended to be used during development and maintenance and seem to keep at least in part their promises [13], [18]. Although Kent Beck states "Maintenance is really the normal state of an XP project" [2] he is aware of the differences and problems of a system under development and a delivered system. He suggests that the effort for changing code in production is almost twice of ideal engineering time and that also XP cannot avoid the entropic death of a software system – all it can do is to extend its lifetime as far as possible.

Therefore, we think that also for XP projects maintainability is a key concern and quality factor. Fred Brooks already claimed [4]: "The total cost of maintaining a widely used program is typically 40 percent or more of the cost of developing it". Other researchers confirmed recently such numbers [7]. Therefore, high maintainability is a long-term success factor for a software product. We think that XP intrinsically guides software engineers to develop products, which are likely to show good quality and maintainability.

Maintainability is a high-level quality metric that combines several internal and external properties of a software product and of the development process [9]. To assess maintainability in this research we use only internal product attributes that are available during development and we monitor their evolution over time. We do not take into account any external product or process metrics.

The paper is organized as follows. In Section 2, we present our research methodology and propose a model for a Maintainability Trend indicator. In Section 3 a case study is presented and discussed; in Section 4 we touch on some issues regarding the limitations of our approach and our future plans. Finally, conclusions and implications of the investigation are drawn in Section 5.

2 A Model to Assess the Evolution of Source Code Quality and Maintainability

In this section we describe the metrics used for assessing maintainability. Afterwards, we develop a model for evaluating how the maintainability of a software system evolves during development.

2.1 Internal Product Metrics That Affect Quality and Maintainability

Our research question is to assess whether XP facilitates the development of high maintainable code or not. Maintainability is a rather vague term for describing certain quality attributes of a software system and can be decomposed into lower-level metrics in different ways [9]. In this research we focus only on internal properties of the software that are considered to be relevant for its maintainability. We use three major sources to identify the metrics to use:

- The Chidamber and Kemerer (CK) set of object-oriented metrics [6]
- Metrics used to assess testability of object-oriented software [15], [5]
- The Maintainability Index (*MI*) proposed by Oman [17]

The motivation for choosing this set of metrics is twofold. First, some of them such as the CK metrics are among the best-understood and validated metrics for object-oriented systems, therefore we can be more confident in their expressiveness. Second, the tool we use for collecting these metrics is able to collect them in an automatic and in a non-invasive way - a fundamental requirement for data collection in an XP process [12].

Several empirical studies put the CK metrics into relationship with software quality and maintenance. Li and Henry [14] for example show that the CK metrics are useful to predict maintainability. Basili *et al.* [3] investigate the relationship between the CK metrics and code quality. Their findings suggest that 5 of the 6 CK metrics are useful quality indicators. However, such studies are rare in XP-like environments and they do not analyze the evolution of the CK metrics during development to see whether there is an observable trend towards an enhancement or degradation of the software in terms of these metrics.

Testability is an important sub aspect of maintainability. Different models have been proposed on how to measure testability in object-oriented systems. Checking the related literature, we found that several authors use the CK metrics and McCabe's cyclomatic complexity [16] as promising indicators for testability [5]. Oman *et al.* [17] propose a Maintainability Index (*MI*) derived by analyzing numerous software systems maintained by Hewlett-Packard. Although the authors claim that it may fit other industrial-sized software systems and the breadth of the work tends to support this claim we were not able to find any validation on object-oriented systems written in Java. Therefore, we think that the *MI* has to be taken *cum grano salis* and should be complemented by standard complexity measures.

Table 1 summarizes the metrics we use in this research as indicators for maintainability.

Table 1. Selected metrics as indicators for maintainability

Metric name	Definition
LOC	Number of Java source code statements
CBO	Coupling Between Objects (CK)
LCOM	Lack of Cohesion Of Methods (CK)
WMC	Weighted Methods per Class (CK)
RFC	Response For a Class (CK)
MCC	Average McCabe's cyclomatic complexity per class
MI	Maintainability Index (based on LOC and Halstead Volume)

Two of the 6 CK zmetrics, namely *NOC* (Number of Children) and *DIT* (Depth of Inheritance Tree) are not included in Table 1. We decided not to consider them since in the project under investigation they show very low values and are mostly constant over time. Moreover, in addition to the CK metrics and complexity we collect also *LOC*, which is used as differential factor in our maintainability evolution equation.

2.2 A Model to Evaluate the Evolution of Quality and Maintainability During Development

In section 2.1 we defined a set of metrics, which is known to be useful as maintainability indicators. However, we do not know a priori the range of values of these metrics that in our case would indicate good or bad maintainability. Analyzing historical data or several similar projects can only – if at all – derive such thresholds. Still, the problem with such thresholds is that if technology or development context change, which is likely in agile contexts, they are not anymore applicable or even misleading.

We follow a different strategy: Intuitively we assume that a fast and increasing growth of the CK and complexity metrics during development would lead to a complex and highly coupled code and therefore deteriorate maintainability; we think it is possible to differentiate between an evolution of the source code, which is healthy for maintainability and one, which is not. Our basic assumption is that all the maintainability metrics we consider grow – in a way we do not know – with the lines of code (*LOC*), but that the way they grow with *LOC* is significant for later maintainability. A bit more formally we can define healthy and unhealthy (regarding maintainability) evolution of a software system as follows.

Let $M_i \in M = \{MCC, WMC, CBO, RFC, LCOM\}$ be a subset of the maintainability metrics listed in Table 1. We consider them at a class level and average later over all classes of the software system. Now we assume that there exists a function f_i that returns the value of M_i given *LOC* and some other – to us unknown – parameters P at time t. Since we are only interested in the dependence of M_i on *LOC* in order to analyze the change of M_i regarding to *LOC* and time we do not require any additional assumptions for f_i and may write:

$$M_i(t) = f_i(t, LOC, P) \qquad (1)$$

Equation (1) simply states that the maintainability metric M_i will change during development and this change will depend on time t, *LOC* and some other parameters P. Now we can express our idea in the following way: If throughout development M_i grows rapidly with *LOC* its derivative with respect to *LOC* will be high (and probably grow) and affect in a negative way maintainability of the final product. Otherwise, if the derivative of M_i with respect to *LOC* is constant or even negative the maintainability will not deteriorate too much even if the system size increases significantly. Formally we can define a Maintainability Trend MT_i for metric M_i and for a time period T in the following way:

$$MT_i = \frac{1}{T} \sum_{t_k}^{T} \frac{\partial f_i(t_k, LOC, P)}{\partial LOC} \approx \frac{1}{T} \sum_{t_k}^{T} \frac{\Delta M_i}{\Delta LOC}(t_k), \; T \text{ is a time period} \qquad (2)$$

To obtain an overall trend we average the derivative of M_i with respect to *LOC* over all time points (at which we compute source code metrics) in a given time period T. This is a very simple approach since it does not consider that for different situations during development such derivative could be different. More sophisticated strategies are subject of future investigations.

We use equation (2) to differentiate between situations of "Development For Maintainability" (DFM) and "Development Contra Maintainability" (DCM):

If the MT_i per iteration is approximately constant throughout development or negative for several metrics i than we do DFM.

If the MT_i per iteration is high and grows throughout development for several metrics i we do DCM and the system will probably die the early death of entropy.

Such classification has to be taken *cum grano salis*, as it relies only on internal code structure and we do not include many important (external) factors such as experience of developers, development tools, testing effort or application domain. However, we think that it is more reliable than threshold based techniques: It does not rely on historic data and can be used at least to analyze the growth of maintainability metrics with respect to size and detect for example if it is excessively high. In such cases one could consider to refactor or redesign part of the system in order to improve maintainability.

2.3 Research Questions

The goal of this research is to determine whether XP intrinsically delivers high maintainable code or not. To this end we state two research questions, which have to be accepted or rejected by a statistical test.

The two null hypotheses are:

H^1_0: The Maintainability Trend (MT_i) per iteration defined in equation (2) for maintainability metric $M_i \in M$ is higher during later iterations (it shows a growing trend throughout development).

H^2_0: The Maintainability Index *MI* decreases monotonically during development.

In section 3 we present a case study we run in order to reject or accept the null hypotheses stated above. If we can reject both of them –assuming that our proposed model (2) and the Maintainability Index are proper indicators for maintainability - we will conclude that for the project under scrutiny XP enhances maintainability of the developed software product.

3 Case Study

In this section we present a case study we conducted in a close-to industrial environment in order to analyze the evolution of maintainability of a software product developed using an agile, XP-like methodology [1]. The objective of the case study is to answer our research question posed in section 2: First we collected in a non-invasive way the basic metrics listed in Table 1 and computed out of them the composite ones as for example the *MI* index; after we analyzed their time evolution and fed them into our proposed model (2) for evaluating the time evolution of maintainability. Finally, we used a statistical test to determine whether or not it is possible to reject the null hypotheses.

3.1 Description of the Project and Data Collection Process

The object under study is a commercial software project at VTT in Oulu, Finland. The programming language in use was Java. The project was a full business success in the sense that it delivered on time and on budget the required product, a production monitoring application for mobile, Java enabled devices. The development process followed a tailored version of the Extreme Programming practices [1], which included all the practices of XP but the "System Metaphor" and the "On-site Customer"; there was instead a local, on-site manager that met daily with the group and had daily conversations with the off-site customer. Two pairs of programmers (four people) have worked for a total of eight weeks. The project was divided into five iterations, starting with a 1-week iteration, which was followed by three 2-week iterations, with the project concluding in a final 1-week iteration.

The developed software consists of 30 Java classes and a total of 1770 Java source code statements (denoted as *LOC*). Throughout the project mentoring was provided on XP and other programming issues according to the XP approach. Three of the four developers had an education equivalent to a BSc and limited industrial experience. The fourth developer was an experienced industrial software engineer. The team worked in a collocated environment. Since it was exposed for the first time to the XP process a brief training of the XP practices, in particular of the test-first method was provided prior to the beginning of the project.

In order to collect the metrics listed in Table 1 we used our in-house developed tool PROM [20]. PROM is able to extract from a CVS repository a variety of standard and user defined source code metrics including the CK metric suite. Not to disrupt developers we set up the tool in the following way: every day at midnight automatically a checkout of the CVS repository was performed, the tool computed the values of the CK metrics and stored them in a relational database. With PROM we obtained directly the daily evolution of the CK metrics, *LOC* and McCabe's cyclomatic complexity, which has been averaged over all methods of a class. Moreover, PROM computes the Halstead Volume (Halstead, 1977) we use to compute the Maintainability Index (*MI*) using the formula given by Oman *et al.* [17].

3.2 Results

In our analysis we consider only daily changes of source code metrics, thus ΔLOC and ΔM_i used in model (2) is the daily difference of *LOC* and M_i. Different time windows would probably slightly change the results and need to be addressed in a future study. Figure 1 shows a plot of the evolution of the daily changes of the maintainability metrics ΔM_i divided by ΔLOC.

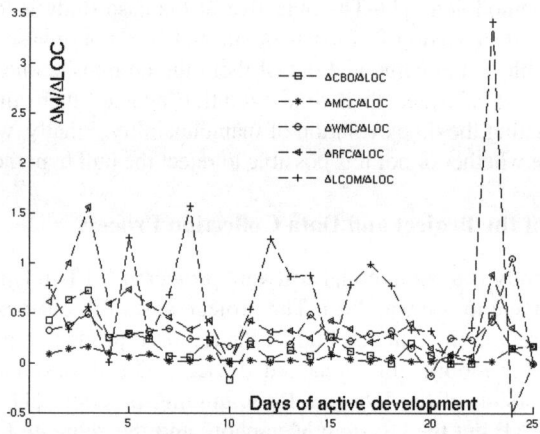

Fig. 1. Evolution of the derivative of maintainability metrics M_i with respect to *LOC*

From Figure 1 it is evident that the daily variation of maintainability metrics with respect to *LOC* – apart from the *LCOM* metric - is more or less constant over development time. Only a few days show a very high respective low change rate. Overall this means that maintainability metrics grow in a constant and controlled way with *LOC*. Moreover, the changes of coupling and complexity metrics have a decreasing trend and converge as time goes on to a value close to 0: In our opinion this is a first indicator for good maintainability of the final product. The cohesion metric *LCOM* shows a somehow different behavior as it has high fluctuations during development. However, several researchers have questioned the meaning of *LCOM* defined by Chidamber and Kemerer [8] and its impact on software maintainability is little understood by today.

If we compute the Maintainability Trend MT_i per iteration we get a similar picture. In iterations 2 and 4 complexity and coupling metrics (*CBO*, *WMC*, *MCC,* and *RFC*) grow significantly slower than in iterations 1 and 3; this is consistent with the project plan as in iteration 2 and 4 two user stories have been dedicated to refactoring activities and we assume that refactoring enhances maintainability [19].

To test whether the Maintainability Trend of metric M_i for the last two iterations of development is higher than for the first three, which is our first null hypothesis, we employ a two-sample Wilcoxon rank sum test for equal medians [11]. At a significance level of $\alpha=0.01\%$ we can reject the null hypothesis H^1_0 for all metrics M_i. This means that on average no one of these metrics grows faster when the software systems becomes more complex and difficult to understand: They increase rather slowly – without final boom - and with a decreasing trend as new functionality is added to the system (in particular the *RFC* metric shows a significant decrease).

In order to test our second null hypothesis we draw a plot of the evolution of the Maintainability Index per release. Figure 2 shows the result: *MI* decreases rapidly from release 1 to 3 but shows a different trend from release 3 to 5. While we have to accept our second null hypothesis H^2_0 – the *MI* index definitely decreases during development meaning that maintainability of the system becomes worse – we can observe an interesting trend reversal after the third iteration: The *MI* index suddenly decreases much slower and remains almost constant during the last iteration. This again can be related to refactoring activities, as we know that in the 4th iteration a user story "Refactor Architecture" has been implemented.

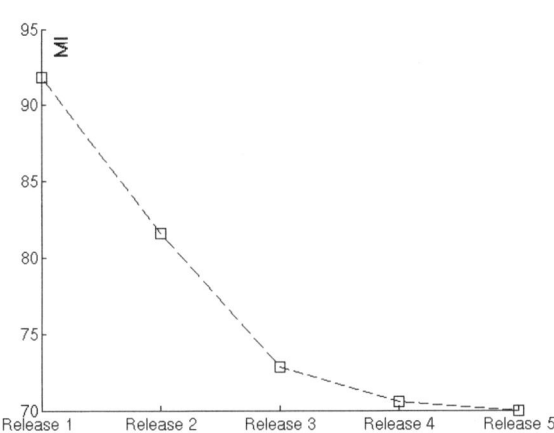

Fig. 2. Evolution of the Maintainability Index *MI* per release

Summarizing our results we can reject hypothesis H^1_0 but not H^2_0. For the first hypothesis it seems that XP-like development prevents code during development from becoming unmaintainable because of high complexity and coupling. For the second one we have to analyze further if the Maintainability Index is applicable and a reasonable measure in an XP-like environment and for the Java programming language.

4 Threats to Validity and Future Work

This research aims at giving an answer to the question whether XP delivers high maintainable code or not. To answer this question we use two different concepts of maintainability: One relies on the findings of other researchers [17] and the other is based on our own model we propose in this research. Both strategies have their drawbacks: The Maintainability Index (*MI*) defined by Oman et al. for example has been derived in an environment, which is very different from XP. Its value for XP-like projects can be questioned and has to be analyzed in future experiments. The model we propose analyzes the growth of important maintainability metrics with respect to the size of the code. We assume that a moderate growth, which shows decreasing trend over time, should result in software with better maintainability characteristics than a fast growth. While this assumption seems to be fairly intuitive, we have not yet validated it. Also this remains to be addressed in our future research. Both approaches have in common that they consider only internal product metrics as maintainability indicators. Of course, this is only half of the story and a complete model should also consider external product and process metrics that characterize the maintenance process.

Regarding the internal validity of this research we have to address the following threats:

- The subjects of the case study are heterogeneous (three students and one professional engineer) and use for the first time an XP-like methodology. This could confound seriously our findings, as for example students may behave very different from industrial developers. Moreover, also a learning effect could be visible and for example be the cause for the evolution of the Maintainability Index in Figure 2.
- We do not know the performance of our maintainability metrics in other projects, which have been developed using a more traditional development style. Therefore, we cannot conclude that XP in absolute terms really leads to better maintainable code than other development methodologies.
- Finally, the choice of maintainability metrics and the time interval we consider to calculate their changes is subjective. We plan to consider variations in metrics and time interval in future experiments in order to confirm or reject the conclusions of this research.

Altogether, as with every case study the results we obtain are valid only in the specific context of the experiment. In this research we analyze a rather small software project in a highly volatile domain. A generalization to other application domains and XP projects is only possible through future replications of the experiment in such environments.

5 Conclusions

This research focuses on how XP affects quality and maintainability of a software product. Maintainability is a key success factor for software development and should be supported as much as possible by the development process itself. We believe that XP has some practices, which support and enhance software maintainability: simple design, continuous refactoring and integration, and test-driven development.

In this research we propose a new method for assessing the evolution of maintainability during software development via a so-called Maintainability Trend (*MT*) indicator. Moreover, we use a traditional approach for estimating code maintainability and introduce it in the XP process. We conduct a case study in order to analyze whether a product developed with an XP-like methodology shows nice maintainability characteristics (in terms of our proposed model and the *MI* index) or not.

The conclusions of this research are twofold:

1. XP seems to support the development of easy to maintain code both in terms of the *MI* index and a moderate growth of coupling and complexity metrics during development.
2. The model we propose for a "good" evolution of maintainability metrics can be used to detect problems or anomalies (high growth rate with respect to size) or "maintainability enhancing" restructuring activities (for example refactoring) (low growth rate with respect to size). Such information is very valuable as it can be obtained continuously during development and used for monitoring the "maintainability state" of the system. If it happens that maintainability deteriorates developers can immediately react and refactor the system. Such intervention – as for an ill patient - is for sure easier and cheaper if recognized sooner than later.

XP as any other technique is something a developer has to learn and to train. First, managers have to be convinced that XP is very valuable for their business; this research should help them in doing so as it sustains that XP – if applied properly – intrinsically delivers code, which is easy to maintain. But after they have to provide training and support in order to convert their development process into an XP-like process. Among other maintainability – one of the killers that precede the death of entropy – will pay it off.

Acknowledgments

The authors would also like to acknowledge the support by the Italian ministry of Education, University and Research via the FIRB Project MAPS (http://www.agilexp.org) and the autonomous province of South Tyrol via the Interreg Project Software District (http://www.caso-synergies.org).

References

1. Abrahamsson, P., Hanhineva, A., Hulkko, H., Ihme, T., Jäälinoja, J., Korkala, M., Koskela, J., Kyllönen, P., Salo, O.: Mobile-D: An Agile Approach for Mobile Application Development. In: Proceedings 19th Annual ACM Conference on Object-Oriented Programming, Systems, Languages, and Applications, OOPSLA'04, Vancouver, British Columbia, Canada (2004)
2. Beck, K.: Extreme Programming Explained: Embrace Change. Addison-Wesley, Reading (1999)
3. Basili, V., Briand, L., Melo, W.L.: A Validation of Object-Oriented Design Metrics as Quality Indicators. IEEE Transactions on Software Engineering 22(10), 267–271 (1996)
4. Brooks, F.: The Mythical Man-Month. Addison-Wesley, Reading (1975)
5. Bruntink, M., van Deursen, A.: Predicting Class Testability Using Object-Oriented Metrics. In: Proceedings of the Fourth IEEE International Workshop on Source Code Analysis and Manipulation (SCAM) (2004)

6. Chidamber, S., Kemerer, C.F.: A metrics suite for object-oriented design. IEEE Transactions on Software Engineering 20(6), 476–493 (1994)
7. Coleman, D., Lowther, B., Oman, P.: The Application of Software Maintainability Models in Industrial Software Systems. Journal of Systems Software 29(1), 3–16 (1995)
8. Counsell, S., Mendes, E., Swift, S.: Comprehension of object-oriented software cohesion: the empirical quagmire. In: Proceedings of the 10th International Workshop on in Program Comprehension, Paris, France, pp. 33–42 (June 27-29, 2002)
9. Fenton, N., Pfleeger, S.L.: Software Metrics A Rigorous & Practical Approach, p. 408. PWS Publishing Company, Boston (1997)
10. Halstead, M.H.: Elements of Software Science. Operating and Programming Systems Series, vol. 7. Elsevier, New York, NY (1977)
11. Hollander, M., Wolfe, D.A.: Nonparametric statistical inference, pp. 27–33. John Wiley & Sons, New York (1973)
12. Johnson, P.M., Kou, H., Agustin, J.M., Chan, C., Moore, C.A., Miglani, J., Zhen, S., Doane, W.E.: Beyond the Personal Software Process: Metrics collection and analysis for the differently disciplined. In: Proceedings of the 2003 International Conference on Software Engineering, Portland, Oregon (2003)
13. Layman, L., Williams, L., Cunningham, L.: Exploring Extreme Programming in Context: An Industrial Case Study. Agile Development Conference 2004, pp. 32–41(2004)
14. Li, W., Henry, S.: Maintenance Metrics for the Object Oriented Paradigm. In: Proceedings of the First International Software Metrics Symposium, Baltimore, MD, pp. 52–60 (1993)
15. Lo, B.W.N., Shi, H.: A preliminary testability model for object-oriented software. In: Proceedings of International Conference on Software Engineering: Education and Practice, 26-29 January 1998, pp. 330–337 (1998)
16. McCabe, T.: Complexity Measure. IEEE Transactions on Software Engineering 2(4), 308–320 (1976)
17. Oman, P., Hagemeister, J.: Constructing and Testing of Polynomials Predicting Software Maintainability. Journal of Systems and Software 24(3), 251–266 (1994)
18. Poole, C., Murphy, T., Huisman, J.W., Higgins, A.: Extreme Maintenance. 17th IEEE International Conference on Software Maintenance (ICSM'01), p. 301 (2001)
19. Ratzinger, J., Fischer M., Gall, H.: Improving Evolvability through Refactoring. In: Proceedings 2nd International Workshop on Mining Software Repositories, MSR'05, Saint Louis, Missouri, USA (2005)
20. Sillitti, A., Janes, A., Succi, G., Vernazza, T.: Collecting, Integrating and Analyzing Software Metrics and Personal Software Process Data. In: Proceedings of the EUROMICRO 2003 (2003)

Inspecting Automated Test Code: A Preliminary Study

Filippo Lanubile and Teresa Mallardo

Dipartimento di Informatica, University of Bari,
70126 Bari, Italy
{lanubile,mallardo}@di.uniba.it

Abstract. Testing is an essential part of an agile process as test is automated and tends to take the role of specifications in place of documents. However, whenever test cases are faulty, developers' time might be wasted to fix problems that do not actually originate in the production code. Because of their relevance in agile processes, we posit that the quality of test cases can be assured through software inspections as a complement to the informal review activity which occurs in pair programming. Inspections can thus help the identification of what might be wrong in test code and where refactoring is needed. In this paper, we report on a preliminary empirical study where we examine the effect of conducting software inspections on automated test code. First results show that software inspections can improve the quality of test code, especially the repeatability attribute. The benefit of software inspections also apply when automated unit tests are created by developers working in pair programming mode.

Keywords: Automated Testing, Unit Test, Refactoring, Software Inspection, Pair Programming, Empirical Study.

1 Introduction

Extreme Programming (XP), and more generally agile methods, tend to minimize any effort which is not directly related to code completion [3]. A core XP practice, pair programming, requires two developers work side-by-side at a single computer in a joint development effort [21]. While one (the Driver) is typing on the keyboard, the other (the Navigator) observes the work and catches defects as soon as they are entered into the code. Although a number of research studies have shown that this form of continuous review, albeit informal, can assure a good level of quality [15, 20, 22], there is still uncertainty about benefits from agile methods, in particular for dependable systems [1, 17, 18]. In particular, some researchers propose to combine agile and plan-driven processes to determine the right balancing process [4, 19].

Software inspections are an established quality assurance technique for early defect detection in plan-driven development processes [6]. With software inspections, any software artifact can be the object of static verification, including requirements specifications, design documents as well as source code and test cases. However, test cases are the least reviewed type of software artifact with plan-driven methods [8], because testing comes late in a waterfall-like development process and might be minimized if the project is late or out of budget.

On the contrary, testing is an essential part of an agile process. No user stories can be considered ready without passing its acceptance tests and all unit tests for a class should run correctly. With automated unit testing, developers write test cases according to the xUnit framework in the same programming language as the code they test, and put unit tests under software configuration management together with production code. In Test-Driven Development (TDD), another XP core practice, programmers write test cases first and then implement code which successfully passes the test cases [2]. Although some researchers argue that TDD is helpful for improving quality and productivity [5, 10, 13], writing test cases before coding requires more effort than writing test cases after coding [13, 14]. With TDD, test cases take the role of specification but this does not exclude errors. Test cases themselves might be incorrect because they do not represent the right specification and developers' time might be wasted to fix problems that do not actually originate in the production code.

Because of their relevance in agile processes, we posit that the quality of test cases can be assured through software inspections to be conducted in addition to the informal review activity which occurs in pair programming. Inspections can thus help the identification of "test smells", which are symptoms that something might be wrong in test code [11] and refactoring can be needed [23]. In this paper we start to examine the effect of conducting software inspections on automated test code. We report the results of a repeated case study in an academic setting where unit test cases, which have been produced by pair and solo groups, have been inspected to assess the quality of test code. The remainder of this paper is organized as follows. Section 2 gives background information about quality of test cases and symptoms of problems. Section 3 describes the empirical study and presents the results from data analysis. Finally, conclusions are presented in Section 4.

2 Quality of Automated Tests

Writing good test cases is not easy, especially if tests have to be automated. When developers write automated test cases, they should take care that the following quality attributes are fulfilled [11]:

Concise. A test should be brief and yet comprehensive.
Self checking. A test should report results without human interpretation.
Repeatable. A test should be run many consecutive times without human intervention.
Robust. A test should produce always the same results.
Sufficient. A test should verify all the major functionalities of the software to be tested.
Necessary. A test should contain only code to the specification of desired behavior.
Clear. A test should be easy to understand.
Efficient. A test should be run in a reasonable amount of time.
Specific. A test failure should involve a specific functionality of the software to be tested.

Independent. A test should produce the same results whether it is run by itself or together with other tests.
Maintainable. A test should be easy to modify and extend.
Traceable. A test should be traceable to and from the code and requirements.

Lack of quality in automated test can be revealed by "test smells" [11], [12], [23], which are a kind of code smells as initially introduced by Fowler [7], but specific for test code:

Obscure test. A test case is difficult to understand at a first reading.
Conditional test logic. A test case contains conditional logic within selection or repetition structures.
Test code duplication. Identical fragments of test code (clones) appear in a number of test cases.
Test logic in production. Production code contains logic that should rather be included into test code.
Assertion roulette. When a test case fails, you do not know which of the assertions is responsible for it.
Erratic test. A test that gives different results, depending on when it runs and who is running it.
Fragile test. A test that fails or does not compile after any change to the production code.
Frequent debugging. Manual debugging is required to determine the cause of most test failures.
Manual intervention. A test case requires manual changes before the test is run, otherwise the test fails.
Slow test. The test takes so long that developers avoid to run it every time they make a change.

3 Empirical Investigation of Test Quality

The context of our experience was a web engineering course at the University of Bari, involving Master's students in computer science engaged in porting a legacy web application. The legacy application provides groupware support for distributed software inspections [9]. The old version (1.6) used the outdated MS ASP scripting technology and had become hard to evolve. Before the course start date, the application had been entirely redesigned according to a four-layered architecture. Then porting to MS .NET technology started with a number of use cases from the old version successfully migrated to the new one.

As a course assignment, students had to complete the migration of the legacy web application. Test automation for the new version was part of the assignment. Students were following the process model shown in Fig. 1. To realize the assigned use case, students added new classes for each layer of the architecture, then they submitted both source code and design document to a two-person inspection team which assessed whether the use case realization was compliant to the four-layered architecture.

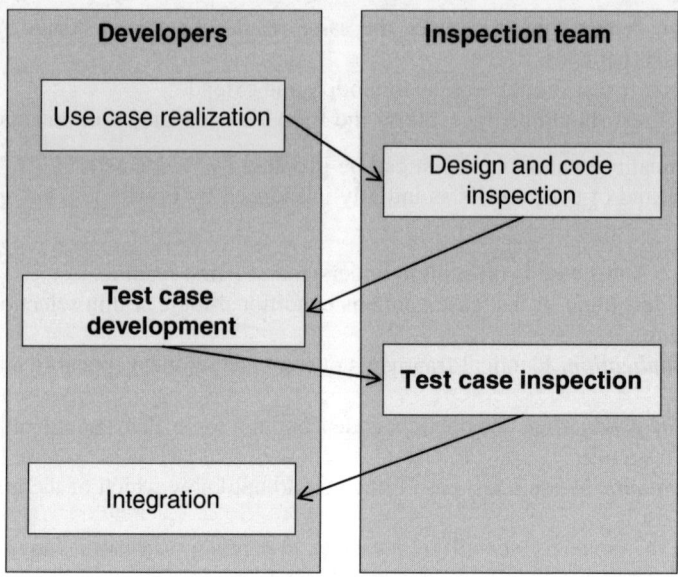

Fig. 1. The process for use case migration

In the test case development stage, students wrote unit test cases in accordance with the NUnit framework [16]. Students were taught to develop each test as a method that implements the Four Phases Test pattern [11]. This test pattern requires a test to be structured with four distinct phases that are executed in sequence. The four test phases are the following:

- *Fixture setup*: making conditions to establish the prior state (the fixture) of the test that is required to observe the system behavior
- *Exercise system under test*: causing the software we are testing to run.
- *Result verification*: specifying the expected outcome.
- *Fixture teardown*: restoring the initial conditions of the system in which it was before the test was run.

In the test case inspection stage, automated unit tests were submitted to the same two-person inspection team as in the previous design and code inspection. This time the goal of the inspection was to assess the quality of test code. For this purpose, the inspectors used the list of test smells as a checklist for test code analysis. Finally, the migrated use cases, which implemented all corrections from the inspections, could be integrated to the baseline.

Table 1 characterizes the results of students' work. Six students had redeveloped four use cases, two of which in pair programming (PP) and the other two use cases in solo programming (SP). Class methods include only those methods created for classes in the data and domain layers. Students considered only public methods for being tested. For each method under test, test creation was restricted to one test case, with the exception of a method in UC4 which had two test cases.

Table 1. Characterization of the migration tasks

	UC1	UC2	UC3	UC4
Programming Model	solo programming (SP)	pair programming (PP)	pair programming (PP)	solo programming (SP)
Class methods	26	42	72	31
Methods under test	12	23	35	20
Test cases	12	23	35	21

Table 2 reports which test smells were found by test case inspectors and their occurrences for each use case.

The most common indicator of problems was the need for manual changes before launching a test. Test cases often violated the Four Phases Test pattern, and this occurred in all the four use cases. In particular, we found that the fixture setup and teardown phases were missing some critical actions. For example, in UC3 and UC4, developers were testing class methods that delete an item in the repository. However, the fixture setup phase were not adding to the repository the item to be deleted, while the fixture teardown phase was missing at all. More generally, when a test case modified the application state permanently, tests failed and manual intervention was required to restore the initial state of the system. This negatively affected the repeatability of tests.

Two other common smells found in the test code were assertion roulette and conditional test logic. The root cause for these issues were developers' choice of writing one test case for each class method under test. As a consequence, a test case verified different behaviors of a class method using multiple assertions and conditional statements. Test case overloading hampered the clarity and maintainability of tests.

Another common problem was test code duplication which was mainly due to "copy and paste" practices applied to the fixture setup phase. It was easily resolved by extracting instructions included in the setup part from the fixture of a single test case to the shared fixture.

Table 2. Results from test case inspections

	UC1 (SP)	UC2 (PP)	UC3 (PP)	UC4 (SP)
Manual intervention	10	10	17	14
Assertion roulette	2	16	15	4
Conditional test logic	1	8	2	6
Test code duplication	1	7	6	1
Erratic test	1	1	2	0
Fragile test	0	0	1	3
Total issues	15	42	46	28
Issue density	1.2	1.8	1.3	1.3

Erratic tests were also identified as they were caused by test cases which depended on other test cases. When these test cases were running isolated they provided different results from test executions which included coupled test cases. Test case inspections allowed to identify those test code portions in which the dependencies were hidden.

Finally, there were few indicators of fragile tests because of data sensitivity, as the tests failed when the contents of the repository was modified.

The last two rows of Table 2 report, respectively, the total number of issues and issue density, that is the number of issues per test case. Results show that there were more test case issues in UC2 and UC3 than in UC1 and UC4. However, this difference is only apparent. If we consider the issue density, which takes into account size differences, we can see that pair programming and solo programming provide the same level of test quality.

4 Conclusions

In this paper, we have reported on an empirical study, conducted at the University of Bari, where we examine the effect of conducting software inspections on automated test code. Results have shown that software inspections can improve the quality of test code, especially the repeatability of tests, which is one of the most important qualities of test automation. We also found that the benefit of software inspections can be observed when automated unit tests are created by single developers as well as by pairs of developers.

The finding that inspections can reveal unknown flaws in automated test code, even when using pair programming, is in contrast with the claim that quality assurance is already included within pair programming, and then software inspection is a redundant (and then uneconomical) practice for agile methods. We can rather say that, even if developers are applying agile practices on a project, if a product is particularly high risk it might be worth its effort to use inspections, at least for key parts such as automated test code.

The results show a certain tendency but are not conclusive. A threat to validity of our study is that we could not observe the developers while working, so we cannot exclude that pairs effectively worked as driver/observer rather than splitting the assignment and working individually. Another drawback of this study is that it represents only a small study, using a small number of subjects in an academic environment. Therefore, results can only be preliminary and more investigations have to follow.

As further work we intend to run a controlled experiment in the next edition of our course to provide more quantitative results about benefits of test cases inspections. We also encourage researchers to replicate the study in different settings to analyze the application of inspections in agile development in more detail.

Acknowledgments. We would like to thank Domenico Balzano for his help in test case inspections.

References

1. Ambler, S.W.: When Does(n't) Agile Modeling Make Sense? http:// www.agilemodeling.com/essays/whenDoesAMWork.htm
2. Beck, K.: Test Driven Development: By Example. Addison-Wesley, New York, NY, USA (2002)
3. Beck, K.: Extreme Programming Explained: Embrace Change. Addison-Wesley, New York, NY, USA (2000)
4. Boehm, B., Turner, R.: Balancing Agility and Discipline: A Guide for the Perplexed. Addison-Wesley, New York, NY, USA (2003)
5. Erdogmus, H., Morisio, M., Torchiano, M.: On the Effectiveness of the Test-First Approach to Programming. In: IEEE Transactions on Software Engineering, vol. 31(3), pp. 226–237. IEEE Computer Society Press, Los Alamitos, CA, USA (2005)
6. Fagan, M.E.: Design and Code Inspections to Reduce Errors in Program Development. IBM Systems Journal, vol. 15(3), Riverton, NJ, USA, pp. 182–211 (1976)
7. Fowler, M.: Refactoring: Improving the Design of Existing Code. Addison-Wesley, New York, NY, USA (1999)
8. Laitenberger, O., DeBaud, J.M.: An encompassing life cycle centric survey of software inspection. In: The Journal of Systems and Software, vol. 50(1), pp. 5–31. Elsevier Science Inc, New York, NY, USA (2000)
9. Lanubile, F., Mallardo, T., Calefato, F.: Tool Support for Geographically Dispersed Inspection Teams. In: Software Process: Improvement and Practice, vol. 8(4), pp. 217–231. Wiley InterScience, New York (2003)
10. Maximilien, E.M., Williams, L.: Assessing Test-Driven Development at IBM. In: Proceedings of the International Conference on Software Engineering (ICSE'03), pp. 564–569 (2003)
11. Meszaros, G.: XUnit Test Patterns: Refactoring Test Code. Addison Wesley, New York, NY, USA (to appear in 2007). Also available online at http://xunitpatterns.com/
12. Meszaros, G., Smith, S.M., Andrea, J.: The Test Automation Manifesto. In: Maurer, F., Wells, D. (eds.) XP/Agile Universe 2003. LNCS, vol. 2753, pp. 73–81. Springer, Heidelberg (2003)
13. Muller, M.M., Tichy, W.E.: Case Study: Extreme Programming in a University Environment. In: Inverardi, P., Jazayeri, M. (eds.) ICSE'05. LNCS vol. 4309, pp. 537–544. Springer, Heidelberg (2006)
14. Muller, M.M., Hagner, O.: Experiment about Test-First Programming. In: Proceedings of the International Conference on Empirical Assessment in Software Engineering (EASE'02), pp. 131–136 (2002)
15. Muller, M.M.: Two controlled experiments concerning the comparison of pair programming to peer review. In: The Journal of Systems and Software, vol. 78(2), pp. 166–179. Elsevier Science Inc., New York, NY, USA (2005)
16. Nunit Development Team: Two, M.C., Poole, C., Cansdale, J., Feldman, G.: http://www.nunit.org
17. Paulk, M.: Extreme Programming from a CMM Perspective. In: IEEE Software, vol. 18(6), pp. 19–26. IEEE Computer Society Press, Los Alamitos, CA, USA (2001)
18. Rakitin, S.: Letters: Manifesto Elicits Cynicism. In: IEEE Computer, vol. 34(12), IEEE Computer Society Press, Los Alamitos, CA, USA, pp. 4, 6–7 (2001)
19. Reifer, D.J., Maurer, F., Erdogmus, H.: Scaling Agile Methods. In: IEEE Software, vol. 20(4), pp. 12–14. IEEE Computer Society Press, Los Alamitos, CA, USA (2003)

20. Tomayko, J.: A Comparison of Pair Programming to Inspections for Software Defect Reduction. Computer Science Education, vol. 12(3). Taylor & Francis Group, pp. 213–222 (2002)
21. Williams, L., Kessler, R.R.: Pair Programming Illuminated. Addison-Wesley, New York, NY, USA (2002)
22. Williams, L., Kessler, R.R., Cunningham, W., Jeffries, R.: Strengthening the Case for Pair Programming. In: IEEE Software, vol. 17(4), pp. 19–25. IEEE Computer Society Press, Los Alamitos, CA, USA (2000)
23. van Deursen, A., Moonen, L., van den Bergh, A., Kok, G.: Refactoring Test Code. In: Proceedings of the 2nd International Conference on eXtreme Programming and Agile Processes in Software Engineering (XP'01) (2001)

A Non-invasive Method for the Conformance Assessment of Pair Programming Practices Based on Hierarchical Hidden Markov Models

Ernesto Damiani and Gabriele Gianini

Dpt.of Information Technology - University of Milan
via Bramante 65, I-26013 Crema (CR)
{damiani,gianini}@dti.unimi.it

Abstract. We specify a non-invasive method allowing to estimate the time each developer of a pair spends over the development activity, during Pair Programming. The method works by performing first a behavioural fingerprinting of each developer – based on low level event logs – which then is used to operate a segmentation over the log sequence produced by the pair: in a timelined log event sequence this is equivalent to estimating the times of the switching between developers. We model the individual developer's behaviour by means of a Markov Chain – inferred from the logs – and model the developers' role-switching process by a further, higher level, Markov Chain. The overall model consisting in the two nested Markov Chains belongs to the class of Hierarchical Hidden Markov Models. The method could be used not only to assess the degree of conformance with respect to predefined Pair Programming switch-times policies, but also to capture the characteristics of a given programmers pair's switching process, namely in the context of Pair Programming effectiveness studies.

1 Introduction

Pair Programming (PP) is one of the key practices of several agile software development methodologies, including eXtreme Programming: it consists in a collaborative development method where two people are working simultaneously on the same programming task, alternating on the use of some IDE, so that while one of the programmers is creating a software artefact the other is committed to assuring quality, by trying to understand, asking questions, suggesting alternative approaches and helping to avoid defects [1,2].

In the standard version of this practice the two developers work on the same machine: it is the so-called *co-located* PP (a distributed variant of PP has also been experimented – see [3,4] – however hereafter we only deal with co-located PP): while a developer plays the role of *actuator*, the other plays the role of *supervisor*. Form time to time the two developers switch their roles according to some prespecified policy.

1.1 Motivation

One of the defining features of the different PP variants is precisely the switching time policy, specifying the amount of time each developer is supposed to spend in each role.

PP, in its different variants, has been claimed to yield, as a part of the extreme programming process, higher quality software products in less time. The claim is supported by anecdotal evidence and by empirical studies [5,6,7,8].

However a more systematic study of the practice would be desirable: one based on real development settings, linking the degree of adherence to the practice to the quality level of software. One of the main problems in this respect is that, whereas several product quality metrics can be defined whose collection is de facto non-invasive to the development process, the collection of PP practice metrics has been so far been rather invasive. Indeed all the studies carried on so far would require either a person playing the role of experiment controller and taking note of the switching times, or the developers taking note of their switching times, either manually or by the equivalent of alternate log-on into some purposely designed and developed log-on system. Those methods are intrinsically either imprecise or invasive or both (for instance it has been reported [9] that, even given a very light-weight *one-click log-on* procedure, the developers would fail to log-themselves on most of the times when switching).

1.2 Approach

In the present work we propose a methodology – based on a non-invasive IDE event log collection – that, given an event log sequence, performs a segmentation procedure, which – exploiting previously automatically acquired knowledge on individual programmer's behaviours – assigns each segment of the sequence to one of the two programmers.

The methodology is based on two key elements. The first one consists in the modelling of the individual developer's behaviour, as seen from the logs, by means of a Markov Chain (a.k.a. Markov Model or Markov Machine): the states of this Markov Model correspond to different event durations[1], we will refer to them as *low-level states*.

The second element consists in modelling the developers' role alternation, within a pair, as a further, higher-level, Markov Chain; the states of the latter, which will be referred to as *high-level states*, correspond to an individual programmer being in the role of actuator.

Notice that the two levels are nested. In fact each high level state, corresponding to one of the two programmers being in the role of actuator, corresponds to the activity of one of the two low-level Markov Machines – the Machine corresponding to the acting developer. Furthermore the high level states (representing

---

[1] The modelling of the individual developer's behaviour by means of Markov Model where the states are represented by the different event durations is based on our previous work [10] on supervised learning of the developer's model and relies on the key observation that each developer appears to have a personal "rhythmic" pattern/fingerprint when interacting with the IDE.

the identity of the actual programmer acting) cannot be seen directly in the logs: therefore the higher level chain is hidden. The overall model can therefore be charategorized, as we will see briefly, as a Hierarchical Hidden Markov Model.

The rationale behind the methodology comes form an observation made in [10]: there it was noticed that if one divides the IDE events into categories according to their duration – e.g. in three categories – considers each instance of a category as a state of a Markov Chain and then learns the corresponding transition matrix from the sequences produced by different programmers, one ends up with different transition matrixes, one for each programmer. Those matrixes can be then used to distinguish a sequence produced by a given programmer from the sequence produced by another one. This fact is exploited by our methodology to segment a given sequence produced by the alternation of two programmers at unknown times into several sub-sequences, each one assigned to a given programmer.

The standard procedure for using the above methodology is given by a preparation phase, a first data gathering phase, a training phase, a second data gathering phase and a sequence segmentation phase: during the preparation phase an event monitor plug-in is activated in the IDE, enabling the logging of the IDE-events' time stamps; during the training phase the Markov Model corresponding to each individual developer is learned from the data collected during the first data taking round; then the second data gathering round takes place; after this phase, which results in a low-level event sequence, the individual developers' Markov Models are used to perform a sequence segmentation and to attribute each subsequence to a given programmer.

1.3 Applications

We suggest two main application for this procedure. It coud be used within PP investigations, for capturing the characteristics of a given programmers' pair switching process, so as to study the link between the degree of respect of the PP practices and the resulting software quality (collected independently). Furthermore it could be used to assess the degree of conformance to some specific PP policy, for instance in the context of outsourcing, when an agreement over the process methodology to be applied has been made.

We will refer hereafter indifferently to both application scenarios.

In the next sections we will recall the definitions of Markov Models (Markov Chains) and Hidden Markov Models (Section 2), then we give a set of relevant PP switching policies (Section 3) and finally (Sections 4 and 5) the procedure for assessing the degree of conformance each policy. A discussion (Section 5) and an outline of possible developments will close the paper.

2 Simple and Composite Markov Models

The dynamics of the software process is stochastic in nature; therefore, in general, non-determinism can and should be used as a key ingredient of the model at every time-resolution level. For the problem under study we are interested in two time-resolution levels: the first is the resolution level of the switching time between programmers, the second is the resolution of level of the events produced by the developer within an IDE, which can be conveniently captured by an IDE plug-in [11,12,13,14,15,16]. The latter could correspond, for instance, to the switch time from one window to another window, from a class to another class, or from a method to another method.

The high level switching event times cannot deterministically be determined in advance, nor can the low-level events: they are rather produced in correspondence to a hidden cognitive path, undertaken by the programmers' pair, during the software artefact construction.

2.1 Markov Models of the Low-Level Event Sequence

However, although neither the category of low-level events nor their timing can be predetermined, an apparent stochastic dependence has been observed among nearby events in experimentally collected fine-granularity event sequences [10] that has hinted for the modelling of the non-deterministic character of the process in terms of local, short-range, step-to-step correlation. In [10] it is shown that by just using the IDE event timing and adopting the event duration as a state, a short range dependence can be found in experimentally collected event traces: a given state in a sequence seems to be stochastically influenced by the few previous states in that sequence.

This fact prompts for adopting a simplifying assumption: that of modelling the sequence of fine-granularity events as a Markov Chain, or Markov Model (MM).

A MM is defined as a stochastic model where the probability of manifestation of a given state, in a sequence, conditionally depends only on a limited number of previous states appeared in the sequence. In other words the probability of a transition of the system to a given state depends only upon the state the system comes from, or upon the few preceding states.

A given MM is characterized by its matrix of state transition probabilities, whose matrix elements p_{ij} represent the probability of the occurrence of a

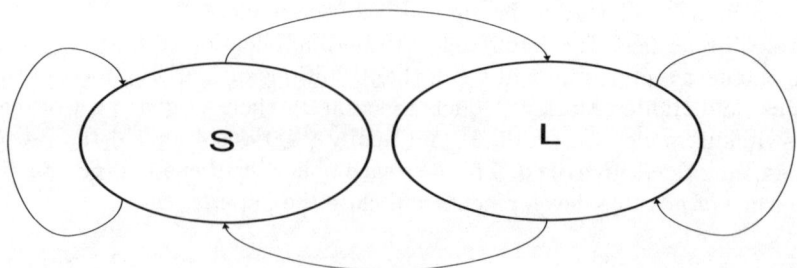

Fig. 1. A schematic view of the event duration Markov machine. The state names S and L stand respectively for Short and Long.

transition from state i to state j: in a first order Markov Model with r states this is a $(r \times r)$ square matrix, in an m-th order Markov Model it is an $r^m \times r$ matrix (in all the following formulas, whenever not explicitly specified we will assume that $i = 1, \ldots, r^m$ and $j = 1, \ldots, r$).

For example a first-order transition matrix where diagonal elements are far greater than off-diagonal events will produce long sequences of identical states: in a set up where the state represents an event duration, this corresponds predominantly into long sequences of events of short duration followed by long sequences of long duration and so on.

In this paper for sake of simplicity we will assume that the transition matrixes of each developer in the PP pair have been learned with a sample of data large enough to allow a sharp estimate of the corresponding matrix elements.

2.2 Markov Models of the High-Level Event Sequence

The paradigm of the Markov Models can be used also for the high level events, with some care. Here each state of the model respresents an individual developer.

The extra care one has to use comes from the following fact: whereas one could assume quite safely that an individual programmer in a programmer's pair is characterized by a steady behaviour – and therefore that his/her dynamics in terms of low-level event generation is correctly described by a matrix transition whose matrix elements are constant in time – the same is not true for high level machines. The probability of a transition from a programmer to another in a PP pair can be considered to increase with time: the corresponding transition matrix is expected to pass from an almost diagonal form at the beginning of the activity of a programmer to an off diagonal form after a while. This could be captured, for instance, by a model where a diagonal element of the transition matrix is proportional to $e^{-\alpha t}$, for some value of α. However, since this would not change the key elemets of our methodology, within this paper we will adopt the approximation of stationarity also for the high-level Markov machine.

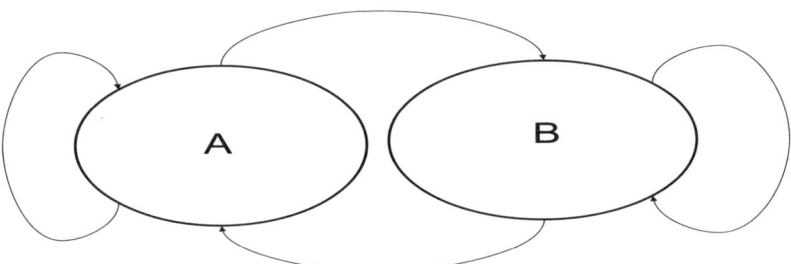

Fig. 2. A schematic view of the two programmers Markov machine. The state names A and B indicate the two programmers of the programming pair, say Alice and Bob.

2.3 Composition of Markov Models: HMMs and HHMMs

The overall stochastic model, responsable for the actual low-level sequence generation, results from the composition of the two levels of Markov Models: the higher level Markov Model representing the switching between developers and the lower level Markov Models, representing the low-level event alternating durations. This composed model belongs to the class of Hierarchical Hidden Markov Models (HHMM).

Hidden Markov Models. Usually the states of a Markov Model, unless differently specified, are intended to be observable: the symbols making-up a sequence, produced by a Markov Model, are in strict one-to-one correspondence to the Markov Model states. A Hidden Markov Model (HMM), instead, is a Markov Model whose states are not directly observable, because the one-to-one correspondence is lost: every state can correspond to one or more observable symbols and the same symbol can be shared by two or more states. In this case one refers to the (hidden) *state sequence* as to the *phenomenon* and to the observable *symbol sequence* as to the *epiphenomenon*: whereas the states of a sequence of states are conditionally dependent on the previous states of the same sequence according to some *transition probability matrix*, the symbols of an observable sequence are not directly dependent from one another but depend only from the underlying state according to some state-to-symbol *emission probability matrix*. One can think of the a HMM as to a model composed of a Markov Model and of a stochastic emission model.

Hierarchichal Hidden Markov Models. One can also compose Markov models with one another. When Markov Models are nested and the lower level model states are not observable due to symbol-to-state ambiguities one speaks of Hierarchical Hidden Markov Models.

The model considered for our methodology fits into the latter class. Indeed, it consists in a high level Markov Model, generating a sequence of higher level states, each mapped into a lower level Markov Model, which in turn generates its own sequence of states; furthermore symbols are shared by the two different low-level machines: whereas given a state of a low-level machine one can map it in only one observable symbol, given an observable symbol one cannot say to which Markov machine it belongs. This is the ambiguity that makes the higher level Markov machine a hidden machine. A schematic representation of the two level model considered here is given in Figure 3.

An example of sequence generated by a Hierarchical Hidden Markov Model with two high-level states, two low-level states for each high level state, and shared observable symbols, can be seen in figure 2.3.

One can see that in this example the higher level sequences of A's states and of B's states display a clear persistence and form almost always long subsequences of identical high-level states; in correspondence with each subsequence one can see a sequence where L and S (or l and s) low-level states alternate, again according to long same-state sequences (this time made by low-level states). In

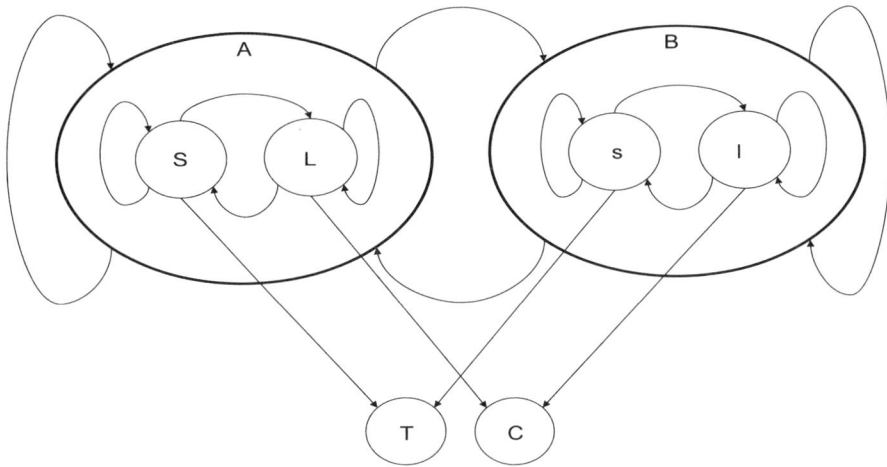

Fig. 3. A schematic view of the two programmers and event duration composite Markov machine. The high-level states are labelled with A and B; the low level states of A are labelled with S and L, standing for Short and Long; the low level states of B are labelled by s and l, again standing for Short and Long. The observabe symbol T corresponds to a short length state either from A or from B; the observable symbol C corresponds to a long duration state either from A or from B. The sharing of the observable symbols between two low-level machines makes it a Hidden Markov Model.

```
BBBBAAAAABBBBBBBAAAAAAAAAAABBBBBBBBBAAAAAAABBBBBAAAAAAAAAAAAAAA
lsslLSSSSssllllsssSLLLLLLSSLLsllllsllssSSSLLLLssll1SSSLLLLLSLLSSSS
CTTCCTTTTTTCCCTTTTCCCCCCTTCCTCCCCTCCTTTTTCCCCTTCCCTTTCCCCCTCCTTTT
```

Fig. 4. An example of sequence generated by a Hierarchical Hidden Markov Model with two high-level states, A and B, and two low-level states for each high level state (S, L and s,l respectively) sharing the observable symbols T (for S and s) and C (for L and l)

correspondence to those low level states one can observe a sequence of symbols: T for S and s, and C for L and l.

3 Pair Programming Switching Policies

The problem of associating sub-sequences of events to one or the other programmer of a PP pair can be recast in our set-up in the problem of segmenting a low level observable sequence into sub-sequences and of attributing each sub-sequence to one of the two Markov Machines, based on their knowledge (their matrix elements learned in the training phase).

Sequence segmentation based on Hidden Markov Models is a consolidated practice in audio segmentation [17], video segmentation [18] and DNA sequence segmentation [19,20] where the Viterbi algorithm is usually used. Futhermore maximum likelihood segmentation procedures for HHMM can be found in [21].

However for the purpose of PP practice assessment we are not interested in the full reconstruction of a high-level state sequence based on the observable symbol sequence. We rather ait to some more modest goal, related to general switching characteristics of the high-level state sequence: which specific goal will depend on the policy we are trying to check for.

Hereafter we mention some relevant PP switching policy. Only in the subsequent section we will deal with the problem of assessing the conformance to each one. However we can anticipate that there will be no need for the application of maximum likelihood segmentation procedures for HHMM from [21]: thanks to the use of domain knowledge on the limited number of switches between programmers one can use a more basic approach that provides the confidence level for each of the possible segmentation hypotheses.

3.1 Prototypical Pair Programming Switching Policies

Among the switching policies of interest for Pair Programming there will typically be a) some that refers only to the *number of programmers' swaps* in a given time interval (for which is available a log sequence, against which the policy has to be checked) , b) some that also mentions some constraints on the *number of events between swaps* and c) some other that constrains the *time between swaps*; one could also define d) *conditional policies*, based on knowledge acquired from outside the experimental sequence: for instance, knowing that *there has been* one swap one could check the compliance to some constraints about its time-location (indirectly in terms of number of events or directly in terms of timing).

Policies About the Number of Swaps Between Programmers. Among the policies checks of the type a) we will consider the following prototypical set: "'Check that in the high-level state sequence corresponding to the observed symbol sequence"'

1) "'there have been no swaps"'
2) "'there has been exactly one swap"'
3) "'there has been at least one swap"'
4) "'there has been more than one swap"'
5) "'there have been exactly two swaps"'
6) "'there have been more than two swaps"'

Policies About the Number of Events Between Two Swaps. Policies of type b) constrain the time of the swap by means the number of events; they relate only un-directly to the elapsed time, however they might be more appropriate in accounting for the effectiveness of the switching practice, since the recorded events in the sequence correspond to actually performed operations, and each operation involves from the side of the developers the use of cognitive resources such as memory and concentration. Among the policies checks of the type b) we will consider the following: "'Check that in the hig-level state sequence corresponding to the observed symbol sequence"'

7) "'there has been one and only one swap exactly after i events"'
8) "'there have been exactly two swaps at indexes i and j"'

Policies About the Time Between Two Swaps. Given a sequence, policies of type c) can be converted in policies of type b) simply identifying which events correspond (approximately) to the switching times specified by the policy.

Policies Sonditional to Some Apriori Knowledge. Policies of type d), or conditional policies, use some knowledge coming from outside the sequence and infer some further knowledge from the sequence. Among the policies checks of the type a) we will consider the following:

9) knowing that there has been exactly one swap, check that the swap took place between event i' and event i''.

4 Switching Time Estimate by Segmentation

4.1 Specific Policy Checking Methods

Hereafter we will assume that the low level states transition matrixes, characteristic of each developer, are known exactly: i.e. we will assume that the transition matrixes of each developer in the pair have been learned with a data sample large enough to allow a sharp estimate of the corresponding matrix elements.

Consider an observed symbol sequence O, made of symbols o_k with $k = 1, , n$, where n is the length of the sequence, and indicate by F the observed sequence of symbol transitions, made by the transitions f_k with $k = 1, , (n-1)$.

For example, in the sample sequence of Fig.2.3 the observed symbol sequence is the n-tuple

(C,T,T,C,C,T,T,T,T,T,T,C,C, . . .,C,C,C,T,C,C,T,T,T,T),

wheras the observed sequence of symbol transitions is

(CT, TT, TC, CC, CT, TT, ... , CT, TT, TT, TT).

We will indicate by $P(f_k|A)$ (by $P(f_k|B)$) the probability that the transition f_k has been caused by A (by B). We will furthermore adopt a short-hand notation for the number of swaps: the probability that there has been exactly one swap in the high-level sequence will be indicated by $P(\# = 1)$.

For each policy we give the expression for the calculation of the probability (or confidence) over policy conformance. Notice that, hereafter, the expressiones are listed in order of derivation, and not in the order used to list the corresponding policies, therefore the policy numbers are not sequential.

1) Check that in the high level state sequence – corresponding to the observed symbol sequence – there have been no swaps.

If there have been non swaps all the transitions have been caused by the same high level state, i.e. by the same Markov machine, either all by A or all by B.

The corresponding probability – if we don't make use of any a-priori knowlegde about the occurrence for A and B so that $P(A) = P(B) = 1/2$ at every k is given by

$$P(\# = 0) = \prod_{k=1}^{n-1} P(f_k|A)/2 + \prod_{k=1}^{n-1} P(f_k|B)/2$$

7) *Check that in the high-level state sequence – corresponding to the observed symbol sequence – there has been exactly one swap in correspondence of the index i.*

If we indicate by i the index at which the swap takes place, we have that, before that index, the responsable for transitions is the Markov machine A, wheras, from that index on, the responsable for transitions is the Markov Machine B, or viceversa.

$$P(idx\,of\,swap = i) = \frac{1}{2}\prod_{k=1}^{i-1} P(f_k|A) \prod_{k=i}^{n-1} P(f_k|B) + \frac{1}{2}\prod_{k=1}^{i-1} P(f_k|B) \prod_{k=i}^{n-1} P(f_k|A)$$

2) *Check that in the high-level state sequence – corresponding to the observed symbol sequence – there has been exactly one swap.*

$$P(\# = 1) = \sum_{2}^{n-2} P(idx\,of\,swap = i)$$

9) *Knowing that there has been exactly one swap, check that the swap took place between event i' and event i''.*

$$P(\# = 1) = \sum_{i'}^{i''} P(idx\,of\,swap = i)$$

3) *Check that in the high-level state sequence – corresponding to the observed symbol sequence – there has been at least one swap.*

$$P(\# \geq 1) = 1 - P(\# = 0)$$

4) *Check that in the high-level state sequence – corresponding to the observed symbol sequence – there has been more than one swap, i.e. at least two swaps*

$$P(\# > 1) = 1 - P(\# = 0) - P(\# = 1)$$

8) *Check that in the high-level state sequence – corresponding to the observed symbol sequence – there have been exactly two swaps in correspondence of the indexes i and j.*

If we indicate by i the index at which the swap takes place, we have that before that index the responsable for transitions is the Markov machine A, wheras from that index on, up to the index j-1 the responsable for transitions is the

Markov Machine B, and afterwards the responsable for the transitions is A again. Another other set of possibilities corresponds to the sequence beginning with B, then switching to A and finally returning to B.

$$P(i,j) = P(idx\ of\ first\ swap = i, idx\ of\ second\ swap = j)$$

$$= \prod_{k=1}^{i-1} P(f_k|A) \prod_{k=i}^{j-1} P(f_k|B) \prod_{k=j}^{n-1} P(f_k|A) \frac{1}{2} +$$

$$+ \prod_{k=1}^{i-1} P(f_k|B) \prod_{k=i}^{j-1} P(f_k|A) \prod_{k=j}^{n-1} P(f_k|B) \frac{1}{2}$$

5) Check that in the hig-level state sequence – corresponding to the observed symbol sequence – there have been exactly two swaps.

$$P(\# = 2) = \sum_{i=2}^{n-3} \sum_{j=i+1}^{n-2} P(idx\ of\ first\ swap = i, idx\ of\ second\ swap = j)$$

6) Check that in the hig-level state sequence – corresponding to the observed symbol sequence – there have been more than two swaps.

$$P(\# > 1) = 1 - P(\# = 0) - P(\# = 1) - P(\# = 2)$$

4.2 An Exhaustive Policy-Checking Method

Before outlining the general procedure involving the policy checking expressions shown in the previous session – that cover the case of a low number of swaps – we mention another approach, that could answer to all the practical policy checking requests, also to those not mentioned above. This is a simple approach consisting considering all the possible high level state sequences and then to compute the likelihood of the high level state sequence given the observed symbol sequence.

Although the corresponding problem is in general exponential, our domain knowledge helps in reducing dramatically its complexity: we know that in most practical cases it is unreasonable to consider programmers' swaps occurring within intervals of less than five-ten minutes; furthermore, real-world programmers' sessions (not only in PP) can be easily seen not to last continuously for, say, four hours, thanks to the distinctive gaps noticeable in the activity from the time stamps of the event log, and corresponding to working pauses. Finally one has to take into account that the "'no-trashing"' policy shared by Agile Methodologies, explicitly asks to avoid long-lasting working sessions: in this work we are not intersted in the evaluation of PP programming policies outside the context of Agile Methodoligies and can therefore assume the presence of easily identifyable gaps in the logs.

All considered, one can safely assume that once gaps are singled out the observed sequences to be considered one at time will be relatively short, say they will correspond typically one-hour sessions, with a number, to be reasonably considered, of swaps between programmers going, say, from zero to five: this would boil the problem down to a more tractable problem and make it possible to perform the exahustive calculation of the probability of each sequence of practical interest in reasonable times.

The simple general procedure for Pair Programming policy checking would then be the following:

I) Consider an admissible high-level state sequence
II) Compute the likelihood with respect of the observed symbol sequence
III) Extract from the high-level state sequence the metrics relevant to the policy (e.g. the number of switches in the high-level sequence)
IV) Add to the metrics distribution the value found for the metrics, weighted with the likelihood
V) Repeat exahustively for every admissible high-level state sequence
VI) Assess the respect of the policy based on the metrics distribution (e.g. say OK if the likelihood that there have been at least n switches is greater than some confidence value)

5 The Overall Pair Programming Policy Checking Methodology

The overall methodology to check the policies mentioned in the previous sessions consists in the following phases.

A) Preparation phase
B) First data gathering phase (or Training data gathering phase)
C) Training phase
D) Second data gathering phase
E) Sequence segmentation/policy checking phase

During the preparation phase an event monitor plug-in such as that of reference [12] is activated in the IDE, enabling the logging of the IDE-events' time stamps.

Then the First data gathering phase collects the controlled data (a low-level timestamped event log sequence) from each programmer, in this phase, the PP programmers are committed to undergo a sort of (possibly minimally invasive) authentication.

During the training phase the Markov Model corresponding to each individual developer is learned from the data collected during the first data taking round. It will correspond to a lower level Markov Model as defined in seciont 2 and capture the dynamics ruling the behaviour of each developer.

Afterwards, the second data gathering round takes place, the low-level event sequence to be used as an input for policy checking.

At this point the individual developers' Markov Models are used to perform policy checking e.g. to perform sequence segmentation into one or two subsequences and to attribute each subsequence to a given programmer.

The invasive character of the procedure is limited to the preparation and the training data gathering phase which, is can be made reasonably short [10].

6 Conclusions and Outlook

In this work we have listed a set of relevant Pair Programming policies and have described a methodology for the assessment of their conformance based on the processing of fine grained log data. Given a sequence of time-stamped log events reporting about IDE events, it is possible to capture the Markov Machine corresponding to each developer, which can then be used to perform a segmentation of the sequence of events produced by a PP pair into subsequences. Each subsequence can then in turn be associated, probabilistically, to each developer based on the likelihood for the sunsequence to have bee produced by a specific developer. The outcome can be used to compute the likelihood that a given policy has been respected.

The method could be used not only to assess the degree of conformance with respect to predefined switch-times policies, but also to capture the characteristics of a given programmers pair's switching process, in the context of PP effectiveness studies.

We plan to extend the present work by exploring the limits of effectiveness of this methodology as a function of the distance between the Markov Machines of the two PP developers: this will be performed by means of simulation and by using semi-syntetic data (e.g. by using two sequences of events produced by two disinct programmers, obtaining subsequences and alternating them). Then we plan to apply this methodology to real PP data.

Acknowledgments. This work was partially supported by contract/grant sponsor FIRB research fund of MIUR, research projects MAPS (Agile Methodologies for Software Production - contract/grant number RBNE01JRK8) and TEKNE (Towards Evolving Knowledge-based interNetworked Enterprise - contract/grant number RBNE05FKZ2_001).

References

1. Beck, K.: Extreme programming explained: Embrace change. Addison Wesley Longman, Inc., Reading, MA (2000)
2. Nawrocki, J., Wojciechowski, A.: Experimental Evaluation of Pair Programming, European Software Control and Metrics (Escom) (2001)
3. Angioni, M., Sanna, R., Soro, A.: Defining a Distributed Agile Methodology for an Open Source Scenario. In: Scotto, M., Succi, G., (eds.) Proceedings of the First International Conference on Open Source Systems Genova, pp. 209–214 (2005)
4. Angioni, M., Carboni, D., Melis, M., Pinna, S., Sanna, R., Soro, A.: XPSuite: tracking and managing XP projects in the IDE Proceedings of the 2004 workshop on Quantitative techniques for software agile process (QUTESWAP 2004) (2004)
5. Lindvall, M., Basili, V., Boehm, B., Costa, P., Dangle, K., et al.: Empirical findings in agile methods. In: Wells, D., Williams, L. (eds.) Extreme Programming and Agile Methods - XP/Agile Universe 2002. LNCS, vol. 2418, Springer, Heidelberg (2002)
6. Melnik, G., Williams, L., Geras, A.: Empirical Evaluation of Agile Processes, presented at XP/Agile Universe 2002, Chicago, USA (2002)

7. Abrahamsson, P., Warsta, J., Siponen, M.T., Ronkainen, J.: New directions on agile methods: A comparative analysis. International Conference on Software Engineering (ICSE25), Portland, Oregon, USA (2003)
8. Abrahamsson, P.: Extreme Programming: First Results from a Controlled Case Study. In: Proceedings EUROMICRO 2003 (2003)
9. Panel of the workshop QUTE-SWAP @ FSE 2004, Newport (CA) (November 2004)
10. Colombo, A., Damiani, E., Gianini, G.: Discovering the software process by means of stochastic workflow analysis. Journal of Systems Architecture 52(11), 684–692 (2006)
11. Sillitti, A., Janes, A., Succi, G., Vernazza, T.: Collecting, Integrating and Analyzing Software Metrics and Personal Software Process Data. EUROMICRO, pp. 336–342 (2003)
12. Sillitti, A., Janes, A., Succi, G., Vernazza, T.: Monitoring the Development Process with Eclipse. International Conference on Information Technology: Coding and Computing (ITCC'04) 2, 133–134 (2004)
13. Scotto, M., Sillitti, A., Succi, G., Vernazza, T.: Non-invasive product metrics collection: an architecture. Workshop on Quantitative techniques for software agile process (QUTE-SWAP04), Newport Beach, California, November 2004, pp. 76–78. ACM Press, New York (2004)
14. Scotto, M., Sillitti, A., Succi, G., Vernazza, T.: A non-invasive approach to product metrics collection. Journal of Systems Architecture 52(11), 668–675 (2006)
15. Sillitti, A., Russo, B., Zuliani, P., Succi, G.: Deploying, updating, and managing tools for collecting software metrics. Workshop on Quantitative techniques for software agile process (QUTE-SWAP04), Newport Beach, California, November 2004, pp. 1–4. ACM Press, New York (2004)
16. Sillitti, A., Succi, G., De Panfilis, S.: Managing non-invasive measurement tools. Journal of Systems Architecture 52(11), 676–683 (2006)
17. Gish, H., Siu, M., Rohlicek, R.: Segmentation of Speakers for Speech Recognition and Speaker Identification. In: Proc. Int. Conf. Acoustics, Speech, and Signal Processing, vol. 2, IEEE, Toronto, Canada, May 1991, pp. 873–876 (1991)
18. Phillips, M., Wolf, W.: Video Segmentation Techniques for News. In: Jay Kuo, C.-C. (ed.) Multimedia Storage and Archiving Systems. Proc. SPIE 2916, pp. 243–251 (1996)
19. Krogh, A., et al.: Hidden Markov models in computational biology. Applications to protein modeling. J. Mol. Biol 235, 1501–1531 (1994)
20. Du, J., Rozowsky, J.S., Korbel, J.O., Zhang, Z.D., Royce, T.E., Schultz, M.H., Snyder, M., Gerstein, M.: Systematically incorporating validated biological knowledge: an efficient hidden Markov model framework for segmenting tiling array data in transcriptional and ChIP-chip experiments. Bioinformatics 22(24), 3016–3024 (2006)
21. Brants, T.: Cascaded Markov Models, EACL 1999 (1999)

Predicting Software Defect Density: A Case Study on Automated Static Code Analysis

Artem Marchenko[1] and Pekka Abrahamsson[2]

[1] Nokia, Hatanpäänkatu 1, FIN-33100 Tampere, Finland
[2] VTT Technical Research Centre of Finland,
P.O.Box 1100, FIN-90571 Oulu, Finland
artem.marchenko@nokia.com, Pekka.Abrahamsson@vtt.fi

Abstract. The number of defects is an important indicator of software quality. Agile software development methods put an explicit requirement on automation and permanently low defect rates. Code analysis tools are seen as a prominent way to facilitate the defect prediction. There are only few studies addressing the feasibility of predicting a defect rate with the help of static code analysis tools in the area of embedded software. This study addresses the usefulness of two selected tools in the Symbian C++ environment. Five projects and 137 KLOC of the source code have been processed and compared to the actual defect rate. As a result a strong positive correlation with one of the tools was found. It confirms the usefulness of a static code analysis tool as a way for estimating the amount of defects left in the product.

Keywords: agile software development, static code analysis, automation, defect estimation, quality, embedded software, case study.

1 Introduction

The number of defects has generally been considered an important indicator of software quality. It is well known that we cannot go back and add quality. By the time you figure out you have a quality problem it is probably too late to fix it. [1]

The embedded software industry faces a number of the specific quality related challenges. The embedded devices software typically cannot be updated by the end user. In the majority of cases the software problems can be fixed only at the authorized maintenance centers. The devices running the embedded software have both hardware and software based components. Nokia and other mobile terminal manufacturers release dozens of mobile phone types a year. It significantly scales the amount of the required maintenance effort and number of software configurations to be supported.

Agile software development teams use automated tools to constantly be aware of the quality of a running system. One of the sources of the metrics analyzed is the static code analysis tools. While these tools are not able to spot all possible defect types, their reports may correlate with the actual number of significant defects in software. If such correlation is found, it will make the static code analysis an important element of the agile team toolbox for getting the quality related view on the developed code. Currently the main drawback of the static code analysis is the lack of empirical evidence of the correlation between the tool reports and the actual defects rate. There is also no explicit evidence in the area of embedded software that the use of automated static source code analysis would yield results that confirm the correlation between the actual defect rate and predicted defect rate.

This paper presents a case study on predicting defects in the domain of embedded software development by use of automated static code analysis tools. The suitability of two particular tools, i.e. CodeScanner and PC-LINT, is tested on a number of components shipped as a part of Nokia smartphone software. The feasibility of a broader study is indicated.

2 Related Literature

Fenton and Neil (1999) outline four general approaches to predicting the number of defects in the system. [2]. This article is based on the approach of finding the correlation between the defect density and the code metrics. The metrics used for the defect rate prediction are produced by the process of static code analysis – the analysis of software statically, without attempting to execute it [3].

There are some studies on the static code analysis effectiveness reporting somewhat controversial results. Dromey (1996) suggests that code analysis can find most of quality defects and report them in a way convenient for the developers to correct the code. [4] Nachiappan and Thomas (2005) found that there was a strong correlation between the number of defects predicted by static analysis tools and the number of defects found by testing [5]. On the other hand Lauesen and Younessi (1998) state that the code analysis can locate only a small percentage of meaningful defects [6].

As shown above, currently, there are virtually no studies on applicability of static code analysis tools in the area of embedded software development as is the case in this study, i.e. Symbian operating system environment. This study focuses on evaluating the ability of the static code analysis tools to predict the number of defects in the software written in C++ for the Symbian operating system.

3 Research Design

In this study a number of components of the mobile phone software have been analyzed. All the components are written in C++ for the Nokia S60 software platform based on the Symbian operating system. The source code has been processed by two static code analysis tools: CodeScanner [7] and PC-Lint [8].

CodeScanner is a tool specifically developed for the Symbian C++ code analysis, while PC-LINT is a general C++ code analysis tool that can be fitted to the particular environment. In this case two sets of in-house built Symbian specific rules have been used to fit PC-LINT to the Symbian code idioms ("normal" and "strict" rule sets).

For the issues reported by the tools the "issue rate" per non-comment KLOC has been computed. The actual defect rate has been obtained from the company defect database. The defects reported within 3 and 6 months after the release date have been taken into account.

The projects have been ranked in the order of the rates. The correlation between the ranks has been computed in order to find out if there is a link between the issue rates and the actual defect rates. Spearman rank correlation has been used for the results analysis, because it can be applied even when the association between elements is non-linear. If rank correlation between the issue rate and the defect rate is positive, then for the projects analyzed, the bigger the issue rate is, the bigger defect rate should be expected.

4 Empirical Results and Discussion

The case study included five components of the 3rd edition of the Nokia S60 platform for smartphones. After the testing and debugging related code exclusion, the size of the code analyzed was 137 KLOC.

Table 1 shows the correlations between the reported issue rates and acknowledged defect rates. The first column presents the CodeScanner results. The next three columns contain PC-LINT results with different variants. The first line presents correlation with critical defects that were reported within 90 days and the second line - with the critical defects reported within 180 days after the release.

Table 1. Correlation results of defects/KLOC

Actual defect rate	Code Scanner rate	PC-LINT strict errors rate	PC-LINT strict errors + warnings rate	PC-LINT normal errors + warnings rate
90 days rate	0.7	-0.7	-0.9	-0.7
180 days rate	0.9	-0.6	-0.7	-0.9

For the projects analyzed there is a strong positive correlation between the CodeScanner defect rate and the actual reported defect rate, i.e. 0.7 in 90 days rate and 0.9 in 180 date rate. Interestingly, there is a strong negative correlation between the PC-LINT defect rate and the actual reported defect rate.

A strong positive correlation between the actual defect rate and CodeScanner reported issues confirms the Nachiappan and Thomas (2003) findings that there is a strong correlation between the static analysis defect density and the pre-release defect density reported by testers of the Windows Server 2003 [5].

A strong negative correlation between the PC-LINT reported issues and the actual defect rate might be a result of the unsuccessful attempt to fit the PC-LINT tool to the Symbian specific issues therefore being a confirmation of the Lausen and Younessi (1998) claim that static analysis tools are able to locate only a small number of meaningful defects [6]. Typical Symbian C++ code significantly differs from the typical Win32 or *nix code. Therefore, it might be so that the closer developers adhere to the industry recommended Symbian idioms, the more issues are reported by PC-LINT.

The CodeScaner tool analyzed in this study has been developed specifically for the Symbian OS C++ code and cannot be applied for other embedded software types.

Therefore the study results are less significant outside the Symbian OS area. For two of the projects analyzed the difference between the corresponding CodeScanner issue rates was less, than 1%. It is unclear how reliable the Spearman rank correlation is in such a situation.

It is also not very clear if the tools examined can be used to predict the defect density of a random sample. A larger case study is needed to address these issues.

5 Conclusions

This study aims at contributing to the problem of estimating the software maintenance costs and of evaluating the software quality. The angle of analysis was the ability for using the static code analysis tools for the software defect rate prediction in the area of embedded software development.

The results indicate that static code analysis tools can be used for helping the agile teams to perform better. If broader studies confirm this paper results, agile teams in the domain of embedded software development will get an important tool for quickly and regularly getting the view on the quality state of the software under development. Future research can be aimed at figuring out which issues detected by the tools correlate with the actual defect rate and which do not.

References

1. Reel, J.S.: Critical success factors in software projects. Software, IEEE 16(3), 18–23 (1999)
2. Fenton, N.E., Neil, M.: A critique of software defect prediction models. Software Engineering, IEEE Transactions on, 1999 25(5), 675–689 (1999)
3. Chess, B., McGraw, G.: Static analysis for security. Security & Privacy Magazine, IEEE 2(6), 76–79 (2004)
4. Dromey, R.G.: Concerning the Chimera [software quality]. Software, IEEE 13(1), 33–43 (1996)
5. Nachiappan, N., Thomas, B.: Static analysis tools as early indicators of pre-release defect density. In: Proceedings of the 27th international conference on Software engineering. St. Louis, MO, USA (2005)
6. Lauesen, S., Younessi, H.: Is software quality visible in the code. Software, IEEE 15(4), 69–73 (1998)
7. Newsletter, S.O.C. Symbian OS Community Newsletter - October 19th, 2004 (2004)[cited 2004 24 January] Available from: http://developer.symbian.com/main/getstarted/newsletter archive/newsletter31.jsp
8. Donner, I.: Computer-Related Inventions: When 'Obvious' is Not So Obvious. Computer 28(2), 78–79 (1995)

Empirical Evidence Principle and Joint Engagement Practice to Introduce XP

Lech Madeyski[1] and Wojciech Biela[2]

[1] Institute of Applied Informatics, Wroclaw University of Technology, Poland
Lech.Madeyski@pwr.wroc.pl
http://madeyski.e-informatyka.pl
[2] ExOrigo Sp. z o.o., Krucza 50, 00025 Warsaw, Poland
Wojciech.Biela@exorigo.pl
http://www.biela.pl

Abstract. Bringing software process change to an organisation is a real challenge. The authors have shown a sample attempt to carry out a process change and then reflected on its results and context. The present reflection points to a need for a set of principles and practices that would support the fragile process of introducing agility. For a start, the authors propose the Empirical Evidence principle exemplified using DICE® and the practice of Joint Engagement of the management and the developers. Both are results of a real-world process change case study in Poland.

1 Background

The company under study is medium-sized (below 200 employees) and employs 30+ programmers in various cities in Poland.

This paper focuses on one project developed in a 2-year period by a remote team. The project was developed by 3 programmers (the team's total was 8) using the Java technology stack. It was a web application, a B2C platform for a trust fund agent.

The project involved various problems, e.g. outdated requirements, system architecture structured but fragile, etc. The team was not using common best practices like loosely coupled code. Usually there was chaotic "code and fix" cowboy coding.

The problems were addressed using a toolkit of agile techniques. One of the authors joined the team to seek out and address problems. At that time, though he had limited experience, he had a strong belief based on of-the-books knowledge and academic projects (e.g. e Informatyka [1]) directed by the co-author of this paper.

Test-Driven Development (TDD) was new and the developers engaged in the project found it to be very effective and rewarding. **Refactoring** was used in the past, but not explicitly and often. Bringing it to a new level let the team implement radical changes without endangering the project. **Pair Programming** (PP) results were inconclusive and managers were reluctant to it. Nevertheless, it helped to share the team's knowledge and halved the time of bringing a new person to the project. **In-process design** sessions required a lot of coaching. **Problem Decomposition** was the most successful technique brought to the team. Dividing the problems into pieces and solving them at that level was really refreshing. **Continuous Integration** and task automation was an obvious benefit. **Darts** or similar group toys are a must-have for any development team. It was another "motivation for regular breaks"[2] and glued the team together. **Communication** still is an issue because the team is remote. Nevertheless, wiki and encouraging people to use Skype helped to some extent.

2 Rolling the DICE® Twice

The authors used the DICE framework [3], created by The Boston Consulting Group, to confirm that the adoption of agile practices actually increases the project's chance of success. The same metric is now used to convince the organisation's top management to conduct further changes.

The DICE framework is a simple empirical evidence-based formula for calculating how well an organisation is or will be implementing its change initiatives [3]. The DICE® framework comprises a set of simple questions that help score projects on each of the four factors: project duration (D), team's integrity (I), commitment of managers (C1) as well as the team (C2), additional effort (E) required by the change process. In DICE®, a project with an overall score between 7 and 14 is considered a *Win*, between 14 and 17 is a *Worry* and between 17 and 28 is a *Woe*. The DICE® formula is $D + 2 * I + 2 * C1 + C2 + E$.

Duration (D) *Before the change (score 2):* There was no notion of iterations, nor project rhythm. *After the change (score 1):* 1–2-week iterations with reviews during the Planning Game sessions. **Integrity (I)** *Before (score 3):* The previous project team leader was not a team leader, he was a sound programmer, but lacked social skills and the will to innovate. *After (score 2):* The current project team leader is capable and eager to implement new ideas. The team is quite self-organising. **Management Commitment (C1)** *Before (score 3):* Management did not involve enough resources for the changes, mainly because they felt the change should take less than the programmers had said. *After (score 2):* Changes took less time (there were fewer bugs), so the management was more supportive. **Team Commitment (C2)** *Before (score 3):* Changes to the project usually met with resistance, because changes usually meant that something else would break then. *After (score 1):* Changes met with much less resistance due to the ability to refactor in a controlled environment (test case safety net). **Effort (E)** *Before (score 3):* Effort required by the change was normal. Upfront design, followed by coding, testing and bug-fixing cycles. *After (score 2):* The overall effort was not as great as before, because although unit-testing and pairing were applied, there was no long design phase and there was less bugfixing. The DICE® score *before* (20) and *after* the change (12) moves the project from the *Woe zone* into the *Win zone*. This suggests that the introduction of agile practices resulted in an environment which facilitates changes more adequately.

The DICE® framework may be also used to measure the responsiveness to change in other contexts, as outlined in [4]. Making use of the experiences of Ziółkowski and Drake [5], the authors used DICE® again – this time to measure the above organisation's capability for carrying out process changes.

Duration *(score 1).* There was no notion of a formal review as it did not fit the agile environment the author was trying to create. Reviews were done frequently by him and his superiors in a more casual fashion. **Integrity** *(score 3).* The change leader (the author) was not given enough resources to achieve his goal. The author was then seriously lacking practical knowledge on how to implement development agility in a concrete situation. **Management Commitment** *(score 3)*. There was some change support from the management. However, they were quite sceptical and did not want to wet their feet (i.e., they wanted it to be a bottom-up approach). They rather wanted the change to use very little or no resources. **Team Commitment** *(score 2)*. The team was aware of the positive results of the changes and was willing to execute them if led properly. They often did not see the long-term consequences and wanted to see effects here and now. But after a discussion and reviewing evidence they usually allowed the change. **Effort** *(score 3)*. The change took a fair amount of additional resources due to the lack of on-site knowledge and proper management support. The DICE® score in this case is 18 *(Woe zone)*. This means that this particular change initiative was carried out in a very unfriendly environment and had good chances for a disaster. Some of the factors are in fact at the developer level (i.e. team commitment), but at this point the authors recognise that this particular change process would need much more top-down support rather than bottom-up. If the change process is not heavily supported by the management, it is likely to fail. This is also in line with the DICE® formula. Differences in the perception of development methodologies deployment by managers and developers were studied by Huisman and Iivari [7].

3 Reflection, Outcome and Conclusions

Rules like good programming style and techniques do not come from managers saying *"use TDD"* or *"program loosely coupled components"*. Management support is substantial (as pointed out in the previous section), but clearly not sufficient. It is the authors' experience that good practices have to come from the developer level. People are more willing to change when they see their peers change with good effect.

To increase the chance of success, process changes need both active management support and the developers' commitment. Without these two forces, the change initiative is likely not to spread enough throughout the organisation and in effect will die on its own. The main issue is to change the attitude of the team and of the managers. As Beck says, XP *"is about social change"* [6]. This is the turning point.

The authors suggest to complement the body of XP with additional practices and principles, which should address the problems that arise in the fragile process of introducing XP. Such practices and principles are needed to shed light on what has to be done to increase the chance of success when trying to implement change. They would not be XP practices and principles, but would rather concern introducing XP. They have to be chosen very carefully. The myriads of existing organizations do have things in common, but they also differ. As the authors' commitment, they propose a principle (*Empirical Evidence*) and an accompanying practice (*Joint Engagement*).

Empirical Evidence means that it is wise to ground on empirical evidence when introducing changes. We search for evidence to confirm whether or not we are on the right track with the process change. With empirical evidence comes the notion of context in which the evidence was obtained, limitations of the empirical studies, etc. One of the widely accepted sources of evidence on the introduction of changes is the DICE® framework. However, other sources of evidence are welcome as well.

Joint Engagement is the new practice guided by the *Empirical Evidence*, as well as the *Accepted Responsibility* [6] principles. Following the *Joint Engagement* practice we begin the change process at various levels of an organisation. The aim is to have the DICE® score in the *Win* zone. We *Win* when we are able to implement changes successfully and permanently. The Boston Consulting Group's studies of the DICE® framework proves that keeping this score low considerably raises the chance of success of the change process [3]. We monitor the DICE® score and try to keep it low. Individuals at the management and at the developer level should be educated and involved in the process. They have to willingly accept their diverse responsibilities in the change process (*Accepted Responsibility* principle). This could be done by means of e.g. the first XP project in the organisation [6]: a meta-project of implementing XP.

The new practice differs from the XP's original *Whole Team* practice in that the latter emphasises diverse team competences rather than the sensible interaction of the lower-level staff with the organization's management during process change programs. Following this new practice and principle is not very surprising for some, but the history of XP itself shows the value of naming and systematizing well-known behaviours into such concrete forms.

Changes to organisations are painful, but experience shows that if proper actions are taken, the change programs, and the introduction of agility in particular, may be very successful. The reflection presented in this paper identifies a need for a set of principles and practices that would support the introduction of agile techniques to organisations. For a start, the authors propose the duo of the *Empirical Evidence* principle and the *Joint Engagement* practice. The authors see a necessity for an assorted and explicit toolkit of introductory practices and principles to help organisations embrace change. They will further investigate this subject to extend this toolkit. Contributions from other practitioners are welcome.

This work has been financially supported by the Ministry of Science and Higher Education, as a research grant 3 T11C 061 30 (years 2006-2007).

References

1. Madeyski, L., Stochmiałek, M.: Architectural Design of Modern Web Applications. Foundations of Computing and Decision Sciences 30(1), 49–60 (2005) http://madeyski.e-informatyka.pl/download/23.pdf
2. Beck, K.: Test Driven Development: By Example. Addison-Wesley, Reading (2002)
3. Sirkin, H.L., Keenan, P., Jackson, A.: The Hard Side of Change Management. Harvard Business Review 83(10), 108–118 (2005)
4. DICE Framework http://www.12manage.com/methods_bcg_dice_framework.html
5. Ziółkowski, B., Drake, G.: Rolling the DICE® for Agile Software Projects. In: Abrahamsson, P., Marchesi, M., Succi, G. (eds.) XP 2006. LNCS, vol. 4044, pp. 114–122. Springer, Heidelberg (2006)
6. Beck, K., Andres, C.: Extreme Programming Explained: Embrace Change, 2nd edn. Addison-Wesley, Reading (2004)
7. Huisman, M., Iivari, J.: Deployment of systems development methodologies: perceptual congruence between is managers and systems developers. Inf. Manage. 43(1), 29–49 (2006)

Power of Recognition: A Conceptual Framework for Agile Capstone Project in Academic Environment

Ville Isomöttönen, Vesa Korhonen, and Tommi Kärkkäinen

Department of Mathematical Information Technology, University of Jyväskylä,
P.O. Box 35 (Agora), 40014 Jyväskylä, Finland
vilisom@jyu.fi

Abstract. Agile methods are finding their way into industry, and also into tertiary education. Approaches on tertiary capstone project are being presented, and questioned, if they provide a supportive learning environment. In this paper, an industrial strength holding, conceptual framework for realizing an agile grounded software project course in academic environment is described and rationalized by pedagogical aspects.

1 Environment-Driven Roles, Goals, and Practices

Environment for a capstone project should be as realistic as possible. *Real customer* is a demand, and at least a nominal price has to be set for the project. Real customer allows to learn to manage real-life uncertainties, see [2], [1]. In [2] it is also noted that students familiar with real-life problems are preferentially sought by industry. Collaboration with real customers implies that certain facilities are required from *physical environment*, for example, mechanisms for handling the customer data safely. A capstone project carried out in *academic environment* is surrounded by lecture-like and research-like conventions in which the practices and context can have a minor role. This does not work when the aim is to produce software for real customer. Time-to-deliver can be derived from academic conventions. Only acceptable finish line, when using a firm project price, is when a semester ends. *Fixed time* budget is suggested in [4] to provide a good learning environment allowing the prioritization of quality. In real customer environment it also forces to recognize the essential activities in ongoing development work. *Studentship* related issues are knowledge, skills, and attitude of the students themselves. Project course may by students' first experience on a realistic SW project. Group cannot build up their ways of living on previous manners. Work hours spent just for the academic credits may cause a problem of motivation. Despite the earlier studies the skill level may vary a lot within the group whose members don't even know each other when the project starts. *The type of customer*, and the depth of the customer's involvement are observable project specific features. Application domain of customer's business, and his experience as a software customer are referred here as customer's type. Also, *application domain (subject) of a single project* may imply particular activities.

Roles. In Fixed Time Real Customer (FTRC) environment *supervisor's* necessary role is a supportive coach. Interestingly, supportive and collaborative activities (active participation, effective use of examples, collaborative problem solving, effective use of feedback, and motivational components) underline modern view of creating deep and durable learning as a teacher [3]. Critical issues has to be recognized and interfered by the supervisor, correspondingly stated in [7]. In less critical issues the team's internal cycle of learning has to be allowed. A major risk is to have too much dependence on the tutor [9]. In FTRC environment supervisor has to sometimes take the role of making the first move. In socio-constructivism this refers to scaffolding. According to pedagogical interpretation of scaffolding initial tasks are supported assuming decreasing need for the support later on, see [9]. Notice that projects following one another accumulates supervisors' understanding of meta-processes within the environment. It is also a necessity to recognize the wider context of the capstone project. Adaptive improvement of pedagogical skills (reflection consisting of students' and customer's feedback, analysis of successful actions, and identifying the open questions) and continuous but critical studying of the state of the art are sources for modifications. Moving between scientific and practical aspects is necessary resulting to reaction skills during the particular projects. In *customer's* role the key issues are that resources have to be allocated and the risk-like challenges of the student environment accepted. Customer may not recognize the properties of the capstone project. Supervisor (coach) can help customer to adapt optimal role leading to the most beneficial results also from customer's point of view. In addition to *students'* developer roles, FTRC environment requires a role for managing the customer interface. Description and organization of these student roles are left in future work.

Goals. Increase in occupational identity is set as the main higher level educational objective for the *students*. On the other hand, understanding of the process model is a more concrete high level item providing a context to particular activities. Assuming that students have had possibility to familiarize themselves with the individual activities of software development (preceding studies), they now concentrate on internalizing the role of the tasks in the process. Correspondingly, one can talk about situated learning. According to Lave and Wenger learning is an integral constituent of social practice [8]. They have further specified the concept of legitimate peripheral participation. In capstone project, the "peripheral" could be related to the fact that students are still learners, not professionals. Thus, despite the affect of authentic environment (use of real customers) on learners, the context is also an academic course. *Supervisor's* goal is to increase the competence in both the personal and organizational level. Complex connections between the environment and the development methods, and also the connections between the pedagogical methods and particular instances of student groups are learned. From *customer's* point of view, novel methods and practices are delivered to customers, and in some cases, these indirectly improve the customers business activities. To another direction, students and university learn from the customer's activities and skills of reaction. Thus, the use of real customers establishes a channel between the university and the industry, which is an organizational goal.

Practices. Presented studentship related environmental features can be interpreted as risks, which are now connected to particular practices. `Inexperience` requires open, immediate, and voluminous communication: supervisor helps the students understand the necessity of communication. Short iterations compensate the inexperience by allowing the use of acquired knowledge during the project: benefits and requirements (e.g. customers involvement and available resources) of short iterations has to be discussed together with the stakeholders. `Lacking operational model`, which has to be rapidly adopted, is a challenge for a novel team (despite the former experiences on SW projects). Again, short iterations force the team to live through the development cycle in early stage of the process. Explicit recognition and agreement on the practices are necessary. The aiding role of the supervisor is emphasized in the beginning of the project to ensure that the team internalizes and applies crucial practices such as planning in customer meetings. `Group of strangers` has to be provided specific tasks that force them to communicate, and hence, ease the group members to become acquainted with each other. These tasks include the role differentiation and the selection of team leader, for example. Coaching is needed to launch and track theses activities. Joint facilities, such as rooms reserved for each group, are environmental features that compel interaction. `Varying skill level` is compensated by providing personal coaching. Coach has to encourage the team to work together, pair programming being one solution. Team-wise communication of problems, and the selection of roles has to be emphasized. Coach has to state these instructions aloud. `Motivation` argues for the the short iterations. It is achieved by completing a piece of concrete software in early stage of the process and obtaining customer feedback of it. Short iterations and coaching, by saying also the positive progress aloud, increase the motivation. Thus, examination of the environment proposed the most valuable practices: coaching, communication, and short iterations. When a student begins the capstone project, an extensive cognitive load is obvious. Short iterations have to be applied also to the learning phase in the beginning of the project. In FTRC capstone project black-box time spans lasting over two weeks are too risky. In the beginning of the project (learning phase) even one-week iterations can be applied. Coaching in turn has to be offered before each activity, proceeding has to be tracked, and repetition applied when necessary. Intensive coaching is required at project's set-up phase. Such coaching enables the operation in FTRC environment, and also the course review becomes more fair. If students are supervised and asked to improve particular activities, they become aware of the need (and have a chance) to reflect and enhance their process.

2   Power of Recognition: Pedagogical Rationale

As the result, power-of-recognition hypothesis is defined as follows: *software can be delivered for real customers within the fixed-time in the context of capstone project, if the students' recognition of environment and project specific features are supported when specifying the method and activities to be applied, and within such framework short iterations, voluminous face to face communication, and coaching make operation possible, reducing the effects of described risks.*

To reason the framework it is connected to a pedagogical paradigm. The socio-constructivism is in agreement with the roles, goals, and practices described. According to [5] it implies that learners are encouraged to: 1. Construct their own knowledge instead of copying it from authority, be it a book or teacher. ⇒ Lecture-like authority has to be avoided. Team-wise and personal coaching has to be utilized. 2. Construct the knowledge in real situations instead of decontextualized. ⇒ The use of fundamental software engineering text books has to be critical, because in such references the context is often abstracted out. Development method has to be determined according to environmental features (context). 3. Construct the knowledge together with others instead of on their own. ⇒ Shared recognition via communication is necessary.

Socio-constructivism seems to support the concept of recognition. It has to be avoided that students would act as copiers without internalization of their operation. This is an important guideline for project course in FTRC environment. The paradigm seems to fit also in the values of agile. More detailed theoretic study focusing on this relation is required. This paper discloses that some of XP's proposals have emerged earlier within the different disciplines (learning, learning theories). The multiple discoveries are inevitable in science [6], and in this particular case the existing learning theories may offer rationale for agile.

References

1. Chamillard, A.T., Braun, K.A.: The software Engineering Capstone: Structure and Tradeoffs. ACM SIGCSE Bulletin 34(1), 227–231 (2002)
2. Ruud, C.O., Deleveaux, V.J.: Developing and Conducting an Industry Based Capstone Design Course. Frontiers in Education Conference, 27th Annual Conference, Teaching and Learning in an Era of Change (1997)
3. Hacker, D.J., Niederhauser.: Promoting Deep and Durable learning in the Online Classroom. In: Weis, R.E., Knowlton, D.S., Speck, B.W. (eds.) Principles of Effective Teaching in the Online Classroom, New Directions for teaching and learning, vol. 84, pp. 53–63. Jossey-Bass, San Francisco (2000)
4. Hedin, G., Bendix, L., Magnusson, B.: Teaching Software Development using Extreme Programming. To appear, Scandinavian Pedagogy of Programming (2006)
5. Kanselaar, G., De Jong, T., Andriessen, J., Goodyear, P.: New Technologies. In: Simons, R., van der Linden, J., Duffy, T. (eds.) New Learning, pp. 55–83. Kluwer Academic Publishers, Boston (2000)
6. Lamb, D., Easton, S.M.: Multiple Discovery. Avebury (1984)
7. Laplante, A.P.: An Agile, Graduate, Software Studio Course. IEEE Trans.Educ., vol. 49(4) (November 2006)
8. Lave, J., Wenger, E.: Situated learning: Legitimate peripheral participation. Cambridge University Press, Cambridge (1991)
9. Wood, D., Bruner, J.S., Ross, G.: The Role of Tutoring in Problem Solving. Journal of Child Psychology and Psychiatry 17, 89–100 (1976)

Agile Commitments: Enhancing Business Risk Management in Agile Development Projects

Mauricio Concha, Marcello Visconti, and Hernán Astudillo

Departamento de Informática
Universidad Técnica Federico Santa María, Valparaíso, Chile
{mconcha,visconti,hernan}@inf.utfsm.cl

Abstract. Agile methods focus on customer satisfaction and delivering business value early, however if flexibility and adaptability are not managed during the development project, agile methods could not assure achieving the overall business expectations. Customers require risk visibility over the main aspects that define its expectations: functionality (scope), budget, time-to-market, and product quality. These risks must be controlled and monitored during the project in order to introduce mitigation actions if needed. In this article, we propose an agile commitments framework based on the definition and follow-up of commitments between customer and developer. This framework aims to improving risk management by enhancing business expectation risk visibility, and also providing a negotiation baseline between customers and developers.

Keywords: Agile development, commitment management, risk management.

1 Introduction

Software is a strategic element to support the business process within organizations, thus software alignment to business goals is an important aspect to be managed. Customer business expectations lead to the development of software, and those expectations are defined at the beginning by the customer in terms of: functionality (scope), time-to-market, budget, and product quality. Those are the aspects the customer is interested in and if some of those items are missing during the project it will cause an unsuccessful project. Flexibility and adaptability are some of the main advantages claimed by agile methods to produce high quality software, however if flexibility and adaptability are not managed during the project, the agile methods could not assure the achievement of all business expectations. Therefore, it is necessary to introduce a risk based approach in order to improve risk management in an agile project.

With the purpose of supporting this risk factor in agile methods, we have defined an approach and a process framework oriented to complement the agile methods with *commitment management*. We have named this approach "Agile Commitments", which finally will provide risk visibility and control to the customer during the whole project. Also, commitment management will provide a baseline for contract negotiation between customer and developers.

We can mention some related work oriented to defining business goals for the project, and to establish the relationship between customer and developers: Agile Contracts [1] [3], Agile Procurement [4], and Risk-Driven Method for XP Release Planning [7].

2 Commitment Management for Agile Methods

Commitment management is an approach that uses commitments between customer and developers to define a list of agreements as baseline for the project, with the goal of mitigating the risk of losing sight of the original project motivations [2]. The commitment specification defines all agreements and a common view of the project among stakeholders. Commitment management is the specification, formalization, and follow-up of commitments during the whole project, with the purpose of aligning the final product with the business strategy and goals that motivate the software project. The term *commitment* is used to refer to goals, forms of cooperation, responsibilities, decisions, and so on, that stakeholders agree upon in a project; commitments scope may include all critical aspects in the project.

The commitment management process has been characterized in the following process areas [2]:

- **Business motivation.** Why is the Project being developed?
- **Project goals definition.** What is delivered and accomplished, when and for how much?
- **Process specification.** How is the Project developed?
- **Risk management.** What are the risks and what do we do?

3 Agile Commitments Framework

The specific objectives of this process framework are to:

- Define and specify the commitments between participants.
- Define and agree on the underlying motivations.
- Manage and control the agreed-upon commitments during the whole project.
- Improve risk management through risk visibility on the business expectation elements: functionality (scope), quality, budget, and time-to-market.
- Provide a negotiation baseline for customer and developers.

The agile commitments framework is made up of two components: a **conceptual schema framework,** which is the conceptual definition of the framework, and describes how the framework is structured; and an **instantiation guideline for project level**, which is a guide to be used by managers in order to implement the agile commitments in a particular project [8].

The framework is divided in 4 process areas, and each one divided in specific goals (see Table 1).

Table 1. Conceptual Schema Framework

Process Areas	Specifics Goals
Business Motivation	Strategic directions and intentions
	Business goals
	Time-to-market
Project Goal	Deliverables and Iterations (value added)
	Schedule and times
	Cost and budget
	Quality
Agile Process Specification	Project management
	Agile process definition (standard or framework)
	Conflict resolution procedures
	Change control procedures
Project Risk Management	Shared assumptions for the project
	Risk analysis and identification
	Scope of risk management
	Accepted risks
	Risk responsibility assignment

4 Achieving Continuous Risk Visibility During the Project

The monitoring of the commitment management framework must be oriented to measuring risk in a qualitative approach; thus, the main problem is to decide which risk metrics should be gathered during the project. For the agile framework, the different phases to assess risk and thus produce the risk visibility are:

- **Initial Scenario:** At the start of the project, all business value goals (functionality, time-to-market, budget, and quality) must be established in terms of *qualitative metrics*, as well as *potential losses* incurred if a business value goal is not met.
- **Current Risk:** The perceived risk at the moment of the measure; it is a subjective assessment. It can be measured using the *perceived probability*, and it must be measured along the whole project execution.
- **Risk Incurred:** The *probability of failure* that the project faced but eventually avoided. Therefore, the problems did not occur because the mitigation efforts worked.
- **Final Scenario:** At the end of the project, it is possible to *compare* the initial business goals taken in the "Initial Scenario" with the final values obtained for business goals (functionality, time-to-market, budget, and quality).

At the end of each project, two important metrics can be collected: the *total risk* incurred during the project for the business goals fulfillment, and the *variation in the final results* obtained for the business goals according to the customer evaluation.

5 Case Studies: Results Using the Agile Commitments Framework

The framework has been evaluated through a number of case studies [8] that allowed us to receive feedback from the customer side on two evaluation levels: 1) the conceptual level, where the framework has been assessed by IT professionals considered as experts in the area because of their expertise in project management; and 2) the project level, where the framework has been instantiated and used in real projects during the full life cycle of a number of academic projects as well as an industry project.

6 Conclusions

Agile methods can be aligned to business goals using commitments management as a complementary activity, to mitigate risk to business value expectations. In this article, we have defined an approach that can be used regardless the agile method implemented in the organization. The proposed solution corresponds to the integration between an agile method and a commitment management technique. Commitment management does not modify the essence of an agile method, commitment management only supports it with complementary practices, and we see at least four benefits from using the proposed agile commitments framework: 1) the agile commitments framework is well-defined and generalized for any agile method; 2) the framework provides a negotiation baseline for customers and developers, as an effective and *agile* alternative to contracts; 3) the framework improves risk management through risk visibility on the business expectation elements: functionality (scope), quality, budget, and time-to-market; and 4) the framework provides a risk-driven decision support tool to the customer during the whole development process.

References

1. Boehm, B., DeMarco, T.: Software Risk Management. IEEE Software (May/June 1997)
2. Kontio, J., Pitkanen, O., Sulonen, R.: Towards Better Software Projects and Contracts: Commitment Specifications in Software Development Projects. In: Procs. International Conference on Software Engineering (ICSE'98) (1998)
3. Beck, K., Cleal, D.: Optional Scope Contracts (1999)
4. Jamieson, D., Vinsen, K., Callender, G.: Agile Procurement: New Acquisition Approach to Agile Software Development (EUROMICRO –SEAA'05) (2005)
5. Schuh, P.: Integrating Agile Development in the Real World, Programming Series, Charles River Media (2005)
6. Hartmann, D., Dymond, R.: Appropriate Agile Measurement: Using Metrics and Diagnostics to Deliver Business Value. In: Procs. of AGILE, Conference (AGILE'06) (2006)
7. Li, M., et al.: A Risk-Driven Method for XP Release Planning, ICSE'06, Shanghai, China. (May 20–28, 2006)
8. Concha, M., Visconti, M., Astudillo, H.: Agile Commitments: Managing Business Expectation Risks in Agile Development Projects. Departamento de Informática, Universidad Técnica Federico Santa María, Technical Report 2007/03 (January 2007)

Usability in Agile Software Development: Extending the Interaction Design Process with Personas Approach

Jukka Haikara

VTT Technical Research Centre of Finland
P.O. Box 1100, FIN-90571 Oulu, Finland
Jukka.Haikara@vtt.fi

Abstract. The current agile software development methods do not seem to address usability and interaction design issues enough, i.e., the interaction design process may remain implicit. However, few studies with positive results have been conducted concerning integrating explicit interaction design process into agile software development. In this study, the interaction design process of Mobile-D^{TM} is extended with the personas approach. Empirical evaluation of the resulting model is performed in a case project. The results provide view points for both industrial and scientific purposes on the applications of interaction design activities in different stages of agile development process.

Keywords: Agile Software Development, Interaction Design, Goal-Directed Design, Personas, Mobile-D.

1 Introduction

According to Constantine [1], no usability communities were invited to the formation of Agile Alliance [2] . Thereupon, Kane [3] has pointed out that the Agile Alliance web-site does not have an article category for usability or interaction design. Nowadays, however, the web-site has a category addressed to usability, which contains twelve articles [2]. This indicates the growing interest on usability in agile software development (ASD). The roles of usability engineering and interaction design process among ASD methods vary. In Extreme Programming (XP) [4], customers are equated to users and their opinions are valued during planning and release days. In Feature-Driven Development [5], well-formed user documentation and extensive on-line help are a part of its usability engineering. In Crystal Methodologies [6], an explicit interaction design process is defined. Nonetheless, this indicates that an interaction design process can be integrated in ASD.

One way to perform interaction design is to utilize personas [7]. Persona is a representation of a hypothetical user, the intended end-user which is constructed by performing research, e.g., interviews, observations or market research. The personas and their goals form the basis of the design. Although Cooper [7] and Beck [4] have discussed the relationship of XP and Personas and disagreed [8], Beck have said that interaction designers can use personas to support the interaction design process. In this study, the interaction design process of Mobile-D^{TM} (Mobile-D) [9] of which practices are based on XP, is extended with personas. A model is constructed by analyzing the contradictions between the principles of the personas and the agile software development. The constructed model is evaluated in one case project.

2 Research Design

The research approach of this study is qualitative. The author participated in the build, implementation and evaluation of the model and acted as a participant-observer in the project. The data was collected and analyzed throughout the project. None of the participants had earlier experience on the personas. After the project four face-to-face interviews were conducted in order to elicit the developers' persona experiences.

The aim was to integrate an explicit interaction design process into ASD. As a result, a model was constructed according to current knowledge in which the interaction design process of Mobile-D was extended. One starting point of the model was to compare agile principles and personas/usability principles. The summary of the contradicting (C) principles and imprecise (I) principles can be seen in Table 1. The differences between principles are categorized as follows: none = nothing; minor = consideration; medium = pay attention to; major = must be paid attention to.

Table 1. Differences of the ASD and personas principles

ASD	Personas	Difference/ ID
Welcome changing requirements…	One set of requirements per one project.	major (C1)
Deliver working software frequently...	One delivery.	major (C2)
Simplicity is essential.	Extensive design up front.	major (C3)
Our highest priority is to satisfy the customer...	Design process iterative, but implementation process not iterative.	medium (C4)
Working software is the primary…	User satisfaction is the primary focus. Working software is a part of using experience.	minor (I1)
Continuous attention to technical excellence…	Design is referred to as interaction design.	none (I2)

3 The Model

The integration of personas method and Mobile-D process is illustrated in Figure 1.

The build and evaluation of the model was based on two criteria: process and usage. Process criteria include the applicability of the proposed model to the used process, i.e., Mobile-D. Figure 1 illustrates how the different stages of the Mobile-D were affected by the adoption of personas. The usage criteria evaluate the satisfaction and awareness of the developers. Satisfaction represents the developers' view on the benefits and problems of applying persona while Awareness reveals how well the developers were aware that the personas exist (e.g., personas and their overall usage).

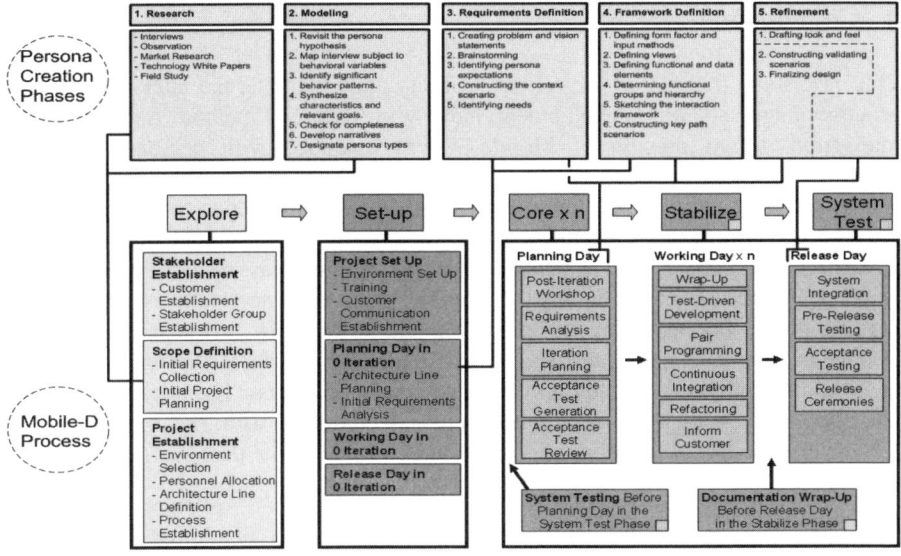

Fig. 1. The integration model of Mobile-D process [9] and Personas [7]

In Table 2, the summary of the empirical findings based on the interviews and participant-observation are identified and aligned with the phases of Mobile-D.

Table 2. Summary of empirical findings

Category	Criteria	Finding
Mobile-D Process	Explore Phase	- In the case project, a calendar month was not enough to perform extensive research and modeling of the personas. - Every negligent matter performed in the explore phase can affect the whole project.
	Planning Day	- The overall target must be set, so that the whole project serves one goal. Iterations are only to refine the product. - The framework definition must be performed carefully to prevent extra work which can cause changes to the interface.
	Working Day	- The developers must be reminded that personas exist. The posters on the wall are an adequate reminder, but when time passes by the personas can be forgotten and therefore interaction design can be misleading.
	Release Day	- The customers should be familiarized (the customer establishment in the set-up phase) with the personas, because otherwise their opinions concerning the end-user's needs interfere with the personas' goals. - The customers were not comfortable adopting roles of the personas: an end-user representative is recommended.
	Other Issues	Because scenarios were not constructed, decisions on interaction design were difficult to conduct.
Usage	Satisfaction	- Personas provide a clear target to focus on. - At first, personas might be a peculiar way to approach designing.
	Awareness	- The goals seemed to be more important than the persona's name as proposed in the literature.

4 Conclusions

This case study focused on the role of usability and extending the interaction design process in agile software development, namely in Mobile-D method. As a result, the interaction design process of Mobile-D was extended with personas activities affecting the explore phase, planning, working and release days. The explore phase was found to be a crucial phase of the project due to its affection to the whole project. Facilitating the customer establishment in the set-up phase should familiarize the customers with the existing personas. In the first planning day, design target, primary persona, is defined. Furthermore, the framework of the interaction design is to be defined in the first planning in order to avoid extra work in the later iterations. Thereafter, the developers can focus on a certain user interface. During the working days the personas were placed on the wall to create awareness. The release days were not successful with customers who were not familiar with the personas. The developers considered personas as a communicative tool. The personas' overall goals were more significant over the personas' names.

Acknowledgments. This research was conducted at VTT Technical Research Centre of Finland, as a part of AGILE-ITEA project.

References

1. Constantine, L.: Process Agility and Software Usability: Toward Lightweight Usage-Centered Design. In: Information Age (2002)
2. Agile Alliance, The Agile Alliance Web-Site. 2001 (Accessed September 19 2005)
3. Kane, D.: Finding a Place for Discount Usability Engineering in Agile Development: Throwing Down the Gauntlet. In: Proceedings of the Agile Development Conference, Salt Lake City, UT, USA (2003)
4. Beck, K., Andres, C.: Extreme Programming Explained:Embrace Change, 2nd edn. Addison-Wesley, Reading (2004)
5. Palmer, S.R., Felsing, J.M.: A Practical Guide to Feature-Driven Development. Prentice-Hall, Upper Saddle River, NJ (2002)
6. Cockburn, A.: Crystal Clear: A Human-Powered Methodology for Small Teams. Pearson Education, Inc. (2002)
7. Cooper, A., Reimann, R.: About Face 2.0: The Essentials of Interaction Design. Wiley Publishing, Indianapolis (2003)
8. Nelson, E.: Extreme Programming vs. Interaction Design (2002)
9. VTT Research Centre of Finland, Mobile-D: Version 1.0. 2005 (Accessed January 6, 2006)

Defining an Integrated Agile Governance for Large Agile Software Development Environments

Asif Qumer

Faculty of Information Technology, University of Technology, Sydney. 2000 Broadway,
NSW, Australia
{asif}@it.uts.edu.au

Abstract. This paper highlights the important aspect of IT governance, with the objective of defining an unaddressed aspect of agile governance, by the application of an iterative, inductive, instantaneous analysis and emergent interpretation of appropriate data-grounded conceptual categories of IT governance. An effective agile governance approach will facilitate the achievement of desired discipline, rationale, business value, improved performance, monitoring, as well as control of large agile software development environments by aligning business goals and agile software development goals.

Keywords: Agile Methods, IT Governance, Agile Governance, Agile Business Value.

1 Introduction

IT governance provides a mechanism for a strategic IT-business alignment to acquire maximum business value delivered by the consumption of IT resources. With the increasing and widescale acceptance of IT products and services in various sectors, the importance of IT governance has been realized. It has been reported that an IT organization's turnover and performance are directly influenced by IT governance practices [16], [19]. It has also been reported that a better IT governance mechanism can earn 20% higher return on assets than an organization with average governance [17]. However, it has been noticed that IT governance has not been discussed in the context of agile software development to any great extent. This paper is an attempt to draw attention to the emerging concept of IT governance by testing this hypothesis: "Although IT governance or agile governance sounds bureaucratic, nevertheless, an integrated agile governance approach in the context of agile software development will bring in sufficient control, discipline and rationale to scale up agile software development methods for large and complex projects".

This paper has been structured as follows. First, it presents the summary of the systematic review and analysis of IT governance to identity the related key concepts. Second, it discusses IT governance in agile environments and proposes a definition of agile governance within a basic agile governance model. Finally, it concludes with a discussion of options for future research.

2 IT Governance: A Systematic Review and Analysis

We have analysed the most up-to-date and comprehensive definitions of IT governance, frameworks, models [1], [5], [8], [9], [10], [13], standards, industry reports [2], [3], [4], [6], [7], [11], [12], [14], [15], [17], [18], a survey, interviews and a focus group feedback, in an attempt to determine the key aspects and importance of IT governance. It has been learnt from the analysis that most of these frameworks are overly bureaucratic (for example COBIT and ITIL) and labour-intensive and, therefore, cannot be applied immediately to agile environments. According to our survey and focus group feedback, 77% (27+38+12) of research participants (Figure 1) reported that with the element of governance, agile methods could be scaled up for large and complex projects. However, 15% of participants thought that governance in an agile environment may give rise to bureaucracy, which may create hurdles on the way to become truly agile. The key distilled concepts of IT governance are summarized in Table 1.

Table 1. Categorization of IT governance key concepts

IT Governance Frameworks	Key Concepts of IT Governance
Control Objectives for Information and related Technology (COBIT)	Performance management Critical success factors (processes) Capability maturity models
IT Audit	Technology risks, capacity, security, scalability and stability issues Human resource (expertise) Project management, change management, IT policies, procedures, software licences and performance management
Six Sigma	Measure, control and improve performance Metrics and measures for staff, product requirements, design and continuous improvement
Application Service Library (ASL)	Functional, technical and application controls
Information Technology Infrastructure Library (ITIL)	Disciplined practices for service delivery and service management
Projects IN Control Environments (PRINCE)	Project organization, management and control practices

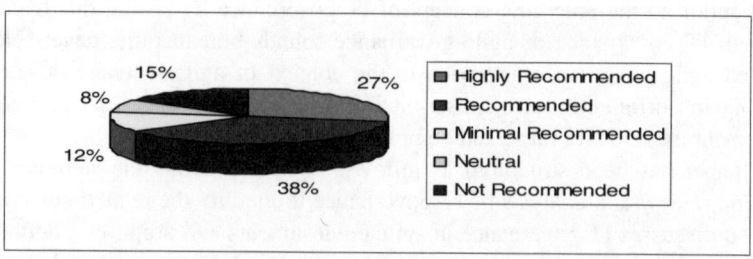

Fig. 1. Importance of IT governance in large agile software development projects

3 Agile Governance

We may define (in the light of the above analysis and discussion) integrated agile governance as:

"an integrated agile governance involves lightweight, collaborative, communication-oriented, economical and evolving effective accountability framework, controls, processes, structures to maximize agile business value, by the strategic alignment of business-agile goals, performance and risk management".

In the light of the above analysis and proposed definition of agile governance, we have developed a simple agile governance model that is called an agile responsibility, accountability and business value governance model (Figure 2). According to this model, the customer is responsible and accountable for providing the product features, executive management is responsible and accountable for agile asset prioritization and procurement, executive management and agile managers are responsible and accountable for the selection of agile principles and agile infrastructure, empowered agile managers and agile teams are responsible and accountable for the selection of the agile software development methodology. Agile teams (empowered) are responsible and accountable for the selection or adoption of specific agile process fragments for agile development. Agile managers and agile teams are responsible and accountable for the delivery of a valuable quality product to the customer. In summary, agile software development proceeds with the factors of responsibility and accountability to achieve a desired business value (Figure 2). This model is a "shared guiding vision" for agilists and will iteratively be assessed and refined with the collaboration of agile stakeholders in agile software development arrangements.

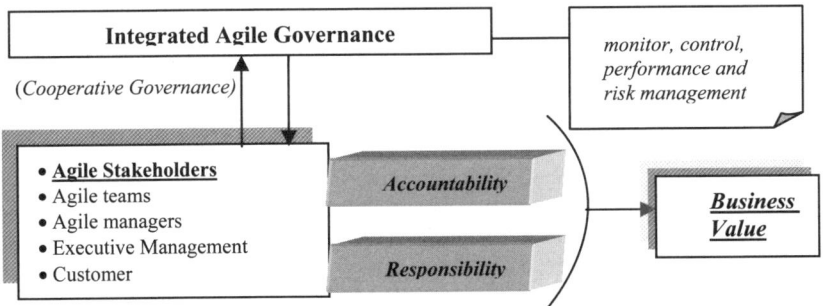

Fig. 2. Agile responsibility, accountability and business value governance model

4 Conclusion

Here, we have highlighted and explained the essential properties of an integrated agile governance and proposed a simple agile governance model. The purpose of this effort is to uncover the potential and important elements of governance for the agile transition from small-medium scale to large and complex scale. We have stressed the issue of maximizing the business value (return on investments) by focusing on decision making, accountability and assessment frameworks for performance and risk management in the context of agile environments. In future, more research is required towards the construction of detailed agile governance frameworks, processes and structure to support large agile environments.

Acknowledgment. I wish to thank the Australian Research Council for financial support under the Linkage Grants Scheme. This is contribution number 07/02 of the Centre for Object Technology Applications and Research. I am also thankful to Prof Brian Henderson-Sellers who helped me with his valuable feedback and experience.

References

1. Behr, K., Kim, G., Spafford, G.: The Visible Ops Handbook: Starting ITIL in 4 Practical Steps, Information Technology Process Institute (2004)
2. Brown, C. V., Magill, S.L.: aligning the IS Functions with the Enterprise: Toward a Model of Antecedents. MIS Quarterly, vol. 18(4) (1994)
3. Grembergen, W.V., Haes, S.D., Guldentops, E.: Structures, Processes and Relational Mechanisms for IT Governance. Strategies for Information Technology, 1-36 (2004)
4. Haes, S.D., Grembergen, W.V.: IT Governance Structures, Processes and Relational Mechanisms: Achieving IT/Business Alignment in a Major Belgian Financial Group. In: Proceedings of the 38th Hawaii International Conference on System Sciences, Hawaii, IEEE (2005)
5. Hammer, M.: Process Management and the Future of Six Sigma. MIT Sloan Management Review, vol. 43(2) (2002)
6. IT Governance Institute: Board Briefing on IT Governance (2003) www.itgi.org
7. Korac-Kakabadse, N., Kakabadse, A.: IS/IT Governance: Need for an integrated model. Corporate Governance 1(4), 9–11 (2001)
8. Linhart, J.W.: A Methodology for Managing and Controlling Information Technology Risks and Vulnerabilities. Journal of Information Systems (2000)
9. Meijer, M.: Application Service Library (ASL) and CMM. The Journal of IT Alignment and Business IT Alignment, vol. 1(1) (2003)
10. OGC: Managing Successful Projects with PRINCE. Office of Government Conference (2005)
11. Peterson, R.A.: Integration Strategies and Tactics for Information Technology Governance. Strategies for Information Technology (2004)
12. Sambamurthy, V., Zmud, R.W.: Arrangements for Information Technology Governance: A Theory of Multiple Contingencies. MIS Quarterly, vol. 23(2) (1999)
13. Sisco, M.: Technology review is the core of IT assessment. TechRepublic (2002)
14. Standards Australia: Draft for Public comment Australian Standard: corporate Governance of Information Technology and Communication Technology, Standards Australia (2004)
15. Webb, P., Pollard, C., Ridley, G.: Attempting to Define IT Governance: Wisdom or Folly? In: Proceedings of the 39th Hawaii International Conference on System Sciences, USA (2006)
16. Weill, P.: Don't Just t Lead, Govern: How Top- Performing Firms Govern IT. MIS Quarterly Executive, vol. 8(1) (2004)
17. Weill, P., Ross, J.W.: IT Governance on One Page. CISR WP 349 (2004)
18. Weill, P., Ross, J.W.: Ten Principles of IT Governance (2004) http://hbswk.hbs.edu/archive/4241.html
19. Weill, P., Broadbent, M.: Leveraging the New Infrastructure: How market leaders capitalize on IT. Harvard Business School Press, Boston (1998)

Enhancing Creativity in Agile Software Teams

Broderick Crawford[1,2] and Claudio León de la Barra[1,3]

[1] Pontificia Universidad Católica de Valparaíso, Valparaíso, Chile
[2] Universidad Técnica Federico Santa María, Valparaíso, Chile
[3] Universidad Autónoma de Madrid, Madrid, Spain
{broderick.crawford, cleond}@ucv.cl

Abstract. The development of new products requires the generation of one or more novel and useful ideas, suitable to implementation in practice. In our research, the agile method eXtreme Programming (XP) is analyzed, evaluated and enhanced from the perspective of the creativity. We believe that a better understanding of concepts related to creative teams (structure, performance and purposes) offers important insights about the use of agile methods in general and XP in particular.

Software engineering is a knowledge intensive process that includes human and social factors in all phases: eliciting requirements, design, construction, testing, implementation, maintenance and project management [4]. No worker of a development project possess all the knowledge required for fulfilling all activities. This underlies the need for communication, collaboration and knowledge sharing support to share domain expertise between the customer and the development team. Since human creativity can be thought as the source to resolve complex problems or create innovative products, one possibility to improve the software development process is to design a process which can stimulate the creativity of developers. There are few studies reported on the importance of creativity in software development. In management and business, researchers have done much work about creativity and obtained evidence that the employees who had appropriate creativity characteristics, were able to work on complex, challenging jobs, and supervised in a supportive, noncontrolling fashion, produced more creative work. In a few publications the importance of creativity has been investigated in all the phases of software development process [2,3] and mostly focused on the requirements engineering [9,6,7]. Nevertheless, the use of techniques to foster creativity in requirements engineering is still shortly investigated. It is not surprising that the role of communication and interaction is central in many of the creativity techniques. Some creativity techniques have been applied in an attempt to bring more creativity to requirements elicitation [7]. However, in requirements engineering the answers do not arrive by themselves, it is necessary to ask, observe, discover and increasingly create requirements. If the goal is to build competitive and imaginative products, we must integrate the creativity as a part of the requirements process. Indeed, the importance of creative thinking is expected to increase over the next decade [5]. In [9,8] an interesting open question is formulated: Is inventing part of the requirements activity? Requirements analysts are ideally placed to innovate. They understand the business problem, have updated knowledge of the technology, will be blamed if the new product does not please the customer and know if inventions are appropriate to the work being studied. In short, requirements analysts are the people whose skills and position allows, indeed encourages, creativity. In [1] the author, a leading authority on cognitive creativity, identifies basic types of creative processes: *exploratory creativity* explores a possible solution space and discovers new ideas, *combinatorial creativity* combines two or more ideas that already exist to create new ideas, and *transformational creativity* changes the solution space to make impossible things possible. Then, most Requirements Engineering activities are exploratory, acquiring and discovering requirements and knowledge about the problem domain. And the Requirements Engineering practitioners have explicitly focused on combinatorial and transformational creativity. The agile principles and values have realized the importance collaboration and interaction in the software development and, by other hand, creative work commonly involves collaboration in some form and it can be understood as an interaction between an individual and a sociocultural context, the study of the potential of concepts and techniques to foster creativity in software engineering is a very interesting issue [3]. The XP methodology includes implicitly diverse central aspects of team work creativity, but we believe that it can be improved from a creativity perspective. In our work, we are trying to answer the following questions:

- related to the structure of the team. What roles (or their functionality) of a creative team are included (or should be included) in the XP team?
- related to the performance and purposes of the team. Is a goal of the XP team to generate novelty ideas?; is the performance (operating) of a XP team equivalent to the creative process (divergent thinking/convergent thinking)?

References

1. Boden, M.: The Creative Mind. Abacus (1990)
2. Glass, R.L.: Software creativity. Prentice-Hall, Inc., Upper Saddle River, NJ, USA (1995)
3. Gu, M., Tong, X.: Towards hypotheses on creativity in software development. In: Bomarius, F., Iida, H. (eds.) PROFES 2004. LNCS, vol. 3009, pp. 47–61. Springer, Heidelberg (2004)
4. John, M., Maurer, F., Tessem, B.: Human and social factors of software engineering: workshop summary. SIGSOFT Softw. Eng. Notes 30(4), 1–6 (2005)
5. Maiden, N., Gizikis, A.: Where do requirements come from? IEEE Softw. 18(5), 10–12 (2001)
6. Maiden, N., Robertson, S.: Integrating creativity into requirements processes: Experiences with an air traffic management system. In: 13th IEEE International Conference on Requirements Engineering (RE 2005), Paris, France, 29 August - 2 September 2005, pp. 105–116. IEEE Computer Society, Los Alamitos (2005)
7. Mich, L., Anesi, C., Berry, D.M.: Applying a pragmatics-based creativity-fostering technique to requirements elicitation. Requir. Eng. 10(4), 262–275 (2005)
8. Robertson, J.: Eureka! why analysts should invent requirements. IEEE Softw. 19(4), 20–22 (2002)
9. Robertson, J.: Requirements analysts must also be inventors. Software, IEEE 22(1), 48–50 (2005)

Investigating Adoption of Agile Software Development Methodologies in Organisations

Antony Grinyer

Department of Computing, Faculty of Maths and Computing, The Open University,
Walton Hall, Milton Keynes, MK7 6AA, UK
arg237@student.open.ac.uk

Prior to the turn of the century, long-standing approaches to software development (see, for example, [1], [2], [3]) provided the models and process heuristics for developing software in industry, but since the late 1990s, these traditional approaches have been challenged by agile methods. But why do practitioners choose to adopt agile approaches, especially given the dearth of any hard empirical evidence as to its efficacy in specific contexts? [4]

The rapid uptake of agile methods seems somewhat akin to the spread of Software Process Improvement (SPI) through the software engineering industry in the 1990s, in that the latter was rapid, attracted a great deal of attention and took place within a context in which little hard empirical evidence had been amassed, published, aggregated or analyzed. In the absence of this evidence, organisations adopted an SPI programme for a variety of reasons, for example, because their customer mandated it or because they wanted to 'jump on the bandwagon' (see, for example, [5]). Informal influences through peer networks and colleagues appear to have been more influential than any other persuasion mechanisms (see, for example, [6] and [7]).

Despite the efforts of empirical software engineers, there is concern [8] in the field of empirical software engineering that the evidence produced by empirical software engineers is having little impact on practice. The reasons for this are speculative and attempts to understand this shortfall have resulted in empirical software engineers questioning why investigations have little influence on practice. Possible reasons are that empirical software engineers are not looking at those aspects of software engineering that are of interest to practitioners, that results of investigations are not communicated suitably to practitioners, and the type of evidence produced by empirical software engineers is not persuasive to practitioners.

In order to influence practice, empirical software engineers need to understand the decision processes within practice and the type of evidence practitioners' draw upon and accept. The rise in popularity of agile methods in the software development community is an attractive case in point. Agile methods have emerged entirely within the practitioner community, and the adoption of agile methods by organisations has not been as a result of weighing evidence of the type produced by empirical software engineers because, until recently, there hasn't been any.

Given these viewpoints, my research seeks to ask:

- What are the factors that influence organisations to adopt agile methods?
- What are the sources and types of evidence that practitioners use in order to decide whether or not to adopt agile methods?

- How does the adoption of agile methods compare with established models of adoption and diffusion (for example, [9])?

From initial investigations [8] and reviewing the state-of-the-art, it is apparent that most of literature concerning agile methods is strongly subjective, that is, most of the evidence supporting agile methods consists mainly of claims and assertions based upon anecdotal evidence from proponents of agile methods. This point, coupled with the fact that there is not much hard evidence from empirical or academic literature regarding agile methods, raises questions as to why organisations adopt agile methods. Nonetheless, the increasing number of reports emerging from organisations adopting agile approaches suggests that agile methods continue to gain popularity and sustain a steady rate of diffusion within the practitioner community despite the dearth of hard evidence. It is this phenomenon that my research wishes to explore.

References

[1] Royce, W.W.: Managing the Development of Large Software Systems: Concepts and Techniques. In: Proceedings of WESCON, Los Angeles (1970)
[2] DeMarco, T.: Structured Analysis and System Specification. Yourdon Press, New York (1979)
[3] Boehm, B.: A spiral model of software development and enhancement. Computer 21(6), 61–72 (1988)
[4] Lindvall, M., Basili, V.R., Boehm, B., et al.: Empirical Findings in Agile Methods. In: Proceedings of XP Agile Universe, Chicago (2002)
[5] Segal, J.: Organisational Learning and Software Process Improvement: A Case Study. In: Althoff, K.-D., Feldmann, R.L., Müller, W. (eds.) LSO 2001. LNCS, vol. 2176, pp. 68–82. Springer, Heidelberg (2001)
[6] Sharp, H., Hovenden, F., Woodman, M.: Tensions in the Adoption and Evolution of Software Quality Management Systems. In: Proceedings of PPIG/EASE 2003, pp. 297–312, Keele University (2003)
[7] Rainer, A., Jagielska, D., Hall, T.: Software engineering practice versus evidence-based software engineering research. In: Proceedings of the REBSE workshop, associated with ICSE 2005, St. Louis, Missouri, USA (2005)
[8] Segal, J., Grinyer, A., Sharp, H.: The type of evidence produced by empirical software engineers. In: Proceedings of the REBSE workshop, associated with ICSE 2005, St. Louis, Missouri, USA (2005)
[9] Rogers, E.M.: Diffusion of Innovations, 5 edn. Free Press (2003)

Agile Software Assurance

Noura Abbas, Andrew M. Gravell, and Gary B. Wills

School of Electronics and Computer Science, University of Southampton
Southampton, SO17 1BJ, United Kingdom
{na06r,amg,gbw}@ecs.soton.ac.uk

1 Research Questions

Since Agile methods were presented in the 90s, many papers, articles and books have been published about Agile. However, little work focuses on Agile Software Quality. Therefore, the main goal of the PhD is to study the quality of Agile projects.

We are trying to answer the following research questions:

1. *What is the quality of Agile Software, importantly, how we can evaluate the quality of Agile Software?*
2. *Can Agile assure the quality under time pressure and with unstable requirements?*
3. *What are the best ways to assure the quality of Agile Software?*
4. *Different organizations interpret words like Agile and iterative in different ways. Therefore, another question is how do organizations understand these terms?*

In order to answer these questions we decided to investigate further Agile Software Assurance, in order to give a clear understanding of the topic, and furthermore, to help people and organizations who work with Agile to produce high quality software.

2 Related Work and Current Solutions

There have been many initiatives relating Agile with quality standards such as CMMI and ISO 9000. Although the results of these initiatives vary, they all shared the same idea of modifying Agile methods in order to be accepted from the standards point of view [1, 2, 3, 5].

An interesting point is whether we really need to modify the method in order to achieve the standards. Instead, why not create a standard which can be suitable for the new methodology. The main reason for introducing CMMI was to modify CMM to be more suitable for modern iterative development, interestingly, because few of the modern principles are in conflict with CMM key process areas [4].

3 Research Approach and Current State

Interviews and questionnaires constitute the appropriate qualitative and quantitative research methods to collect as much data as possible about Agile in practice. We have started with developing two questionnaires. The first one will be to understand *what organizations mean by the term "Agile", and how Agile they are*. Then the second questionnaire will be to find out *how organizations assure the quality of Agile software products, and what are the reasons behind their success.*

As a start, the questionnaires will be conducted on 10 Agile projects that use Agile in different percentage. In the next stage the questionnaires will be improved and the range of the organizations will be broader.

We have started interviewing people from two organizations and half of dozen individuals who had experience with Agile projects. The interviewees are involved in different roles within the organizations: project managers, developers, testers, architects, and domain experts. The projects were chosen from a range of software development organizations in the UK (where uptake of Agile methods has been slower than in the US). The projects are of different sizes, from a variety of application domains, mainly middleware, web services, electronic design automation, and banking management systems. Our initial findings showed that the final products had different levels of quality. In addition, organizations use different Agile practices to assure the quality: testing, re-factoring, pair programming, recruiting skilled people, and continuous communication with the customer. Importantly, those organizations have different understanding of Agility, and probably this is one of the important reasons behind having "Agile" software with different levels of quality.

The next step will be to analyze the collected data, in order to understand how people used Agile. Furthermore to find out how this usage affects the quality of the final products. The final step will be to bring all the findings together and inform the model which will describe how to improve the quality of Agile projects.

4 Significance of the Research

This research will help software development organizations to have deeper understanding of Agile Methods, principles and practices. Moreover, identifying critical links between conditions of success and reasons of failure to achieve high quality Agile software could be a potential research finding. Furthermore, this research will help to evaluate the quality of Agile projects.

From this point of view having a successful quality assurance model for Agile projects will increase the successful use of Agile in both industry and academia.

References

1. Anderson, D.: Stretching Agile to fit CMMI level 3, Microsoft Corporation (2005)
2. Royce, W.: CMM vs. CMMI: From Conventional to Modern Software Management, Rational Software (2002)
3. Vriens, C.: Certifying for CMM Level 2 and ISO9001 with XP@Scrum. In: Proceedings of the Agile Development Conference (ADC'03) (2003)
4. Nawrocki, J., Jasinski, M., Walter, M., Wojciechowski, A.: Combining Extreme Programming with ISO 9000. In: Shafazand, H., Tjoa, A.M. (eds.) EurAsia-ICT 2002. LNCS, vol. 2510, pp. 786–794. Springer, Heidelberg (2002)
5. Turner, R., Jain, A.: Agile Meets CMMI: Culture Clash or Common Cause? In: Proceedings of the XP/Agile Universe 2002, pp. 153–165. Springer-Verlag, Heidelberg (2002)

User Stories and Acceptance Tests as Negotiation Tools in Offshore Software Development

Ivan Chubov and Dmitri Droujkov

Phenix Solutions, Inc
3117 Twin Leaf Drive
Raleigh, NC 27613, USA
{ichubov,ddroujkov}@phenixsolutions.com

Abstract. This experience report talks about applying agile tools, namely, user stories and acceptance tests, to resolve problems in offshore software development. These tools help to formulate and to better understand results and goals of projects, and to avoid miscommunications about expectations. The report shows the importance of discussing technical project limitations.

Keywords: offshore development, user stories, acceptance tests, collaboration with customers.

1 Project Background

In March 2006, our team was asked to help another team of developers to make a part of functionality for their project. The project was about a web site where visitors, that is, guests and registered users, can perform complex calculations. Having this general understanding of the project and a small task to do, our team started working on the task.

2 The Development Story

The small task we were assigned was completed pretty fast. QA has verified the part we developed as a separate piece of the project against created requirements. As the next step, the customer asked our team to make the code integration in spite of the fact that the second team knew the application code better than we did. The code integration contained lots of detailed, line-by-line programming work as we were not given access to the code repository of the second team. When we showed results to the customer, he was very angry, as his expectations were not fulfilled at all. He reported new issues again, and again. Making fix in one place introduced bugs in five other places. We were charged with all of the issues, as we did the code integration. Developers and the QA team were blamed for creating and missing bugs. Customer was blamed by the team for "inventing" new issues and features. For the project success it was necessary to have the customer and the team on the same side. And we had one great advantage, namely, the customer was really interested in the project. He was willing to communicate and to work with the team.

As a start, we decided to be extremely open with the customer. We explained to him everything that we thought and knew about the project. At an online conference, we convinced him that we needed to discuss and to describe, step by step, every part of the project. We suggested a redesign of the project architecture and defining the requirements set in a parallel. To begin, the customer created a short high level description of the overall system, which was going to be a frame for the full description. A project manager or a QA member took each small part of the functionality, gave it a name, and described it with acceptance tests. All this data were put into TWiki for the customer review. Every unclear place or emerged question was reported as an open issue via the bug tracking tool Mantis, and then assigned to the customer. Almost every day the customer reviewed assigned issues and communicated them with the manager. In addition he inspected new stories acceptance tests in TWiki, and reported any unclear or incorrect places in Mantis. This work went on in advance of the development work, so that developers had a clear vision of what to do next.

This stage took us about two months. But this was not the end of the journey! At the point when most of the acceptance tests passed, the customer told us that he could not accept the work: its performance was much slower than the original application's.

The new customer request could be satisfied by significant code changes. We realized it was a big mistake not to ask the customer about technical requirements. What to do? We decided to rely on the old approach: to treat the performance request as a new set of user stories and to develop, with the customer, the set of acceptance tests. Now they were about the loading speed. This work has taken almost two months to complete. Finally, the project was ready for beta release.

From the start to the beta release, the project took about six months, which is four times shorter than the development that took place before our team got involved. Currently the project is open to a group of beta users, and we are waiting for the usability feedback by the customer.

3 Conclusions

We came a long way from the point when everything seemed to fail to the successful project beta release. The first conclusion: be extremely open with customers and try making customers a part of the team. It is especially important if you work in an offshore team: encourage customers to work with you as much as possible. Next, document all of the details you discuss with customers in user stories and acceptance tests. They will be core parts of the project artifacts: developers will know what to do, and QA and customers will be able to validate that everything works as expected. It is important to remind yourself that user stories, along with acceptance tests, as well as the project code, evolve throughout the project lifecycle. And finally, don't forget to discuss the quality of service requirements with the customer at early stages. The standard approach used for business requirements – user stories and acceptance tests – can be applied to handle technical requirements.

A Case Study of the Implementation of Agile Methods in a Bioinformatics Project

Xueling Shu[1], Andrei Turinsky[2], Christoph Sensen[2], and Frank Maurer[1]

[1] Computer Science Department, University of Calgary,
Calgary AB T2N 1N4, Canada
{shu,maurer}@cpsc.ucalgary.ca
[2] Sun Center of Excellence for Visual Genomics, University of Calgary,
Calgary AB T2N 4N1, Canada
{aturinsk,csensen}@ucalgary.ca

Abstract. From July 2005 to August 2006, a bioinformatics project experienced a substantial transformation by adopting Scrum and some XP practices. The paper reveals project risks, previous challenges faced by the team and results from this one-year exploratory case study. The paper presents a discussion of the lessons learned from the perspective of both the project manager and the on-site agile advisor, and recommendations on speeding up the adoption process for other projects.

Keywords: Agile Methods, Lessons Learned, Java 3D™, Bioinformatics.

1 Introduction

Ethnography recommends collecting data from "participant observations, interviews, documents, and informal contact with participants" over an extended period [1]. Through embedding agile researchers into a bioinformatics development team during an approximately one-year case study, we developed a deep understanding of the implementation strategies for agile methods from long term observations.

The observed team has been developing a software tool that allows medical researchers to view a complete image of disease mechanisms in a 3D environment. Several project risks existed: technical novelty, limited resources, ineffective interpersonal communication, and reluctant user support. One of the goals of the project is *commercialization* of leading edge bioinformatics research software. Therefore, high software quality and solid management practices are essential.

Some of the earlier projects in the lab faced various challenges. Developers struggled with debugging of unstable research prototypes that focused on proof-of-concept demonstrations, facing substantial requirement churn. Acceptance of some papers that presented new software tools was delayed when peer reviewers tested the software and found bugs in it. Overall, the management was not satisfied with progress and software quality.

2 Result

The adoption of Scrum and XP practices brought substantial improvements in two aspects: management process and intra-team communication. User stories now describe features more clearly. Developers pick the stories by themselves rather than being assigned the stories, which helps the team form a self-organization culture. Test automation saved considerable amount of effort and improved software quality. Product backlog facilitated the management of specification obsolescence. Story-oriented meeting style improved the meetings efficiency considerably. Task coordination became a team-wide effort. With the problems being cleared away step by step, the morale has also improved both professionally and personally.

3 Lessons Learned

The on-site agile advisor must be a proactive gentle(wo)man. Disagreements continued throughout the duration of the project. The resolution lies in being a proactive listener with patience and actively yet carefully analyzing the environment.

The on-site advisor should try to benefit from her technical expertise. Demonstration of skills tells people that you really can help them solve problems and build up the team confidence in the advisor's suggestions.

"Down, and touch the ground". Benefits of a new idea will not be accepted easily by simply talking about theories from books. For example, we showed the benefits of test automation by actually writing test code for the project. After the lab wide seminar on test automation, some developers either started coding tests for their own project or were willing to learn how to write the code.

The project manager should focus on most tangible agile improvements, especially at the beginning. One of our biggest concerns was to ensure that the suggested changes are both timely and relevant to the project deliverables, and are demonstrably valuable. In our case, these turned out to be the introduction of automated development-support tools for automated testing, Java code-standard checking, and iteration planning by the on-site agile advisor.

The project manager should try to pair the agile advisor with another developer. Such pairing may overcome the steep learning curve for the advisor, and also broaden the social support base for the advisor within the team, making subsequent changes easier to introduce.

The biggest problem we observed is the advisor was considered "just a student", instead of an outside expert. For other agile practitioners, we would strongly recommend start higher-up in their teams: add a process consultant as an advisor or as a PM so that the power structures are actually set up to impact a change faster.

Reference

1. Myers, M.: Investigating Information Systems with Ethnographic Research. Communications of the AIS, vol. 2(4) (December 1999)

Adapting Test-Driven Development for Innovative Software Development Project

Deepti Mishra and Alok Mishra

Department of Computer Engineering, Atilim University,
Ankara, Turkey

Abstract. In Test-Driven development, first test is made according to the customer requirement and then code is prepared to execute this test successfully. In this approach, design is not done exclusively before preparing test cases and coding. Design emerges as software evolves but this may result in lack of design quality. We adapted TDD by incorporating exclusive architectural design phase in the successful implementation of an innovative, large scale, complex project.

1 Project Background and Development

When the decision was taken to develop supply chain management software, a team that includes a marketing expert, project manager and a domain analyst contacted many customers in order to define potential customer sectors and required services and functionalities. We analyzed the product and domain characteristics as following:

- Large scale and high complexity of project
- Insufficient and volatile requirements
- Variety of customers and quick release was important to get an edge in the market
- Many development teams concurrently developed different parts of SCM software.

As the evidences show that this project is an inventive project and it should be developed within the motivation of agile iterative methods. In order to control unpredictability, the key is iterative and incremental development as well as adaptive development. It was observed that the product will consist following parts:

- Core (solver and many heuristics for the optimization)
- Support (Geographical Information System, storage of data, reports and GUIs)

A research was conducted to gain knowledge and decide whether these parts should be developed from the scratch or by integrating a pre-developed library or product. The result of the research concluded that the core part should be developed from scratch because of performance and other reasons. For the report and GUIs components, open source library was chosen to be integrated and used into supply chain management software. The main functionalities were provided by the library; all other required functionalities were developed by team members.

Initially, we conducted interviews with customers in many sessions and collected information was analyzed by a team (includes domain expert, project manager and development team representatives) in a brain storming meeting. These requirements were stored in a centralized repository where they can be viewed prioritized, and "mined" for iteration features. Requirements should also be readily accessible to all team members, to be enhanced and revised over time, and remain reasonably current to create test cases and subsequent coding. There were other critical non-functional requirements also such as performance, portability, usability, reliability. As this project was innovative, and complex, it was not possible to get all requirements by conducting interviews alone. Rate of change in requirements was also high so a more flexible approach like prototyping needs to be used to gather additional requirements and refine the old ones. Also, quick release of software was important to have an edge in highly competitive market so we started developing software with the initial set of requirements by using iterative and evolutionary approach. These iterations had short timeframes. These evolutionary prototypes of software were used to get the feedbacks from customers that helped in extracting new requirements and further refinement of previous requirements.

Preliminary architectural design was done with requirement engineering using the initial requirements to get a common picture and avoid confusion between many development teams working concurrently on different parts of SCM software. This was the structure that specifies the whole system as major components, modules; responsibility of each module, collaborations, interactions and interfaces between them. Object-Oriented design techniques were used to document this structure and it was also allowed to change as a result of customer's feedback from future iterations. Then development was done using Test Driven Development. The programming language used during development was pure java based on full object-oriented structure. For each iteration (new functionality, defect fix, changing) during the development, the requirements were selected from the repository according to their priority and defined functionality for that iteration. Unit tests are implemented before the code and run continuously. Then restructuring of the system was done by removing duplication, improving communication, simplifying and adding flexibility. Customers did the functional tests.

2 Conclusion

As Supply chain management software was an innovative project, key practices of XP such as test-driven development, refactoring, incremental delivery of software, feedback from expert users, emphasis on face-to-face communication, pair development, daily integration, self organizing teams, and periodic tuning of methods helped significantly to achieve its successful implementation. XP provide flexibility so it encourages the development teams and individuals towards creativity which is essential for the successful implementation of innovative projects. We used TDD for the development of supply chain management software but it was adapted according to the characteristics of the project. In TDD, we usually don't have a design at start; it emerges as we make software. However, the TDD practice is flexible and can be adapted to any process methodology, including those that specify low-level (detailed) upfront design phases. As it was innovative, large scale, high risk project, we formally did the architectural design along with documentation. This design played an important role in the successful implementation of this project and it will be helpful in the maintenance phase also.

Learning Agile Methods in Practice: Advanced Educational Aspects of the Varese XP-UG Experience

Federico Gobbo, Piero Bozzolo, Jacopo Girardi, and Massimiliano Pepe

DICOM – Dipartimento di Informatica e Comunicazione, Università dell'Insubria,
via Mazzini 5, 21100 Varese, Italy
federico.gobbo@uninsubria.it, varese-xpug@googlegroups.com

Abstract. In Italy the public adoption of agile practices in software planning, design and development is still in an infancy state. Local XPUGs are few – notably, the most active ones are in the cities of Milan and Rome. After an informal meeting of the participants of the first edition of ESSAP, the Varese XP-UG was born in 2006, October[1]. This XP-UG is the first experience in Italy spread from an academic environment with specific learning purposes, applying agile methods in an advanced education setting in computer sciences. In particular, preliminary observations of a University ad hoc open source web application called Examinando are given.

Keywords: agile development of open source software, education and training, practitioners' experience reports.

1 Examinando, the First XP User Group Experience

For most members of the Varese XP-UG (eXtreme Programming User Group), the first edition of ESSAP (European Summer School on Agile Programming) represented the first experience of agile methods and practices. In particular, the pomodoro technique by [1] and the XP planning game learnt directly from [2] raised great enthusiasms: some undergraduate and graduate students in computer science at the University of Insubria started to apply them in their individual work and study. Afterwards, a new XP-UG in Varese was established, in order to share ideas and experience and improve what learned during the summer school. Every Varese XP-UG meeting lasts two hours, in which three pomodoros are spent. In this team, each pomodoro lasts 25 minutes plus 5 minutes having a break, to avoid work overload. 13 meetings in total occurred until March 2006 (approx. 6-8 participants per meeting), more or less on a weekly basis, for a total running time of 26 hours. Examinando was proposed originally in the ESSAP 2006 as a real-case laboratory for agile practices. In fact, it is a web application for classroom reservation within the University of Insubria, which is currently inefficient (a lecturer must call the classroom administrator by phone or email messages). The main goal is to let lecturers reserve classrooms and resources by themselves if they want to do so, avoiding unwanted reservation overlappings. 24 pomodoros were spent on the planning game and user stories design,

---

[1] Permalink of the Varese XP-UG: http://varese-xpug.has.it

with the help of dialogue mapping [3], while 119 pomodoros were spent in development (77% of the total). Participants play different roles: in the case of seniors, a coach is always on site as the customer (proxy), while juniors play the role of software designers and developers. Pair programming revealed to be central, as the most efficient solutions were found through dialogue. The development team decided use Ruby on Rails as the development framework, as it is easy for new team members to become ready for active contribution [4].

2 Preliminary Conclusions and Further Directions

Since 2007, meetings always started with a stand-up meeting. Furthermore, a wiki and a mailing list were set up to improve the team organization. People learned to use the pomodoro technique effectively – the number of broken (i.e. lost) pomodoro drastly reduced. However, pomodoro estimates made by programming pairs are still too optimistic. Stand-up meetings also increased efficiency, as it greatly helps people not being late. In the future, the whole team plan to pay more attention to the user stories description writing. In particular, acceptance tests should be written with more precision and regularity, possibily with the help of a ubiquitous language as the "backbone of the model" [5]. Furthermore, user stories should intertwine strictly with the pomodoro tracking and the design should be more interface-oriented. The team members plan to publish the first release of Examinando during ESSAP 2007, for more extensive testing and feedback. The general feeling of Varese XP-UG members is that, throughout this experience, productivity in software design and – more important – quality of working life, has changed in better.

Acknowledgments. The Varese XP-UG members thank Matteo Vaccari for his invaluable teaching and help.

References

1. Cirillo, F.: La Tecnica del Pomodoro v1.1. Technical Report. XPLabs Italy (Published October 23, 2006) http:// www.xplabs.it
2. Van Cauwenberghe, P., Peeters, V.: The XP Game Explained. In: Succi, G., Marchesi, M., Wells, D., Williams, L. (eds.) Extreme Programming Perspectives, pp. 311–322. Addison-Wesley, Boston (2002)
3. Concklin, J.: Dialogue Mapping: Building Shared Understanding of Wicked Problems. John Wiley and Sons, Chichester (2006)
4. Thomas, D., Heinemeier Hansson, D.: Agile Web Development with Rails. The Pragmatics Programmers L.L.C., Raleigh Dallas (2006)
5. Evans, E.: Domain-Driven Design: Tackling Complexity in the Heart of Software. Addison-Wesley, Boston (2003)

Overcoming Brooks' Law

Kealy Opelt

Menlo Innovations
kopelt@menloinnovations.com

Abstract. Most programmers are familiar with the notion that adding new resources to a project will most likely slow down progress if not bring it to a complete stop while new team members are brought up to speed. Unfortunately, in business situations there are often important opportunities missed or dollars lost if a software development team cannot increase the rate at which they complete functionality. Surprisingly, many of the practices of Extreme Programming also help teams overcome Brook's Law and actually increase production by adding resources. If more software development teams successfully demonstrated this phenomenon, then many business sponsors would be interested in supporting the practices used by these teams.

1 Introduction

Brooks summarized his law, "The bearing of a child takes nine months, no matter how many women are assigned." It is possible that he never imagined software development in an open environment such as Extreme Programming (XP). Menlo Innovations, a custom software design and development shop, finds that the XP practices create on the job training and constant communication within the team, where new developers learn faster and contribute to the team productively within weeks rather than months. Teams can reap these benefits through an XP environment, overcoming Brooks' Law and directly benefiting each software project's production and its members.

2 Brooks' Law

Brooks' Law states "Adding manpower to a late software project makes it later" and that increasing the output of an expanded team is crippled by the "added burden of communication" where "communication is made up of two parts, training and intercommunication"[1]. Adding members to a team would increase the burden of communication for team members in some of the following ways:

- explaining code to another developer
- training on the specific technical tools of the project
- learning the architecture of the code
- learning how to detect failures when code is changed
- learning the business domain
- reading the design specifications
- being interrupted to answer questions from other team members

Clearly all of these things can have a negative impact on productivity, and if that negative impact is large enough, a team that is increased significantly would produce less output.

3 The Doubling Experience

While all of the above challenges are real, of Menlo's experience is different. An XP team with eight developers doubled to a team of sixteen developers in the period of less than three weeks. The choice to increase the team was based on the customer's desire to complete more functionality with an already established deadline. As each new developer joined the team they spent the first few weeks pairing with developers who were familiar with Menlo's process, the architecture, tools and project domain. As new team members paired in to the team their pair discovered they were less efficient, completing fewer stories. They spent more time explaining existing code, architecture, and guiding progress on new features. However experienced team members found that they did not stop producing output to bring new team members up to speed. Instead they learned what they needed by the way they worked. Reflecting about why this was possible the team concluded the XP practices helped them to overcome the challenges.

On the following page table 1 shows the challenges new programmers faced when joining the team and the XP practice the team discovered helped decrease the high cost of communication.

Table 1. Developer Challenges with Decreasing Practice

Challenges For New Developers	Practices That Reduce The Negative Impact
How do I know who owns the code?	Collective Code Ownership
How do I decide if my change broke something else?	Test Driven Development
How can I estimate my story cards if I don't know the code yet?	Estimation Every Iteration, Team Co-location
What should the architecture for new features look like?	Simple Design, System Metaphor, Design Improvement as Needed
How do I quickly communicate with my team members?	Team Co-location, Pair Programming
How do I gain the respect of my peers?	Pair Programming
Who can I turn to for help?	Team Co-location, Pair Programming
How do I add new features in code I don't know yet?	Simple Design, System Metaphor, Design Improvement as Needed, Team Co-location, Pair Programming
How do I merge my code with everyone else's?	Continuous Integration

Table 1. (*Continued*)

What am I allowed to work on?	Planning Game, Collective Code Ownership
What story should I work on first?	Planning Game
How do I fix a bug with out being punished for failing?	Collective Code Ownership
How do I get my work done with out "burning out" from working too many hours?	Sustainable Pace

Even while the team was experiencing the practices as solutions, more than one programmer noticed their slow down and raised the question to the project managers; did it really make sense to add more resources, when it was obviously less efficient? Some team members and some of the sponsoring managers gathered around a white board to explore the topic, eventually creating the following figure.

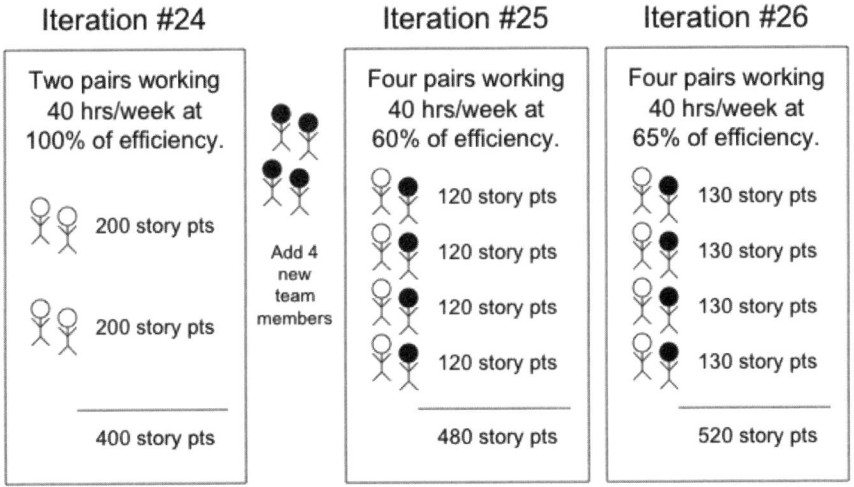

Fig. 1. Depiction of mature XP team the iteration before doubling the team and the effects of story points completed two iterations after

Figure 1 of a team doubling separates the issue of increased output from decreased productivity. The team at two pairs are working at 100% productivity accomplishing 400 story points. When they are doubled to four pairs each pairs productivity decreases to 60% then only accomplishing 120 story points. However, overall story points increase to a total of 480 story points. This makes the choice to increase the team a business decision of whether cost or deadline is more important and not about what how many story points a pair can complete. Apparently many programmers focus on the cost and low personal efficiency, making them refer to Brooks' Law, when increasing the overall team productivity should be a choice made by the business.

4 Conclusion

Why should a business person care about the software development methodology you use? Perhaps they would if you could provide software with fewer bugs, software at a lower cost, or provide completed software sooner. When a business sponsor asks if software can be delivered sooner there are two obvious potential solutions; reduce the scope of the project or increase the size of the team. But when software developers are asked to increase the size of the team, most refer to Brooks' Law and declare that adding resources will simply slow the project down. Spending over a year on an XP team that rapidly changed size several times based on business deadlines creates the thought; can all mature XP teams easily overcome Brooks' Law.

Reference

1. Brooks, S., Frederick, Jr., P.: The Mythical Man-Month Essays on Software Engineering Anniversary Edition. Addison Wesley Longman, Inc, Boston, 18, 25 (1995)

Project Bid on Iteration Basis

Juanjuan Zang

Abstract. A different way of bidding for contract work is introduced and discussed in this paper. The bid is priced on a per iteration basis. The throughput goal of each iteration is estimated in story point format based on projected load factor, planned work days, and staff plan. The development team is responsible for achieving the target throughput goal of each iteration. Though pricing bid this way gains client trust quickly, key lesions are learnt and advice are given specifically on estimation, load factor projection, and client education.

Keywords: Agile, Iteration, Release, Story, Story Point, Estimation, Load Factor, Velocity.

1 Introduction

Do you have to bid on a contract with a client who is concerned about delivery capability? Traditionally, there are essentially two types of billing for contract work: Fixed Bid or Time & Materials. Both have their advantages and disadvantages. Fix bid allows a defined set of work to be delivered for a fixed amount of money. Fix bid shifts more risk to the bidder, especially when scope increases. A Time & Materials contract is similar to providing hourly employees, in that you are paid a set rate for the actual hours that you worked. Time & Material shifts the risk to the client, especially when the team is inefficient.

Company X was facing market share losses caused by its competitors. To increase revenue by attracting more customers, they asked us to redesign and implement their S application to make it more flexible and manageable. To accommodate their situation, we introduced a new way of pricing a bid on a per iteration basis in accordance with the project release plan projections.[1] While cost per iteration is calculated using hourly billing rates and number of team members, the throughput goals are estimates. Throughput is estimated to increase progressively in successive iterations via productivity and increase in team scale. The requirements are captured as Agile stories and are estimated in points.[2] The development team was accountable for the throughput goals of each iteration. Throughput targets were revisited by the parties on a monthly basis, and adjusted as needed.

2 Background

The Company X's S system is currently implemented as a multi-tier J2EE product, delivering much greater volume of new customer traffic than it encountered just two

---

[1] See Table 1 "Release Plan Projections" on page 3.
[2] Story points are a pure measure of story size.

years prior. The S system is limiting this dramatic growth and is therefore of significant concern to the business. The application is specifically failing in the following areas:

1. **Extensibility** – Company X is unable to economically realize alterations to the S system workflow. New or different features require months to deliver, while the business needs far quicker response.
2. **Cost-of-ownership** – The complexity of the S system creates a steep learning curve for new developers and significantly lengthens coding and defect resolution processes.
3. **Cost-of-change** – The product's elaborate dependency configuration significantly impedes deployments, further increasing the latency of new feature deployment.

With the goal of achieving simple interaction, friendly user experience, incrementalism[3] and managerial utility for its S application, Company X made the call to us. Before we priced a solution, the team collaborated with Company X in a four week formal inception exercise. The result of this process was to identify a complete, high-level list of user stories associated including priority and estimate. Additionally, the team created release plan projections based on the projected team size, work days, and load factor.[4] Our challenge for bidding this project was:

1. Engender Company X's trust in our delivery capability: It takes time and effort to get Company X fluent with the Agile process. Simultaneously, Ruby was selected for this project which required several developer spikes.

3 Our Approach

The company produced a bid on a per iteration basis. We targeted throughput in points per iteration based on planned team size, work days and projected load factor which is expected to improve over time. See Table 1 for projected throughput per iteration.

Table 1. Release 1 Plan Projections

Iteration	Days (Real)	Number of developers	Expected Load Factor	Target Throughput (Velocity)	Cumulative
0	10.0	8.0	-	-	
1	9.5	8.0	0.22	17	17
2	7.5	10.0	0.25	19	36
3	9.5	10.0	0.27	26	62
4	5	10.0	0.29	15	77
5	8.5	12.0	0.31	32	109

---

[3] Incrementalism means the application can accommodate the incremental requirement changes easily and quickly.
[4] Load Factor is an adjustment that helps one convert from the unit of estimation to Velocity.

Table 1. (*Continued*)

6	8.5	12.0	0.33	34	143
7	9.5	12.0	0.36	41	184
8	9.5	12.0	0.39	44	228
9	9.5	12.0	0.00	-	228
10	9.5	12.0	0.00	-	228

Remark 1. The cost per iteration is calculated on unit billing rate and number of staff, and the targeted iteration throughput was scheduled to be revisited on a monthly basis.

Remark 2. The formula to calculate the targeted throughput for each iteration:

$$\text{Days} * \text{Number of developers} * \text{Expected Load Factor} = \text{Targeted Throughput} . \qquad (1)$$

Remark 3. Code delivery time for Release 1 is the end of Iteration 8. Iterations 9 and 10 are reserved for testing and bugfixing and are completed before Release 2 begins.

4 Conclusion

This approach successfully provided more flexibility and supervision for the client. Meanwhile, we had been struggling with several problems:

1. The original estimate for each story is a variable: Our bidding approach was actually based on that the total original estimation of all stories determines the complete scope of Release 1. The total scope for the first release of this project was 228 points in story points / 145 stories. However, the original estimate was done during the exploration phase (the "Inception"). Most of the stories needed to be re-estimated later because the lack of knowledge of the domain, complexity of integrated system, and unfamiliarity of back end code made the original estimation very inaccurate.
2. The projected load factor is also variable. The project load factor is based on previous project data, and should be adjusted every iteration based on actually team performance. The expected load factor listed in the table above is a judgment call based on past experience. It doesn't necessarily apply to the actual team.
3. Team size and real work days are variable, too. The team size could be changed since staffing may not happen as planned. Real works days will also change since team members usually take unplanned days off.

Based on the projected velocity,[5] team size and real work days, by iteration 8, or Release 1, the team should finish all 145 stories since the accumulated throughput by then is equivalent to the scope of 228 points. However, once the project started, we faced a couple of challenges:

---

[5] Velocity is defined as the number of units that can be implemented within a development iteration.

1. The original estimation is inaccurate as many stories were underestimated. But because of the way the project was bid, no new points could be introduced. We can only *redistribute* rather than *reestimate* stories in Release 1. The relative scale among stories can be adjusted, but the estimation for each story can not be adjusted. This causes concerns. For example, after redistribution, a story is estimated at 12 points. But if this story is split into multiple stories due to a better understanding, then all split stories will have to share the 12 points even though one story may worth 12 points alone. This might lead to scope creep.
2. It is very hard to evaluate whether the team achieves the committed throughput by iteration when stories end up in hangover. In Agile, hang over cards are not counted points for that iteration though the cards may have already been played. Thus it is very common to see the project burn up charts[6] bump up and down dramatically through iterations, especially if there are lots of carry over cards with large story point values.

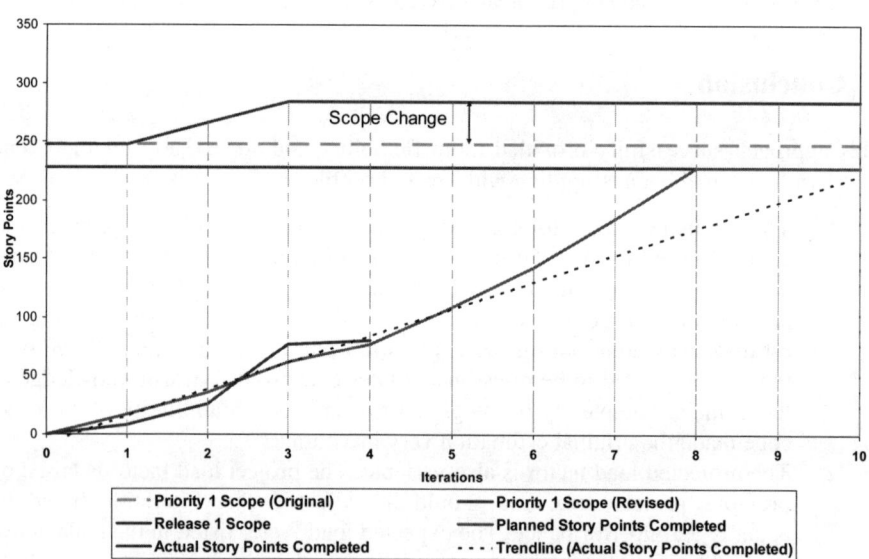

Fig. 1. Trend line (*black dotted line*) is generated based on the actual completed story points (*blue solid line*). The planed story points completed (*green solid line*) is the target throughput calculated on projected load factor and staffing plan (1). The figure projects that iteration 10 would be the most possible completion date instead of the originally planned iteration 8 based on team's performance by iteration 4.

Overall, this approach incurred lots of discussions and estimation refactoring, since each story point has significant financial consequences. Before taking on this approach to a project bid, consider the following:

---

[6] See Figure 1 on page 4.

1. Be very confident in your scope and estimate from the beginning
2. Make a realistic load factor projection
3. Go to great lengths to educate the client in Agile terms, specifically iteration, points, velocity, and load factor
4. Adjust estimates as early as possible

References

1. Cohn, M.: User Stories Applied: For Agile Software Development. Addison-Wesley Professional, Reading (2004)
2. Back, K.: Extreme Programming Explained: Embrace Change. US Ed edition. Addison-Wesley Professional, Reading (1999)
3. Back, K., Fowler, M.: Planning Extreme Programming, 1st edn. Addison-Wesley Professional, Reading (2000)
4. Martin, R.: Agile Software Development, Principles, Patterns and Practices, 2nd sub edn. Prentice Hall, Englewood Cliffs (2002)
5. Cohn, M.: Agile Estimating and Planning. Prentice Hall PTR, Englewood Cliffs (2005)

Making the Whole Product Agile – A Product Owners Perspective

Dharmesh Raithatha

British Broadcasting Company, Future Media and Technolgy,
201 Wood Lane, London, United Kingdom
draithatha@gmail.com

Abstract. This experience report is from the viewpoint of the product owner and covers how a successful product was created by trying to be Agile throughout all aspects of product development and how other processes were incorporated with Scrum[1], including Prince 2[2] (a generalised project management process), a User Centred Design[3] process and an Innovation process. The report also covers how different disciplines were involved with the agile process to create a product.

Keywords: Agile, User Centred Design, Innovation, Scrum, Product Owner.

1 Introduction

The Product Owner of this project noticed a distinct lack of focus in the agile literature of how to be a good product owner working within a multi-disciplinary team. Most texts seemed to start from a prioritised backlog of user stories and most examples tended to focus on the software development aspect. So what the product owner wrestled with was how to build and develop a good product and how to keep to the philosophies of Agile throughout, while incorporating or working with other processes where necessary. The rest of this report describes the processes and how they were used on this project.

1.1 Project Background

The product is the BBC's primary Social Media software platform. A managed service, it allows multiple community and user generated content propositions to be developed and launched quickly and provides enterprise level moderation and user management tools to ensure that the quality of content is maintained. It was the first project within the BBC to use Scrum (over 4 years now) and is in continual development with a team of 8 software engineers, 2 Client Side Developers and Designer. It runs on SQL Server 2005 with a C# and C++ application layer and uses very complex XSLT templates for the presentation layer.

1.2 Prince 2 and Scrum

While using Scrum the product owner found that it did not give sufficient answers for the complete cycle of product development, for example project initiation and project end were not comprehensively described. It was found that incorporating Prince 2 with its concept of stages was extremely useful. Prince 2 is a complete general project management process that has many different stages and describes key roles that need to be filled.

Describing the process, before user stories were identified they had a 1 page document where clients or sponsors were asked to describe what they wanted and what the expected benefit was and how it could be measured. It was found that this alone filtered out many features which the team might have otherwise spent time on. The process also used the key Prince 2 roles like the executive, senior user and senior supplier (normally the product owner) and made sure they were identified before progressing.

After this stage high level requirements were captured from all stakeholders and converted into user stories and these formed the initial product backlog. They aimed for no more than 50 regardless of the project complexity. Depending on the feature they would initiate a research phase including competitor analysis and ethnographic research.

The product owner's aim was to ensure that the feature that was developed had potential value outside of the single client (in order to maximise value), fitted into the product's overall vision and was focused on doing one thing well. This formed the second stage of the process where work could stop or be given permission to continue by the project board.

For the next stage they conducted a risks brainstorm and represented these risks and their associated mitigation tasks as user stories and added them to the product backlog. The backlog was then prioritised, estimated at a high level and divided into sprints to give a rough indication of how long the work would take. At this point the product owner worked hard to identify the core stories that delivered the feature and that anything thing else had a lower priority.

Key members from all disciplines then sat down together to work out a conceptual model for the system. Most of this work was very quick (maximum a week) but was important as some thinking had to occur before development and architecture decisions took place, even if they were working within an agile process.

Scrum sprints were then used to deliver the project and at the end of each sprint the product could (and often would) change direction or in more severe circumstances the project could be stopped.

At the end of a particular project they had an end of project review.

1.3 Scrum and User Centred Design

On previous projects the team had used Scrum for the developers but the product features were defined outside of Scrum in a separate User Centred Design Process (UCD) and run by the design team. The idea of UCD is to put the user at the heart of the process. Involving such techniques such as persona development, user research and validating ideas with user testing.

Working in this way the team seemed to naturally fall into a waterfall development process, with large wireframe documents for requirements and a separation of disciplines causing the projects to overrun and to not be successful.

Below are key parts of the current unified process which has been far more successful:

- **Combine both processes and teams completely.** Designers and developers are part of the same team.
- **User Stories are the requirements.** Our requirements are always expressed as user stories and are personalised by developing personas for each role.
- **Solve integration issues early.** This ensured that communication between teams and software components were solved very early on.
- **Have a few clear Sprint Goals for the whole team.** Each sprint had 1 or 2 clear goals the stories into tasks generated by all disciplines. A UCD task might be to create a simple wireframe, user testing, or visual design work. Prototyping was encouraged throughout the process as wireframes were often insufficient.
- **Prototyping and user testing flowed into development tasks for a story.** It was found that of the 2 goals in a sprint, some tasks would be for production work and other tasks would be for prototyping, conceptual work and user testing. The key idea was that the team were working in the same sprint which ensured good communication and teams were not separated into prototyping and production work.
- **User testing was part of the sprint.** User testing was planned towards the end of a sprint so that this could inform the product owner whether to reprioritise the product backlog.
- **Be sensitive to the needs of different disciplines.** Different disciplines still struggled with daily meetings and sprint planning especially where the tasks were irrelevant to them. The product owner had to be very sensitive to this and sometimes allowed team members to not attend. They kept daily meetings short and tight to help the situation.
- **Launch with the minimum and iterate.** The product owner always tried to launch early with less features as it was difficult to predict how the product would actually be used.

1.4 Innovation and Scrum

Innovation was and is critical to ensuring that the product remains useful. The product owner also wanted the team (who have been working on the product for years) to feel that they could make the product their own and give them additional motivation and a sense of play. Following is how they added innovation to their development process.

1.4.1 Innovation Planning Meetings

The innovation planning meeting is where the team brainstorm ideas (6 months to 2 years out max). The product owner kept the concepts loosely around the product area as it was important to show that the ideas could add value to the business. Clients could also add ideas but these would have to be backed by the team. These ideas formed an innovation backlog managed by the product owner. The product owner would also seek to stimulate the teams thinking by organising events, bringing in speakers or showcasing what their competitors were doing.

1.4.2 Research Questions

The innovation backlog consisted of "Research Questions" rather than "User Stories". This was to encourage exploration rather than producing work ready to be released. The team were encouraged to produce working prototypes rather than written reports.

Once the tasks were identified they put 20% of their time into the sprint planning sessions as normal, however, innovation time was time-boxed to this 20%. All tasks in a sprint were given a priority from 1 to 3 and innovation tasks were given a priority of 2 to ensure that business critical work was done first. The product owner would ensure that where possible priority 1 tasks accounted for only 60% of a sprint.

1.4.3 Innovation Reviews

In the same cycle as the sprints, but not on the same day, the team had an innovation review. This was a formalised point where team members show what they have learnt and built and where new ideas could be discussed and then reprioritised in the innovation planning meetings.

Every quarter they had a special review where clients were invited to use the prototypes. This alone provided a certain amount of pressure to the team, however, the team were also given a night out if they thought that they had made good use of the time.

2 Lessons Learned

The product owners role is key to a successful product. They must have a strong understanding of all the processes that the team uses when they work. By getting everyone to work off the same backlog and having the daily meetings, the product owner ensured that communication and understanding between the disciplines was high.

The product owner found that it took the team a few sprints to get used to doing innovation work. However, after a few sprints the motivation and energy of the team was greatly increased and quality prototypes were produced.

The product owner had to experiment around the principles of Agile to ensure that you the team were building the right product.

With Scrum there was a danger that the team lost sight of the product, especially if they are working on it for many years. They came to meetings, they got stories and tasks, they completed the tasks and then moved on. In this routine the product owner had to come up with ways to get them more involved in the product shaping. They had regular points where they thought about where the product could go. The product owner invited the team to meet clients and to go to user testing sessions. The team wrote a team manifesto[4]. This alone made a big difference to the team feeling as a single unit.

By adapting different process and combining them with Agile the product owner was able to produce a successful product with a happy productive team.

References

1. Schwaber, K., Beedle, M.: Agile Software Development with SCRUM. Prentice Hall, Englewood Cliffs (2001)
2. Norman, D.: The Design of Everyday Things, Basic Books (2002)
3. Office of Government Commerce.: Managing Successful projects with Prince2
4. Cagan, M.: 12 Product Management Tips www.svproduct.com

Financial Organization Transformation Strategy

Juanjuan Zang

Abstract. Major challenges IT department in investment banking industry faces include but not limited to frequently changing requirements, last minute change request, frequent emergency release request and unavailability of business users. The paper addresses those challenges with tailored strategies, specifically focusing on four areas including requirement capture and flush out, iteration and release planning, project status tracking and build automation. The paper also listed strong management support, team advocate and more involvement of business users as the key successful contributors.

Keywords: Agile, Iteration, Release, Story, Ideal Days, Prioritization, Estimation, Build, Load Factor, Velocity, Pair.

1 Introduction

What will be the best strategy to introduce and apply agile methodology to an investment banking industry, nature of which is reputed for continuously changing requirements, continuously changing priorities, last minute requirement request, and unavailability of business users. Meanwhile, the business mandates the flexibility for emergency releases at any time if needed. In May 2006, we were brought in by Company B to help with an organization transformation effort by providing best agile practices, specifically for its risk portfolio management team. We identified the pain points, the challenges the team faced, and then ironed out a tailored approach which successfully bought in the team with iterative development best practices. This approach improved transparency to the team and business users, introduced test driven development concept and automated the build process.

2 Background

In May 2006, Company B called us in to help with its organization transformation. This specifically included:

1. Run project using Iterative Development Methodology
2. Provide best practices consulting for Company B's project managers, developers and development leads including:
    a. Iterative project planning and management
    b. Story-based requirements development
    c. Software engineering best practices
3. Enable Company B staff to hold Iterative Development roles and responsibilities
4. Demonstrate the value of Iterative Development to the business
5. Provide metrics to compare project's performance to other projects

We came in and worked specifically with Company B's risk management team as a pilot project. When we stepped in, the risk management team and its project manager had been struggling with team status report, urgent release requests, obscure requirements, strenuous and long-haul build, labor intensive manual testing, and code versioning, etc. Basically, their main pain points were:

1. Requirements are not captures as stories in business user's tone. Nor are they captured in use cases or any standard format
2. New feature requirements, defects and enhancements are all bundled together without differentiation
3. Requirements gathering process isn't streamlined
4. No process of iteration and release planning
5. No process for prioritization of requirements
6. No estimation process for requirements including new features, defects and enhancements
7. No visibility or transparency to outside parties including business users or management team regarding to the team's velocity[1], development progress and time loss impact
8. No acceptance testing criteria for each requirement
9. Manual build process
10. Infrequent code check in and manual merging of code between branches

3 Our Approach

Considering time and resources constraints, we generated a list of tasks and bucketed them into "what we have to do", "what we can do", and "what we should do" by prioritization. We then identified the approaches as how to implement those tasks and eventually address the pain points the team was having. We mainly tackled the following four areas:

1. Requirement capture and flush out
2. Iteration and release planning
3. Project status tracking
4. Build automation

The rest of the paper takes the "Iteration and release planning" area as an example to show the issues the team faced and how we approached and addressed them.

3.1 Challenges

The challenges the team faced when planning iterations and releases were:

1. Story priority is hard to weigh and changes very often
    a. Over 90% of the stories are prioritized as Priority 2
    b. Incoming production defects usually take the precedence over prioritized stories

---

[1] Velocity is defined as the number of units that can be implemented within a development iteration.

2. Stories for future iterations and releases are quite volatile and usually can only be planned a week before the actually iteration starts
3. Stories are swapped between iterations and releases very often
4. Emergency releases[2] happen all the time
5. Huge story estimation variance due to
    a. Less business user interaction
    b. Unfamiliar with business domain, code base and work flow
    c. Poor understanding of business requirements
6. Huge time loss due to
    a. Unexpected time loss due to production support, data migration, user requests, etc
    b. Team member juggle with multiple teams and multiple tasks
    c. Time loss on SWAT:[3] fix defects rejected from quality assurance (QA) and user acceptance testing (UAT)
7. Technical tasks such as build automation, test driven development (TDD) coaching continue through all iterations

3.2 Approaches

Targeting all the identified challenges, we, as a whole team, tailored our agile practices which became resorted "solutions":

1. Continuously check and reprioritize stories with customer proxy
2. Only plan stories for next two upcoming iterations
    a. Verify with team leads and customer proxy specifically on stories of the latter of the two iterations
3. Keep track of time loss on a daily and weekly base
4. Adjust load factor[4]
    a. Adjust load factor based on historical data and team experience
    b. Book certain hours each iteration for SWAT if needed
5. Schedule some buffer stories (back up stories) in iteration in case the following happen
    a. Development sometimes is completed ahead of schedule
    b. Development sometimes halts due to the dependencies on other teams
6. Improve estimation accuracy
    a. Have estimation done as team
    b. Have developers break down stories into multiple subtasks
    c. Factor time spent on writing test cases in estimation
    d. Use ideal days instead of actual days

---

[2] Emergency Release refers to the releases which are not planned and scheduled. Those releases go to production without going through formal testing procedures such as UAT (user acceptance testing).
[3] SWAT (Special Weapons And Tactics, originally Special Weapons Assault Team), is used here to refer to fire fighting urgent defects activities.
[4] Load Factor is an adjustment that helps one convert from the unit of estimation to Velocity.

7. Plan and prioritize technical stories[5] along with functional stories for each iteration
8. Put aside fixed number of hours each iteration for recurring story card and story card which can't be estimated

At the end of the project, we checked each of the four areas "before the Agile process adoption" against that "after the process adoption". We provided the comparison report to the team and stake holders.

Table 1. Planning Iteration Workload

Iteration	Development Start	Expected Load Factor	Team Sz. (Developers)	Developer Vacation Days	Capacity for this iteration in Ideal Days	Estimates for the cards assigned to this iteration	Hangover Estimate	Over/Under
1	Wednesday, July 05, 2006	0.30	5.0	2.0	7	7	0	
2	Wednesday, July 12, 2006	0.30	5.0	2.0	7	8	0	
3	Wednesday, July 19, 2006	0.35	4.0	0.0	7	8	2	
4	Wednesday, July 26, 2006	0.40	5.0	2.0	9	12	3	
5	Wednesday, August 02, 2006	0.50	5.0	2.0	12	12	3	
6	Wednesday, August 09, 2006	0.50	5.0	2.0	12	12	2	
7	Wednesday, August 16, 2006	0.50	4.0	1.5	9	9	0	
8	Wednesday, August 23, 2006	0.50	5.0	3.0	11	11	0	
9	Wednesday, August 30, 2006	0.50	5.0	2.0	12	12	2	

Remark 1. This is the iteration planning tool used for iteration kick off. This gives a quick snap shot on team capacity vs. work assigned. Red *(Over/Under)* indicates the team doesn't have enough capacity to accomplish the work assigned in that iteration, while green indicates the team could finish the planned work.

$$\text{(Team size} * 5 \text{ days per week} - \text{vacation days} - \text{other time lost)} * \text{expected load factor} = \text{capacity for iteration}. \quad (1)$$

Table 2. Calculated Load Factor

Iteration	Development Start	Ideal Days completed	Calendar Days Worked	Calculated Load Factor
1	Wednesday, July 05, 2006	7	23	0.30
2	Wednesday, July 12, 2006	6	23	0.26
3	Wednesday, July 19, 2006	7	20	0.35
4	Wednesday, July 26, 2006	12	23	0.52
5	Wednesday, August 02, 2006	12	23	0.52
6	Wednesday, August 09, 2006	14	23	0.61
7	Wednesday, August 16, 2006	9	19	0.49
8	Wednesday, August 23, 2006	9	22	0.41

Remark 1. This is the actual load factor for each iteration. Team can adjust the future expected load factor based on the team performance in the past

$$\text{Ideal days completed / calendar days worked} = \text{calculated load factor}. \quad (2)$$

---

[5] Technical Stories, sometimes also referred as technical debts. Examples are data migration, data mapping, exception handling framework, etc.

4 Conclusion

Not only we coached the team as how to scope and flush out stories, how to conduct iteration and release planning, how to keep team's agility to accommodate urgent requests and emergency releases, how to prioritize and estimate stories, and how to track project status and improve the transparency, we also made the team feel very comfortable and confident with adapting to the process and sustaining the process beyond the project. We also provided valuable data and matrix to its PMO office, which improved the transparency greatly to the business user and stake holders outside of the team. Most important, the experience and knowledge learnt by the team could be leveraged by other teams within the organization. What we have learnt in order to make the process succeed is:

1. Gain strong support from the project manager
2. Have strong team advocate
3. Get business users more involved
4. Have business user or customer proxy available and accessible
5. Make team dedicated
6. Pair with the peer of the team

References

1. Demarco, T., Lister, T.: Waltzing With Bears: Managing Risk on Software Projects. Dorset House Publishing Company, Incorporated (2003)
2. Demarco, T., Lister, T.: Peopleware: Productive Projects and Teams. 2nd edn. Dorset House Publishing Company, Incorporated (1999)
3. Cohn, M.: User Stories Applied: For Agile Software Development. Addison-Wesley Professional, Reading (2004)
4. Back, K.: Extreme Programming Explained: Embrace Change. US Ed edition. Addison-Wesley Professional, Reading (1999)
5. Back, K., Fowler, M.: Planning Extreme Programming, 1st edn. Addison-Wesley Professional, Reading (2000)
6. Martin, R.: Agile Software Development, Principles, Patterns and Practices, 2nd sub edn. Prentice Hall, Englewood Cliffs (2002)
7. Cohn, M.: Agile Estimating and Planning. Prentice Hall PTR, Englewood Cliffs (2005)

An Agile Approach to Requirement Specification

Tom J. Bang

Bekk Consulting, Norway
tom.bang@bekk.no

Abstract. This experience report is about how one project in Norway made an agile approach to specifying software requirements for a new intranet. Rather than spending months on trying to detail all requirements and aspects of the solution, the team spent a few weeks specifying a prioritized list of high-level requirements. Further details will emerge by face-to-face communication through the iterations of the project quickly turning in to valuable working software for the customer.

The customer and the team

The customer is a student welfare organisation that provides a wide range of services to make the student life easier. With their 650 employees, divided into various service areas, they provide services to approx. 40,000 students in Oslo, Norway.

During the pre-study phase the core team consisted of:

- The customer's project manager (60-80%)
- A technical architect (a man week)
- A graphic designer (a man week)
- Project manager and solutions architect (100%)

In addition the following groups where established to support the project:

- A steering committee (representatives from the top management)
- A project group (key resources in the company)
- A reference group (representatives from all service areas within the company)

The challenge

The customer's current intranet is based on legacy technology, where the company who build it no longer exists. They wanted help moving the current intranet (content and functionality) over to a new technical platform. It was agreed on performing a pre-study phase over a few weeks to deliver:

- A specification of the user interface (wireframes[1])
- Graphical design for a couple of example web pages.
- A list of system requirements
- Vendor selection (application server, portal and content management system)
- An estimate and a project plan

---

[1] In web design, wireframes are a basic visual guide used to suggest the layout and placement of fundamental design elements in the interface design (Wikipedia).

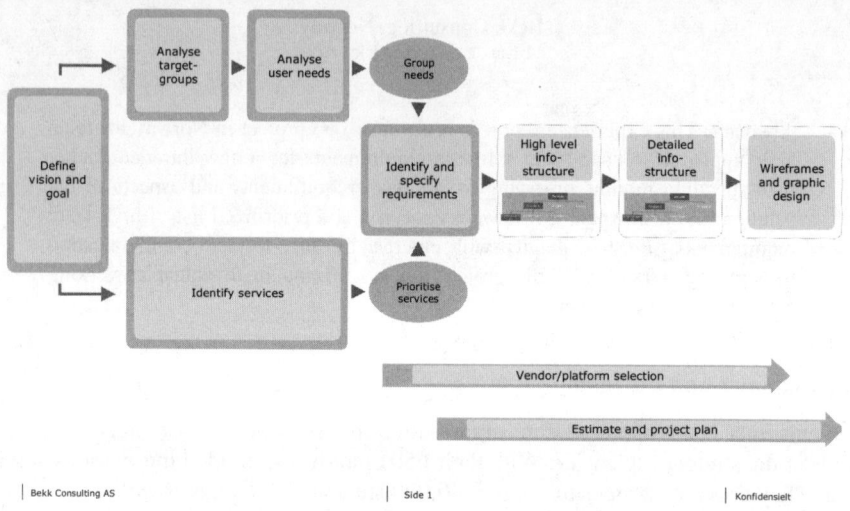

Fig. 1. Process

In order to achieve this in a few weeks the team chose an agile approach to the requirement specification. This meant identifying requirements, prioritising them and describing the at an high-level (the most valuable with more detail than the less valuable). To avoid wasting precious time, a clear vision and set of goals were established for the new intranet. In addition a structured and delivery-focused process was agreed upon.

The process

Together with the customer's project manager and members from management the team identified the people who could help define the vision and goals for the new intranet and identify the needs. The team toured the company, performing a number of workshops, interviews and a questionnaire, trawling[2] requirements. After these sessions the information was structured and workshops were performed with a smaller group of people to identify, specify and prioritise the information to create high-level specifications of the systems behaviour – User Stories.[3]

At first we only wrote simple, single, sentences on yellow post-it notes to describe the behaviour. An example is "SHOW COMPANY NEWS". This was easy for the customer to understand and they could express themselves like in their day-to-day job.

---

[2] Trawling is a fishing technique using a net pulled behind a boat (from Mike Cohn's book "Agile planning and estimating").

[3] A user story is a software system requirement formulated as one or two sentences in the everyday language of the user.

To help us we used the INVEST-principle as a reminder when writing the stories. A story should be Independent, Negotiable, Valuable, Estimatable, Small and Testable.

After identifying all user stories a first high-level prioritisation was performed, using the MoSCoW[4] technique. To aid the group some guidelines were given in order to utilise the technique:

MUST: Will be implemented
SHOULD: Implemented if time and money
COULD: Considered in the next phase/version
WON'T: Will probably never be implemented.

After the prioritisation 70-80% of the user stories were categorised as either "MUST" or "SHOULD". These were used as the basis for the next round of prioritisation, but first they were developed and described further. Inspired by Mike Cohn's excellent book: "Agile Estimating and Planning", the user stories were specified using the following formula:

As a [ROLE]
I need [FEATURE]
So that [VALUE]

This gave a more complete description of the requirement:

As an EMPLOYEE
I need TO READ THE COMPANY NEWS
So that I AM UPDATED ON WHAT IS HAPPENING IN MY COMPANY

Writing the User Stories we decided on only having two kinds of users, employees and editors.

Planning Poker[5] was chosen for estimation.

The following roles attended the workshop:

- Representative from IT-department
- Customer's project manager
- Technical Architect
- Front End Developer
- Project Manager (and solution architect)

There were five sets of cards, with each set containing the following values: ½, 1, 2, 3, 5, 8, 13, 20, 40 and "?". Each player was given a set.

The user representative explained the user story and provided a short overview. The team was given an opportunity to ask questions to clarify assumptions and risks.

For each user story we played planning poker:

- Each player laid down a card (face down) representing his or her estimate in ideal days of effort.

---

[4] MoSCoW is a method used in business and particularly in software development to get an understanding with the customer on the importance they place on the delivery of each functional requirement (Wikipedia).
[5] Planning Poker is explained in Mike Cohn's book "Agile Estimating and Planning".

- Everyone showed his or her card simultaneously.
- People with high estimates and low estimates discussed their justification for their estimate.

The estimation process was repeated until a consensus was reached. In less than four hours about 50 User Stories were estimated – the whole first release and some more.

The team revisited the vision and goal to make sure the user stories were supporting these prior to the final prioritisation and presenting the results before the steering committee. Even the members of the steering committee, with little or no experience from IT-projects, had few problems understanding the meaning of the user stories. They could easily help us perform the final prioritisation in order to accept the project and create the budget.

Preliminary Results

After about six weeks we finished the pre-phase with the following results:

- A set of wireframes drawn on flip-charts and captured with a digital camera (main page and five main section pages).
- A high-level description of the information architecture (site map).
- Three graphical designed web pages, based on wireframes.
- Application server, portal and content management system selected.
- An estimate for first release.
- A project plan for the first release.

...and about 50 User Stories identified, specified and prioritised (requirements sufficient for two releases). In addition the project identified a set of more technical requirements.

The identification, specification and prioritisation were about half of the time spent during the pre-phase – more or less three man weeks. We have now finished the initial phase with the deliverables described above. No thick documents. No nitty gritty details. Only simple and clear defined goals, user stories, estimates and a high-level plan for the project well anchored with the sponsors – and employees. The final report contains 23 pages, almost half of which consists of pictures and illustrations. The project is accepted and will now continue with the detailing of user stories to acceptance tests for implementation along the iterations, in a BDD-manner[6] - until the customer has the intranet they need.

Lessons learned

Some lessons learned:

- Everyone can understand the process of describing User Stories, and the User Stories themselves without having to learn a new language. And we avoid fooling ourselves by adding lots of details we can't be sure of – only giving us false sense of security.

---

[6] BDD stands for Behaviour-driven development. For more information visit: http://www.behaviour-driven.org

- Planning Poker is an efficient way to do high-level estimation. For estimating and planning a full release (or more) up front, it is much less time consuming and probably as trustworthy as a more scientific, detailed, bottom-up approach.
- You need to have a customer that trusts you, and wants to "row" the project together with you – in the same direction. Only this way will they accept such a high-level approach to approve and budget a project.
- You need to have a customer that understands that one can only specify requirements up front to a certain level of detail before you get lost, and start wasting time and money.
- When basing the requirements on high-level descriptions you are depending on having the same key people available throughout the project to avoid starting old discussions over again (wasting even more time…).

The Application of User Stories for Strategic Planning

Lawrence Ludlow

Intelliware Development Inc., 1709 Bloor Street West, Suite 200, Toronto, Ontario, Canada
M6P 4E5
lawrence@intelliware.ca

Abstract. In agile development stories are typically used to define small, independent pieces of functionality that have value for the customer. They are most often used to define requirements for future development. This paper describes a project where stories were used on a much broader scale as part of a strategic planning exercise to identify a long-term development roadmap for a new system. Stories were used not only to define what needed to be built but also to document existing functionality and gaps with current systems. This resulted in the generation of a large number of stories, which created challenges with managing and keeping the stories up to date as the project proceeded.

1 Introduction

This experience report describes how user stories were utilized as a key component in the development of a strategic roadmap plan for a new system. A roadmap represents a comprehensive plan for a development exercise to address a particular business issue or objective. A roadmap can be used as part of a business case to secure funding for a project or as the starting point for more detailed planning and development.

A user story is defined by Beck [1] as "Something the system needs to do. The stories are written on index cards, with a name and a short paragraph describing the purpose of the story." Jeffries et al. [2] also defined a story as "...a short description of the behavior of the system, from the point of view of the user of the system." For the project described in this paper stories were used for requirements for the new system plus also functionality provided by existing systems and known gaps with those systems. The existing function and gap stories established a baseline for future planning.

The client company was a large international financial services firm that was created by a joint venture involving divisions of two large banks. This resulted in the client's internet presence being delivered by several existing, disparate systems each providing differing levels of functionality and appearance. The objective of the project was to develop a roadmap for a new enterprise-wide Web portal capable of delivering a consistent user experience to all of the client's customers. Intelliware was engaged by the client group responsible for defining and delivering the new Web presence and interfacing with other key stakeholders, such as senior management and product group representatives.

2 Project Approach and Methodology

The project was split into four main phases:

1. Internal State Assessment – Documentation of current capabilities and known gaps
2. Future State Engineering – Documentation of high level Strategic Alternatives
3. External State Assessment – Third party investigation to define best practices for an online client experience
4. Strategic Options – Identification of project options and development of a high level plan for the preferred Strategic Alternative

Stories were used during all 4 phases of the project, resulting in nearly 900 stories being identified. The following sections summarize each phase.

Internal State Assessment. Internal state involved the identification of current functionality and known gap stories. The existing systems were reviewed in detail and stories were written for each major piece of functionality. The resulting current functionality stories were then validated by reviewing the cards with key operations and business representatives. The cards were updated as needed and the final versions were posted on the project Web site for further review by the client.

Also, existing product and system documentation was reviewed and stories were written for the functional gaps that were identified. Follow up reviews were held to validate the gap stories with managers from the appropriate product groups. New gap stories identified were added to the overall list and posted on the project Web site.

Future State Engineering. Future State Engineering involved weekly meetings with client representatives to discuss future requirements and write stories. Once an initial set of stories was identified, product experts were brought in to review the stories relevant to them to ensure their known future requirements were represented.

Towards the end of the Future State phase several Strategic Alternatives were identified and presented to the project Steering Committee. The preferred alternative was an evolutionary approach that involved developing a new system to deliver core functionality provided by two key existing systems and retiring those systems as soon as possible. Functionality provided by other systems and net new functionality were considered to be longer term objectives for after the first major release.

External State Assessment. The External State assessment was initially completed by a third party company contracted by the client. When the assessment was completed the final report was reviewed by the Intelliware project team to identify:

1. Requirements represented by existing Future State stories
2. New requirements which necessitated the addition of new stories to Future State

The new stories were reviewed with the client and added to the Future State list.

Strategic Options. The objective of the Strategic Options phase was to identify project options and develop high level plans for the preferred Strategic Alternative. The planning process to do this involved the following steps:

1. Reviewed all Internal State existing functionality and known gap stories and linked them to equivalent Future State stories. Several new Future State stories were

added to ensure all Internal State requirements were covered. Also, several Internal State gap stories were found to be redundant and not useful and were removed.
2. Identified all Future State stories linked to current functionality stories for the two target systems. This was done by filtering the Future State stories to exclude all stories that were not linked to Internal State current functionality stories for the two key systems. This resulted in a smaller sub-set of core Future State stories.
3. Reviewed the core Future State stories with the client to identify gaps and add additional stories where needed. Several new stories were identified because the smaller set of core stories enabled the client to better visualize the system.
4. Prioritized the core Future State stories with the client as must haves (Priority 1), should haves (Priority 2) and nice to haves (Priority 3). The other non-core Future State stories were categorized for future development.
5. Estimated the relative sizes of the Priority 1, 2 and 3 stories. Client representatives were not involved in this step; estimating was done by the Intelliware project team.
6. Used the estimates to derive duration for the Priority 1, 2 and 3 stories using an assumed velocity and created an initial plan for 2007 and beyond. The resulting plan is shown in Figure 1.
7. Reviewed the plan with key project stakeholders and refined it where necessary.

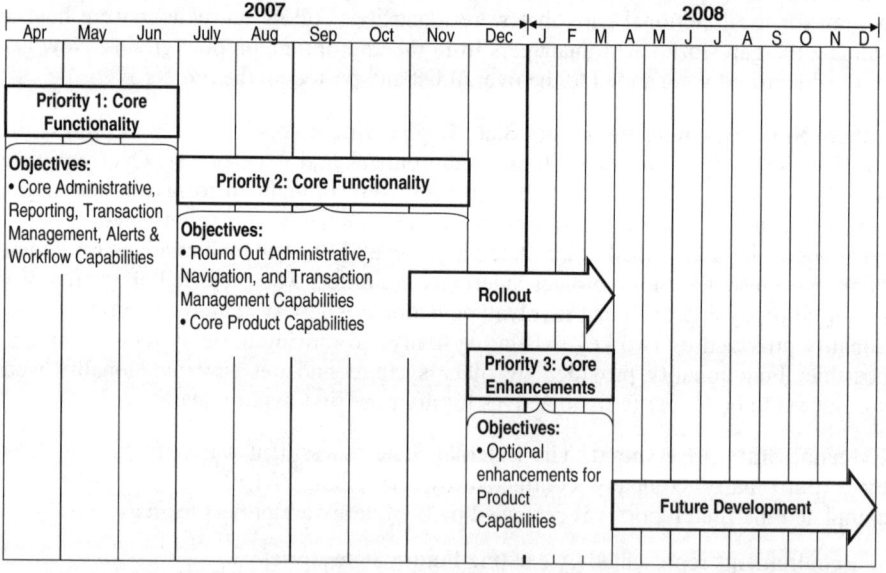

Fig. 1. Simple bar chart of the roadmap showing future planned development iterations

3 Findings

During the project several significant observations were made proving that stories can be successfully used on a strategic planning project.

Stories were found to be an effective tool for documenting not only future requirements but also existing functionality and known gaps with existing systems.

Stories allowed the project team to easily inventory functionality provided by and gaps associated with existing systems and identify overlaps and common themes. These findings could then be effectively illustrated to the client by organizing the story cards in certain ways on the table during review meetings.

The ability to effectively present project findings to the client was greatly facilitated by the conceptually simple nature of stories. This was most evident during story validation reviews with system operations and business representatives. Typically these meetings would include a description of stories at the beginning, but often it was not certain whether or not the attendees really grasped the concepts. However, once the cards were spread out on the table the situation would quickly turn around. The participants would soon start asking questions and pointing out missing or incorrect stories, and in some cases they would even start writing on them. After one session our client contact noted that the review was so effective that it felt like the business representative that we met with was given a tutorial on his system.

User stories were also effective for presenting and reviewing the draft plan with stakeholders at many levels. Having a rough plan backed up by stories made it possible to have both high level and very detailed discussions on what would be delivered and when. Detailed discussions were facilitated by laying the cards on the table.

Tools were essential for managing the large numbers of stories that were generated. For this project two tools were used, Microsoft Excel spreadsheets to track and document stories and a Word mail merge template for generating printable story card files. The spreadsheet was set up with one row per story and the columns represented story attributes such as name, description, size, etc. The mail merge template was connected to the spreadsheet as its data source with embedded link fields representing the story attributes. A new story cards file could be generated any time using the "Merge To New Document" function in Word. A typical story card generated in this fashion is shown in Figure 2.

intelliware.ca business application development	Web Strategy Roadmap	Status	Priority	Size	Print Date
		FSE	1	2	3/27/2007

List Standard Reports

Description:
List all pre-defined Report Definitions that the user can access.

Notes:
- User can either view a Report or modify the Definition.
- Allow user to pick a report and save it to the Saved Report screen

Project Phase	Application	Functional Area	Story ID
FSE	Generic	Reporting	FSE-Generic-Reporting-1

Fig. 2. Example story card generated from the Word template and Excel spreadsheet data file

Using spreadsheet files it was possible to define additional attributes for stories, such as priority, product area and functional area for Future State stories. This facilitated organization, categorization and analysis of the stories. The stories lists could easily be sorted and filtered to generate sub-sets organized by product area, functionality, priority, etc. Also, using spreadsheets facilitated the cross-reference linking between the Internal and Future State stories.

The second tool, the Word mail merge template, was useful for generating new cards for various review meetings. Using hand written cards was not an option given the number of reviews that took place and the number of times that the cards were written on by different stakeholders. The Word template could be configured to include filters for different story attributes, making it possible to create custom card files for specific product or functional areas. Corporate logos were added to the template to give the cards a more professional look, which helped earn credibility with client representatives who didn't know us very well.

4 Conclusions

User stories proved to be an effective tool not only for identifying and documenting future requirements but also for inventorying both current functionality and known functional gaps. They also provided significant business value in terms of planning, allowing the client to effectively distill a myriad of requirements into a concise plan that could easily be communicated to a large and diverse audience of project stakeholders. By using stories, detailed discussions on what would be delivered and when could be facilitated by simply laying the cards out on the table and organizing them by release.

Conceptually stories are very simple and can be created by hand by writing functions on standard index cards. However, for a large project involving hundreds of stories and many review sessions there are advantages to using tools such as spreadsheet and word processor applications to help organize and categorize stories and create clean copies of cards for review sessions.

References

1. Beck, K.: Extreme Programming Explained: Embrace Change. Addison-Wesley, Reading (2000)
2. Jeffries, R., Anderson, A., Hendrickson, C.: Extreme Programming Installed. Addison-Wesley, Reading (2001)

Introducing Agile Methods into a Project Organisation

Tom J. Bang

Bekk Consulting, Norway
tom.bang@bekk.no

Abstract. Bekk Consulting (BEKK), a Norwegian IT- and management consulting company changed their way of running projects from traditional waterfall to a more agile approach. It took more than a year getting the whole company onboard and more than two years to convince most of the customers. We are still learning, adjusting and improving the way we run our projects – with focus on the outcome over delivering features.

BEKK is a Norwegian IT- and management consulting company leveraging on the intellectual capital of their more than 160 employees. With specialist like graphic designers through system developers, usability experts, project managers and management consultants we create cross-functional teams running projects to high business value solutions, based on internet technology.

We will later in this report discuss what were the drivers for this transition, but first we need to understand that **it's about creating VALUE for the customer.**

Some history

Agile methods were known among some developers in our company back in 2000-01, but limited to testing (JUnit and some home made test frameworks), continuous integration and automation with Ant, and XP. Open Source projects were early adopters and our company participated on these.

Some of the first attempts were related to introducing XP-techniques (2003), but only among developers. But as there was no good understanding of agile at that time, Management and sales viewed XP and agile as a hackers dream.

The author's first encounter with an agile/iterative project approach was back in 2002, but unfortunately it was too heavy on RUP so it didn't really become very agile.

And like this project, most ended up waterfall...

With the waterfall method projects sometimes ended up with a Big Surprise! Developing features and functionality according to a giant requirement specification, testing was often saved for last, making it an extremely tough challenge to assure quality.

To build software of higher quality, we needed to involve the customer much more and not put all our trust in written documentation and formal sign-offs. Communication based on written documentation and limited dialogue was misinterpreted several times during the development life cycle and lead to surprises late in the project.

We needed to create an environment based on trust.

So, what where the main change drivers for introducing Agile Methods?

- **Communication:** Communication based on written documentation and limited dialogue was misinterpreted many times during the development life cycle and led to surprises late in the project.
- **Changes:** The environment changes, thoughts and ideas mature and both the customer and the supplier increase their domain knowledge. Acknowledging this made us understand that the requirements shouldn't stay fixed.
- **Learn and reflect:** The fact that we gain more knowledge during the project is not reflected in the final software: The design is finished and there is a tight schedule to construct the software – we had no time to think and reflect on feedback (if any…).
- **Decide late:** Too much design up front (BDUF): i.e. drawing GUI mock-ups two months before we started to implement the GUI. Many details were lost during the time lag. Large parts of the budget was spent on early design and left no room for changes later in the project.
- **Eliminate risk – focus on what you don't know:** Insufficient risk reduction early in the project. Often assuming how two systems could be integrated instead of actually integrating them. Waiting for the last minute setting up test and production environment.

Our goal

Our overall goal was to improve (external) quality with regard to both "fitness for use" and "conformance to requirements".

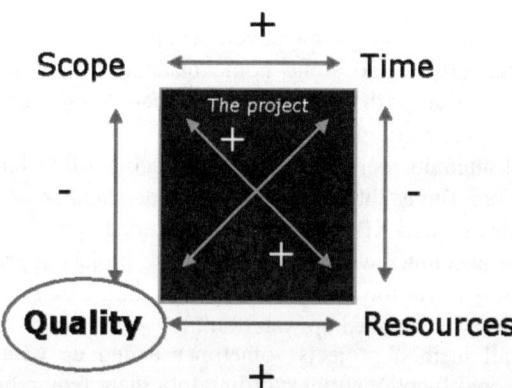

There are various agile methods "out there". BEKK did not choose one specific method, but chose to use the Unified Process (not RUP) as a framework to enhance communication internally – and with customers.

Working with large companies with complex organisations and politics it is necessary to adapt the process accordingly. We adapt the process in every project basing the approach on the values and principles in the Agile Manifesto and focus on the purpose and objective.

Where did our change-drivers lead us?

Communication: Communication based on written documentation and limited dialogue was misinterpreted many times during the development life cycle and led to surprises late in the project.

We had to involve the customer more and not put all our trust in written documentation and formal sign-offs

Change: The environment changes, thoughts and ideas mature and both the customer and the supplier increase their domain knowledge. Acknowledging this made us understand that the requirements shouldn't stay fixed.

We had to create an environment where changes were welcome so that the final product better matches true desires (and time-to-market)

Learn and reflect: The fact that we gained more knowledge during the project was not reflected in the final software: The design was finished and there was a tight schedule to construct the software – no time to think and reflect on feedback (if any...)

We had to create an environment where creativity was not a "been there – done that"

Decide late: Too much design up front (BDUF): i.e. drawing GUI mock-ups two months before we were actually going to implement the GUI. Many details lost during the time lag.

We must design the system as we go based on the accumulated knowledge

Eliminate risk - focus on what you don't know: Insufficient risk reduction early in the project: assuming how two systems could be integrated instead of actually integrating them

We must have early risk mitigation and discovery – tackling the hardest, riskiest problems first

The journey

When introducing agile methods into our organization we tried to **avoid** the following syndrome:

> "Sure, we don't apply waterfall – everyone knows it doesn't work. We've adapted <iterative method X> and are into our first project. We've been at it for two months and have the use case analysis nearly finished, and the plan and schedule of what we'll be doing each iteration. After review and approval of the final requirements set and iterations schedule, we'll start programming."

With support from management BEKK established an internal project called **BAM!** (BEKK Agile Movement), run by people representing all functional areas:

- Management
- Sales
- Information Architecture
- Project Management
- System Development
- Front End Development
- Graphical design
- Management Consulting

BAM! coordinated activities for increasing the knowledge and understanding and enabling the implementation of agile methods into an organization. Some of the activities where:

- Agile Competency Day (internally, for the whole company)
- Monthly meetings discussing agile topics
- Weekly/bi-weekly meetings within each competency group
- Seminars and presentations for our customers

Even though spending time going through the values and principles of the Agile Manifesto, the main focus in the beginning was on the techniques and practices of agile methods (iterations, iteration planning, stand-up meetings, burn-down charts etc). Still getting familiar with this new way of thinking and running projects, it was hard going to our customers and convincing them. Usually the projects adapted some agile practices and tested them out, without calling it an agile project. Step by step our projects evolved into agile projects.

Today

Almost all software development projects are based on Agile methods, though most are based on "waterfall"-contracts. Sales and Project Management are leading the way, trying to find contract models more suitable for Agile projects (fighting the old "waterfall"-contracts). BEKKs employees have a good understanding of Agile methods and have embraced it. Agile is not spoken about as something new anymore, and is not being compared against the waterfall approach – it is now the default way of running projects.

But still, some are doing agile practices without really understanding the purpose of them, which is often related to the fact that they don't fully understand the values and principles in the Agile Manifesto.

It took us 2-3 years of hard work and dedication before we could call ourselves an Agile Company.

Lessons learned

- Involve management, sales and other stakeholders who will be affected (not only developers)
- Find the ambassadors first and use them!
- Don't become "religious" – Agile methods does not alone guarantee success (it's not a silver bullet)
- You need the understanding and trust from the customer
- Don't try to do all at once – listen to your needs

Last, but not least, it's not about producing working software as fast as possible. It's about creating the most value for the customer!

Agile Development Meets Strategic Design in the Enterprise

Eric Wilcox, Stefan Nusser, Jerald Schoudt, Julian Cerruti, and Hernan Badenes

IBM Almaden Research
650 Harry Road
San Jose, CA 95120 USA
{eric_wilcox,nusser,jschoudt,jcerruti,hbadenes}@us.ibm.com

Abstract. In this paper we present our approach to design and develop an enterprise email application called bluemail. We describe our development process that is orchestrated for fast, iterative deployments and aimed at offering increased transparency to our internal user community. We finish by discussing the relationship between iterative design and agile development practices.

Keywords: Agile programming, email, collaboration, research, software engineering methods.

1 Introduction

The motivation for writing this experience report stems from a recently initiated research project called bluemail. The goals of the project are two-fold. Firstly, we wanted to explore alternatives to the well established forms of email-based collaboration. Secondly, we were interested in looking at Ajax web client technologies for rich browser based applications in the enterprise.

It turned out that the software development approach we chose became a critical consideration in contrast to our goals. Broad interest in email encouraged us to find an approach that integrated our internal user community throughout our development cycles. This was particularly important to us since we launched the bluemail effort without requirements from product or service divisions.

To create an engaging and viable email client we also had a constraint to develop quality code with rich functionality. We wanted a transparent, fast-paced, iterative development process geared specifically towards hosted applications.

In this article we describe how we drew on Agile development methodologies to shape our own development process and tooling. We also look at how iterative design practices can be integrated at different levels throughout the process to maintain a consistent and desirable user experience.

2 Development and Design Process

Our development process borrows freely from the Agile family methodologies [1]. We tailored our practices to take advantage of how hosted applications are deployed and used. We focused on continuous deployment and rapid exploration of ideas. The key characteristics are the following:

- **Continuous integration and rapid iterations.** Each creating functional, working code. This principle is at the heart of all Agile development methodologies. It implies that all features get broken down into the smallest possible set of functionality that are each independently deployable. Once that nucleus of functionality is implemented, it is completed by iterative refinement. We also rely heavily on continuous integration [2], building our application several times daily.
- **Continuous deployment.** We further extend the concept of continuous integration by adding an automated deployment step. This makes the application in its current state available to end users on a dedicated development site or in a sandbox as described below.
- **Parallel development efforts with sandboxes.** A sandbox is conceptually a complete clone of the source code repository including associated continuous integration and deployment capabilities. We aggressively use sandboxes for all changes that go beyond what can be completed in a day. The sandbox not only contains code, but also a running instance of the application.
- **Gradual and independent stabilization of features.** Newly implemented features become robust by moving from sandboxes to more stable instances of our application. Along the way, the feature gets exercised by the internal team and our users. The more stable instances serve a larger audience. Introducing a bug has later in the chain has more severe implications. Thus, update cycles become longer as a change migrates from a sandbox through the development instance and the prerelease instance to our production server.

As a result of these principles, our development process has a high degree of transparency. The development team and our user community have, at any point in time, complete insight into the status of all development activities.

3 Putting These Principles to Work – The Bluemail Development Environment

Our development and design process is supported by a development environment that provides the necessary tooling to make source code management, building, and deployment a largely automated process.

We leverage several publicly available tools. Subversion provides the source code management capabilities [4]. Trac, a wiki based project management tool, is used to track bugs and features. We use Cruise Control to monitor source trees and automatically trigger builds upon newly committed modifications [3, 5]. Additionally, we extend this set to automatically deploy and unit test application builds.

Developers can initiate the **creation of a sandbox** from a web-based interface. When this happens, several automated steps are performed:

- Creating a new branch of code is triggered at the source code management level.
- Cruise Control is set to monitor and perform automated builds and unit tests.

- A deployment environment for the sandbox is created which is equivalent to a new instance of the application server with its own URL.
- The sandbox is added to what we call the switchboard – a dynamically generated list of active sandboxes.

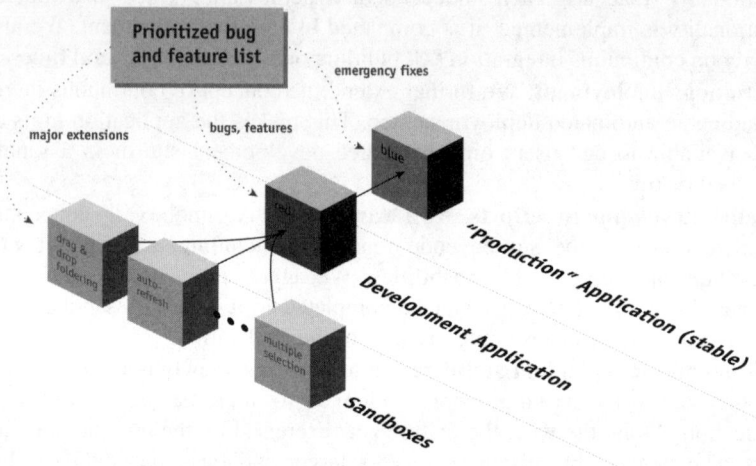

Fig. 1. The sandbox deployment model

As developers commit changes to the main line of code, the isolated branch in the sandbox will become more out of synch. To address this we added tooling support to allow **refreshing the sandbox** with updates from main line of code. Developers perform this process every other day on average. All updates that do not cause merge conflicts are automatically integrated, leaving only a few changes to be manually merged. Committing the refresh triggers a build and execution of our unit test scripts.

One advantage of frequent refreshes is that **dissolving a sandbox** is relatively easy. After going through the refresh procedure described in the previous paragraph, the sandbox and main line of code differ only by the set of changes added in the sandbox. We provide an interface to trigger change merges into the main line. The steps taken are similar to the operation described above except that source and target are reversed.

Sandboxes are intended for changes that take at least one or two days of work. Smaller changes and bug fixes are usually committed directly to the main code.

Periodically, we move the current set of changes from a development instance to a more stable pre-production instance to serve a larger user community. We time it such that we dissolve sandboxes at the beginning of the cycle. Relevant features sit in our development instance for a few days before the code is promoted to the pre-production application version. In Subversion, the level of code on the pre-production instance corresponds to a tagged set of changes. We move current items out of the pre-production instance to live production as newer changes roll in from sandboxes.

It is not uncommon in our environment to have bug fixes go directly into the pre-production instances, forward-fit to the development instance, and back-fit to active sandboxes. Occasionally, a bug has to get fixed directly in the production instance, corresponding to an earlier tagged set of changes in Subversion. As an alternative, the production instance can always be reverted to the previous level of code.

To summarize, our development environment allows us to flexibly work on multiple features in parallel while moving the main line of code forward. It provides opportunity for feedback from developers, designers, and the user community.

4 Strategic Design

Traditional software development models often favor up-front design. Significant resources are spent early in the process to define requirements and architect a system before committing to any lines of code. Design's role often involves producing comprehensive user interface and interaction specifications. Many user-centered design methods (contextual inquiry, card sorting techniques, and participatory design) have been developed that aim at grounding up-front design in user needs and desires. One downfall to these methods is the time necessary to prepare, conduct, and analyze results [6, 7]. In preparing to design bluemail, we felt traditional methods would only result in identifying mostly predicable and well documented problems in email.

Instead of following a path from users to requirements to articulated value and specification, the early design aimed to quickly illustrate a core vision. Light-weight competitive analysis was conducted to see how web-based consumer-driven clients were changing the email landscape. Are there ways to apply these practices to the enterprise? What unique opportunities open up by developing within a company firewall? Answers to these types of questions coupled with a deep understanding of key gaps in product roadmaps enabled the design team to focus on a handful of core values. As coding rolled forward on implementing core email functionality, the vision evolved and was vetted across research, product, and service divisions through a series of presentations. Traditional design artifacts (scenarios and UI mockups) were used as communication tools to position bluemail in regards to product roadmaps.

4.1 Maintaining Vision Across Sandboxes

As bluemail began to take shape through development efforts, design has played a valuable integration role. Design provides a common ground for things to progress in their short-term isolation while maintaining the cross-cutting trajectory for features across sandboxes. When possible, design is able to aid the team by anticipating how two or more elements will merge, and can design each accordingly. An example of this in bluemail involved a goal of providing richer context to messages through linking to shared documents. The email composition header design became a key integration point. One sandbox focused on providing attachment support while another looked to incorporate links and ties to an activity-based document store. Design was able to provide a consistent behavior to both capabilities, and by the time the sandboxes merged, they both employed a consistent user interaction.

Design, in this and many more cases, acted as a middle-man between the high-level vision and bottom-up innovations under development.

4.2 Closing the Loop with End-Users

Once the core mail features had reached a high enough level of maturity, we deployed the bluemail system to a broader number of early adopters. As mentioned earlier, the software as a service deployment model is well suited to take advantage of implicit usage statistics as well as explicit user feedback. Upon rolling out the initial system, we were able to see that people were running into problems during the initial sign-up and login phase. In less than a day, we were able to provide and rollout a fix that incorporated a more guided interaction to users.

As deployment becomes broader, usage patterns play an increasing role in design decisions. As new concepts are experienced by users, we can track their success or failure and use the numbers we record as grounding for future design decisions and a continued dialog with stakeholders in the product and service organizations.

5 Conclusions

The development process described in this experience report has allowed us to implement significant functionality within a few months time. We have begun to build a user community around bluemail and several of our users are engaging in our development effort by using sandboxes. Exploring design alternatives in this way has added grounding to decisions and increased acceptance by our user community.

Sandboxes have also proven to be useful for our geographically distributed development team. Each team member's process becomes transparent to the entire team. Design feedback and code reviews can happen in a targeted manner while feature implementation nears completion in the sandbox.

We plan to apply the process learned here to a different project with a larger team in the coming year.

References

1. Cockburn, A.: Agile Software Development. Addison Wesley, Reading (2002)
2. Fowler, M., Foemmel, M.: Continuous Integration, martinfowler.com/articles/continuousIntegration.html
3. CruiseControl http://cruisecontrol.sourceforge.net/index.html
4. Michael Pilato, C., Ben Collins-Sussman, Fitzpatrick, B.W.: Version Control with Subversion, O'Reilly Media (2004)
5. The Trac User and Administration Guide http://trac.edgewall.org/wiki/TracGuide
6. Lievseley, M.A., Yee, J.S.R.: The Role of the Interaction Designer in an Agile Software Development Process, work in progress report, CHI 2006 (2006)
7. McInerney, P., Maurer, F.: UCD in Agile Projects: Dream Team or Odd Couple? In: Interactions, vol. 12(6), ACM Press, New York (November + December 2005)

An Agile Approach for Integration of an Open Source Health Information System

Guido Porruvecchio[1], Giulio Concas[1], Daniele Palmas[2], and Roberta Quaresima[1]

[1] Dipartimento di Ingegneria Elettrica ed Elettronica, Università di Cagliari,
Piazza d'Armi, 09123 Cagliari, Italy
{guido.porruvecchio,concas,roberta.quaresima}@diee.unica.it
[2] dnlplm@gmail.com

Abstract. In this paper we examine the close relationship that can be established between Agile methodologies and the FLOSS (Free-Libre Open Source Software) development model, by integrating a Health Information System (HIS) into the IT environment of an Italian hospital (a so-called software *verticalization*). We followed XP approach during development of new features. This approach allowed us not only to contribute to the original Open Source project, helping it to become increasingly mature, but also to evaluate in a quantitative manner the effort devoted to the international project, to the national context and to the specific health care organization.

1 Introduction

Care2x [1] is an Open Source project commenced in 2002, for the purpose of creating an integrated health care environment for hospitals and health care organizations. It is based on four major components - a Health Information System, a Practice Management System, a Central Data Server and a Health Exchange Protocol. In this paper we describe an experience with the Care2x HIS, a web application based on PHP and Javascript technologies, which uses an Open Source DBMS (MySQL or PostgreSQL). Its design is modular and can be easily extended by plug-ins. We chose the University Hospital of Cagliari as the environment for integration and testing of the new features we implemented, limiting the scope to a single ward. The result of this activity is a fork of Care2x HIS, named FLOSS-HIS. This is not the first time a health care organization is involved in the deployment of an Open Source IT infrastructure [2], but in this case it is intended to stress the importance of adopting an agile methodology in such activities.

2 The Development Process

Choosing the XP approach for the development allowed us to track the process in detail, obtaining useful information about the development effort, which will be analyzed later in this paper. In this paragraph we describe the two main phases of the development process:

1. Requirements elicitation and coding
2. In-ward testing

Following XP guidelines [3], the iterations in the development were quite short (one or two weeks), allowing us to receive enough feedback from the customer to satisfy his needs [4]. The development team comprised a senior and a junior programmer, with the support of a senior coach, and the developers strictly followed the pair programming practice [5] during the entire coding activity.

2.1 Requirements Elicitation and Coding

During this phase, our customer was one of the hospital's IT managers; he developed the HIS currently used and his knowledge of the information flow through the hospital areas enabled us to better focus on the missing features to be implemented and on the necessary minor tweaks to the code. User stories were the main tool in this phase [6], and all the results of our work were built thereon. Indeed, by estimating the time needed for each task and recording the actual time needed for its implementation, we were able to collect all the data presented in this work. We also used XPSwiki software [7], which helped us to track and record the user stories related data; it can also generate XMI exports for further elaboration [8].

The main additions to Care2x system implemented in this phase, not considering the minor changes and bug fixes, can be summarized as follows:

- **User access control:** it is now possible to manage and fine-tune the access privileges to the various application functionalities, taking into account the user role (i.e., doctor, nurse, system administrator, etc.). To develop this feature we used phpGACL [9], an Open Source PHP library which provides the classes to implement a powerful access management system, using the Access Control List pattern.
- **Laboratory interface:** an interface between the HIS and laboratory machines was implemented to automate the acquisition, storing and printing of the exams requests and results.
- **ICD9CM codes:** ICD (International Classification of Diseases) is the international standard diagnostic classification for epidemiologic and health management. We needed to implement the ICD version currently adopted in Italy, because Care2x uses the latest version, ICD10.
- **Clinical exams integration:** the exam list was far from complete, so we had to add a lot of exam types to the application, especially those used in the ward where we tested the software.

2.2 In-Ward Testing

After the first phase, the software was ready to be installed on a server machine and tested by hospital personnel. Initially, we concentrated our efforts on activities like software and database installation/configuration, data migration and user training (creating a simple manual for the most common tasks). Then new requirements were collected from the medical personnel who helped us in this phase (as new customers), so further features were developed, mainly regarding functionalities too specialized to be reused outside the local context. The feedback from the users was very important for fully understanding how to satisfy their needs. We found a further demonstration of the importance of communication between users and developers to improve software quality and customer satisfaction. This is true also in the Open Source development model, were the attention is focused more on the communication among the developers of the community [10].

3 Results: Analysis and Discussion

We extracted from the user stories the data about the development effort (in practice, the time needed to complete each task of each story, expressed in man-hours), to highlight the kind of contribution each feature provided in terms of reuse, considering its scope (local, national, international). For this purpose, we made the following effort classification:

1. **International:** New features and bug fixes that can be presented to Care2x developers community and integrated into a future software release. This represented the main contribution to the Open Source project, and its "international" value as far as our work is concerned.
2. **National:** Features that are considered mandatory in order to adapt the software to the Italian context.
3. **Local:** Features and customizations aiming to satisfy specific needs of the University Hospital, whose reuse in another environment might be quite complicated, due to different practices; this constitutes the software verticalization.
4. **Support:** Care2x code analysis and understanding, creation and configuration of tools for the development team.

We included in the first category user access management, other minor functionalities (like a browser extension to enable kiosk mode) and bug fixes.

Regarding the national context, the most relevant modification is the ICD9CM codes implementation. In general, these two categories include functionalities that were developed during the first phase, while most of the hospital-related features were requested, and developed, during in-ward testing.

As far as the last category is concerned, this consists mainly of the study tasks (used to understand the code we had to modify) and marginally of other activities, like IDE configuration and test framework development. This contribution may at first be considered of marginal utility, but the importance of software knowledge becomes clear in case of further deployments.

Overall, the team worked for 154 man-days; the following tables show the distribution of effort across the process phases.

During the first phase, the major effort was spent in developing highly reusable modules (international and national context); this is a predictable result, because the first features added were those rated as key features by the customer (i.e. user access management), so they had to be developed as soon as possible. Also a great deal of time was spent studying the software code, as it was at the beginning of the project.

Table 1. Effort spent during requirement elicitation and coding phase

Category	Man-days	Share
International context	53.5	40.5%
National context	18.7	14.2%
Local verticalization	26.7	20.2%
Support activities	33.1	25.1%
TOTAL	**132**	**100%**

Table 2. Effort spent during in-ward testing phase

Category	Man-days	Share
International context	3	13.6%
National context	7	31.8%
Local verticalization	11	50.0%
Support activities	1	4.6%
TOTAL	**22**	**100%**

Table 3. Total project effort

Category	Man-days	Share
International context	56.5	36.7%
National context	25.7	16.7%
Local verticalization	37.7	24.4%
Support activities	34.1	22.2%
TOTAL	**154**	**100%**

As expected, in-ward testing produced mainly hospital-related functionalities (sometimes ward-related) because, as already mentioned, the doctor who provided the requirements focused his attention on specific needs of his hospital and his ward. In addition, we were at a more advanced project phase, so the most important features had already been developed, and there was little need to spend further effort in system understanding.

Another kind of data we were able to extract from user stories is how the effort distribution evolved with iterations (Fig. 1):

The graphs clearly show a predominance of the international contribution and of the system study at the beginning of the project, while during the later iterations we focused mainly on the local side of the project. We observed the same behavior on a larger scale, examining the entire development process. The data regarding the national aspect are not very meaningful, because they contain too few features, so do not follow a specific trend.

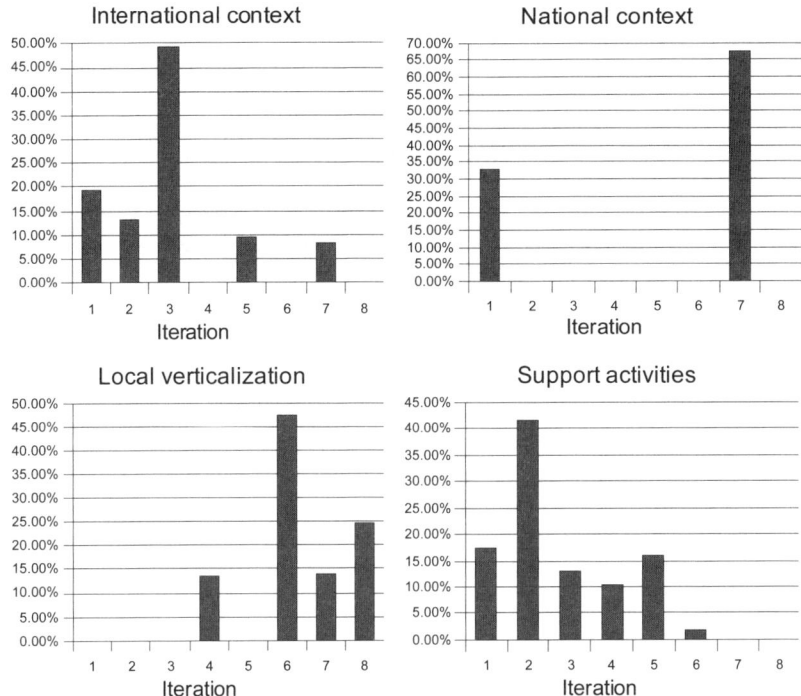

Fig. 1. Effort distribution during the first phase iterations

4 Conclusion

The experience described in this paper shows that adopting an agile methodology not only results in the developers producing better quality software, but it can also help to explore the various implications an Open Source project can have. Thanks to the information provided by user stories, we were able to evaluate to what extent the effort spent during the development was reusable, so as to identify in which context it could bring real benefits. In this specific experience, we found that a project like FLOSS-HIS, conceived as a software verticalization with only local scope, provided instead a significant contribution to the originating Open Source project as a whole.

References

1. Care2x Project Home Page, http://care2x.org
2. Fitzgerald, B., Kenny, T.: Developing an information systems infrastructure with open source software. IEEE Software 21(1), 50–55 (2004)
3. Beck, K.: Extreme Programming Explained: Embrace Change. Addison Wesley, Reading (2004)
4. Martin, A., Biddle, R., Noble, J.: The XP customer role in practice: three studies. Agile Development Conference (2004)

5. Williams, L.A., Kessler, R.: Pair Programming Illuminated. Addison Wesley, Reading (2002)
6. Cohn, M.: User stories applied for Agile software development. Addison Wesley, Reading (2004)
7. Pinna, S., Lorrai, P., Marchesi, M., Serra, N.: Developing a Tool Supporting XP Process. In: Maurer, F., Wells, D. (eds.) XP/Agile Universe 2003. LNCS, vol. 2753, Springer, Heidelberg (2003)
8. Cau, A., Concas, G., Mannaro, K., Marchesi, M., Pinna, S., Serra, N.: XMI for XP project data interchange. In: Proceedings of QUTE SWAP workshop on QUantitative TEchniques for SoftWare Agile Processes (2004)
9. phpGACL Project Home Page http://phpgacl.sourceforge.net
10. Hemetsberger, A., Reinhardt, C.: Sharing and creating knowledge in Open Source community – The case of KDE. The fifth European conference on Organizational Knowledge, Learning and Capabilities (2004)

Agile Practices in a Large Organization: The Experience of Poste Italiane

Mauro Sulfaro[1], Michele Marchesi[2], and Sandro Pinna[2]

[1] Poste Italiane S.p.A, Chief Information Office System Management, Polo Tecnologico Piemonte Liguria e Valle d'Aosta
sulfarom@posteitaliane.it
[2] Dipartimento di Ingegneria Elettrica ed Elettronica, Università di Cagliari,
Piazza d'Armi, 09123 Cagliari, Italy
{michele,pinnasandro}@diee.unica.it

Abstract. In this paper we show how agile practices have been used at the Poste Italiane for building a monitoring system of its complex IT infrastructure. The system, called Datamart, is built upon the existing monitoring infrastructure. A testing framework has been developed for performing assertion checking either on existing legacy modules or on the new functionalities. This framework is currently used, and is able to process data coming from 100,000 distributed computers, enabling and improving their centralized control.

1 The Context

In this paper we present an experience regarding the adoption of agile practices in Poste Italiane, a large organization which offers a complete range of postal services and a large number of financial services in Italy. This complex organization comprises several thousand business units distributed throughout Italy and linked up through the group's IT infrastructure.

A business unit may be either a post office in a city or in a remote village, or an important regional or national business center, all sharing a basic model based on the lifecycle of a single atomic entity: the single workstation (or the server).

The main problem of such a large organization is to be able to satisfy business demand in a continually changing market. To achieve this goal we need to manage more than 100.000 units all over Italy.

This would be a simple matter if we could disregard the dynamic feature of this system. Unfortunately (but fortunately for our project) the changes, either business driven or technology driven, occur everyday and in our experience the need to support these changes is the primary requirement for our organization. To this purpose, we have in place a number of infrastructures, each of them being responsible for managing a single aspect of our ICT business. These vertical layers could be regarded as a single competence, so we speak vertically of Antivirus Platform, Asset Management Platform, Software Distribution Platform, Cash Dispenser Platform, System Management Platform and so on, up to the next vertical layer (the future, as yet unknown platform that the business will require).

2 The Project Datamart

In this context it was decided to experiment agile methodologies to develop a monitoring system, called Datamart, aimed to ease the use and leverage the existing complex infrastructures.

And now for the figures: Poste Italiane has more than 100.000 computers (servers & clients) spread over more than 20.000 subnets and from the outset the company equipped its ICT infrastructure with systems able to monitor their hardware devices, applications and services.

In this huge context, we experienced some difficulty in effectively tracking the dynamic behavior of the system and found that the functionalities of each infrastructure could be improved by cross-correlating the information provided by each subsystem. This is the aim of the Datamart project described herein.

We implemented the Datamart system using an incremental and iterative approach, guided by user stories. The first release was guided by the high-level schedule goal[1] : "Every subsystem needs to collaborate to describe the management domain". At the end of the first release we found that there were a large number of machines that were not recognized by any subsystem, thus obtaining the first valuable outcome: each subsystem, initially described only in terms of internal infrastructure metrics, could be more exhaustively reviewed in terms of a more realistic overall metric derived by integrating the data shared among all the subsystems.

The next schedule goal: "The system must drive the transition among states, triggering certified actions" creates the basis for all subsequent development, including refactoring of the interfaces of the vertical layers quoted in the previous section. The goal is to be able to identify the basic events to be shared among all infrastructures in a simple, certified way.

The first problem that developers have to face is a communication problem due to the lack of a shared vocabulary of domain specific terms. Starting from the XP lessons that enable the spread of knowledge among team members, it was decided to model the domain in order to establish not only a common vocabulary, but also a common approach between business units.

The functionalities have been analyzed and collected using user stories. CRC cards have also been used to better explain responsibilities and intermodule collaboration.

Finally, some state diagrams have been written for effectively representing and standardizing the dynamic behavior of the basic entities.

In order to modify such a complex system one must ascertain that the modifications do not introduce errors in the modules or result in the loss of existing functionalities. The XP addresses this problem by prescribing the writing of unit and acceptance tests that are automatically executed each time there is a system change.

The context in which the Datamart operates is that of an infrastructure composed of numerous subsystems, each one with its own legacy monitoring infrastructure. The Datamart system is able to integrate and manage the data generated by these subsystems. So, writing a testing framework for such system was a challenge, as pointed out in the next section.

---

[1] John Kern, "Goal-centric Process and Project Management", The Coad Letter, Issue 104, 7 Nov 2002.

3 The Practices

In order to test the functionalities of the existing legacy systems and the new added features, an ad-hoc test framework was created that allowed to execute assertions in an automated and repeatable way. A peculiar characteristic of Datamart system is that the assertions are not simply used during development as regression tests; in fact the framework triggers execution of the assertions during normal operation, so as to collect metrics from the meta-model. Metrics have been defined at a meta-model level and can therefore be replicated for every subsystem. They contribute to finding the number of entities that mismatch assertions, helping to identify the causes and adopt corrective measures.

Another characteristic of the test framework is that it is able to activate, in a supervised manner, the actions for given triggering conditions. As an example, an action could be the addition of a new workstation in a specific subsystem or the deletion of a workstation from all the subsystems.

Datamart has been developed following an iterative and incremental approach; this approach allowed the team to give value to the customer from the very first steps of the development phase. Moreover, this turned out to be a winning approach because it enabled to obtain feedback from the customer early on. The requirements have been collected in an agile way using the user stories.

The Pair-Programming technique and the continuous feedback have in this case brought systems development from mere encoding carried out by the developers to a precise understanding of all codifications, sharing an advanced level of Business Process Rules (BPR).

Another important result of Datamart has been standardization of the interfaces for interaction with the subsystems, based on a model shared that the suppliers have to use to enable them to supply new functionalities to the system.

In this way, technology changes can now be encouraged, maintaining the BPR previously defined at the model layer.

4 Conclusion

The shared model proved to be an excellent communication tool. The test framework was useful for writing regression tests and also for collecting the metrics important for system monitoring.

The iterative and incremental approach has been perceived as a major innovation compared to the traditional methods. It has also been appreciated by management because of the possibility it offers to obtain value early on and of providing early feedback to the team, laying out the basis of its further adoption in other projects.

Acknowledgement

This work was supported by MAPS (Agile Methodologies for Software Production) project, of FIRB research fund of MIUR; contract number: RBNE01JRK8.

Multi-tasking Agile Projects: The Focal Point

Ruud Wijnands and Ingmar van Dijk

MiPlaza, Philips Researh Laboratories, HTC 29,
5656AE Eindhoven, Netherlands
{Ruud.Wijnands,Ingmar.van.Dijk}@philips.com

Abstract. This paper outlines what happens when a team has to work on more than one project at a time. It explains how time can be divided, the team's challenges and how to priorities can be set when more projects are approaching deadlines at the same time.

Keywords: release planning , iteration planning, iteration length, challenges, escalation, deadline pressure.

1 Introduction

Together we have 8 years of agile software development experience working on various projects within Philips Research. Philips is Europe's largest electronics company and owns one of the world's major private research organizations with laboratories spread throughout the world. These laboratories create value and growth for Philips through technology-based innovations in both the healthcare and lifestyle domains. Deliverables of Philips Research are standards, patents and publications, each accompanied by hardware and/or software prototypes as a proof of concept.

2 The Context

Some of our customers only have budget to pay for a single software developer up to a particular deadline. Since we do XP/SCRUM we require at least two developers to work on a project to facilitate pair programming. This non-ideal situation does not allow the developers to switch pairs, but we have found it to be far more optimal than not being able to pair program at all.

The consequence of this requirement is that the budget is consumed twice as fast. The work also gets done at least twice as fast with respect to the original timeline.

Additionally, many of our customers create joined collaborations with other parties to get to a prototype or a product. This means that the software development teams are basically one of their suppliers. Often the team needs to collaborate with one or more of these partners of the customer.

2.1 Dividing Your Time

The increased velocity is sometimes not acceptable to our customers. You might think: "Huh?" Well, the explanation is that our customers also have a timeline and often require input from other partners too. These partners often have milestones that may fit the original timeline of our customer. Consequently, our developers are sometimes waiting for deliveries of other parties.

To solve this issue we let our developers work on that project for 50% of their time to reduce deviations of the original schedule of our customer. When this happens, we have to find some other project we can do in the remaining 50% of our time to assure people are booked fulltime.

This gets our developers in the situation where they have to find a way to do agile planning and tracking for two projects in parallel.

3 Iteration Length and Allocation

As always the team has to choose an iteration length for each project and they will have to decide when an iterations starts and when it ends. When the team works 50% on one project and 50% on the other, then two week iterations are not a nice option for the customers unless they are alternating over 4 weeks periods.

We have tried several options. The first option was to have the team work three days on project A and the other two on project B and then the next week the other way around. This proved hard to most team members because this resulted in a context switch during the week.

The next option we tried was working two week iterations by working one week on project A and the other week on project B. This worked out relatively fine, but also was not very nice for the customer, because this sometimes lead to unfinished user stories during the first week. Consequently, the customer would only have partial user stories finished.

The next option we tried was to work in iterations of one week starting on Monday and ending on Friday. Let's say every even week on project A and every odd week on project B. This seems to have a number of unexpected advantages. First of all this challenges the team to create small user stories, so they are sure they can finish a number of them and also complete all of them. The second advantage is that since the user stories are so small, it is easy to get started, stay focussed and finish them. A third advantage is that the team is less tempted to do gold-plating. A fourth advantage is that the customers have a week in between. This gives them the opportunity to more often change the priorities in the backlog and this appears to be advantages in a more research like environment like ours.

A disadvantage is, that this way of working is harder and definitely not for everyone. We believe it requires more experienced extreme programmers, because here the team's discipline is tested to a larger extend. And of course we should not forget that the team still has to cope with the context switches. This brings us to the next advice: make sure your iterations run from a Monday until the Friday. Do not have iterations that e.g. start on Wednesday to Wednesday the next week. In the latter case teams will be more easily tempted to work over the weekend, just to get some extra stories finished. In the view of sustainable pace people should avoid doing that as much as possible. Additionally, in the first case the context switch takes place during the weekend and this has its advantages, since most people have a context switch then anyway.

Due to the short iterations having a proper plan becomes more important, consequently acceptance criteria should be available at the start of a new iteration and not half way during the iteration. Effectiveness is influenced in case of doing more than one project in parallel. The team will be challenged in producing an equally large output compared to a single project with a two-week iteration as a result of reduced effectiveness and reduced velocity.

4 Single Point of Escalation

When a team works on more than one project, it can make a whole lot of difference when they are dealing with a single or with multiple customers.

4.1 A Different Customer for Each Project

When executing more than one project with the same team, it is very important that the team can get the priorities right. When each project has its own customer, this can be a challenge. Basically, both customers need to be setting the priorities as always in agile projects.

However, customers are people too (yeah... really!) and they will always try to get as much as possible. So reducing scope just before a deadline is sometimes hard for them. They must choose and depending on the maturity as a manager, they will either choose or they will say something like: "It does not matter in which order you will implement the stories; I need all of them anyway." You can image that this is not helping the team and this also increases the pressure.

In case you deal with a different customer for each project, you should make it very clear that there is not a trivial option to let people work overtime, just to get what they want. Working overtime shall only be used in very exceptional cases. It should be clear to the customer, that the only options he has during the time that the team works for him, is to either add more people to the team or to reduce scope.

The first option of adding more people usually does not help a team that is already under pressure. It becomes clear from the release planning meetings that something like this may be needed on the long run and new team members can be added to the team before the pressure is increased. But for the first period of 1 to 3 months the new staff will be a net liability.

The second option is easier than you might expect, but also requires a bit of educating your customer. Eventually, when time is up your customer can only get what is done. If not all user stories are done and your customer was one of those who did not want to choose, he will be confronted with this fact of life. The problem with this option is that motivated developers usually feel very uncomfortable with it and will be tempted to do more as we outlined before.

Working for multiple customers can be a problem when deadlines are approaching. Customers generally are willing to help out another customer by allowing the team to work more on the project that is nearing the deadline. But when two customers want to meet a deadline and the team feels it cannot make both of them, we always try to make sure the team leader has a single point for escalation. This person then has to decide where priorities lie. Usually, this is possible for a team creating in-house software.

4.2 A Single Customer for Both Projects

When a team is working for a single customer on more than one project, then things are easier. The customer can be confronted with an additional level of prioritizing.

Namely, when one or more projects are under time pressure, he not only has to prioritize the user stories, but also should prioritize between projects.

The customer can choose which project gets the highest priority and can allow a team to do more work for the project under pressure. When both projects are under pressure, it is basically the problem of the customer to choose between the two of them. In the previous case where there are multiple customers involved, the team is challenged in their negotiation skills to make things work. This challenge is not present when your team works for a single customer.

5 Dependencies and Risk Management

Most software projects have dependencies to people, hardware or other software. When handling more than one project, it requires more skills to make sure that everyone or everything is available to the team.

In case the customer collaborates with a number of partners to get to a product, the software team often has to communicate about outcomes with these partners too.

With less experienced teams it is sometimes a better idea to make this the customers' responsibility. In such a case the team is responsible for clearly communicating any dependencies they have with respect to deliverables by partners. The team is also responsible for making clear what the impact is to their planning and schedule when partners are not able to deliver in time, deliver something else than expected or needed or do not deliver at all.

Agile teams are usually quite strong in finding alternative solutions, so when communicating the iteration and release plan, they should identify possible dependencies and create mitigation plans together with the customer just in case partners do not deliver as expected.

With a more experienced team it is better to leave identifying risks and mitigation to the team. It is not uncommon that an agile team finishes early with respect to schedules of others. Consequently, an agile team can be slowed down by others. When the team can track dependencies and mitigation plans themselves, they can make this an integral part of their iteration and release planning and deal with this as user stories.

We have found that experienced teams prefer this way of working to avoid waiting time or sudden big bang integrations. Experienced agile teams are often quite capable of helping partners to deliver in time. By the way, this is fun for a team too, since the pressure is with others and not with them.

The latter is only advisable when the team has already built a trusting relationship with the customer. Such a relation is usually only present when a customer has worked with the team for a longer period of time.

References

1. Watt, R.J., Leigh-Fellows, D.: Acceptance Test Driven Planning, Extreme Programming and Agile Methods – XP/Agile Universe 2004. In: Zannier, C., Erdogmus, H., Lindstrom, L. (eds.) XP/Agile Universe 2004. LNCS, Vol. 3134, Springer, Heidelberg (2004)
2. Cohn, M.: Agile Estimating and Planning. Robert C. Martin Series, Prentice Hall, Englewood Cliffs

Extreme Programming Security Practices

Xiaocheng Ge[1], Richard F. Paige[1], Fiona Polack[1], and Phil Brooke[2]

[1] Department of Computer Science, University of York, UK
{xchge,paige,fiona}@cs.york.ac.uk
[2] School of Computing, University of Teesside, UK
pjb@scm.tees.ac.uk

Abstract. Current practice suggests that security is considered through all stages of the software development life cycle, and that a risk-based and plan-driven approach is best suited to establish security criteria. Based on experience in applying security practices, this paper proposes two new security practices, security training and a fundamental security architecture, for applying Extreme Programming.

1 Introduction

Software security means different things to different people in different contexts. On one hand, software security is about delivering secure software: designing/implementing/testing software to be secure, and educating software developers, architects, and users about how to fulfil security tasks. On the other hand, software security is about protecting software and their surrounding systems in a post facto way, i.e., after development is complete.

General security evaluation criteria and guidelines, such as the Common Criteria [1], presume that security must be considered from the start of a development process, because security, like safety or dependability, is a system-wide emergent property that requires advance planning and careful design. But modern software projects also recognise that change is inevitable; for example a sudden change in the business environment might change the course of the project. The operational environment is so integral to security that a change of environment is likely to expose the system to new or unforeseen threats.

Agile methodologies, such as Extreme Programming (XP) [4] attempt to respond to change in a productive manner. Security, like other quality attributes, is not a native consideration of any existing Agile process. Indeed, security considerations clash with many of the intrinsic development goals (e.g., efficiency and usability). There is a range of work addressing the addition of security considerations to Agile development processes, e.g, [2,3,5,6,11]. Whilst these start to address the tensions between agility and the existing security practices and evaluation, the state-of-the-art is still a loose collection of ideas and techniques with little evidence that they reliably produce systems with the desired security attributes. Based on our experience, we are exploring a synthesis of these ideas into *agile practices* that can be tailored to the needs of software projects where security is a concern.

2 Security Practices in the Planning Game

As practitioners become more aware of software security's importance, they are increasingly adopting and evolving a set of best practices to address the problem. Security engineering aims to ensure that security concerns should be taken at every stage of software development life cycle. In the cases of applying agile methods, the obstacles are studied in [3,5,6,11]. At a certain level of abstraction, almost all agile methods follow a loose iterated process: *planning, designing, coding,* then *testing.* Among these phases, *planning* is especially important because it always determines the course of the software project, and it is the key element which makes the method differs from plan-driven methodology.

XP is based on simple rules and a small number of practices. In *planning*, the practices used are as follows: user stories are written; release planning creates the schedule; make frequent small releases; measure project velocity; divide the project into iterations; iteration planning commences each iteration; move people around; start each day with a stand-up meeting; and fix XP when it breaks.

Based on our experience in applying XP, and more generally in building a variety of secure information systems, we suggest that there are two essential security practices that are compatible with XP. They are:

- *Security training* for all participants of the project, including the customer. The customer and developers need appropriate security knowledge from the start of the project. They must understand basic terminology (e.g., risks, vulnerabilities, assets) and notions of risk assessment. We suggests that the likelihood that the system will satisfy its security requirements will be correlated to the relevant security knowledge of the customer and team members. Whilst specifics of security training differ across projects, common themes that are compatible with XP are: writing a security story; understanding common security attacks and vulnerabilities; avoiding known poor practice in programming; and performing security testing.
- A *fundamental security architecture* is defined before iterations commence. The fundamental security architecture is of critical importance, as it outlines what security mechanisms are available in the IS platform (e.g, DBMS access control mechanisms etc.), and how these mechanisms relate to identified risks and vulnerabilities [6]. Moreover, a fundamental security architecture encodes best-practice and proven experience: a system architect can apply experience from other software projects. A fundamental architecture could, for instance, be represented as a collection of engineering patterns.

3 Security Training

The reality is that establishing software security is an exercise in security risk management. Security practitioners often point out that security is not a purely technical problem. Problems are inevitable if participants in a project team are not security-aware. This problem is exacerbated in people-oriented processes such as XP. Improving the security awareness of the whole project team is obviously important.

The practice of security training is focused on improving organisational security capabilities and providing appropriate technical knowledge. In addition to security professionals or experts, the human roles involved in an software project can be classified into:

- *Stakeholders*, including several roles in XP: customers, coaches, trackers, and manager. They always provide the stories that form the metaphor of the development, and answer subsequent questions.
- *Developers*, including metaphor, programmers and testers. They work from the requirements of stakeholders and security experts, with the goal of delivering an appropriate system.

The requirements of security training vary for different roles. Training for stakeholders are the more general, focusing on how to respect security policies when requesting new functionality, and ultimately when using the system. Developers need technical training for specific system architectures, explaining built-in or add-on security mechanisms. They also need training that enables them to modify existing mechanisms, and to design and install new mechanisms where necessary.

System attacks rarely create security holes; they simply exploit existing ones. Unidentified security vulnerabilities are typically the result of poor software design and implementation, whilst the exploitation of identified vulnerabilities is the result of poor risk assessment. Improving the security knowledge and awareness of developers can mitigate these vulnerabilities and risks. However, enhanced security awareness by project participants is not normally a sufficient substitute for a security lead in the development team. A security specialist brings deep understanding of security issues and of software development, and acts as a resource for the development team. In some cases, the security specialist takes a role of coach in the project.

4 Fundamental Architecture

Software security is a system-wide issue that takes into account both system architecture (such as the model of access control) and concrete security mechanisms (such as the implementations of access control). Whilst many security vulnerabilities arise through poor implementation, significant mitigation can be achieved by a strong fundamental security architecture.

The key to meeting the security requirements of a system is risk management; to manage security risk, threats must be identified early, and it must be possible to analyse their implications. This is facilitated by incremental development of a security-focused architecture, or high-level platform design, that allows assessment of risks and rigorous security testing of deliverables. The security architecture captures the experiences of the similar system developments. It provides a basis on which to address the trade-off between security requirements and functional user stories.

The practice of creating the fundamental architecture is not incompatible with the spirit of XP (see [7]), and related XP values, especially simplicity. [6] shows that a security architecture can be constructed incrementally, and demonstrates that the practice of constructing a security architecture itself is agile too.

Several artifacts and tasks can help to create a fundamental architecture:

1. Architectural risk analysis. The central activity of architectural risk analysis is to build up a consistent view of the target software system at a *reasonably* high level. The most appropriate level for this description is the typical "white board" view of boxes and arrows describing the interaction of various critical components of software system.
2. Practical security handbooks on software systems, such as [12], and programming languages, such as [9], which either implicitly or explicitly document security best-practice.
3. Experience and knowledge of other software projects. These are not always formally documented but they are transmitted to every participant in the project by security training.

The practice of fundamental architecture is also supported by recognised security tactics, such as *defence in depth* and *fail securely*. To conform to XP values, the fundamental architecture should be as simple as possible, e.g., a basic outline for the first release, with new features incrementally added in later iterations.

5 Conclusion

Proven principles and practices for building secure software build on hundreds of years of security experience in a variety of situations, from military defence to software engineering.

In addressing the need for seamless integration with agile practices, we analysed common elements of established security practices in two ways:

1. By qualitative argument that the security practices are *not incompatible* with the agile values, principles, and technical practices.
2. Through experiments and case studies.

Both are necessary – the first demonstrates a conservative form of *compatibility* between a specific agile process and the security practices, whilst the second demonstrates the *practicality* of adding new practices to an existing process.

We conducted a review of the security practices used in [8,10,13,12] and elsewhere, with the aim of identifying a sufficient set to integrate with XP for software development. For each practice, we identified whether it supported each of the five XP values. We found that many of the security practices are compatible with XP's values. For instance, security reviews emphasise communication and feedback, whilst a simple security solution is always preferred because it is less likely to have unintended side-channels, and is easier to demonstrate to external assessors. Furthermore, nothing in the security practices reviewed contradicts the values of courage and respect. A summary of this review is in Table 1.

Table 1. The embodiment of XP Values by Security Practices

	Security Training	Fundamental Architecture
Communication	√	√
Simplicity	n/a	√
Feedback	√	√
Courage	√	n/a
Respect	√	n/a

We then considered similarity to the key XP practices dictating simplicity, embracing change, and incrementation. At the end, we selected the two essential security practices used in planning. Our approach was specifically focused on low-risk systems which are commonly developed using agile methods.

References

1. Common criteria for information technology security evaluation, version 2.5. ISO/IEC 18405 (2005)
2. Aydal, E.G., Paige, R.F., Chivers, H., Brooke, P.J.: Brooke. Security planning and refactoring in extreme programming. In: Abrahamsson, P., Marchesi, M., Succi, G. (eds.) XP 2006. LNCS, vol. 4044, pp. 154–163. Springer, Heidelberg (2006)
3. Baskerville, R.: Agile security for information warefare: a call for research. In: Proc. ECIS2004, Turku, Finland, June (2004)
4. Beck, K., Andres, C.: Extreme Programming Explained: Embrace Change. 2nd edn., Addison-Wesley, Reading (November 2004)
5. Beznosov, K.: Extreme security engineering. In: Proc. BizSec Fairfax, VA (October 2003)
6. Chivers, H., Paige, R.F., Ge, X.: Agile security using an incremental security architecture. In: Baumeister, H., Marchesi, M., Holcombe, M. (eds.) XP 2005. LNCS, vol. 3556, pp. 57–65. Springer, Heidelberg (2005)
7. Fowler, M.: Is design dead? (May 2004), http://www.martinfowler.com/articles/designDead.html
8. Graff, M., van Wyk, K.: Secure Coding, Principles, and Practices. O'Reilly (2002)
9. Kumar, P.: J2EE Security for Servlets, EJBs, and Web Services. Prentice Hall PTR, Englewood Cliffs (2004)
10. Pfleeger, C.P.: Security in Computing, 2nd edn. Prentice Hall, Englewood Cliffs (1997)
11. Siponen, M., Baskerville, R., Kuivalainen, T.: Integrating security into agile development methods. In: Proc. 38th HICSS (2005)
12. Tracy, M., Jansen, W., McLamon, M.: Guidelines on securing public web servers. Technical report, NIST 800-44 (September 2002)
13. Viega, J., McGraw, G.: Building Secure Software. Addison-Wesley, Reading (2002)

Multi-tasking Agile Projects: The Pressure Tank

Ruud Wijnands and Ingmar van Dijk

MiPlaza, Philips Researh Laboratories, HTC 29,
5656AE Eindhoven, Netherlands
{Ruud.Wijnands,Ingmar.van.Dijk}@philips.com

Abstract. This paper explains how teams and their customers try to save time when under time pressure when a deadline is approaching. We explain how best-practices and team communication are influenced by time pressure. Furthermore we also explain how team leads or SCRUM Masters can help a team during such a time.

Keywords: project, simultaneous, time pressure, deadline, SCRUM, best-practice, retrospective, pair programming.

1 Introduction

Together we have 8 years of agile software development experience working on various projects within Philips Research. Philips is Europe's largest electronics company and owns one of the world's major private research organizations with laboratories spread throughout the world. These laboratories create value and growth for Philips through technology-based innovations in both the healthcare and lifestyle domains. Deliverables of Philips Research are standards, patents and publications, each accompanied by hardware and/or software prototypes as a proof of concept.

2 The Context

It is not uncommon that software development teams can work under non-ideal circumstances. Working on more than one project simultaneously is sometimes unavoidable and although agile teams are usually very flexible it is often still quite a challenge. Except the problem of how to plan the teams' time, there are several other challenges which we will discuss here.

3 Temptation Island

Multitasking influences the team's output. It often results in a drop in the team's velocity, but this is not the only effect. Once the pressure for a deadline increases, the team will be tempted to increase the output to satisfy the customer. Of course we know that the customer should reduce the scope in case the team cannot finish all stories before a deadline. In most cases the customer is not the problem. More often it happens that the team is so motivated that they really want to try and finished more than they expect that can be done. Basically, everyone should be happy in such a situation, right? Well, some second thoughts might be appropriate here. When the team gets into this mode of persisting to finish more user stories, they tend to loose focus on code quality and when acceptance tests may not be sufficiently clear, they tend to be tempted to fill-in the details themselves. You might be thinking here: "Hey, they are pair programming and therefore continuously reviewing the code, so what's the problem?" Right, the problem is that in these cases most developers become more flexible and allow pairs to split and work (test, code, refactor) separately. Even though they know solo work has its influence on the code quality and they almost always admit this. So why are they doing this? Most of the time they fall back into old habits and start believing again that when two programmers do stuff in parallel, things will go faster. Hey, you're working on two things at a time, so you must be faster, right?

We would be lying to say this is wrong. In some cases it is true. When two developers are working on something they have done many times before and it is really obvious to both of them what needs to be done and how it needs to be done, then working separately can increase velocity. In most cases, however it is not. Temporarily, they seem to increase speed and they do finish more user stories. However, after the specific deadline we see teams need more refactoring compared to when they pair all the time.

4 Pair Programming Challenged

Pair programming is very intensive, as most developers who ever used it will know. Switching pairs is also intensive and can be a challenge when two developers have different levels of experience. Pair programming also results in task switching. One moment you are working a user story A and after the switch you may be working on user story B. This type of switching may involve some learning time too when you switch to a user story that requires different domain knowledge. Consequently, the pair may be slowed down temporarily because one of the pair needs some time to explain stuff to his new partner.

We have seen that pair switching sometimes occurs less often when pressure increases. What happens is that team mates that prefer each other tend to pair more often and longer with each other.

You need to be careful with this, because it may influence the quality of the deliverables. One way of dealing with this we have found to work quite well, is that a pair must switch at least between every two user stories. This means that a pair is allowed to work together on a single user story and finish it together too. This reduces the spreading of knowledge, but it is ok when user stories are small. To us small user stories take no more than half a day to finish for a pair.

5 Inter –and Intra Team Communication

When a team is multi-tasking over projects, communication becomes more important than ever and it also becomes harder than ever. Team members will be challenged on the level of their inter-personal communication skills.

We believe a team lead or a Scrum master can get a feeling over 'Agile Maturity Level' of a team when the pressure increases. During such a moment, it becomes tempting to fall back into 'old' habits and to lose discipline. This discipline is meant to help teams to keep their heartbeat going. Teams with a high 'Agile Maturity Level' stay disciplined and continue following the process even under pressure.

The chance of miscommunication increases when people start skipping stand-up meetings. It helps to explicitly schedule the stand-up meeting to avoid any excuses about being in another meeting.

Time seems to be such a valuable resource that sometimes teams try to reduce the time spent on iteration -and release planning meetings. We have seen teams skip the release planning meetings to save time with in mind that they will make up for it when the pressure is released. This reduces the face to face communication with the customer and consequently the risk of developing the wrong software increases.

The customer plays a very important part in this and sometimes needs to be educated a bit. Customers naturally tend to focus on the number of features that will be in the release and understandably prefer not to reduce the scope. Consequently, they will try to reduce the amount of time spend in meetings even when it is for their own good.

We feel it is important to stick to the natural rhythm of the iteration and release planning meetings and even increase customer involvement during high pressure times. However, it is possible to reduce the total amount of time spent by all team members for these meetings without jeopardizing the quality of the communication with the customer. This can be achieved by having the team lead talk to the customer about the next iteration during the current one. He should discuss all new user stories including the acceptance tests upfront on his own with the customer. He can then already ask most relevant questions and get answers to them. Additionally, he can gather questions during the current iteration that may influence user stories in the next iteration and also get these answered. During the iteration planning meeting everyone must be present again. However, the time spend in explaining user stories and defining acceptance tests can be reduced, because all user stories and acceptance tests already have been clarified to the team lead. This type of iteration preparation results in fewer open issues that need to be covered during the iteration planning meeting.

Team leads and SCRUM Masters should look for any signs of reduced stand-ups, pair programming, release planning and iteration planning meetings and immediately act on it and help the team to maintain these practices.

6 Retrospectives

Usually we advise teams to do a retrospective at least every iteration (of two weeks or more). In case pressure increases, it is easy to get tempted to skip the retrospectives from time to time. "Hey, we are doing stand-up meetings too, you know? "

We have learned that when time pressure increases, teams are much more likely to skip the practices that will help them most. People tend to fall back into old habits as long as new behavior is not yet a real habit. Many of our experienced agile developers still have more years of experience with conventional software development processes than with agile processes. As a result, they still sometimes fall back into 'what they know best' when they are challenged most.

A team may be temped to skip iteration planning, release planning, stand-up's, test driven development etc. All those wonderful practices to help to keep them from becoming stressed are sometimes easily abandoned. Consequently stress increases and the quality and quantity of the team's output reduce. Retrospectives help to bring these type of 'time savers' to the surface and should therefore never be skipped.

Our advice is to keep the heartbeat and schedule your retrospectives at a fixed time and for a fixed length each iteration. Keep a scoreboard and track your pitfalls. Discuss the scoreboard each day during your daily stand-up meetings and when you detect you are off track, discuss what it costs and plan actions to get back on track.

7 Mental Challenges

We have noticed that many of our developers experience more pressure when working on more than one project. Even when the pressure is not even real.

It appears that developers sometimes unconsciously think for their customer and make up pressure that is not really there when looking at their situation from a more objective point of view.

As we said before, teams tend to focus on getting as many features done as possible in the release. More focus on one thing often leads to less focus on another thing. Sometimes teams forget that they should ask their customer to decide on the priorities and reduce scope when necessary. Often the customer is very much willing to prioritize and trade one feature for another. Especially when it is clear that the team will not be able to finish all the desired features before the deadline.

By not asking the customer to prioritize and reduce the scope the team increases the pressure on themselves. This is often followed by a reduced focus on best-practices like: pair programming, test-driven development, stand-up meetings, release planning and iteration planning meetings to find more time for implementing features.

Additionally, we have seen reduced code quality. Developers are more willing to accept code duplication and are less driven to refactor to excellence. They are more temped to quickly hack additional features into the code base and forget about testing.

We have also noticed an upside to this pressure. We all know the principle of 'the simplest thing that could possibly work'. We have seen developers rely much more on this principle when under pressure. The focus on maximizing the number of features also seems to increase the focus on simplifying solutions. As a result, even though code quality may not be as excellent as can be, the designs sometimes simpler.

References

1. Watt, R.J., Leigh-Fellows, D.: Acceptance Test Driven Planning, Extreme Programming and Agile Methods – XP/Agile Universe 2004. LNCS. Springer-Verlag, Berlin Heidelberg New York (2004)
2. Cohn, M.: Agile Estimating and Planning. Robert C. Martin Series, Prentice Hall, Englewood Cliffs

The Creation of a Distributed Agile Team

Paul Karsten and Fabrizio Cannizzo

British Telecom PLC, BT Centre, 81 Newgate Street, London (UK), EC1A 7AJ
{paul.karsten,fabrizio.cannizzo}@bt.com
http://web21c.bt.com

Abstract. This report tells the story of a project started one and a half years ago in BT and how the enthusiasm and dedication on applying agile methodologies has allowed the team to grow while successfully delivering on their goals. It describes the process that has been put in place to manage the project and develop the software; it also tells how some of the practices initially applied have been then changed and adapted to make them fit for the distributed and unique nature of the team.

Keywords: Agile, distributed team, scrum, extreme programming, SOA, web services.

1 Introduction

In 2004 Al-Noor Ramji was named CIO of BT Group. He immediately began to institute policies intended to change the way that IT was done within BT. As part of that program[1] Al-Noor brought in agile development methodologies. This report reports the experience of a software development team that has been created in the wake of those changes.

In January 2006 BT and Microsoft brought 7 teams together in Reading (England) for the first Imagine Cup Accelerator Workshop[2]. One of the direct results of the event was the idea for BT to expose a variety of services to the global development community in order to make it easier for entrepreneurs such as these to add traditional telecom features to their applications.

Thus hatched the project Web21c SDK (http://web21c.bt.com): a small team (also know as Delta Tau Chi[3]) was formed including members from in and around London (England), Denver (USA) and Bangalore (India) with the goal to produce a proof of concept for a set of web services and an associated SDK to ease the consumption of those services. The proof of concept that was approved by management and in April 2006 the first planning session was held. The objective was to present the first release

---

[1] http://www.btplc.com/Innovation/Strategy/IT/index.htm
[2] http://www.btplc.com/News/Articles/Showarticle.cfm?ArticleID=93dd63c7-709d-443a-82b1-b1d644c7db37
[3] http://en.wikipedia.org/wiki/Delta_Tau_Chi

of the services and SDK to the public at the Microsoft TechEd[4] conference in Barcelona (Spain) in November of 2006.

The team was ultimately successful in achieving many of the goals set out for them and the presentation at the TechEd[5] was well received by the public and by BT senior management. Since then, it has continued to work its next goal which was to take the services from a free sandbox environment to a pay for use commercial model.

2 Maintaining Vision

One of the keys to achieving our goals has been the level of communication that happens within the team. We use planning sessions to gather the entire team together and plan the next project release. These occur approximately 3 times a year and last for 3 days. The activities performed in the three days mainly involve understanding goals and vision for the next release, planning of the release, discussion of the stories, socialization.

We have found as we have grown that it has become harder to maintain the ultimate vision and to keep everyone up to date with the progress of each of the sub-teams. To that end we have modified the structure of subsequent sessions to put in place activities focused to improve the level of communication and understanding of each member of the team, but ultimately to help producing better software. Practices recently introduced are the institution of a 30 minutes presentation held by each team to show the deliveries of the previous release, and to discuss the deliveries for the next release. This allows know-how to be shared and dependencies and impediments to be identified.

At each planning session part of the sub-teams are reshuffled. This not only helps us with maintaining intra team communications but has increased our Truck Number[6]. It also keeps team members fresh and challenged.

3 Separation of Concern

Coordinating the work of distributed teams is difficult at best most of the times. Rather than attempting to create teams that can work around the clock (which rarely, if ever, works) we have taken the approach of creating local sub-teams working on various components whose interfaces are loosely coupled in order to minimize the dependencies between the various sub-teams. When an interface does have to change, the updated service is placed in a common integration area where the other teams can update their references during their next Sprint.

For the most part this has worked well. Teams have been able to make use of Mocks and Stubs[7] while developing against the defined interface points. However, even with our use of Continuous Integration techniques, we have found that integration still is not trouble free and we have to allocate time in each Sprint in order to validate and consolidate the changes.

---

[4] http://www.skyscrapr.net/blogs/arcasttv/archive/2006/11/12/445.aspx
[5] http://www.flickr.com/photos/web21csdk/sets/72157594387229319/
[6] http://c2.com/cgi/wiki?TruckNumberFixed
[7] http://www.martinfowler.com/articles/mocksArentStubs.html

4 Working Ways

We use a combination of Scrum and XP in our team. We use Scrum and Sprints for planning and story maintenance and XP practices in our day-to-day development activities. Sprints last two weeks and releases occur at most 90-days after each planning session. The tools and practices used to develop are described below.

The Beginning and the End of a Sprint. At the beginning of each Sprint the sub-teams work with their customer proxy to identify a set of stories that are to be worked on during that next Sprint and define the acceptance criteria, in the form of "happy" and "sad" scenarios. Stories are prioritized and teams then plan their sprints and report back to the customer if there are issues (Yesterday's Weather[8] is used to determine how many stories each team can complete during that cycle).

Acceptance criteria are coded into automated acceptance tests that are used during the Acceptance session at the end of each Sprint to demonstrate stories delivery. They have also been used by other teams integrating with our services as source of documentation to understand the behavior of those services.

Tools and Development Practices. Since the start of the project teams have been using tools and practices that have been fine tuned along the way. Some of these tools and practices have been found useful and productive so that they have been mandate to all the sub-teams. Examples of standardized tools and practices include the Continuous integration environment, build scripts, project website template, a common set of reusable libraries.

However each sub-team is permitted to deviate from the norm if they find a new tool or practice that helps. The sub-team then introduces that to the wider team for adoption if appropriate. Sometimes "committees" have been formed to spike on new technologies or on find a solution to a common problem.

Code quality is monitored across the several sub-team artifacts by providing metrics[9] that translate into a Red, Amber and Green (RAG) status. This has allowed components built in different languages to have the same build report and has increased visibility with our immediate management.

Scrum Practices. We have one dedicated Scrum Master that spans all of the sub-teams. His role is to provide mentoring and guidance with regard to the team's agile practices, to check that the wider team is adhering to the principles we set forth by attending stand-ups and looking for areas where we can use Big Visible Charts[10] to change behavior[11], to chair the Scrum-of-Scrums[12] (meetings held to identify impediments and dependencies and to share know-how across the wider team.)

In addition each sub-team appoints one person to act as both team member and a local Scrum Master. Some sub-teams keep the same person for an entire release, some

---

[8] http://www.cutter.com/research/2005/edge051122.html
[9] Main metrics used are: the number of failed unit tests, the percentage of code coverage, the number of statically detectable bugs and the number of cyclical dependencies.
[10] http://c2.com/cgi/wiki?BigVisibleChart
[11] One example is the creation of our build light board, remotely accessible via web-cam, where everyone can see the build status of each component.
[12] http://www.mountaingoatsoftware.com/scrum_team

rotate the responsibility. The local Scrum Master is responsible for interacting with the customer to make sure that the sub-team is getting the information they need. They also make sure that each sub-team holds a retrospective[13] at the end of each Sprint to identify what is working well and what is not and the information shared.

Relation with the customer. The biggest departure from pure XP is our lack of a traditional customer. Originally, we were unable to find a sponsor from the business who had the time or the ability to provide stories and guidance; hence, we identified one of the original team members from the first Accelerator to act as the customer proxy (the wider development community). Since the launch of our sandbox environment we have begun engaging with internal and external customers as the project has evolved and are bringing them into our planning sessions.

We also have taken a page from many of the open source projects and use our Portal – the forum and the issues list – as another customer, allowing users to provide feedback to the team with regard to the use of our services and desired future direction.

5 Distributed Working

In the early 2000's BT embarked on a policy that permitted and sometimes encouraged developers to work from home. One of the obstacles that we encountered early on was prevalence of home working and the geographic spread of our team. During retrospectives we found that people valued and enjoyed working together so much that they insisted that we find ways to work co-located more. In the end we instituted a policy whereby sub-teams co-locate at least 3 days a week. No mean feat in a company that is trying to consolidate real estate or in places (like Denver) where there is no physical office. Through the judicious use of coffee shops, meeting rooms, people's houses, and what space we could beg, borrow or steal, we have been able to keep together. In fact our space in the UK is being redesigned from the traditional UK office desks into an "Agile paradise" including white walls (not just boards), pairing stations, Wi-Fi, and web cams.

Communication is one of the keys to any working group. More so in distributed working groups. When creating or re-organizing teams we try to be cognizant of geographic boundaries to make sure that teams can co-locate. Occasionally in order to promote more cross fertilization, we do geographically split teams.

Another way we try to keep communication flowing is that we make extensive use of Wiki[14] technology to document discussions and decisions. Teams also use this to create information for other related teams to use. RSS readers allow us to keep track of changes as they occur.

We often make use of web meeting technologies to facilitate paring when pairs are not able to co-locate or when working with a member of another sub-team. While not optimal this can be used periodically and we found being effective when there's an established work relationship with the individual on the other end. Without our co-location and period gatherings, this style of pair would not be sustainable.

---

[13] http://c2.com/cgi/wiki?IterationRetrospective
[14] http://www.wiki.org/wiki.cgi?WhatIsWiki

6 Continued Education

BT has an internal Scrum training program staffed by Certified Scrum Master trainers. We have been able to send all members through this program after their first few months with the team.

Another mechanism to foster communication and learning is our weekly Brown Bag[15] sessions. During these 90 minute sessions members of the team present a technology, an idea, a book, or a technique related to the work that we are doing. We again use web meetings to share this meeting with everyone on the team. These Brown Bag sessions have been extremely useful for sharing ideas and for encouraging people to keep themselves up to date with the latest technologies and trends.

In addition to the Brown Bags the team is given time, usually about two weeks, after each release and prior to the next planning session to sharpen the saw[16]. This time is often used to catch up on literature, learn a new tool, or on a demonstration intended on impacting the project moving forward. This "free" time has not only contributed innovation to the overall project but we believe has contributed to the enthusiasm the team continues to demonstrate.

7 Expanding the Horizons

The team is growing. From the original 12 that attended the accelerator in January of 2006 to the 40+ people working on the project now. The team is also beginning to take an active role in the process of bringing on additional members. The team runs "gauntlet" sessions where prospective employees are interviewed by pairs. Prospects are also asked to work on some piece of code with another pair. This not only allows us to verify that the prospect has the ability to work in a team environment, but is critical to maintaining the team culture.

8 Conclusions

As discussed in this report, high bandwidth communication is one of the most critical aspects of software development, especially, as in this case, when the group is distributed geographically. But through commitment in adopting agile methodologies and judicious use of travel, co-location, and new technologies it is possible to create an environment where teams can survive, grow and thrive all, delivering quality software quickly.

---

[15] http://idioms.thefreedictionary.com/brown-bag
[16] http://www.leaderu.com/cl-institute/habits/habit7.html

Distributed Scrum in Research Project Management

Michele Marchesi, Katiuscia Mannaro, Selene Uras, and Mario Locci

DIEE, University of Cagliari, Piazza d'Armi,
09123 Cagliari, Italy
{michele,mannaro,s.uras,mario.locci}@diee.unica.it

Abstract. Can research projects be agile? In this paper we describe our proposal of applying Scrum for the management of an European research project aimed at developing an agent-based software platform for European economic policy design. The use of an agile, adaptive methodology is justified because successful research projects are complex, unstable processes, that should be continuously adapted along their way. We describe in detail the roles, artifacts and practices of the proposed process, and the first steps of its adoption.

Keywords: Scrum, project management, distributed team, research project.

1 Introduction

Can research projects be agile? This paper describes our experience implementing an agile process for managing a research project called Eurace, aimed at developing an agent-based software platform for European economic policy design with heterogeneous interacting agents. In particular, the Eurace project proposes an innovative approach to macroeconomic modeling and economic policy design according to the new field of agent-based computational economics (ACE). The Eurace project is, by its very nature, multidisciplinary. The partners are Research Units composed of engineers, computer scientists, economists, physicists and mathematicians.

Like any research project, Eurace is a complex, unstable process. This means that none of its actions, practices or techniques are simple or repeatable, its predictability is limited and it is difficult to control. The activities may require constant changes in directions, new tasks may be added or it may require unforeseen interactions with many other participants.

Activities such as scientific research, innovation, invention and software development, typically exhibit this behavior, common in a so-called "empirical" process. Agile Methodologies (AM) were devised to deal with this kind of issues. They are able to manage continuous changes in project requirements, technologies and organization following an approach based on feedback and adjustments, and not on up-front analysis and planning, as more traditional methodologies. AM are considered very successful in the realm of software development.

The structure of the Eurace project and its objectives require adequate management and a tool for exchange and coordination throughout the duration of the project. Our goal is to provide an effective management system for the project as a whole as well as for the coordination of the individual members of the Consortium. The assumption is that this scientific project is an empirical process, in other words the project cannot be well defined and uncertainty is inevitable. In order to manage this complexity, we propose the use of a process derived from Scrum: a lightweight process that can manage and control software and product development. So we transfer the software engineering approaches to manage a research project.

2 Method

We propose Scrum because it is scalable from single process to the entire project. Scrum controlled and organized development and implementation for multiple interrelated products and projects, with over a thousand developers and implementers. Moreover Scrum can be implemented at the beginning of the project or in the middle of the project, or when product development effort that is in trouble. It has a track record going back as far as 1995 and earlier.

As far as we are aware, this is the first time an Agile Methodology is applied to the management of a distributed research project such as EURACE. This is a major challenge. However, the effectiveness of AM for controlling software – and not only software – projects and for managing changes in the requirements even late on in the development, is appealing. Most project management methods and techniques are very prescriptive. They tie us down to a fixed sequence of events and do not consider variations. The rules and practices from Scrum are few, straightforward, and easy to learn. To adapt Scrum to the management of a research project, however, we must bear in mind the analogies and differences between a development project and a research one.

2.1 Scrum

The term Scrum [1], [2], [3] comes from a 1986 study by Takeuchi and Nonaka [4]. In that study they note that projects using small, cross-functional teams historically produce the best results, and state that these high-performing teams were like a team of players in the Scrum formation in Rugby. When Jeff Sutherland and others developed the Scrum process at Easel Corporation in 1993, they used Takeuchi and Nonaka's study as the basis for team formation and adopted their analogy as the name of the process as a whole. Ken Schwaber [5], [6] formalized the process in the first published paper on Scrum at OOPSLA 1995.

Scrum is a simple and adaptable framework that has three roles, three ceremonies, and three artifacts:

- **Roles:** Product Owner, Scrum Master, Team;
- **Ceremonies:** Sprint Planning, Sprint Review, and Daily Scrum Meeting;
- **Artifacts:** Product Backlog, Sprint Backlog, and Burndown Chart.

Scrum projects are organized following an iterative, incremental approach. Iterations are called Sprints, and typically last one month. Every day the team holds a Scrum, a 15 minute update meeting, that helps the project flowing smoothly.

3 Implementation of EURACE Scrum

Although Scrum was intended to be used for the management of software development projects, its has already been used to manage other kinds of industrial developments. We believe it can be applied to any context where a group of people need to work together to achieve a common goal, and this is the case of a scientific research project.

The Scrum methodology is designed to be quite flexible and the controlled involvement of the whole team is facilitated.

The following roles have been formalized in the Eurace Scrum project:

1. Project Owner (formerly Product Owner): this person has in control the whole project, and controls that the artifacts delivered by the process are in line with the research project aims and the required deliverables. A natural candidate for this role is the project coordinator.
2. Scrum Master: in a distributed research project the Scrum Master is a person who is responsible for enforcing the rules of the process, helping to remove impediments and ensuring that the process is used as intended.
3. Unit Coordinator: this is a new role, specific to a distributed research project. He is the person who coordinates the Team Members belonging to a research unit and controls that the artifacts delivered by the unit are in line with the required deliverables. The Unit Coordinators, together with the Project Owner, decide feature prioritization.
4. Unit Members: the people working on the project. Each member belongs to a Research Unit.
5. Research Unit: a group of people working in the same location, including the Unit Coordinator. Each unit has specific duties in the project, being responsible for features and deliverables. Units are cross-functional, having different skills, and work together to turn requirements into features, and features into deliverables and a working system.

The main artifacts of EURACE Scrum are Project Backlog, Sprint Backlog, Impediment List, Project Increment and Burndown Graphs. The Project Backlog is a prioritized list of project requirements with estimated times to turn them into parts of project deliverables and/or completed system functionality and the Sprint Backlog a list of tasks that defines a team's work for a Sprint. Moreover we have an Impediment List of anything around a Scrum project that impedes its productivity and quality. At the end of every Sprint the team should have delivered a production quality increment of the deliverables or of the system, demonstrated to the Project Owner and, at each project review, to external reviewers (Project Increment). Finally the Burndown Graphs show the trend of work remaining across time in a Sprint, a release or the whole project. Other reports on project status, bug status, etc. may be necessary.

3.1 How Does Eurace Scrum Work?

Eurace Scrum was designed to allow average participants to self-organize into high performance teams. The Eurace Scrum process is based on specification of what has to be done through a list of features. Each feature is assigned an estimated value for the project, an estimated effort and a responsible person. Project advancement occurs using time-boxed iterations called Sprints. Sprint duration is 6 weeks. Each Sprint (iteration) implements a subset of the Project Backlog, in other words a list of features prioritized according to their value, effort and risk. This is done by the Project Owner together with Unit Coordinators. Finally Sprints are grouped into Releases. A Release covers one year of work, and delivers official project deliverables.

At the beginning of each Sprint, a Sprint Planning Meeting decides what features to implement in the Sprint, and decomposes them into the Tasks needed to implement the feature. Tasks for a sprint must be well quantified and assigned to one individual, and if the task is shared it is strategic to give one person the primary responsibility. The Sprint Planning Meeting is held through the Internet or, when possible, through a physical meeting. During the meeting the team members synchronize their work and progress and report any impediments.

The Daily Scrum should be done among Unit Members, but this is a choice left to them. Every one or two weeks, a Scrum Meeting is held via instant messaging among all project researchers, to synchronize the work and to report impediments.

The Sprint Review meeting provides an inspection of project progress at the end of every Sprint and the Sprint Retrospective meeting is held after each Sprint to discuss the just concluded Sprint and to improve the process itself. The Sprint Review and Sprint Retrospective Meetings are held through the Internet or, when possible through a physical meeting. They typically precede the Sprint Planning Meeting deciding about the next Sprint.

4 Adoption of Eurace Scrum and Conclusions

The EURACE Scrum process described in this paper has been proposed to Eurace partners, and its adoption is in progress. The first steps we performed to set up the process were:

1. A virtual place where to put project management documents (Project Backlog, Sprint Backlog, etc.) has been created in Eurace project's Wiki.
2. Templates for the Project Backlog and the Sprint Backlog have been prepared using a spreadsheet, and put on the virtual place.
3. A first list of prioritized features describing the goals and characteristics of the project has been prepared. This list in not complete, but the features of the first couple of Sprints are detailed enough. The Project Owner and the Unit Coordinators were in charge of this activity. Each feature is also assigned to a research unit responsible for it. They are listed in the Project Backlog template and are available to all project members.

In the next project meeting, which will be held at the end of the month, we will revise and estimate the features, and start the first Sprint.

The use of an Agile Methodology such as Eurace Scrum has been warmly accepted by project partners, some of whom are not software engineers but economists, as a way to keep in control a distributed scientific project. We believe Scrum provides better project management than the conventional management theory [7]. Everything is visible to everyone, team communication improves, a culture is created where everyone expects the project to succeed.

We all are aware that this is a risky experiment, but we are determined to go ahead. In the case of problems and impediments, We trust the Sprint Retrospective, a (virtual) meeting held after each iteration of the process, to be the right place to discuss drawbacks and limitations of the method, and propose changes and improvements.

We are also developing an automatic support tool to help manage Eurace Scrum on the Internet, based on XPSwiki [8], a tool originally introduced for supporting XP process. This tool is based on a Wiki and will be very lightweight and easy to use. It will be able to keep in contact people through the Internet, easing the production of graphs and reports. This tool will be finalized only after the first Sprints will have been concluded, and after feedback will be gained on the whole process.

We will give more details of the advancement and status of this project at XP2007 conference.

Acknowledgment

This work was supported by EURACE E.U. STREP project #035086, under FP6-IST-2005-2.3.4 (xi), IST FET PROACTIVE INITIATIVE, "SIMULATING EMERGENT PROPERTIES IN COMPLEX SYSTEMS".

References

1. http://www.agilealliance.com
2. http://www.controlchaos.com/
3. http://www.scrumalliance.org/
4. Takeuchi, H., Nonaka, I.: The New New Product Development Game (1986)
5. Ken, S.: Scrum Development Process (1997)
6. Ken, S.: Agile Project Management with Scrum. Microsoft Press, Redmond, WA (2004)
7. Guide to the Project Management Body of Knowledge - PMBOK Guide 2003 Edition, Project Management Institute, Pennsylvania (2003)
8. Pinna, S., et al.: Developing a tool supporting XP process. In: Marchesi, M., Succi, G. (eds.) XP 2003. LNCS, vol. 2675, pp. 151–160. Springer, Heidelberg (2003)

Multiple Perspectives on Executable Acceptance Test-Driven Development

Grigori Melnik and Frank Maurer

Department of Computer Science, University of Calgary, Canada
{melnik,maurer}@cpsc.ucalgary.ca

Abstract. This descriptive case study is about the dynamics of a software engineering team using executable acceptance test-driven development in a real world project. The experiences of a customer, a developer, and a tester were discussed. The observed consensus among multiple stakeholders speaks of the effectiveness of the practice in the given context.

1 Introduction

Acceptance testing is an important practice regardless the type of the process followed. Acceptance testing is conducted (preferably by the customer) to determine whether or not a system satisfies its acceptance criteria. The objective is to provide confidence that the delivered system meets the business needs of the customer.

In the agile world, the iterative nature of the processes dictates automation of the acceptance tests (i.e. producing "executable acceptance tests") as manual regression testing at the customer level is too time consuming to be practical and feasible given the short timeframes of agile iterations. Furthermore, eXtreme Programming (XP) and Industrial XP advocate writing these tests in the test-first/TDD fashion. As a result, *"executable acceptance test-driven development"* (EATDD), or *"story-test driven development"* as it is called sometimes, makes it possible to formalize the expectation of the customer into an executable and readable contract that programmers follow in order to produce and finalize a working system [4].

This investigation set out to characterize and validate, in a given context, the main proposition: *executable acceptance testing is an effective tool for communicating, clarifying, and validating business requirements on a software project*. Even though we did not impose our definition of "effectiveness" on the respondents, we recognized that an effective practice and tool must address several aspects of communication. Those aspects include clarity of requirements, ability to deal with complex, end-to-end scenarios, ease-of-learning and ease-of-use. Therefore, we structured the interview guides accordingly to unveil these facets.

2 Context

The team was collocated and consisted of an on-site full-time product manager who was a domain expert (the "Customer"), a project manager, 10–12 developers, 1–4 QA engineers, and one consultant who introduced the methodology, the practices, and who also performed specialized work. All development was done in-house. The team worked on a single greenfield project (no project switching) – the implementation of an EDI transaction platform to allow users to define business rules around delivery of certain critical documents (for example, purchase orders) via a Web interface, to execute those rules, and to notify some parties who needed to be notified. It is important to stress that this was not a simple rule engine. To give the reader a sense of the project caliber, there were about 7,000 acceptance tests.

The team adopted XP (with a coach) and diligently carried out all practices of XP. The iterations were two weeks long. The project lasted 10 months, and despite some difficulties and growing pains, it was successful – the team was able to release a high-quality, feature-complete application on time (as unanimously recognized by all respondents – the Customer, the Tester, and the Developer). In addition, the marketing was satisfied and accepted the system, the existing clients of this vendor were happy with the product and the vendor even managed to sign up new clients.

Three members of the team took part in this study: (1) *the Customer*, whose job was to identify a high-value set of user stories for each iteration and do what was necessary to help the developers understand and implement these stories; (2) a lead QA engineer (*"the Tester"*), whose job was to review acceptance tests specified by the Customer, suggest new scenarios, find problems, and in any other way help the team to understand what was going on; (3) a lead developer (*"the Developer"*), whose job was to implement the system that met business requirements of the Customer.

It is important to note that the Customer had an information systems background. While he was not a software developer, he was performing a job similar to what a business analyst would do. Therefore, this report does not make any speculative generalizations on whether a non-technical customer would be as capable as the one we interviewed. In fact, the chances are likely that it would not be the case.

3 Discussion

3.1 Learning the Practice

The team adopted executable acceptance test-driven development and the FIT framework [2] with no prior experience in the practice. A 4-hour intro was given to all team members. During the first iteration, the consultant assisted the team with writing user stories and acceptance tests. After that, the team felt comfortable specifying their business rules in the form of acceptance tests. According to all three respondents, learning the technique and the framework was easy. According to the Tester, after a couple of days of "playing" with FIT, the team could operate the framework and write basic test scenarios. Everyone on the QA team caught on within a week and was able to get on their own with the job of writing and running acceptance tests. The learning curve was quite short. The Tester enthusiastically noted that "FIT is simple!"

3.2 Reflection on the Practice

Because of the inherent complexity of the domain, for each iteration meeting, the Customer would prepare an "info-sheet" – a short (one- to three-page), informally-written document with plenty of diagrams, callouts, and, most importantly, mock screen shots. It was meant to describe characteristics, behavior, and logic around a coherent set of features. It was not meant to be an authoritative specification and no official signoffs were used. The iteration planning meeting would involve the following: (1) Discuss the info sheet and talk about functionality; (2) Resolve any general questions about functionality; (3) Define a user story; (4) Define acceptance tests (criteria) for that story; (5) Repeat 3, 4. Notice, defining acceptance tests did not mean coding them in FIT. Initial "sketching" of the test was done at the back of an index card. When the list of possible test cases got longer, the testers suggested recording them in a spreadsheet – "something that we could later go back to". Later, either the Customer or the Tester would create an actual FIT table. The Customer explains: "We defined all requirements in general groups. I went into the planning meetings with well-described 'featurelets' and came out with stories and ideally acceptance tests." An example of a story could be "Rule: deadline dates are all treated as Eastern time". The team then identified all places in the system where the time was relevant (the UI, database, email, etc.) They stopped – that was enough to write an acceptance test. The developers could start their work based on the user story and acceptance test summary. They would have the detailed tests before their implementation was completed. This story-by-story procedure, including the invention of the info-sheets, matches the pattern of specifying business rules with executable acceptance tests the investigators expected. Importantly, the test-first paradigm of development was truly adopted and followed throughout the project.

We pursed the line of inquiry to understand why the info-sheets were necessary. The Customer aimed the info-sheets "at where they needed to be – to communicate the context to developers". Stories were isolated and stand alone. So the team talked about the stories, but "stories and talking are not great for communicating the details that should persist". The info-sheets would help to answer the questions why the developer was doing this or that and what this piece connects to. This is illustrative of a common concept that the customer needs to come to the iteration planning meetings prepared and have a very concrete understanding of what he wants from the upcoming iteration. This understanding can be documented upfront (if the customer thinks that this is beneficial – which was the case with this project and this customer).

Testers and the Customer paired up often with developers when specifying test scenario details (what data to use, what actions to execute, etc.) "Sitting down with the developers and giving feedback to them – they didn't need much more than that". Everybody agreed that "it was very interactive between the developers, the QA, the Customer – everyone!" The Tester pointed out that the "open space led a lot to XP thinking and very open communication. Everybody knew what everybody else was doing". It is worth reminding that the team size was ideal for this type of the process (13 – 18 people) and in a different setting (larger team or non-collocated team), the results may have been different.

While working on a story, the team may have realized that they had missed several cases. In this event, additional acceptance tests would be written. This occurred 30-50% of the time. The phenomenon can be explained by the nature of continuous learning about the domain and the system through testing (this aspect of continuous learning is emphasized by the thought leaders and practitioners of the context-based school of testing, and exploratory testing, in particular [1]). During iteration planning, one often cannot think of all acceptance test scenarios, but as the person dives in the story implementation, other things become apparent and new scenarios are added.

3.3 Acceptance Test Authoring

All acceptance criteria were specified by the Customer and the QA. When it came to actual authoring of tests in the form of FIT tables, about 40% of all FIT test pages were written by the Customer, 30% by developers, and the remaining 30% by testers (based on the estimates provided by the Customer and the Tester). The Customer found that "in practice, it was best if the Customer wrote acceptance tests. This is related to the fact that going from a general description to a test has some fluidity in interpretation." Because of the domain complexity, the customer either had to communicate in greater details what the test should be and then review it, or simply do it himself. The Tester reported specifying acceptance tests in pairs with the actual developers of a story or with the Customer. If it was with the Developer, the acceptance tests would be reviewed by the Customer in an informal review session (that usually took no more than 10 minutes and was done on the fly). This was possible due to team collocation and informal communication flow.

The Developer indicated that for negative tests, they wrote sophisticated error messages (and comprehensive checks) to convey the meaning of what may have caused that error. Moreover, the developer went beyond functional tests in FIT. They extended the FIT framework to capture runtimes and do basic load testing.

3.4 Challenges in Specifying Requirements in the Form of Acceptance Tests

Several experts in the industry question the expectation of the agile teams for the customer to write acceptance tests (see, for example, [5]). Therefore, the customer's opinion of the difficulty of specifying executable acceptance tests was especially important to this investigation. The Customer testifies: "[It was] not particularly hard... Because we were all there (developers, testers, and I [the Customer]) talking about the story. So, the acceptance test was a natural segway." Apparently, the difficulty was not the practice itself, but the discipline of doing it. "Once functionality was discussed and the stories were defined, the team wanted to be done. Forcing ourselves to think in detail about what tests needed to be performed and what the logic of those test scenarios should be, was hard". Devoting proper attention to the tests at the beginning was something the team had to work on. This question of discipline was intriguing, so the researchers pursed the line of questioning further. The Customer recognized that putting off writing an acceptance test was "a dangerous thing" (even if it did not happen frequently). He paraphrased from the book "Zen and the Art of System Analysis" by Patrick McDermott [3]: "We delay things because they are either difficult or unpleasant. Difficult things become easier over time, and unpleasant thing become more so". The question was whether the team was postponing writing the acceptance tests because they were "difficult" or because they were "unpleasant". It turned out that it was usually because of the "unpleasant" aspect. The Customer explained: "It was complicated stuff to test, and the thought of diving into that complexity, just when we thought we were done, was unpleasant." The team did realize that it had to put discipline into this.

All in all, both the Customer and the Tester were quite enthusiastic about EATDD and, specifically, FIT. The following testimony of the Customer illustrates one of the reasons for this enthusiasm: "FIT is definitely more accessible and I could write FIT tests. That was huge!" Doing so helped the Customer and the team to discover a lot of missing pieces or inconsistencies in a story. The FIT tests were concrete.

4 Conclusions

The Customer and the Tester decisively recognized the effectiveness of the executable acceptance test-driven development for specifying and communicating functional business requirements. In his own characterization, the Customer "was happy". The Tester enthusiastically declared "It [EATDD] made the whole testing process more focused. It made it more unified – everybody agreed on the tests – it was the same tests running over and over again. It made our code a lot cleaner. When we found bugs in our system, we would go and update our FIT tables related to that particular function, so that we could catch it the next time it [the bug] transpires… It was just a good, fresh, new way to run the testing process. The other thing that I loved about it is, when you found a defect and you wrote a test around it, if it was a quality test, it didn't happen again – it was caught right away. Obviously, it made my job [as a QA] much easier and made the code a lot better."

Furthermore, the Customer did an internal survey of the team and found that the developers felt that the info-sheets together with iteration planning meeting were quite effective. As mentioned earlier, the developers may have been less enthusiastic about FIT from time to time as they deemed writing acceptance tests in FIT required more effort than implementing them in JUnit. However, there was no argument about the value of FIT tests from the perspective of making the tests "as English as possible" (i.e. readable and intuitive). This is remarkable as it clearly demonstrates the consensus among all three interviewees – the Customer, the Developer, and the Tester – on the value and effectiveness of executable acceptance testing.

References

[1] Bach, J.: Exploratory Testing Explained. Online: http://www.satisfice.com/articles/et-article.pdf
[2] Fit: Framework for Integrated Test. Online: http://fit.c2.com/
[3] McDermott, P.: Zen and the Art of Systems Analysis: Meditations on Computer Systems Development, 2/e, 3. Writers Club Press, Lincoln, NE (2003)
[4] Reppert, T.: Don't Just Break Software, Make Software: How Story-Test-Driven-Development is Changing the Way QA, Customers, and Developers Work. Better Software 6(6), 18–23 (2004)
[5] Sepulveda, C.: XP and Customer Tests: Is It Fair? Online: http://christiansepulveda.com/blog/archives/cat_software_development.html

Test Driving the Wrong Car

Ingmar van Dijk and Ruud Wijnands

MiPlaza, Philips Researh Laboratories, HTC 29,
5656AE Eindhoven, Netherlands
{Ingmar.van.Dijk,Ruud.Wijnands}@philips.com

Abstract. Test-Driven Development (TDD) is a practice that can be applied in almost all software development projects. It is a great tool to write working code and end up with clean designs. When writing code we make choices about the technologies we use and the underlying architecture. Sometimes the consequences of unfortunate choices do not show up for a while. TDD does not prevent us from making big mistakes. This paper is about such an unfortunate choice, the process of writing code based on this choice and the result. Finally, we discuss the lessons learned that can help us to avoid making big mistakes or to get a quick indication of such a mistake.

Keywords: Test-Driven Development, mistakes, non-functional tests, feedback.

1 Introduction

Test Driven Development [1] (TDD) is one of the practices from eXtreme Programming [2] (XP) that can be applied in almost all software development projects. It is a great tool to write working code and end up with clean designs. Another benefit is that TDD makes you go faster. How? The tests are documenting how to use the code. This decreases the time needed to comprehend what the code currently is doing. Additionally, the tests bring focus: only writing code to make a failing test pass helps us to stay away from gold-plating our code.

When writing code we make choices about the technologies we use and the underlying architecture. Sometimes the consequences of unfortunate choices do not show up for a while. TDD is not going to prevent us from making big mistakes. This paper is about such an unlucky choice, the process of writing code based on this choice and the result. Finally, we discuss the lessons learned that can help us to avoid making big mistakes or to get a quick indication of such a mistake.

2 Context

In our example we needed to convert one form of XML file into another. Using XSLT was not an option, because we needed to perform too many calculations on the data. Therefore, we decided to develop a Java application to convert the XML file. Because our department is doing XP@SCRUM [3] we used TDD to develop the application.

Since this application was only a small one, it took us no more than a single iteration to write a first version.

3 The Process

Writing user stories [4] for the application was simple. For each element in the source file we had a story that described the conversion to the target format. When we completed writing down the stories and prioritized them, we could start writing the code. The development of the code was done according to the following process:

1. Write a unit test to check the conversion of one element into the required format.
2. Implement the code to really do the conversion and make the test pass.
3. Refactor to excellence [5] and start over at step 1 for the next story.

After we had written the first unit test, we needed to decide how to implement the production code. We had several options, one of which was to write our own XML parser and builder classes, which seemed not so smart. So we decided to use an existing technology: the DOM parser. Unaware of the consequences of this choice, we continued writing tests and producing code. All unit tests were in memory only tests, no file access was required and therefore we were able to run them extremely fast. Many times, the tests pointed out small mistakes we had made in the conversions and we were able to quickly make good progress. Eventually, all tests were passing and we were able to convert all elements into the desired XML format.

Next to writing unit tests, we also had written some acceptance tests to check we were able to really read some XML files from disk and to write them back. The XML files we used in acceptance tests were only subsets of the original files we wanted to convert. We had done this on purpose to simplify the verification of the output XML file. Again we were not aware of the consequences of this choice.

4 What Happened?

Now comes the good part. The first time we ran the application on the file we wanted to convert it did not work! How could that be? We had written tests all the time, so our code should be working. Unfortunately, when trying to convert our XML file we got an 'Out of memory' error. The input file was just too big. Because we had used a DOM parser it was not possible to work with large files.

Why had we not noticed this earlier? The first answer to this question is, we had no test for working with big files. All our acceptance tests were based on small subsets of the original files and unit tests are by default not supposed to work with large datasets. Next to that, the DOM parser had been able to perform all operations we had written tests for.

Suppose the choice of technology is like the choice for a car to get to a destination. We had chosen for a Formula 1 car and whenever we wanted it to turn left it could turn left, when we asked it to turn right it was able to do so. A left or right turn can be compared to the conversion of one element in our XML file. However, we had never tested whether the car could also drive the distance we required! And Formula 1 cars are not built to drive long distances. We had not checked for the distance we had to drive with our car. If we had, we could have seen that the engine of our Formula 1 car could only last for around 1000km while we needed to go for a 20000km drive. With that knowledge we would have better been off going for a comfortable limousine.

Fortunately, we were able to rewrite the code based on a SAX parser more suited for large files. Our acceptance tests still were useful, because we could also run them with the new code. Eventually, the application had quickly been rewritten and we had only 'wasted' a single iteration.

5 Lessons Learned

How could we have avoided running into these problems? Well, if we had tried to convert our large file earlier, we would have been able to notice that it was not possible to work on big files. It is all about getting quick feedback. When doing TDD, you get quick feedback on whether the code just written is working as required. However, the code is only doing the things it was tested for. Therefore, if bigness is one thing to take into account: try to find out if it is going to be an issue or requires a special kind of solution as soon as possible. In general, the unit tests produced with TDD are not suited for checking non-functional requirements like performance, scalability, memory usage, etc. We advise developing some acceptance tests to check the non-functional requirements.

The quick feedback provided by the unit tests definitely helps in avoiding the small mistakes. Off by one errors show up immediately and can be corrected right away. This saves us from spending a lot of time in the debugger trying to figure out why the code is not doing what it is supposed to do. The unit tests point out the small mistakes and therefore the developer can focus on the big problems.

Next to that, the acceptance tests we had written for the conversion application were of great help in rewriting the code. We could get the tests to green one at a time, and quickly we had a working system again, with the same functionality as the first version but now also able to handle large files.

References

1. Beck, K.: Test-Driven Development by Example. Addison-Wesley, Reading (2003)
2. Beck, K.: Extreme Programming Explained: embrace change. Addison-Wesley, Reading (1999)
3. Mar, K., Schwaber, K.: Scrum with XP. Prentice Hall, Englewood Cliffs (2002)
4. Cohn, M.: User Stories Applied for Agile Software Development. Addison-Wesley, Reading (2004)
5. Hill, M.: Testing and Refactoring Workshop, Industrial Logic

Epistemological Justification of Test Driven Development in Agile Processes

Francesco Gagliardi

Department of Physical Sciences — University of Naples *Federico II*
Via Cintia — I-80126 Napoli, Italy
francesco.gagliardi@libero.it

Abstract. In this paper we outline a methodological similarity between test driven software development and scientific theories evolution. We argue that falsificationism and its *modus tollens* are foundational concepts for both software engineering and scientific method. In this perspective we propose an epistemological justification of test driven development using theoretical reasons and empirical evidences.

Keywords: Software Testing; TDD; Agile Programming; Epistemology; Falsificationism; Modus Tollens.

1 Introduction

The reality of software engineering, in our view, *"is more about science than it is about computer science"* as J. Bach argued in [5], but software development, and in particular software testing, are not generally regarded as a scientific enterprises, even though theirs practices do not match strongly in a neat framework of mathematics or computer science, while they can be usefully framed in experimental activities.

So we draw the relationship between the scientific method and software development, starting from the problem of software testing.

2 Theory of Software Testing

In *computability theory* a mathematical proof concludes that the programs correctness problem is undecidable.

The need to do testing based on sound and systematic principles led researchers to develop *theory of software testing* ([1], chp. 6) in which concepts, such as *program correctness*, *test set* (or *suite*), *selection criteria* and theirs *consistency* and *completeness*, are formalized.

It is also defined an *ideal test suite* T as a test suite such that: *"if a program S is incorrect, there is at least an element of T such that S fails on T"* or, in other words, if program passes an ideal test suite then it is correct.

It is proved that an ideal test suite exists for any program, but unfortunately it is also proved that there is no constructive criterion (i.e. algorithm) to derive a test suite satisfying that property.

The incomputability of ideal test suite is the primary cause of the existence of several empirical criteria to define the test suite such as category partition, boundary analysis, special values detection, an so on.

So the main goal of testing is restricted to show the presence of failures because testing can never completely establish the correctness of an arbitrary program.

Then the methodology of software testing is well rooted in *modus tollens* (Latin: *mode that denies*) rather than in *modus ponens* (Latin: *mode that affirms*) which is the well known deductive argument.

Modus tollens is the formal name for contrapositive inference and it can also be referred as *denying the consequent*, it is a valid form of argument and is antithetical to *modus ponens* which can be referred to as *affirming the antecedent*.

Modus tollens has the following argument form:

> *If P, then Q.*
> *Q is false.*
> *Therefore, P is false.*

In the software testing field it becomes:

> *If (Program is Correct) then (Whatever Test Suite Passes).*
> *(A Test Suite Fails)*
> *Therefore (Program is Incorrect).*

These theoretical results can be well summarized by *Dijkstra's thesis* [2]: *"Program testing can be used to show the presence of bugs, but never to show their absence!"*

3 Epistemology and Software Development

In epistemology the foundational problem of experimental validation of scientific theories was faced by Karl Popper in his *Theory of Falsificationism* [3]. In this theory *modus tollens* plays a key role, indeed, in experimental sciences no number of positive outcomes at the level of experimental testing can confirm a theory, but a single counter-instance shows that the scientific theory, from which the implication is derived, is false.

Thus despite software development is not explicitly defined as scientific enterprise, it has a close resemblance to the way in which experimental sciences work. Indeed, no number of passed test suites can proof the correctness of a program but a single failed test suite shows the program to be incorrect. Then, falsification *à la* Popper with experimental implementation of *modus tollens* is just as essential to software testing as it is to scientific theories and this is not just an analogy.

In a way, scientific theories are computational models of nature and software systems can be seen as computational models of business processes.

According to this 'naturalistic' unifying viewpoint Kaner et al. ([4] pg. 359) argue that a effective testing requires *"an empirical frame of reference, rather than a theoretical one"* and they refer to test cases as *"miniature experiments"* (see also [7]) and Pettichord [6] about development and scientific method argues *"developing software is much like creating theories"*.

As matter of fact testers design 'experiments' to test if the software (i.e. 'theory') fit with data of test suite, while developers build a 'model' (i.e. software) to fit with and to generalize the data specified in the test suite.

So testers have more an empirical attitude while developers more a theoretical one. We can think that software testing is experimental science in the field of software development, while software development is theoretical science.

In traditional software development methodologies these two activities are kept strongly separated. Moreover from organizational and sociological viewpoint we have often two separate teams with different skills, different attitudes and sometime in open contrast between them.

4 Test Driven Development and Agile Methodology

In *Test Driven Development* (TDD) practice, developers and testers are the same people (or a couple in close interaction according to agile practice of *pair programming*), so we have a true 'scientists team at work', it is able to perform in close and synergetic interaction both theoretical and empirical thinking.

In agile context, programmers translate claims about the program into testable assertions about how it will behave under known conditions and then check its behavior. Also they are able to theorize about required behaviour to implement code and to re-engineer it (the *refactoring* phase in TDD) to improve underlying model.

In this cognitive cycle programmers produce *model-based* software which adheres to behavioral data, specified pragmatically by test case, as well as scientists 'design' a theory to model experimental data.

In fact TDD is not a simply technique of "code and fix", as scientific activities are not simply based on "trial and error" method, but they are *"reflection-in-action"* as argued by Edwards [8], because in each of them there is a quest to model and to generalize empirical data.

TDD with agile practices of pair programming and collaborative ownership create a method in which synergy between theoretical and empirical thinking implement the scientific method in software development.

4.1 Dependability

As we argued above, it cannot be proved that scientific theories and computer programs are absolutely true or correct, respectively. It is sometimes possible to detect and then eliminate their wrong behaviour by using falsificationism of *modus tollens*. But if the behaviour turned out as predicted, the model is only confirmed and cannot be proved.

Scientific theories and programs advance through continuous testing while eliminating bad features and improving some others. Continuous testing is a continuous attempt to "falsify" a theory or a software and its failure (the program passes the test suite) increases our dependability.

So the empirical 'validation' by means of testing increases our dependability of a scientific model or a software system, although this dependability can never be established with absolute certainty.

In agile programming the software is designed from the start to work and to iteratively evolve, adhering with increasing data of test suite; so the practice of TDD and continuous testing increase our dependability of developed system more than one single big test suite passed at the end.

5 Concluding Remarks

The methodology of software production, for mathematical theoretical reasons concerning the undecidability of programs correctness proof, is based in a non eliminable way on *modus tollens*.

This firmly links software development to methodologies of natural sciences and to epistemology, in particular to theory of falsificationism by Popper. And we need to adopt this perspective if we want to increase the comprehension of methodology and practice of software development.

In this perspective TDD is the unique 'scientific' methodology to develop software systems because it uses the falsificationism and embraces continuous testing.

Summarizing, the successful of TDD in agile processes is based on the rediscovery of scientific method.

References

1. Ghezzi, C., Jazayeri, M., Mandrioli, D.: Fundamentals of Software Engineering. 2nd edn. Prentice-Hall, Englewood Cliffs (2003) (ISBN: 0133056996)
2. Dijkstra, E.W.: Notes On Structured Programming. 2nd edn., T.H.-Report 70-WSK-03, Technological University Eindhoven, Department Of Mathematics, The Netherlands (1970), (Url: http://www.cs.utexas.edu/users/EWD/ewd02xx/EWD249.PDF
3. Popper, K.R.: The Logic of Scientific Discovery (Translation of Logik der Forschung). Hutchingson, London (1959)
4. Kaner, C., Falk, J., Nguyen, H.Q.: Testing Computer Software, 2nd edn. John Wiley and Sons, Chichester (1999) (ISBN 0471358460)
5. Bach, J.: What software reality is really about. IEEE Computer 32(12), 148–149 (1999), doi:10.1109/2.809258
6. Pettichord B.: Testers and Developers Think Differently. STQE magazine, vol. 2(1), pp. 42-46 (2000), (Url: http://www.stickyminds.com/sitewide.asp?Function=edetail&Object Type=ART&ObjectId=506)
7. Coutts, D.: The Test Case as a Scientific Experiment. (url: http://www.stickyminds.com/sitewide.asp?ObjectId=8965&Function=DETAILBROWSE&ObjectType=ART)
8. Edwards, S.H.: Using software testing to move students from trial-and-error to reflection-in-action. SIGCSE Bull. 36(1), 26–30 (2004), http://doi.acm.org/10.1145/1028174.971312

How Does Readiness for Agile Development Relate to Team Climate and Individual Personality Attributes?

Tali Seger[1], Orit Hazzan[2], and Ronen Bar-Nahor[3]

[1] Ruppin Academic Center, Emek Hefer, Israel
talis@ruppin.ac.il
[2] Department of Education in Technology and Science, Technion, Haifa, Israel
oritha@techunix.technion.ac.il
[3] Amdocs, Ra'anana, Israel
Ronen.Bar-Nahor@amdocs.com

Abstract. In this short paper we present our research idea on relationships between specific indices of organizational climate (team/management climate), level of individual self-efficacy as a personality attribute, and software practitioners' readiness for agile software development. Research results can help organizations predict the readiness of employees to implement agile methods and/or to work effectively in an agile environment.

1 Introduction

Agile software development is a relatively new software project management paradigm. On the one hand, the positive results of implementing the agile approach are well known[1]; on the other hand, the literature reports resistance expressed towards its implementation in software organizations (for example, [1]). This resistance can be explained by the fact that agile software development introduces a new software development culture, which is mainly (but not only) expressed by redefining the roles of software engineers, software team leaders as well as other role holders, such as QA people, system analyzers and designers. The research idea presented in this paper attempts to explain the source of this resistance by exploring how organizational climate and individual personality attributes are related to software practitioners' reactions towards the transition to agile software development.

For this purpose, several hundred software practitioners working in a leading Israeli hi-tech company, are observed with respect to their readiness to adapt to the change required when shifting to agile software development, both on the team/management level and on the individual level. With respect to team/management climate we refer to factors such as managerial thoughtfulness, team collaboration, intimacy and moral; whereas on the individual level, we refer to individual self-efficacy.

---

[1] See, for example, the *VersionOne*'s *Agile Development: Results Delivered* report at http://www.versionone.net/pdf/AgileDevelopment_ResultsDelivered.pdf

2 Research Background

2.1 Changes Introduced by Agile Software Development

The concept of "Agile development" emerged against the backdrop of the changing global environment. Individual status has become superior to the system; clients have become empowered and increasingly receive the full attention of service providers. Furthermore, technological developments, economic prosperity and new cultural trends have all created a new industrial environment that is centered on communications and information revolution [6].

In general, changes in the work environment are a kind of stress factor for employees [7]. In particular, moving to agile software development requires a change in the software practitioners' mind set, which in turn might lead to even greater stress. Main changes introduced by agile software development include: team empowerment, moving from a command and control structure to self-managed teams, applying very rigid (although simple) guidelines that all must follow, using social pressure to align the team members' behavior, accountability and taking responsibility, openness to criticism, willingness to share knowledge and expertise, willingness to admit to failures, seeking improvements, and goals orientation – willingness to do what ever is needed (testing, development, design, documentation, etc.) in order to meet the objectives.

2.2 Coping with Changes and Threats in the Work Environment

Folkman and Lazarus [7] defined coping as a factor that mediates between the stress experienced by the individual and the individual's performance. In order to cope and function more effectively when experiencing change, the individual mobilizes, or is affected by, individual personality attributes (for example, self-efficacy in this study), in addition to environmental resources (team climate components, in this study).

Researchers who studied the effects of organizational climate on employees found that a positive managerial climate in the work environment is an empowering and facilitating factor for employees (for example, [4, 11]). Thomsen, Soares, Nolan, Dallender and Arnetz [12] compared the effect on employee performance of environmental resources, such as managerial thoughtfulness, team collaboration etc. on the one hand, and individual personality attributes on the other hand. They found that the effect of environmental resources on employees was at least as strong as the effect of individual attributes. In the present study we examine both aspects.

3 Research Model

Based on previous findings described in Section 2, Figure 1 presents a schematic description of the research model examined in this study.

The dependent variable in the present study is the *practitioner's readiness for agile software development*; the independent variables are *team-management climate* and individual personality attributes, focusing at this stage only on *individual self-efficacy*. In what follows we describe the research hypotheses.

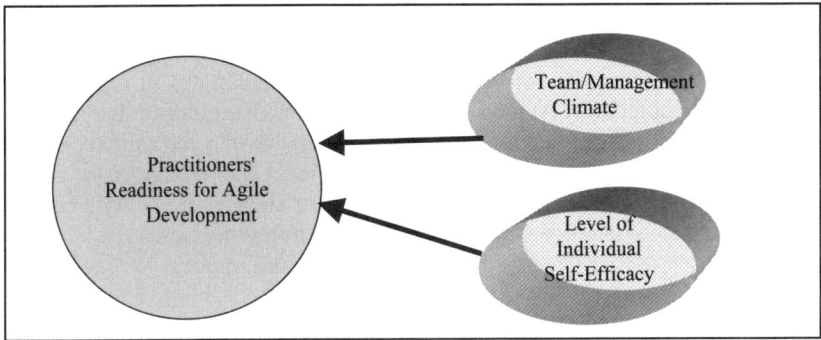

Fig. 1. Proposed model for software practitioners' readiness for agile development

3.1 Team-Management Climate

The first hypothesis is based on findings that posit a relationship between positive team climate, empowering managerial style and employee performance. Gillen, Baltz, Gassel, Kirsch and Vaccaro [8] found a positive correlation between positive departmental climate perceptions and employee performance, and coping with stress and pressure at work. As mentioned, moving to agile software development emphasizes both the need for team cooperation and the dependencies between team members. Accordingly, the following hypothesis was formulated:

Hypothesis 1: Negative correlations will be found between perceived positive team climate indices and the level of rejection of agile development; in other words, *perceived positive climate relates to a high level of readiness for agile development.*

3.2 Individual Self-efficacy

The second hypothesis relates to individual self-efficacy, which is defined as an individual characteristic that distinguishes between individuals according to their tendency to perceive hard events as challenging and to perceive themselves as capable of accomplishing almost anything [2, 3]. Accordingly, the following hypothesis was formulated:

Hypothesis 2: Software practitioners with high levels of self-efficacy will exhibit high levels of readiness for agile software development perceptions.

4 Research Methods

Questionnaires are being distributed to several hundred male and female software practitioners. The questionnaire includes the participants' demographic information, followed by three sections that correspond with the study topics, based on the questionnaires developed by Halpin and Croft [9], Chen and Eden [5] and Hazzan and Dubinsky [10].

5 Conclusion

We are currently at the data-gathering stage. The updated status of research will be presented at the conference. Among other contributions, we propose that the research results will have broad implications for the management of agile initiatives. For example, if a significant relationship between self-efficacy and readiness for agile software development is found, technological/software organizations will be able to measure applicants' self-efficacy as part of the recruiting processes.

References

[1] Auer, K., Miller, R.: Extreme Programming: Taming the Resistance. Addison-Wesley, London (2001)
[2] Bandura, A.: Self-efficacy mechanisms in human agency. American-Psychologist 37, 122–147 (1982)
[3] Bandura, A.: Self-efficacy: The Exercize of Control. W.H Freeman, New York (1997)
[4] Bradley, J.R., Carwright, S.: Social support, job stress, health and job satisfaction among nurses in the United Kingdom. International Journal of Stress Management 93, 163–182 (2002)
[5] Chen, G., Eden, D.: General self-efficacy and self-esteem: Toward theoretical and empirical distinction between correlated. Journal of Organizational Behavior 25, 375–395 (2004)
[6] Crook, K.S., Pakulski, J., Waters, M.: Post modernization: Change in Advanced Society. Sage, London (1992)
[7] Folkman, S., Lazarus, R.S.: Coping as a mediator of emotion. Journal of Personality and Social Psychology 54, 466–475 (1988)
[8] Gillen, M., Baltz, D., Gassel, M., Kirsch, L., Vaccaro, D.: Perceived safety climate, job demands, and coworker support among union and un-union injured construction workers. Journal of Safety Research 331, 33–51 (2002)
[9] Halpin, A.W., Croft, D.B.: The organizational climate of schools. Chicago: Midwest Administration Center of the University of Chicago (1963)
[10] Hazzan, O., Dubinksy, Y.: Clashes between culture and software development methods: The case of the Israeli hi-tech industry and Extreme Programming. In: Proceedings of the Agile 2005 Conference, Denver, Colorado, pp. 59–69. IEEE computer society, Los Alamitos (2005)
[11] Lok, P., Crawford, J.: Antecedents of organizational commitment and the mediating role of job satisfaction. Journal of Managerial Psychology 168, 594–613 (2001)
[12] Thomsen, S., Soares, J., Nolan, P., Dallender, J., Arnetz, B.: Feelings of professional fulfillment and exhaustion in mental health personnel: The importance of organizational and individual factors. Psychotherapy and Psychosomatics 683, 157–164 (1999)

Communication Flow in Open Source Projects: An Analysis of Developers' Mailing Lists

Selene Uras[1], Giulio Concas[1], Manuela Lisci, Michele Marchesi[1], and Sandro Pinna[1]

DIEE Department of Electrical and Electronic Engineering
Universita' di Cagliari, Piazza d'Armi 1,
Cagliari, 09123, Italy
[1]{s.uras,concas,michele,pinnasandro}@diee.unica.it,
manuelalisci@gmail.com
http://agile.diee.unica.it

Abstract. Team work is defined by different factors: team size, members role, interactions and communication. In Agile Methodologies communication plays a fundamental role. Some research studies have found that the involvement of team members in a project also depends on the information provided. Communication also depends on the tool employed. The aim of this paper is to analyze communication among team members of the 9 most active projects on Sourceforge provided of a developers' mailing list. In particular we tried to investigate how and why members post to developers' mailing list and the use that different members make of these mailing lists.

Keywords: Communication flow, social network, Open Source.

1 Introduction

Team work is defined by different factors: team size, member skills, member roles, interactions and communication. Some researchers [5] have found that the team member performance also depends on the information given on the project: better knowledge corresponds to greater involvement.

In XP teams, communication is also a value and it can change in accordance with team displacement. Communication is maximized in co-located teams but sometimes a team has to work in a dislocated manner, as in Open Source teams [1] [2].

In the latter case, there are different tools for facilitating on line communication such as chats, instant messengers, forums, wikis and mailing lists. In OS projects a specific tool is often used: the developers' mailing list.

This tool is used like a (virtual) space in which developers can exchange ideas and share information about project development. The aim of this work is to investigate communication in Open Source communities. The attention was focused on the big stage where actors-community members communicate: the developers' mailing list.

The aim of this work is to identify and evaluate the utilization of developers' mailing list of mainstream Open Source projects, to get insight on communication patterns among developers and the users of the list.

2 Data Collection

This analysis is focused on nine projects chosen among the most active on Sourceforge website.[1]

We examined more than 70 projects in order to find a sufficient number of projects.

In fact, when we looked for developers' mailing lists, we found that most of these projects had none.

This can be easily explained considering the kind of use software development teams make of Sourceforge [4]. Many teams started to use Sourceforge at the beginning of their projects, but later, as the project size rapidly increased, they preferred to use their own website with specific tools (CMS, wikies, forums...) in place of Sourceforge. At the same time, a large amount of these projects uses Sourceforge website as a means for making their product better and more widely known So, it is very likely that they use a developers' mailing list not available on Sourceforge web site.

Only 9 projects out of 70 seem to actually use Sourceforge developers' mailing list. These projects are shown in Table 1.

Table 1. The nine projects studied. All have activity level at 99.90%

Project	Topic	Number of analysed mails
Arianne	Multi player on line engine to develop games	1159
Gaim	Instant messaging application	8954
Gallery	Web based photo gallery	3997
Geotools	Open source java GIS toolkit	11076
Gimp-Print	Package of printer drivers	7816
Licq	Instant messaging application	4715
Mingw	Tool for importing libraries and header files	2690
Miranda	Instant messenger application	1045
Netatalk	Daemon for sharing files and printers	4678

In order to investigate the developers' mailing lists chosen we implemented a specific parser that enabled automatic data analysis.

The parser was written in Java. It was created to extract key data from the repository of a developers' mailing list.

For each e-mail, we extract the sender, the subject and the time, and for each thread the ID of the starter. Different queries can be made to query the repository.

3 Data Analysis

First of all, it is interesting to point out that two subgroups participate in discussions in developers' mailing list: the sub-group of users and the sub-group of developers.

Preliminary, we checked and resolved e-mail addresses and user names: about 50\% of community members (both developers and users) use different user names

---

[1] All the data reported are extracted from www.sourceforge.net

and e-mail addresses to post to the same mailing list (there are people who use even 5 different identities!).

3.1 E-Mails

Neither users nor developers are consistently the most active in sending e-mails.

In fact, the e-mails sent by the two subgroups change for each project.

In four projects users' sub-group is the most active, in another three the most active is the developers' sub-group, while in the remaining two projects the amount is evenly distributed. We believe that this matter warrants further investigation.

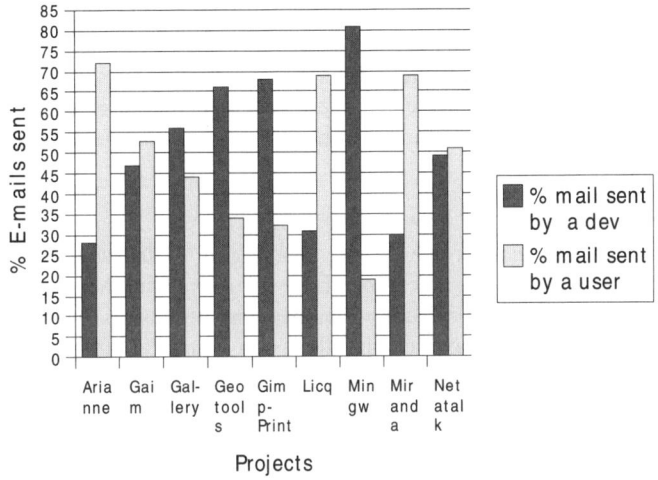

Fig. 1. Percentage of e-mails sent by developers and users

There are some developers who send from 5% to 20% of the total number of e-mails. So just a small number of developers are the main suppliers of e-mails in their mailing lists.

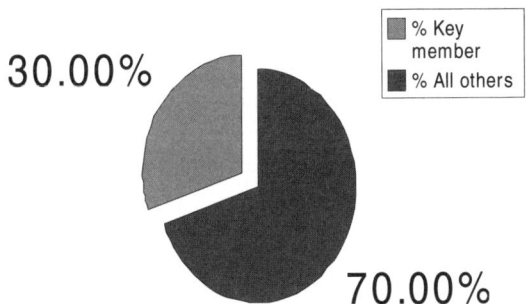

Fig. 2. E-mail sent by a "key member" vs other members

These active developers play a "key role" in the communication process. In fact, these "key members" are either project managers, support managers or developers.

Their "key role"[3] is to know everything about the project and to share information and provide explanations to users.

3.2 Threads

The users, usually, start about 65% of all the threads. In these threads the users ask for information, answer other users' questions when they solved the same or a similar problem and, sometimes, report a bug.

On the contrary the developers, on average, start about 35% of all the threads. In these threads, developers used to announce new releases, report a bug and discuss new features.

Note that, in each project a single developer, on average, starts a number of threads ranging from 5% to 30% of all threads. These developers are also the "key members" (see previous paragraph) and this again confirms the fundamental role of those members.

3.3 Links

A link is a connection between two members belonging to the same developers' mailing lists. Two members share a link if they have participated in the same thread.

Analyzing links between community members can help us to understand the communication [6] among team members and their consequential effort and involvement in the project.

Links between users are about 60% in four projects, while they range from 13% to 43% for the remaining ones. This does not mean that each user communicates, on average, with many of other users.

In fact if we look at a single thread it is evident that each user communicates, on average, only with two other users. We can state that a lot of users participate in communication in developers' mailing lists but only a few keep in direct contact. So the network formed by user communication is very poor and scattered.

We generally found a similar behavior in communication among community members (users and developers together).

On the other hand the links between developers are about 15% for four projects, about 5% for the other three projects, with two outsiders too: one with 39% and the other with 2%.

If we look at single thread we find that a developer communicates, on average, with 3 other developers. This suggests that there is a dense communication net and a great deal of information sharing among these developers, who are also the "key members". The network formed by their communication can be considered like an entity: the core of the communication.

4 Conclusion and Further Work

Justinian said "Nomina sunt consequentia rerum"(Names are sequent to the things named), so analyzing these developers mailing lists we initially expected to find e-mail exchange only among the project developers themselves.

But surprisingly both users and developers post there. We also found that a significant percentage of e-mail traffic was to be attributed to users.

To analyze the data we split the community into two sub-groups: developers' and users'.

Users utilize this space to spell out their problems concerning software utilization and to receive explanations on the software developed; at the same time, developers seem to understand and support this vision of the developers mailing lists, providing suggestions and information.

So we can say that users' sub-group and developers' sub-group are complementary.

Data analysis revealed that not all the developers' mailing lists behave in the same way about sending e-mails, starting threads or establishing relationships.

Some developers are "key members" of the community: they share information with the other members. These "key members" keep in contact with each other creating a dense communications network.

The users on the other hand only create a scattered network.

So this kind of distribution seems to suggest a dichotomous communication pattern in which the core is composed of developers and the periphery of users.

One very interesting topic for further research would be to compare the different indicators for each project like programming languages, development status, number of releases, for example so as to identify a specific communication pattern.

Acknowledgments

This work was supported by MAPS (Agile Methodologies for Software Production) research project, contract/grant sponsor: FIRB research fund of MIUR, contract/grant number: RBNE01JRK8.

References

1. Camplani, R., et al.: A comparison between co-located and distributed agile. In: Proceedings of the First International Conference On Open Source Systems (2005)
2. Camplani, R., et al.: Using extreme programming in a distributed team. Proceedings of the First Internationall Conference On Open Source Systems (2005)
3. Crowston, K., Howison, J.: The social structure of free and open source software development. First Monday, vol. 10(2) (2005)
4. Crowston, K., Scozzi, B.: Open source software projects as virtual organizations: competency rallying for software development. In: Proceedings of the First International Conference On Open Source Systems, vol. 1 (2002)
5. Gupta, M., Singh, R.: An integration-theoretical analysis of cultural and developmental differences in attribution of performance. Developmental Psychology 17, 816–825 (1981)
6. Wasserman, S., Faust, K.: Social network analysis: methods and applications. Cambridge University Press, Cambridge (1994)

Community Reflections

David Hussman

SGF Software, USA
david.hussman@sgfco.com

Abstract. The agile community/movement is growing and changing faster every day. As the initial agile flavors blend, the community continues to reach out, gathering new ideas from other communities and disciplines. One such practice, retrospectives/reflections, is an example of the agile community embracing an idea that harmonizes with the core principles of agile. As retrospectives and reflections are now a mainstay for many agile communities, this session is a way for the community to share in this practice. Using the fishbowl format, the session will start with a discussion among long time players in the agile community. Once the conversation is rolling, anyone interested may join the discussion, sharing their experiences or opinions. The moderator will be gathering questions for the fishbowl and keep the conversation flowing through the many topics present at the conference and during the session. Over all, this is a place for the community to meet and reflect on where we have been, what we have learned, and discuss topics and paths for the future.

1 Length

90 minutes.

2 Audience

This session is aimed at the entire conference. The hope is that people new to agile will have a chance to hear long time practitioners share their experiences as well as have the opportunity to engage in dialog with other member of the agile community.

3 Goal

Create a forum for the community to share experiences and a place where new comers can hear the experience of veteran practitioners. This session will also introduce people new to the community to the wonderful format of the fishbowl (in case there are no other fishbowl sessions).

4 Process

Each person in the initial fishbowl will start with a short introduction and answers to the following questions:

- What are the 2 things you like most about agile?
- What 2 things have you discovered that are the most unexpected and why?
- What 2 things would you like to see change or investigated in the agile community?

Once the initial fishbowl has finished their introductions, the moderator may ask them to discuss one of the answers given, or move on to ask questions gathered from the audience. Topics will be allowed enough time for discussion, but the moderator will keep the conversation moving, while allowing for spontaneous discourse within the fishbowl. Once the discussion is moving, the standard fishbowl format will be used.

5 Moderators Qualifications

David Hussman has been part of many conferences and has moderated fishbowl discussions at XP2003 - XP2006, XP Universe 2003, XP Universe 2004, Agile 2005 - 2007, AEG gathering in Mpls, and various companies in the US, Canada, and Europe.

To Certify or Not to Certify

Angela Martin, Rachel Davies, David Hussman, and Michael Feathers

Abstract. One of the problems the agile community is currently facing is how do we encourage the things that are agile and discourage those that are not? As agile software development has grown in popularity we discover that some people claim to "do agile" and yet "do not", and no one calls them on it. The principles of the Agile manifesto and the practices within each of the methods becomes diluted and lost. Is certification the answer? Tom DeMarco comments that *"though the rationale for certification is always societal good, the real objective is different: seizure of power. Certification is not something we implement for the benefit of the society but for the benefit of the certifiers"*. So certification is clearly a complex and interesting area and ripe for debate. This panel brings together industry practitioners with differing perspectives and experiences of certification; the audience should come prepared to both ask and answer questions.

Keywords: Certification, Community Direction.

1 Audience

This discovery session is aimed at anyone who is interested in the direction of the agile community including: project managers, testers, programmers and customers.

2 Content Outline

2.1 Set-Up

The student volunteer(s) will distribute index cards and pens on each table within the room 10 minutes prior to the start of the session. The student volunteer(s) will then also hand index cards and a pen to as many attendees as possible as they enter the room.

2.2 Introduction (10 Minutes)

The moderator of the panel will begin the panel by explaining the topic of the panel and introducing the "Question Time" [1] panel format. We have selected this format as we have found it produces the most interesting and in-depth panel discussions.

During the introduction the moderator will cover how audience members should ask questions: – by writing the question on an index card and raising it in the air.

---

[1] For further information please refer to
http://www.martinfowler.com/bliki/QuestionTimePanel.html

Student volunteer(s) will then collect the question cards and give them to the moderator.

The moderator will guide the audience to write their initial questions as she begins to (briefly) introduce each of the panellists.

2.3 Discussion (70 Minutes)

The discussion will begin with a pre-prepared question to allow time for the audience to begin to generate their questions.

During the discussion the moderator and panellists will work together to ensure that all sides of the issue are explored. If one perspective is not presented then the moderator will request a panellist to specifically debate or present that perspective as though they held it themselves. This will ensure that the topic receives a full and interesting discussion.

The moderator will consolidate and organise the questions from the audience into a good conversational flow.

2.4 Wrap-Up (10 Minutes)

This time will be reserved to allow panellists and the moderator to summarise the discussion and lessons learnt during the panel.

3 Presenters

Angela Martin, Martin IT Consulting Limited

Angela will be the moderator of this panel. She has a number of years of facilitation and moderation experience, both in industry and as a conference panel moderator.

Angela Martin is a London based consultant with over twelve years of professional software development experience; she works directly with programmers and customers on agile projects to deliver software that works. She is also completing her PhD research at Victoria University of Wellington, New Zealand, supervised by James Noble and Robert Biddle. Her research utilises in-depth case studies of the XP Customer Role, on a wide range of projects world-wide. Angela is also an Agile Alliance Board Member and can be reached at angela@martinitconsulting.com

Rachel Davies, Agile Experience Ltd (www.agilexp.com)

Rachel Davies is an XP practitioner and makes her living training and coaching agile teams in industry. She is also a director of the Agile Alliance.

David Hussman, SGF Software

David Hussman has designed and created software for more than 13 years in a variety of domains: digital audio, digital biometrics, medical, retail, banking, mortgage, and education to name a few. For the past 6 years, David has mentored and coached agile teams in the U.S., Canada, Russia, and Ukraine. Along with leading workshops and presenting at conferences in North America and Europe, David has contributed to numerous publications and several books (including "Managing Agile Projects" and "Agile in the Large"). David co-owns the Minneapolis based SGF Software, is a senior consultant with The Cutter Consortium, and has contributed to the agile curriculum for Capella University and the University of Minnesota.

Mike Feathers, Object Mentor

Michael Feathers has been involved in the XP/Agile community since is inception. While designing biomedical instrumentation software in the late 1990s, he met several of the members of the Chrysler C3 team at a conference and was persuaded by them to try XP practices.

Subsequently, he joined Object Mentor where he has spent most of his time transitioning teams to XP. Michael is also the author of 'Working Effectively with Legacy Code.

Learning More About "Software Best Practices"

Steven Fraser[1], Scott Ambler[2], Gilad Bornstein[3], Yael Dubinsky[4],
and Giancarlo Succi[5]

[1] Senior Staff, QUALCOMM, San Diego, USA
sdfraser@acm.org
[2] Practice Leader, Agile Development, IBM, Toronto, Canada
scott_ambler@ca.ibm.com
[3] Staff Manager/Engineer, QUALCOMM, Haifa
giladb@qualcomm.com
[4] Visiting Researcher, The Department of Computer and Systems Science,
University of Rome La Sapienza, Italy
dubinsky@dis.uniroma1.it
[5] Professor and Director, Center of Applied Software Engineering at the Faculty of Computer
Science, Free University of Bozen-Bolzano, Italy
giancarlo.succi@unibz.it

Abstract. What constitutes a *software best-practice* and what are the best strategies to become aware, learn, adopt and adapt such practices? This fishbowl will bring together seasoned professionals who will meld a mix of academic and industry perspectives with an agile flavor.

1 Steven Fraser (Fishbowl Impresario)

STEVEN FRASER joined QUALCOMM's Learning Centre in 2005 in San Diego, California – with responsibilities for tech transfer and technical learning. From 2002 to 2004 Steven was an independent software consultant on tech transfer and disruptive technologies. Previous to 2002 Steven held a variety of software technology program management roles at Nortel and BNR - including: Process Architect, Senior Manager (Disruptive Technology and Global External Research), Advisor (Design Process Engineering), and Software Reuse Program Prime. In 1994 he spent a year as a Visiting Scientist at the Software Engineering Institute (SEI). Steven holds a Doctorate in Electrical Engineering from McGill University in Montreal, Canada. Steven is a Senior Member of the IEEE and a member of the ACM.

This year marks the 20th anniversary of Frederick P. Brooks' Jr paper "*No Silver Bullet – Essence and Accidents of Software Engineering*" which appeared in IEEE Computer's April (Vol 20, No. 4) 1987 issue. Brooks considered complexity, conformity, changeability, and invisibility to be the challenges inherent in software systems. Has anything changed in the past twenty years? – Are there new software practices to address these and other challenges? – A non-exhaustive list of software practices with their historical roots (not necessarily definitive) is listed in Table 1– whether they are "best" depends on context and perspective. This fishbowl will discuss and debate what we've learned and adopted – or learned to avoid – in the past twenty years.

Table 1. Software Practices and Historical Roots

Software Practice	Historical Roots
High Level Languages	50's Backus & FORTRAN
Pair Programming	50's von Neumann & IBM
Project Planning	60's NASA
Risk Management	60's NASA
Software Architecture	60's Brooks + Dijkstra + Parnas
Software Reuse	60's McIlroy
Coding Standards	70's Kernighan & Plauger
Collective Ownership	70's Unix + Open Source
Continuous Integration	70's IBM FSD Integration
Data Hiding & Abstraction	70's Parnas
Development Processes	70's Royce + Boehm
Documentation	70's Parnas
Incremental Releases	70's Basili & Turner
On-site Customer	70's Mills & IBM FSD
Reviews	70's Fagen + Gilb
Simple Design	70's Basili & Turner
Software Metrics	70's Gilb + Halstead
Testing	70's Meyers
Evolutionary Design	80's Gilb
Maturity Models	80's SEI + Humphreys
Patterns	80's DeMarco & Lister + GoF
Peopleware	80's DeMarco & Lister
Refactoring	80's Opdyke + Fowler
Metaphor	90's Beck & Fowler & Cunningham
Retrospectives	90's Kerth & Rising

2 Scott Ambler

SCOTT W. AMBLER is the Practice Leader: Agile Development in IBM Rational's Methods Group and is the founder of the Agile Modeling (AM), Agile Data (AD), Agile Unified Process (AUP), and Enterprise Unified Process (EUP) methodologies. Scott is the (co-)author of several books, including *Refactoring Databases*, *Agile Modeling*, *Agile Database Techniques*, *The Object Primer 3rd Edition*, and *The Enterprise Unified Process*. Scott is a columnist with *Dr. Dobb's Journal*.

The idea of software *best practices* is arguably one of the most damaging concepts ever inflicted upon the IT community. The term *best practice* is nothing more than marketing rhetoric designed to sell products, services, publications, and seats in conference panels. The effectiveness of a practice is contextual: in some situations it is a *best practice* and in others arguably a *worst practice*. Consider logical data modeling. On traditional projects using structured technology it may be a best practice, yet on projects using object-oriented technology it ranges from irrelevant busy work to an impediment to delivering working software. Clearly logical data modeling presents a range of usefulness, yet many data professionals consider it a best practice and seem to have little compunction inflicting it upon teams which clearly will not benefit from its application. There are many agile practices, such as database refactoring and Agile Model Driven Development (AMDD), which prove to be very effective practices on agile teams, but are they truly *best practices* in all situations? This seems doubtful. The agile community would be well served to forgo the term "best practice" and thereby help to remove the scourge of this marketing term from our vocabulary.

3 Gilad Bornstein

GILAD BORNSTEIN has worked at QUALCOMM Israel for nine years as a developer, team leader and a Scrum Master. For the past two years he has successfully combined the conservatism of the embedded software world with the modernism of Agile programming. Gilad is focused on improving his organization's software process by coaching his peers and educating the younger generation. Gilad holds a BSc in software engineering from Technion Institute of Technology.

Over the years working as a software engineer I have faced many managerial and technological challenges that required me to develop and collect a bag of best practices to assist me with my work. Eventually, every engineer will have such a collection; It is just a matter of how long will it take him or her to gather it. One of my current organizational roles is to help new engineers learn and adopt as many practices as possible – as early as possible.

4 Yael Dubinsky

YAEL DUBINSKY is a visiting member of the human-computer interaction research group at the Department of Computer and Systems Science at La Sapienza, Rome, and for more than ten years she is the instructor of a project-based course in the Department of Computer Science at Technion Institute of Technology. She is also affiliated with the Software and Services group in IBM Haifa Research Lab (HRL). Her research interests involve aspects in software engineering and information systems. Yael has a significant experience with guiding agile implementation processes in the industry and academia. She has presented her work (since 2002) and co-facilitated tutorials (since 2005) in Agile and XP conferences.

My experience shows that software *best* practices are these that keep high levels of *tightness* in all relevant aspects. For example, 'short iterations' is a best practice since it gives high level of tightness to the project management. Another example is - 'exhaustive testing' is a best practice since it gives high level of tightness to the product quality. The tightness is necessary since software is a complex product that regularly changed. Following this rule, software *worst* practices are these that produce low levels of tightness. For example, a distributed team, in which the product management and the quality assurance departments are in one country and the developers team is in another country (another time zone; another culture), gives low level of tightness to the project management and in most cases also to the product quality.

5 Giancarlo Succi

GIANCARLO SUCCI is a Professor and the Director of the Center of Applied Software Engineering at the Faculty of Computer Science, Free University of Bozen-Bolzano,

Italy. Previously he was a Professor at the University of Alberta, Edmonton, Alberta, Associate Professor at the University of Calgary, Alberta, and Assistant Professor at the University of Trento, Italy. He was also chairman of a small software company, EuTec. Giancarlo's research interests included: open source development; agile methodologies; experimental software engineering; and software reuse.

Software best practices should be really called "reasonable practices:" they codify reasonable actions that can be used to approach wicked projects, where an optimal solution does not exist. Quite like medical semeiotic, such reasonable practices define plausible approaches to attack highly intractable issues. Therefore, the ability of the software engineer is to identify from a very sketchy description of a problem (the symptoms) which reasonable practices could be employed. It is quite ironic that after years where software engineering have tried to "automate" the development process so that it could work with any kind of "average workforce" we have now come to the conclusion that such software engineering semeiotic, all based on personal experience and personal skills, play a substantial role in a successful project.

Author Index

Abbas, Noura   165
Abrahamsson, Pekka   137
Ambler, Scott   271
Astudillo, Hernán   149
Atkinson, Colin   28

Badenes, Hernan   208
Bang, Tom J.   193, 203
Bar-Nahor, Ronen   257
Barra, Claudio León de la   161
Bellettini, Carlo   74
Biddle, Robert   9, 62
Biela, Wojciech   141
Bornstein, Gilad   271
Bouillon, Philipp   101
Bozzolo, Piero   173
Brooke, Phil   226

Cannizzo, Fabrizio   235
Cerruti, Julian   208
Chubov, Ivan   167
Colombo, Alberto   74
Concas, Giulio   213, 261
Concha, Mauricio   149
Crawford, Broderick   161

Dajda, Jacek   70
Damiani, Ernesto   74, 123
Davies, Rachel   268
Deng, Chengyao   93
Dobrowolski, Grzegorz   70
Dourambeis, Nicola   17
Droujkov, Dmitri   167
Dubinsky, Yael   271

Elshamy, Ahmed   46
Elssamadisy, Amr   46

Feathers, Michael   268
Ferreira, Jennifer   9
Fraser, Steven   271
Frati, Fulvio   74

Gagliardi, Francesco   253
Ge, Xiaocheng   226
Gianini, Gabriele   123

Ginez, Estaban   38
Girardi, Jacopo   173
Gobbo, Federico   173
Goldman, Alfredo   84
Gotel, Olly   24
Gravell, Andrew M.   165
Grinyer, Antony   163

Haikara, Jukka   153
Hazzan, Orit   257
Hummel, Oliver   28
Hussman, David   266, 268

Isomöttönen, Ville   145

Kärkkäinen, Tommi   145
Karsten, Paul   235
Kolenda, Henning   38
Kon, Fabio   84
Korhonen, Vesa   145
Krinke, Jens   101

Lanubile, Filippo   115
Leip, David   24
Lisci, Manuela   261
Locci, Mario   240
Ludlow, Lawrence   198

Madeyski, Lech   141
Mallardo, Teresa   115
Mannaro, Katiuscia   240
Marchenko, Artem   137
Marchesi, Michele   219, 240, 261
Martin, Angela   268
Maurer, Frank   1, 38, 54, 93, 169, 245
McDowell, Sandra   17
Melnik, Grigori   245
Meyer, Nils   101
Mishra, Alok   171
Mishra, Deepti   171
Morgan, Robert   38
Moser, Raimund   105

Noble, James   9
Nusser, Stefan   208

Opelt, Kealy   175

Author Index

Paige, Richard F.   226
Palmas, Daniele   213
Pepe, Massimiliano   173
Pinna, Sandro   219, 261
Polack, Fiona   226
Porruvecchio, Guido   213

Quaresima, Roberta   213
Qumer, Asif   157

Raithatha, Dharmesh   184

Sato, Danilo   84
Schoudt, Jerald   208
Scotto, Marco   105
Seger, Tali   257
Sensen, Christoph   169
Shu, Xueling   169
Sillitti, Alberto   105
Steimann, Friedrich   101

Succi, Giancarlo   105, 271
Sulfaro, Mauro   219

Tessem, Bjørnar   54
Turinsky, Andrei   169

Uras, Selene   240, 261

van Dijk, Ingmar   222, 231, 250
Visconti, Marcello   149

Walny, Jagoda   38
Whitworth, Elizabeth   62
Wijnands, Ruud   222, 231, 250
Wilcox, Eric   208
Wills, Gary B.   165
Wilson, Patrick   93

Zang, Juanjuan   179, 188
Zannier, Carmen   1

Printing: Mercedes-Druck, Berlin
Binding: Stein+Lehmann, Berlin

Lecture Notes in Computer Science

For information about Vols. 1–4466

please contact your bookseller or Springer

Vol. 4600: H. Comon-Lundh, C. Kirchner, H. Kirchner (Eds.), Rewriting, Computation and Proof. XVIII, 273 pages. 2007.

Vol. 4591: J. Davies, J. Gibbons (Eds.), Intergrated Formal Methods. IX, 660 pages. 2007.

Vol. 4581: A. Petrenko, M. Veanes, J. Tretmans, W. Grieskamp (Eds.), Testing of Software and Communicating Systems. XII, 379 pages. 2007.

Vol. 4574: J. Derrick, J. Vain (Eds.), Formal Techniques for Networked and Distributed Systems – FORTE 2007. XI, 375 pages. 2007.

Vol. 4573: M. Kauers, M. Kerber, R. Miner, W. Windsteiger (Eds.), Towards Mechanized Mathematical Assistants. XIII, 407 pages. 2007. (Sublibrary LNAI).

Vol. 4569: A. Butz, B. Fisher, A. Krüger, P. Olivier, S. Owada (Eds.), Smart Graphics. IX, 237 pages. 2007.

Vol. 4549: J. Aspnes, C. Scheideler, A. Arora, S. Madden (Eds.), Distributed Computing in Sensor Systems. XIII, 417 pages. 2007.

Vol. 4547: C. Carlet, B. Sunar (Eds.), Arithmetic of Finite Fields. XI, 355 pages. 2007.

Vol. 4546: J.H.C.M. Kleijn, A. Yakovlev (Eds.), Petri Nets and Other Models of Concurrency – ICATPN 2007. XI, 515 pages. 2007.

Vol. 4543: A.K. Bandara, M. Burgess (Eds.), Inter-Domain Management. XII, 237 pages. 2007.

Vol. 4542: P. Sawyer, B. Paech, P. Heymans (Eds.), Requirements Engineering: Foundation for Software Quality. IX, 384 pages. 2007.

Vol. 4541: T. Okadome, T. Yamazaki, M. Makhtari (Eds.), Pervasive Computing for Quality of Life Enhancement. IX, 248 pages. 2007.

Vol. 4539: N.H. Bshouty, C. Gentile (Eds.), Learning Theory. XII, 634 pages. 2007. (Sublibrary LNAI).

Vol. 4538: F. Escolano, M. Vento (Eds.), Graph-Based Representations in Pattern Recognition. XII, 416 pages. 2007.

Vol. 4537: K.C.-C. Chang, W. Wang, L. Chen, C.A. Ellis, C.-H. Hsu, A.C. Tsoi, H. Wang (Eds.), Advances in Web and Network Technologies, and Information Management. XXIII, 707 pages. 2007.

Vol. 4536: G. Concas, E. Damiani, M. Scotto, G. Succi (Eds.), Agile Processes in Software Engineering and Extreme Programming. XV, 276 pages. 2007.

Vol. 4534: I. Tomkos, F. Neri, J. Solé Pareta, X. Masip Bruin, S. Sánchez Lopez (Eds.), Optical Network Design and Modeling. XI, 460 pages. 2007.

Vol. 4531: J. Indulska, K. Raymond (Eds.), Distributed Applications and Interoperable Systems. XI, 337 pages. 2007.

Vol. 4530: D.H. Akehurst, R. Vogel, R.F. Paige (Eds.), Model Driven Architecture- Foundations and Applications. X, 219 pages. 2007.

Vol. 4529: P. Melin, O. Castillo, L.T. Aguilar, J. Kacprzyk, W. Pedrycz (Eds.), Foundations of Fuzzy Logic and Soft Computing. XIX, 830 pages. 2007. (Sublibrary LNAI).

Vol. 4528: J. Mira, J.R. Álvarez (Eds.), Nature Inspired Problem-Solving Methods in Knowledge Engineering, Part II. XXII, 650 pages. 2007.

Vol. 4527: J. Mira, J.R. Álvarez (Eds.), Bio-inspired Modeling of Cognitive Tasks, Part I. XXII, 630 pages. 2007.

Vol. 4526: M. Malek, M. Reitenspieß, A. van Moorsel (Eds.), Service Availability. X, 155 pages. 2007.

Vol. 4525: C. Demetrescu (Ed.), Experimental Algorithms. XIII, 448 pages. 2007.

Vol. 4524: M. Marchiori, J.Z. Pan, C.d.S. Marie (Eds.), Web Reasoning and Rule Systems. XI, 382 pages. 2007.

Vol. 4523: Y.-H. Lee, H.-N. Kim, J. Kim, Y. Park, L.T. Yang, S.W. Kim (Eds.), Embedded Software and Systems. XIX, 829 pages. 2007.

Vol. 4522: B.K. Ersbøll, K.S. Pedersen (Eds.), Image Analysis. XVIII, 989 pages. 2007.

Vol. 4521: J. Katz, M. Yung (Eds.), Applied Cryptography and Network Security. XIII, 498 pages. 2007.

Vol. 4519: E. Franconi, M. Kifer, W. May (Eds.), The Semantic Web: Research and Applications. XVIII, 830 pages. 2007.

Vol. 4517: F. Boavida, E. Monteiro, S. Mascolo, Y. Koucheryavy (Eds.), Wired/Wireless Internet Communications. XIV, 382 pages. 2007.

Vol. 4516: L. Mason, T. Drwiega, J. Yan (Eds.), Managing Traffic Performance in Converged Networks. XXIII, 1191 pages. 2007.

Vol. 4515: M. Naor (Ed.), Advances in Cryptology - EUROCRYPT 2007. XIII, 591 pages. 2007.

Vol. 4514: S.N. Artemov, A. Nerode (Eds.), Logical Foundations of Computer Science. XI, 513 pages. 2007.

Vol. 4513: M. Fischetti, D.P. Williamson (Eds.), Integer Programming and Combinatorial Optimization. IX, 500 pages. 2007.

Vol. 4511: C. Conati, K. McCoy, G. Paliouras (Eds.), User Modeling 2007. XVI, 497 pages. 2007. (Sublibrary LNAI).

Vol. 4510: P. Van Hentenryck, L. Wolsey (Eds.), Integration of AI and OR Techniques in Constraint Programming for Combinatorial Optimization Problems. X, 391 pages. 2007.

Vol. 4509: Z. Kobti, D. Wu (Eds.), Advances in Artificial Intelligence. XII, 552 pages. 2007. (Sublibrary LNAI).

Vol. 4508: M.-Y. Kao, X.-Y. Li (Eds.), Algorithmic Aspects in Information and Management. VIII, 428 pages. 2007.

Vol. 4507: F. Sandoval, A. Prieto, J. Cabestany, M. Graña (Eds.), Computational and Ambient Intelligence. XXVI, 1167 pages. 2007.

Vol. 4506: D. Zeng, I. Gotham, K. Komatsu, C. Lynch, M. Thurmond, D. Madigan, B. Lober, J. Kvach, H. Chen (Eds.), Intelligence and Security Informatics: Biosurveillance. XI, 234 pages. 2007.

Vol. 4505: G. Dong, X. Lin, W. Wang, Y. Yang, J.X. Yu (Eds.), Advances in Data and Web Management. XXII, 896 pages. 2007.

Vol. 4504: J. Huang, R. Kowalczyk, Z. Maamar, D. Martin, I. Müller, S. Stoutenburg, K.P. Sycara (Eds.), Service-Oriented Computing: Agents, Semantics, and Engineering. X, 175 pages. 2007.

Vol. 4501: J. Marques-Silva, K.A. Sakallah (Eds.), Theory and Applications of Satisfiability Testing – SAT 2007. XI, 384 pages. 2007.

Vol. 4500: N. Streitz, A. Kameas, I. Mavrommati (Eds.), The Disappearing Computer. XVIII, 304 pages. 2007.

Vol. 4499: Y.Q. Shi (Ed.), Transactions on Data Hiding and Multimedia Security II. IX, 117 pages. 2007.

Vol. 4497: S.B. Cooper, B. Löwe, A. Sorbi (Eds.), Computation and Logic in the Real World. XVIII, 826 pages. 2007.

Vol. 4496: N.T. Nguyen, A. Grzech, R.J. Howlett, L.C. Jain (Eds.), Agent and Multi-Agent Systems: Technologies and Applications. XXI, 1046 pages. 2007. (Sublibrary LNAI).

Vol. 4495: J. Krogstie, A. Opdahl, G. Sindre (Eds.), Advanced Information Systems Engineering. XVI, 606 pages. 2007.

Vol. 4494: H. Jin, O.F. Rana, Y. Pan, V.K. Prasanna (Eds.), Algorithms and Architectures for Parallel Processing. XIV, 508 pages. 2007.

Vol. 4493: D. Liu, S. Fei, Z. Hou, H. Zhang, C. Sun (Eds.), Advances in Neural Networks – ISNN 2007, Part III. XXVI, 1215 pages. 2007.

Vol. 4492: D. Liu, S. Fei, Z. Hou, H. Zhang, C. Sun (Eds.), Advances in Neural Networks – ISNN 2007, Part II. XXVII, 1321 pages. 2007.

Vol. 4491: D. Liu, S. Fei, Z.-G. Hou, H. Zhang, C. Sun (Eds.), Advances in Neural Networks – ISNN 2007, Part I. LIV, 1365 pages. 2007.

Vol. 4490: Y. Shi, G.D. van Albada, J. Dongarra, P.M.A. Sloot (Eds.), Computational Science – ICCS 2007, Part IV. XXXVII, 1211 pages. 2007.

Vol. 4489: Y. Shi, G.D. van Albada, J. Dongarra, P.M.A. Sloot (Eds.), Computational Science – ICCS 2007, Part III. XXXVII, 1257 pages. 2007.

Vol. 4488: Y. Shi, G.D. van Albada, J. Dongarra, P.M.A. Sloot (Eds.), Computational Science – ICCS 2007, Part II. XXXV, 1251 pages. 2007.

Vol. 4487: Y. Shi, G.D. van Albada, J. Dongarra, P.M.A. Sloot (Eds.), Computational Science – ICCS 2007, Part I. LXXXI, 1275 pages. 2007.

Vol. 4486: M. Bernardo, J. Hillston (Eds.), Formal Methods for Performance Evaluation. VII, 469 pages. 2007.

Vol. 4485: F. Sgallari, A. Murli, N. Paragios (Eds.), Scale Space and Variational Methods in Computer Vision. XV, 931 pages. 2007.

Vol. 4484: J.-Y. Cai, S.B. Cooper, H. Zhu (Eds.), Theory and Applications of Models of Computation. XIII, 772 pages. 2007.

Vol. 4483: C. Baral, G. Brewka, J. Schlipf (Eds.), Logic Programming and Nonmonotonic Reasoning. IX, 327 pages. 2007. (Sublibrary LNAI).

Vol. 4482: A. An, J. Stefanowski, S. Ramanna, C.J. Butz, W. Pedrycz, G. Wang (Eds.), Rough Sets, Fuzzy Sets, Data Mining and Granular Computing. XIV, 585 pages. 2007. (Sublibrary LNAI).

Vol. 4481: J. Yao, P. Lingras, W.-Z. Wu, M. Szczuka, N.J. Cercone, D. Ślęzak (Eds.), Rough Sets and Knowledge Technology. XIV, 576 pages. 2007. (Sublibrary LNAI).

Vol. 4480: A. LaMarca, M. Langheinrich, K.N. Truong (Eds.), Pervasive Computing. XIII, 369 pages. 2007.

Vol. 4479: I.F. Akyildiz, R. Sivakumar, E. Ekici, J.C.d. Oliveira, J. McNair (Eds.), NETWORKING 2007. Ad Hoc and Sensor Networks, Wireless Networks, Next Generation Internet. XXVII, 1252 pages. 2007.

Vol. 4478: J. Martí, J.M. Benedí, A.M. Mendonça, J. Serrat (Eds.), Pattern Recognition and Image Analysis, Part II. XXVII, 657 pages. 2007.

Vol. 4477: J. Martí, J.M. Benedí, A.M. Mendonça, J. Serrat (Eds.), Pattern Recognition and Image Analysis, Part I. XXVII, 625 pages. 2007.

Vol. 4476: V. Gorodetsky, C. Zhang, V.A. Skormin, L. Cao (Eds.), Autonomous Intelligent Systems: Multi-Agents and Data Mining. XIII, 323 pages. 2007. (Sublibrary LNAI).

Vol. 4475: P. Crescenzi, G. Prencipe, G. Pucci (Eds.), Fun with Algorithms. X, 273 pages. 2007.

Vol. 4474: G. Prencipe, S. Zaks (Eds.), Structural Information and Communication Complexity. XI, 342 pages. 2007.

Vol. 4472: M. Haindl, J. Kittler, F. Roli (Eds.), Multiple Classifier Systems. XI, 524 pages. 2007.

Vol. 4471: P. Cesar, K. Chorianopoulos, J.F. Jensen (Eds.), Interactive TV: a Shared Experience. XIII, 236 pages. 2007.

Vol. 4470: Q. Wang, D. Pfahl, D.M. Raffo (Eds.), Software Process Dynamics and Agility. XI, 346 pages. 2007.

Vol. 4469: K.-c. Hui, Z. Pan, R.C.-k. Chung, C.C.L. Wang, X. Jin, S. Göbel, E.C.-L. Li (Eds.), Technologies for E-Learning and Digital Entertainment. XVIII, 974 pages. 2007.

Vol. 4468: M.M. Bonsangue, E.B. Johnsen (Eds.), Formal Methods for Open Object-Based Distributed Systems. X, 317 pages. 2007.

Vol. 4467: A.L. Murphy, J. Vitek (Eds.), Coordination Models and Languages. X, 325 pages. 2007.